The W-Hollow Cookbook

Naomi Deane and Jesse Stuart

The W-Hollow Cookbook

Compiled by
Glennis Stuart Liles
With the assistance of
Betty Stuart Baird

Edited by
Chuck D. Charles

The Jesse Stuart Foundation

Naomi Vivian Keeney

To the memory of Naomi Vivian (Bibbie) Keeney,
a favorite niece of Jesse's and an excellent cook.
She was never happier than when she had several
feet under her table.

Second Edition

ISBN 0-945084-18-8

Published by
The Jesse Stuart Foundation
P.O. Box 391
Ashland, Kentucky 41114
1990

Foreword

In 1987, Jesse Stuart's youngest sister, Glennis Stuart Liles, called me at home one Sunday afternoon and announced that she had an idea for a new money-making project for the Jesse Stuart Foundation. "I want to do a cookbook! I've wanted to do one for years, and all the family will participate!"

I did not doubt Glennis's ability to prepare a good book, but I asked myself all the questions a publisher normally asks. The world is full of cookbooks. National and state organizations do them. So do local clubs and family associations. Would there be a market for another one? Could we afford the time and money to edit and publish a cookbook, when we were absolutely covered up with financing, editing, publishing, and marketing Jesse Stuart's many out-of-print works and unpublished manuscripts? However, Glennis was both persistent and persuasive. I concluded that there would be a market for the unique cookbook she proposed, and that the Jesse Stuart Foundation would take on the task of publishing it.

I tried to recommend a practical methodology. "Develop a standardized recipe format," I advised. "That way you won't have so much editing and retyping to do." "I can't do that," Glennis responded. "A lot of these older folks aren't going to follow any guidelines. They're going to write out recipes their own way." And she was right! She wrote to Stuarts all across America, and recipes arrived in many forms. Glennis, assisted by Betty Stuart Baird, then spent more than a year sorting out and testing recipes and soliciting additional text and photographs. Although editors later standardized the recipe format, this book still retains a charming informality.

Glennis eventually placed an enormous typescript in my hands. As I examined it, I found that it was more than a cookbook. It was part family history and part social history, too. It stands, as Glennis had intended, as another way of perpetuating her brother Jesse's legacy. At another level of analysis, it is a tribute to great families, like the Stuarts, that provide much of the cooperative strength and spirit of Appalachian society.

By 1989, the compilation was complete, and the production processes began. At that point, several friends, as well as my office staff, became involved. Jim Marsh, Manager of Creative Services at Ashland Oil, Inc. and one of his employees, Carolyn Kersey, did the photography for the cover. Barbara Nicholls, an English teacher at Ashland Community College, edited the narrative por-tions of the text, and Chuck D. Charles, JSF Director of Sales and Marketing, edited the recipes. My office staff—Mr. Charles, Mary Jo Smith, Bonnie Clay, Gladys Franz, and Shirley Crisp—then proofread the manuscript at several stages. Rocky Zornes and Bruce Kabalen, who operate ZAK productions in Lexington, Kentucky, made the book camera-ready for printing.

Mr. Charles, the project director and primary editor, deserves special praise for his attention to detail and for his patience, good humor, and professionalism. Thanks to Chuck Charles and Glennis Liles, the First Edition of the W-HOLLOW COOKBOOK was published in time for holiday sales, 1989.

The Jesse Stuart Foundation published 2100 copies of the First Edition. With the enthusiastic support of 178 family members who had contributed to the book, more than 1000 copies had already been sold before the First Editions arrived at my office on December 7, 1989.

Within two months, two thousand copies were sold! Glennis Liles and her husband, Whitey, sold almost 400 copies, Mrs. Jesse Stuart's energetic sister-in-law, Lucille Norris, sold almost 250 copies. Loretta Benner sold more than one hundred copies, and Helen Shultz and Nancy Lake sold more than fifty copies. Many others made a significant contribution to the sales effort.

Preparations for a second edition began immediately after Christmas 1989. A new edition, rather than simply a second printing, enabled us to make necessary corrections and also allowed us to include some additional recipes and descriptive material.

The First Edition of the W-HOLLOW COOKBOOK was popular and well received, and I am confident that the second edition of this family cookbook is even better. Bon Appetit!

James M. Gifford, Ph.D.
Executive Director
Jesse Stuart Foundation
P.O. Box 391
Ashland, KY 41101
February 7, 1990

Introduction

For several years Jesse's wife, Naomi Deane, planned to write a cookbook. But because of her busy schedule, she never found the time. A niece, Naomi Vivian Keeney, also had an idea to do one but didn't live to carry out her plan. About two years ago my daughter, Melissa, asked me to do a book of my favorite recipes for our family. So in March, 1987, I sent letters to all the family members I could reach asking them to help me do a family cookbook for The Jesse Stuart Foundation. The response was excellent.

This book is concerned with good plain cooking, but it is not just a collection of recipes. We have tried to incorporate memories, photographs

Naomi Deane Stuart and Jesse Stuart

and quotations from six generations of the Jesse Hilton Stuart family to make it interesting and helpful to collectors of Jesse Stuart memorabilia.

It covers a time period from cooking on the open fire or wood-burning stove in iron pots, preserving pork by the old salt-cure method, and milking cows by hand to modern day microwave cookery. Underneath it all lies many years of experience in learning how to use different kinds of kitchen equipment and experimenting with methods of cooking in order to perfect mouth-watering foods for you to enjoy.

The recipes included were collected from the Stuarts (some spelled Stewart); from Jesse's mother's family, the Hiltons (also spelled Hylton); from his maternal grandmother's family, the Penningtons; and his wife, Naomi Deane's family, the Norrises.

The names of the people who so willingly contributed their prized recipes are listed throughout the book along with their relationship to Jesse. He once told a cousin, Ila Shanks, that he had no "second" cousins. So none have been removed; they are all cousins, regardless of how close or distant, as are nieces and nephews.

I owe a special thanks to other family members and friends for sharing their time, talent, and photographs in the preparation of this book: sister-in-law-Naomi Deane Stuart; and her sister Laura Avanelle Norris Callihan; sisters, Sophie Keeney and Mary Nelson; brother, James Mitchell Stuart; daughters, Anne O'Hare and Melissa Liles; husband, Herbert (Whitey) Liles; cousins, Mary Belle Johnson, Helen Shultz, Jimmy E. Stewart (East Liverpool, OH), Ila Shanks, Faye Lester, Dorothy and William Holbrook, Fred Hilton, Joyce (Jimmie) Carter McKinney, Frank Hilton, Marie Hilton Ellington, Ethel Hilton Porter, and Phyllis Hilton Parker; and Karen Belt, typist.

Our family has grown closer through the collecting of the material for this book. Some cousins have met for the first time. Some have given recipes never before shared outside the immediate family. Some gave old, old recipes which had to be converted for modern measurements and cooking equipment. A few said we could even change the spelling of their names if we needed to. We sincerely appreciate the support, concern, and enthusiasm shown by all who contributed to make this book a worthwhile family project.

Glennis Stuart Liles

Table of Contents

Appetizers

Snappy Cheese Appetizers
Cheese Ball I
Cheese Ball II
Cheese Ball III
Holly Cheese Ball
Cheese Balls
Cheese and Sausage Balls
Cheese Biscuits (for parties)
Clam Dip
Club Cheese
Duck Butter
Horseradish Cheese Spread
Teriyaki Meat Balls
Stuffed Mushrooms
Pizza Snacks

Porcupine Balls
Roll Ups-Hors D'oeuvres
Salmon Balls
Smoked Salmon Ball
Sandwich Spread
Hot Sausage Appetizers
Sausage Balls
Shrimp Butter
Shrimp Dip
Treet Salad
Tuna Cheese Triangles
Barbecued Weiners
Vegetable Dip
Fresh Vegetable Dip
Tarty Dip for Vegetables

For Mitchell Stuart

I've seen him go among his corn at night
After his day was done-By lantern light
He went, unless it was light of the moon,
And a bright moon was up-He's broken soon;
Lines are grooved on his face at fifty-two.
The work he does would get the best of you.
And now his love is wind among the corn;
His love is whispering, talking, green corn blades.
His love is cornfields when the summer fades,
Oak leaves to red and fodder blades to brown.
His love is autumn raining dead leaves down
And going out on autumn morns to salt the stock.
He loves his mules and whispering corn at night-
Buff-colored corn in full autumn moonlight.

*Stuart, Jesse, Land of Honey-Colored Wind, (Morehead, Kentucky: The Jesse Stuart Foundation, Inc., 1981), p.135.

L to R. Glennis, James, Mary, Jesse, Sophie, Martha and Mitchell Stuart

Excerpts from *My World*
by Jesse Stuart

My father, Mitchell Stuart, known as "Mick," married Martha Hilton in Greenup County. They lived together forty-nine years before my mother's death. My father's death was three years later. In those forty-nine years they lived in six different houses, all within a one-mile radius. My father's plow and my mother's hoe turned over all the pebbles and stones and much of the ground on hill and bottom in this valley.

My mother had seven children. Two of my brothers died young, but two boys and three girls still live. We grew up on the foods we grew from this soil, most of which is considered poor land. My mother and father rented land and share-cropped until I was twelve, when my father bought fifty acres of land. That was all he ever owned. But he told me I should buy land while I was a young man and hold on to it. Land didn't grow, he said, but populations did and we had to save our land for the generations to come.

So piece by piece, over a period of twenty-eight years, I have bought all the land my parents ever rented. Now I have approximately a thousand acres. This land will never be destroyed, nor will its timber and wildlife, as long as I live. My sisters, nephews, nieces, and I now own nearly all of W-Hollow. We have one of the most beautiful little valleys in Greenup County, in the eastern mountains of Kentucky, in all of Kentucky, in the United States, in any country of the world. This is saying a lot, I know. But I

have visited many times in Scotland, England, Wales, Ireland, Germany, France, and Switzerland. I have seen the small valleys in these countries. But they are not like W-Hollow.

I grew to manhood here, eating food grown from this soil. We never bought anything from the stores but salt, pepper, soda, baking powder, and sometimes sugar, for we often sweetened with sorghum and wild honey in the early days. Our mother nursed her children; never was one of us on a bottle. In the early days we had wild game, then later our own pork, beef, and mutton. On this food I grew into a broad-shouldered block of a man, just over six feet, weighing 225 pounds. My brother James grew to six-feet-five, a broad-shouldered 200 pounder. Our three sisters grew to be husky women, mentally and physically energetic.

God's Oddling was about my father, my mother, and our family. It told how we worked and struggled. Through its pages, W-Hollow covered the world. My father never read a book. He never wrote a letter or read one. Intelligent as he was, he couldn't read or write. But the Stuarts of W-Hollow leveled with the world.

Jesse Stuart. *My World.* (Lexington. Kentucky: The University Press of Kentucky, 1975)

3

Appetizers

Snappy Cheese Appetizers
Cousin-Francis Hilton Hunt - Bloomfield, KY

2 sticks pie crust mix
1 (4 oz.) pkg. (1 c.) shredded sharp natural cheddar cheese
1/4 tsp. dry mustard
2 tsp. Worchestershire sauce
30 small stuffed green olives
2 tsp. paprika

Prepare pie crust mix according to pkg. directions, thoroughly mixing in cheese, mustard, Worchestershire sauce and paprika, till mixture forms a ball. Divide dough in half. Using one half, wrap about one tsp. dough around each olive. Roll other half out on floured surface to 12 x 8 inch rectangle. With pastry wheel or knife, cut into sticks 1/2 inch wide and 4 inches long. Place olive balls and cheese sticks on ungreased baking sheet. Bake in hot over (425°) 10 to 12 minutes or till golden brown. Serves as appetizers, snacks, or salad accompaniment. Makes 2-1/2 dozen balls and 4 dozen sticks.

Cheese Ball I
Niece-Naomi Vivian Keeney - Greenup, KY

2 (4 oz.) Roquefort (Blue cheese)
2 (5 oz.) jars processed cheddar
2 (8 oz.) cream cheese (recipe calls for 12 oz. but I found a little extra doesn't harm the taste and makes it more spreadable)
2 T grated onions
1 tsp. Worchestershire sauce
1/2 c. finely chopped parsley
1 c. pecans

Let all cheese soften in a large bowl at room temperature. Mix well add onions, Worchestershire. Mix well. If you use the extra cream cheese, the mixture tends to be sticky. It is best to refrigerate before making ball and attempting to roll in parsley and pecans.

Cheese Ball II
Niece-Barbara Keeney Oney - Raceland, KY

2 (8 oz.) pkgs. cream cheese
2 c. shredded cheddar cheese
1 T pimentos
1 T green pepper
1 T chopped onions
2 T Worchestershire sauce
1 tsp. lemon juice
dash of salt and pepper
1 c. chopped pecans

Combine softened cheese. Mix well. Add all other ingredients and mix well. Shape into ball and roll in pecans. Refrigerate before serving.

Cheese Ball III
Cousins-David and Thomas Adkins - Lucasville, OH

1 pkg. chipped beef
1 small bunch of green onions, stems and all
1 pkg. extra sharp cheese
2 (8 oz.) Philadelphia cream cheese

Chop beef fine. (Use scissors to cut it.) Chop onions and add sharp cheese and cream cheese with beef and onions until well blended. Shape into 2 balls or 2 logs.

Holly Cheese Ball
Cousin-Marie Hilton Ellington - Ashland, KY

3 (8 oz.) pkgs. Philadelphia cream cheese
3 T freeze dried chives
1 tsp. garlic salt
2 tsp. salt
1 tsp. Worchestershire sauce
1/2 c. nuts

Soften cream cheese. Mix above ingredients. Put well mixed cheese on waxed paper. Pull paper up around cheese and pat into ball. Roll cheese ball in nuts and sprinkle with dried or freshley chopped parsley.

Cheese Balls

Cousin-Grace Carter - Sophie, WV

1 c. grated cheese
1/4 c. butter
1/2 c. flour
1 tsp. paprika
1/4 tsp. salt

Melt butter and add cheese. Mix flour, paprika, and salt. Add to cheese mixture. Roll into balls. Bake 425° from 10-15 minutes or until brown. Refrigerate 20-40 minutes.

Cheese and Sausage Balls

Cousin-Janet Stewart Mayo - Kenova, WV

8 oz. cheddar cheese, grated
1 lb. sausage
3 c. bisquick

Work together with hands. Roll into med. size balls and bake 20 min. at 400° or until done.

Cheese Biscuits (for parties)

Sister-in-law-Lucille Norris - Greenup, KY

2-1/2 c. flour
1/2 c. finely chopped pecans
1/2 lb. margarine
1/2 lb. old English cheese
pinch of salt
pinch of red pepper

Soften margarine and cheese. Mix together like cheese ball. Add flour and chopped pecans. Shape in 2 small rolls and chill well. Slice when firm into little cookies and bake in moderate oven on ungreased cookie sheet till lightly browned.

Clam Dip

*Sister-in -law-Laura Avenell Norris Callihan
Greenup, KY*

1 (8 oz.) cream cheese
1 can minced clams drained
1 tsp. Worchestershire sauce
1 tsp. grated onion
Tiny bit salt and pepper

Mix. Add clam juice to thin if needed.

Club Cheese

Cousin-Susan Shultz Arnold - Portsmouth, OH

1 (12 oz.) container cheddar cheese (room temp.)
3 oz. cream cheese (room temp.)
2/3 c. large curd cottage cheese
1 T finely minced onion
1 tsp. Worchestershire sauce
1/4 tsp. Tabasco sauce
1/2 tsp. caraway seeds

Mix all ingredients with electric mixer. Chill covered for 24 hours. Serve with crackers.

Duck Butter

Cousins-David and Thomas Adkins - Lucasville, OH

2 (8 oz.) cream cheese (softened)
4 cloves garlic, grated fine
1/4 med. onion grated fine
2 T Worchestershire sauce
1/4 tsp. Tabasco sauce
dash salt

Combine all ingredients, serve with crackers or melba toast.

Horseradish Cheese Spread
Cousin-Lynn Hunt Newton - Hamilton, OH

1 lb. Velveeta cheese
1 c. mayonnaise
4 drops Tabasco
4 oz. pure horseradish

Melt cheese. Add remaining ingredients. Put in crock and refrigerate. Serve with crackers or cornchips.

Teriyaki Meat Balls
Niece-Martha Deane Callihan North - Champaign, IL

3 lbs ground beef

sauce:
1. c. Soy Sauce
1/2 c. water
2 T ginger
garlic powder to taste

Form beef into 1" balls and place on large roasting pan. Pour sauce over beef balls. Bake 1 hour at 275°. Yields 100 balls.

Stuffed Mushrooms
Niece-Ruth Nelson - Greenup, KY

12 lg. mushrooms
3 T butter, melted
1/2 tsp. finely chopped onion
1-1/2 T flour
1/2 tsp. finely chopped parsley
nutmeg, salt and pepper to taste
buttered bread crumbs

Brush or wash mushrooms then dry on a paper towel. Cut off the stems and chop them fine. Combine mushroom stems and onion and saute for 10 minutes. Add flour, nutmeg, parsley, salt and pepper. You may choose chicken stock, tomato juice, or cream to moisten. Cool. Fill mushroom caps, rounding well over the top. Cover with buttered bread crumbs. Bake 15 minutes at 425°

To vary: Add finely chopped cooked chicken, turkey, ham, celery, or cheese.

Pizza Snacks
Cousin-Norma Jean Pennington Darnell - Greenup, KY

1 lb. sausage
1 lb. ground beef
1 lb cheese
1 tsp. oregano
1 tsp. garlic powder
1 onion, chopped,
1 pepper, chopped
Party bread

Brown meat and drain. Add cheese and cook until melted. Put 1 tsp. of mixture on bread. Put in oven for 10 to 15 minutes on 350°.

Porcupine Balls
Niece-Connie Keeney - Greenup, KY

1 lb. ground chuck
1/2 c. rice
1/2 c. water
small chopped onion
salt, celery salt, garlic powder, (to taste)

Sauce:
1 can tomato sauce
1 c. water
2 tsp. Worchestershire sauce

Form balls-Top with sauce and cover with foil. Bake at 350° for 45 minutes. Uncover and bake for 15 minutes.

Roll Ups - Hors d'Oeuvres
Cousin-Goldie Adkins - East Liverpool, OH

1 pkg. (10 slices) Oscar Meyer Salami
1 (8 oz.) Philadelphia Cream Cheese
Kosher Dill Pickles Spears (Vlasic)

Spread cheese on each slice of salami. Place pickles on salami slice and roll up. Then slice rolls into thin pieces.

Salmon Balls

Cousin-Marie Pennington Hardymon - Greenup, KY

1 (16 oz.) can salmon
1 egg
1/4 c. milk
1 tsp. salt
1/8 tsp. pepper
1/8 tsp. celery salt
1/2 tsp. Worchestershire sauce
1 c. soft bread crumbs

Drain salmon, flake fine. Lightly beat egg, add milk, salt, pepper, celery salt, and Worchestershire sauce to egg; mix. Mix salmon and bread crumbs together. Stir in egg-milk mixture. Make into 1-1/2 inch balls. Fry at 365° in deep shortening in heavy skillet for 5 minutes or until brown. Yields 8 servings.

Smoked Salmon Ball

Cousin-Steven W. Stewart - Kenova, WV

1 (15-1/2 oz.) can salmon
1 (8 oz.) pkg. cream cheese
1 T lemon juice
1 T horseradish
1/4 tsp. salt
1/2 c. finely chopped onion
1/4 tsp. liquid smoke

Remove bones and skin from salmon. Place in bowl and flake with fork. Add softened cream cheese, lemon juice, horseradish, salt, onion and liquid smoke. Mix well. Shape into ball then roll in parsley flakes. Wrap in plastic wrap and store in refrigerator, until ready to serve.

Sandwich Spread

Cousin-Beverly Jane Benner Murphy - Lucasville, OH

Use grinder:
4 lb. hot dogs
1 lg. can fruit cocktail, drained well
1 lg. jar sweet pickles, drained well
small amount pancake syrup
sprinkle brown sugar
mayonnaise-2 c. or more to proper consistency.
salt and pepper to taste

Mix and refrigerate. Serve 48.

Hot Sausage Appetizers

Cousin-Donna Stewart Broscious - Ravenswood, WV
Cousin-Pat Stewart - Ravenswood, WV

1 lb. hot sausage
1 sm. jar cheese whiz
3 c. Bisquick mix
1/2 c. milk

Combine all ingredients in lg. mixing bowl. Shape into one inch balls and place on ungreased cookie sheet. Bake in a preheated oven at 400° for 15 to 20 minutes. These can be prepared ahead and frozen. Allow to reach room temperature and bake in oven at 400°.

Sausage Balls

Cousin-Betty Stewart Walker - Huntington, WV

1 lb. sausage
3 c. Bisquick mix
1 (8 oz.) jar cheese whiz
1/2 c. milk

Mix ingredients thoroughly and roll into small balls. Bake at 400° for 15-20 minutes on an ungreased cookie sheet. Can be made and frozen for later use.

Shrimp Butter

Niece-Regina Nelson Stout - Greenup, KY

1 (8 oz.) cream cheese
1 stick butter
1 c. popcorn shrimp
2 T mayonnaise
1 sm. onion, grated fine

Blend butter, cream cheese, and mayonnaise. Add onion and shrimp. Serve at room temperature on assorted crackers.

Shrimp Dip

Sister-in-law-Laura Avenelle Norris Callihan
Greenup, KY

1 lg. pkg. cream cheese
1 c. or 6 oz. can shrimp
1 tsp. Worchestshire sauce
1 tsp. lemon juice
2 tsp. horseradish
Grated onion

Mix. Thin with cream (I use milk).

Treet Salad

Cousin-Brenda Stewart Marcum - Kenova, WV

2 cans Treet
4 sweet pickles
4 dill pickles
1 onion
3 T Kraft shredded cheese
1 tsp. mustard
3 T mayonnaise (more if desired)

Grind up Treet and add pickles, onions, cheese, mayonnaise, and mustard. Mix well until all ingredients are blended. Makes approximately 24 sandwiches.

Tuna Cheese Triangles

Niece-Theresa Darby - Normantown, WV

1 can refrigerated quick cresent dinner rolls
1 can (7 oz.) tuna, drained and flaked
1-1/4 c. shredded cheddar cheese
1/3 c. chili sauce
1/4 c. pickle relish
1/4 tsp. chili powder

Unroll cresents and put 4 rectangles on cookie sheet. Press edges together to form a 13-1/2 x 7-1/2" rectangle. Bake in 375° oven for 8 minutes. Mix remaining ingredients, reserving 1/4 c. cheese, and spread on rectangle. Sprinkle with remaining cheese. Put back in oven for 5 minutes. Cut in triangles and serve hot. Makes 2 dozen.

Barbecued Weiners

Niece-Martha "Marty" Abdon - Greenup, KY

4 lg. size onions (sliced)
3/4 c. vinegar
1 bottle catsup
1/2 bottle Worchestshire sauce
3/4 c. sugar

Combine and cook until onions become tender. Add 2 lb. sliced weiners. Boil. Ready to eat.

Vegetable Dip

Cousin-Geraldine Holbrook - Greenup, KY

8 oz. Philadelphia cream cheese
2 T milk
2 T french dressing
1/3 c. ketchup
1 T minced onion
8 drops tabasco sauce
4 drops red hot sauce

Mix until smooth, chill, serve with cauliflower, carrots, celery, radishes, and green peppers.

Fresh Vegetable Dip

Cousin-Alma Martin - Racine WS

1 c. sour cream
1 c. real mayonnaise
1 T Bleu Monde
1 T. parsley
1 T onion powder
1 T dill weed

Mix well and let stand at least 2 hours. Will keep in refrigerator up to 5 weeks.

8

Tarty Dip for Vegetables

Cousin-James Stewart - E. Liverpool, OH

May be prepared in advance

1/4 c. Kraft Catalina dressing
8 oz. pkg. cream cheese (Philadelphia)
1/4 c. Heinz catsup
1 tsp. onion powder
2 T milk
A pinch of salt (optional)

Soften cream cheese at room temperature. Whip all ingredients together with electric mixer until thoroughly mixed.

Beverages

Bloody Mary
Bloody Mary (without vodka) Bloody Shame
Chocolate Syrup for Milk
Mulled Cider
Holiday Eggnog
Homebrew
Mint Julep
Christmas Cranberry Punch
Holiday Punch
Lemon Balm Punch
Lime-Pineapple Punch

Punch-Easy and Good
Sunshine Punch
Tea, Country Mint
Sassafras Tea I
Sassafras Tea II
Sassafras Tea III
Spiced Tea
Sumac Ade
Tea (hot) - Tea (iced)
Iced Tea - Three Easy Ways

R. to L. Betty Stuart Baird, Jesse Stuart and Glennis Stuart Liles

L to R. Niece Nancy Sue Darby and Jane Stuart (They were
very close playmates)

x Their only child

Jesse Stuart

Naomi Deane Stuart

13

Beverages

Bloody Mary

Sister-in-law-Lucille Norris - Greenup, KY

Large glass frosted in freezer with salt on rim
1-1/2 oz. vodka
1/2 glass Mr. and Mrs. T
1/2 glass homemade tomato juice
heavy dash aunt Jane's crazy salt
generous squeeze of fresh lime
dash of tabasco and Worchestershire

Serve with celery stick

Can be made in pitcher and laced with vodka or gin or plain. Jesse said I could make better Bloody Marys than anyone until after he had his first stroke. Then he said I had lost my touch.

Bloody Shame (without vodka) Bloody Mary

Sister-in-law-Lucille Norris - Greenup, KY

1 can beef motto
1 can clam motto
1 T beef bullion
1 tsp. lemon juice
1 tsp, orange juice
6-1/2 tsp. Worchestershire
Cayenne pepper sauce to taste
1-1/2 c. vodka or gin (optional)

Mix in pitcher. Dip glasses in rock salt around rim and set in freezer before using.

Chocolate Syrup for Milk

Niece-Melissa Liles - Greenup, KY

Boil for 5 minutes:
2 c. water
2 c. sugar

Make paste of:
1 c. cocoa
cold water

Add paste to syrup and boil 10 minutes. Use 2 T syrup per cup of hot or cold milk.

Mulled Cider

Nephew-John Baird - Wadestown, WV

3 qts. cider
2/3 c. brown sugar
12 cloves
6 whole allspice
2 cinnamon sticks
pinch ground nutmeg

Simmer ingredients for at least 5 minutes. Strain through fine sieve. Serve in heated mugs with fresh grated nutmeg. Serves 12.

Holiday Eggnog

Nephew-Mike Lake - Berea, KY

6 eggs, separated
1/2 c. sugar
2 c. milk
2 c. whipping cream
1/2 to 1 c. brandy or bourbon (optional)
2 T dark rum
1/4 c. sugar
ground nutmeg

Beat egg yolks until thick and lemon colored; gradually add 1/2 c. sugar and beat until dissolved. Beat in milk, cream, brandy and rum; cover and refrigerate overnight. Just before serving, beat egg whites (at room temp.) until soft peaks form. Gradually add 1/4 c. sugar, beating until stiff but not dry; gently fold into egg yolk mixture. Pour into punch bowl and sprinkle with ground nutmeg. Yield: 10 cups.

Homebrew

Nephew-Mitchell Nelson - Greenup, KY

5 gallon distilled water
5 lb. sugar
3 lb. can hop-flavored malt extract (light or dark)
2 pks. yeast (or 1 cake)
1 potato, raw and quartered, placed inside old sock
(clean)

Mix ingredients in 8 gallon crock or equivalent thereof. Cover crock with clean cloth held in place with large rubber band. Let stand for about 5 days undisturbed at 70-75° until fermentation slows. To boost alcohol content, add 1 tsp sugar to each sealable bottle or jar before carefully siphoning brew from the top of the crock so as not to disturb the sediments in the bottom. Seal and store undisturbed in cool; dry location for three weeks. This is important to keep bottles from exploding. Chill brew before drinking, taking care not to disturb the yeast in the bottom when pouring.

Mint Julep

Sister-Glennis Stuart Liles - Greenup, KY

Put a few sprigs of mint into a tin, dry, warm tumbler. Add a T of sugar, and fill the tumbler with shaved ice, add more mint springs and stir until glass frosts over on the outside. Just before serving the flavor can be improved by shaking a little rum over the top of the crushed ice.

Christmas Cranberry Punch

Cousin-Katherine Stewart Martin - Racine WS

1 (3 oz.) pkg. cherry jello
1 c. boiling water
1 (6 oz.) can frozen lemonade
3 c. cold water
1 qt. cranberry juice
1 lg. bottle ginger ale
1 qt. cranberry sherbert

Mix first 5 ingredients in order given. Add ginger ale and sherbert just before serving.

Holiday Punch

Cousin-Grace Carter - Sophie, WV

2 pkg. kool-aid
2 c. sugar
2 qts. water
1 lg. can pineapple juice
1 can frozen orange juice
1 (liter) 7-up
1/2 gallon pineapple sherbert

Mix.

Lemon Balm Punch

Niece-Melissa (Lissie) Liles - Greenup, KY

1/4 c. sugar
1/4 c. boiling water
1/2 c. fresh lemon balm leaves, finely chopped
1/2 c. fresh mint leaves, finely chopped
1/2 c. lemon juice
4 qts. ginger ale, chilled
orange slices (optional)
fresh lemon balm leaves (optional)

Combine sugar and water, stirring until sugar dissolves. Combine sugar mixture, chopped lemon balm leaves, mint leaves and lemon juice in a small bowl; cover and let stand overnight. When ready to serve strain syrup mixture in a large punch bowl or pitcher; pour in ginger ale, stirring gently. Garnish with floating orange slices and additional lemon balm leaves, if desired.

Lime-Pineapple Punch

Sister-in-law-Laura Avenell Norris Callihan
Greenup, KY

2 pkgs. lime kool-aid
2 c. sugar
46 oz. can of pineapple juice
2 qt. water
2 qt. ginger ale

Mix ingredients. Serve over ice.

Punch-Easy and Good

*Sister-in-law-Laura Avenell Norris Callihan,
Greenup, KY*

1 (6 oz.) can frozen orange juice
1 (6 oz.) can frozen lemonade
1 (6 oz.) can frozen lime ade or pineapple juice
4 c. cold water
1 lg. bottle ginger ale-add last
Red Cherries

This is a tart zippy punch. Combine all ingredients. Yields:
12 to 15 cups.

Sunshine Punch

*Cousins-Steven Meyers and Michael Adkins
Defiance , OH*

1 can (46 oz.) pineapple juice (chilled)
1 can (6 oz.) frozen lemonade (thawed)
1 can (6 oz.) frozen orange juice (thawed)
4 c. cold water
3 (28 oz.) bottles ginger ale (chilled)

In chilled punch bowl combine all ingredients. Ladle out
5 qts. to make ice rings. Pour this in small ring molds and
freeze. Food coloring can be added to make more color-
ful. Also orange and lemon slices can be used as a garnish.
Delicious!

Tea, Country Mint

Niece-Nancy Sue Darby Lake - Berea, KY

1 part crushed spearmint
1 part crushed peppermint
1 part crushed lemon balm

If using dried leaves, measure 1 or 2 tsp. per cup plus 1 tsp.
for the pot. If using fresh herbs, measure 1 T per cup. Pour
boiling water over herbs. Cover and let steep 5 to 10
minutes. Herb teas are light in color, so strength must be
judged by taste, not appearance. If tea is too weak, add
more herbs. Do not steep too long.

Sassafras Tea I

Sister-Sophie Stuart Keeney - Greenup, KY

Wash roots well. Put six roots in pan or coffee pot in about
a qt. of water. Soak overnight. Then place on fire and boil
until fairly strong. Weaken and sweeten to taste. Serves 5-
7 thirsty children.

Sassafras Tea II

Sister-Sophie Stuart Keeney - Greenup, KY

One small handful of roots. 3-4 inches in length, dropped
into 2 or 3 qt. enameled pan and covered with as much
water as desired depending on number you wish to serve.
Let boil until the tea is dark in color. The flavor increases
with successive boilings.

Sassafras Tea III

Nephew-Sam Darby - Normantown, WV

4 sassafras roots, each about 2 inches long
1-1/2 qts. of water

Dig sassafras roots early in the spring, before the sap rises.
Wash the roots. Then scrub them with a brush, rinse and
then scrape bark into a large saucepan. Add the roots and
water to the bark scrapings in the pan. Bring to a boil and
then reduce heat to simmer. Simmer gently for 15 minutes. Remove from heat and allow to steep ten minutes.
Strain and serve hot or cold. Sweeten if desired.

Spiced Tea

Cousin-Valerie Hilton Kerr - Ashland, KY

1 (18 oz) jar of Tang
1 lg. pkg. Wyler's Lemonade Mix
1 c. instant tea
1 tsp. cloves
1 tsp. cinnamon
1 tsp. allspice
1-1/2 c. sugar

Mix together-store in closed container.

Use two heaping T per cup with hot water.

Sumac Ade

Nephew-Stacy Nelson - Greenup, KY

3 large or 6 small staghorn sumac clusters
2 qts. water
4-6 T honey

Steep sumac berries in the water overnight. Seive the sumac berries through several thicknesses of cheese cloth. Add honey to the drink to sweeten. Chill and serve the sumac ade with cracked ice and a sprig of mint in a tall glass.

Tea (Hot)

Niece -Betty Baird - Wadestown, WV

Allow 1 teaspoonful of tea to 1 cupful of boiling water. Scald teapot, put in tea and 1 cupful of boiling water, keep hot to almost boiling; let it steep or "draw" five minutes. Then fill up with as much boiling water as is required. Better if served in a porcelain or china teapot.

Tea (iced)

Niece -Betty Baird - Wadestown, WV

Use black or green and black tea mixed, never just green. Make tea with fresh boiling water, using 1/2-tsp. tea to a cup of boiling water, let stand five minutes to steep. Fill glasses with cracked ice. Pour hot tea directly on ice and serve with sliced lemon and sugar. If care is taken that the hot tea is poured on the ice and does not touch the glass there is no danger of breaking the glass.

Iced Tea-Three Easy Ways

Niece-Theresa Darby - Normantown, WV

1. Bring 1 qt. cold water to a full boil. Remove from heat and add 15 tea bags or 1/3 c. of loose tea leaves. Stir, cover and let stand 5 minutes. Stir again and strain into a pitcher holding another quart of cold water. Makes 2 qts.

2. To 1 quart of cold water add 8-10 tea bags (remove tags). Seal and refrigerate at least 6 hours or overnight. Remove bags. Recipe may be doubled.

3. For instant tea allow 2 rounded teaspoons instant tea powder for each qt. of cold water. Stir to dissolve. If using a flavored iced tea mix, use 1/2 c. (2 envelopes) to a quart of cold water.

Breads

Biscuits

Biscuits (for freezer)
Angel Biscuits
Baking Powder Biscuits
Beer Biscuits
Uncle Jesse Hilton's Pan Biscuits
Sour Milk or Soda Biscuits

Corn Breads

Corn Fritters
Puffy Corn Fritters
Corn Sticks
Crackling Bread
Crusty Corn Bread
Deluxe Cornbread
Fried Corn Pone
Grandma's Corn Bread
Jalapeno Cornbread
Mexican Corn Bread I
Mexican Corn Bread II
Mom's Corn Bread
Quick Corn Bread

Muffins

Apple Muffins
Spiced Apple Muffins
Bran Muffins
Do-Ahead Bran Muffins
Honey-Corn Muffins
Pumpkin Muffins
Raisin Bran Muffins
Six Week Bran Muffins

Quick Breads

Fresh Apple Nut Bread

Apricot Bread
Banana Bread
Banana Nut Bread
Cranberry Bread
Kentucky Bourbon-Fruit Loaf
Herbed Beer Bread
Pumpkin Bread
Zucchini Bread I
Zucchini Bread II
Zucchini Bread II
Popovers

Yeast Breads

Buns, Orange Blossoms (from Frozen Dough)
Cinnamon Leaf Coffee Ring
Swedish Coffee Ring
Dill Bread
Buttermilk Doughnuts
Oatmeal Yeast Loaves
Whole Wheat Pita Rounds
Hot Rolls I
Hot Rolls II
Hot Rolls III
Ice Box Rolls
Out of this World Rolls
Potato Rolls
Yeast Rolls
Sally Lunn
Freezer White Bread

Other Breads

Dumplings
Lemon Bread
Indian Fry Breads
French Toast
Buckwheat Pancakes
German Pancakes
Bugs Bunny Bread

L to R. Betty Stuart, Jesse Stuart, James Stephen Stuart and Naomi Deane Stuart at a family reunion.

Jesse and Deane at The Kentucky Derby

Uncle Jimmie Stuart and Family - L to R. 1st row - James Edward Stump, James Stewart (Mitchell's brother), Paul Douglas Johnson, Clara Wright, Wilma Wright. Seated in rocker is James' wife Clara Gertrude Johnson Stewart. In 2nd row and standing behind her father is Myrtle Allen Stewart Stump.

Biscuits

Biscuits (for Freezer)
Wife-Naomi Deane Norris Stuart - W-Hollow, KY

4 c. self rising flour
1-1/2 c. Crisco
2 tsp. baking powder
2 c. sweet milk

Mix flour and baking powder. Cut in Crisco. Add milk and mix. Roll and cut into biscuits. These can be made ahead and frozen. Freeze on cookie sheets; then place in freezer bags.

Angel Biscuits
Niece-Lori Ann Stuart - Greenup, KY

5 c. flour
3/4 c. Crisco
1 tsp. soda
1 tsp. salt
2 c. buttermilk
3 tsp. baking powder
1 cake or pkg. yeast
1/2 c. lukewarm water
3 T sugar

Dissolve yeast in water. Sift dry ingredients together. Cut in shortening until it is mixed well. Add buttermilk and yeast and stir with a large spoon. Grease a large bowl. Put in dough. Cover and refrigerate until ready to use. Take out as much dough as needed and roll about 1/2 inch thick on floured board. Cut with biscuit cutter. Let rise. Brush top with butter. Bake at 400° for 10-15 minutes.

If you prefer a double biscuit, roll dough thinner, cut, brush top of one with butter and place a second one on top.

Baking Powder Biscuits
Niece-Carrol Keeney Abdon - Greenup, KY

2 c. sifted all-purpose flour
1 T baking powder
1/2 tsp. salt
1/4 c. shortening
3/4 c. milk

Sift flour, baking powder and salt together into a bowl. Then use your fingers, fork or pastry blender to blend the shortening and flour into very fine particles. Add the milk and stir just enough to make the particles cling together. Should be a very soft dough. Turn out on a floured surface and knead for about a minute, then either roll or pat out. If you want thick fluffy biscuits, dough should be 1/2 to 3/4 inch thick, and if you want thin crusty biscuits it should be be about 1/4 inch thick. Cut in rounds. For crispy biscuits, place far apart on ungreased cookie sheet; for fluffier biscuits place close together on ungreased cookie sheet. Bake in preheated oven 450° for about 12 to 15 minutes. About 12 biscuits. Note: For drop biscuits, add another 1/4 c. milk, drop by spoonfuls onto a buttered baking sheet, and bake the same way.

Beer Biscuits
Almost like Marshmallows
Cousin-James Stewart - E. Liverpool, OH

2 c. Bisquick
1 (6 oz.) can of beer
1 T sugar

Mix all together (will look like bread sponge). Put in muffin tins, preferable med. size and bake until brown (about 400°).

Uncle Jesse Hilton's Pan Biscuits

Niece-Betty Stuart Darby Baird - Wadestown, WV

3-1/4 c. plus 2 tsp flour
1-1/2 T baking powder
3/4 tsp. baking soda
1 tsp. salt
1/2 c. solid shortening
1-1/2 c. buttermilk

Grease 9 x 9 x 2 inch bread pan. In large bowl, sift together the 3 1/4 c. flour, baking powder, soda and salt. Cut in shortening with fork or tips of fingers until mixture is crumbly. Add buttermilk all at once; stir lightly just until dough is blended.

Turn dough out onto floured surface and knead a few times. Pat evenly into greased pan. With knife, score top of dough 1/4 inch deep and 3 inches apart to form 9 squares. Sprinkle remaining 2 tsp. flour over top. Bake in hot preheated oven 450° about 35 minutes or until golden brown. Note: Very good with honey and butter or sorgum and butter.

Sour Milk or Soda Biscuits

Sister-Mary Stuart Nelson - Greenup, KY

2 c. flour
1/2 tsp. soda
2 tsp. baking powder
2 tsp. fat
1/2 tsp. salt
3/4 c. sour milk or buttermilk

Mix and sift dry ingredients. Rub in fat with tips of fingers or chop with a knife. Add milk gradually to make a soft dough. Toss on a well-floured board. Pat or roll to one inch thickness and cut with biscuit cutter dipped in flour. Place close together on an oiled pan and bake in hot oven, 450°, 10-15 minutes.

Corn Breads

Corn Fritters

Cousin-Vicki Hotopp Caserta - Dayton, OH

3/4 c. sifted flour
2 tsp. baking powder
1 scant tsp. salt
16 oz. can whole kernel corn, drained
1 egg, beaten
1/2 c. milk

Combine beaten egg, milk, and corn. Add mixture to sifted dry ingredients and mix until flour is moistened. Drop by level T into hot deep oil (350°). Fry 4 to 5 minutes until golden brown. Drain on paper towel. Serve hot.

Puffy Corn Fritters

Cousin-Cynthia Smith Lewis - West Portsmouth, OH

1 -1/3 c. flour
1-1/2 tsp. baking powder
3/4 tsp. salt
1 T sugar
2/3 c. milk
1 egg, beaten
1 can whole kernel corn, drained

Sift together flour, baking powder, salt and sugar. Add milk and egg gradually to the flour mixture. Stir in the drained corn and drop by T into deep hot fat. Fry until golden brown. Drain on paper towel and serve with maple syrup.

Corn Sticks

Nephew-Roy Abdon - Greenup, KY

1/2 c. all-purpose flour
2 T sugar
1 c. cornmeal
1/2 stick melted butter
2 tsp. baking powder
1/2 tsp. salt
1 large egg
1 c. milk

Heat oven to 450°. Sift dry ingredients into mixing bowl. Beat egg well with milk and butter. Stir into dry ingredients. Grease and heat corn stick pan (for 1 doz. sticks). Spoon batter into hot pans, filling each space about 2/3 full. Bake 15-20 min. Makes 12 sticks. Serve while hot.

Crackling Bread

(made by mother, Martha Hilton Stuart)
Sister-Glennis Liles - Greenup, KY

Sift together 2 cups of cornmeal and a small handful of flour, 1/2 teaspoonful of soda and a good-sized dash of salt. Add 1 cup of sour milk and blend well. Then add 1 cup (more or less) cracklings. Stir lightly with your hands. Make into small oblong pones, and bake in hot oven. Cracklings are the remains of rendering lard. There is some fat remaining and therefore no fat is used in this recipe.

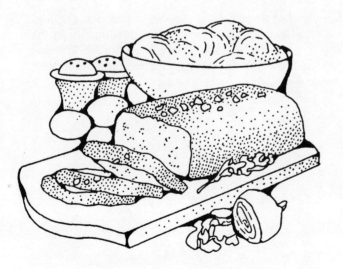

Crusty Corn Bread

Sister-in-law-Betty Stuart - Greenup, KY

1 c. cornmeal
1/2 c. all-purpose flour
1 T sugar
1 T baking powder
1/2 tsp. soda
1/2 tsp. salt
1 egg, beaten
1 c. buttermilk
1/4 c. bacon drippings

Method: Combine first 6 ingredients, mix well. Add egg and buttermilk. Stir until smooth. Place bacon drippings in 9 inch skillet. Heat at 425° for 5 minutes. Remove skillet from oven, pour part of hot drippings into batter and mix well. Quickly pour batter into skillet. Bake at 425° for 20 to 25 minutes or until golden brown. 8 servings. Note: This recipe may be used for yellow meal or white meal.

Deluxe Cornbread

Cousin-Faye Hilton, Frankfort, KY

2 eggs
1 (8 oz.) carton commercial sour cream
1 c. cream style corn
1/2 c. vegetable oil
1 c. self rising meal

Beat eggs. Add remaining ingredients, blending well. Bake in pre-heated 10 in. iron skillet (greased) at 425° for 30 min. or until browned. Refrigerate what isn't eaten and it warms up well.

Fried Corn Pone

Brother-James M. Stuart - Greenup, KY

1 egg
1 T baking powder
1 tsp. soda
1 tsp. salt
2 c. cornmeal
1 3/4 c. buttermilk

Mix and fry into cakes.

"On cold winter days Mom would quilt in front of the fire. Many times I fried corn cakes on the open fire because we wouldn't have a fire in the cookstove. I often added leftover soup beans from the day before to make bean cakes. They were very good with cold sweet milk for lunch."

Grandma's Corn Bread

(Mary Hylton Johnson)
Cousin-Helen Shultz - Portsmouth, OH

2 c. corn meal
1-1/2 c. all purpose flour
3/4 tsp. baking soda
2 tsp. baking powder
2 c. buttermilk
1 egg, beaten
1 tsp. salt
1 T sugar

Combine all dry ingredients and mix well. Add buttermilk and egg, stirring well. Meanwhile add 3 T bacon or ham drippings to 9 x 9 inch square baking pan and heat to piping hot in oven. Pour excess fat into cornbread mixture leaving enough to coat bottom and sides of pan. Mix well. Pour into pan and bake about 30 minutes in 375° oven.

Jalapeno Cornbread

Cousin-Mary Arnold - Hillsboro, OH

3 pieces bacon, fried and crumbled
1 c. yellow cornmeal
3 tsp. baking powder
1-1/2 tsp. salt
2 eggs, beaten
1 c. sour cream
1/2 c. vegetable oil
1 c. cream style corn
3 to 4 jalapeno peppers, minced, remove seeds
1 to 1 1/2 c. cheddar cheese, grated

Blend corn meal, baking powder, salt; add beaten eggs, sour cream, oil and corn. Mix well. Pour half the batter into a greased, heated pan. Spread some of cheese, peppers, and bacon in middle. Pour remaining batter on top. Sprinkle remaining cheese, peppers, and bacon on top.

Mexican Corn Bread I

Cousin-Ethel Stewart Terry - Ceredo, WV

1 c. corn meal (hot rise)
1 c. flour
1/2 c. cream style corn
1/4 c. sugar
1/4 c. onion (chopped)
1 c. longhorn cheese (diced or shredded)
3/4 c. oil
green pepper, cut up
3 banana peppers, cut up
1 c. sweet milk

Mix well and bake in large iron skillet. Bake for about 45 minutes or until brown on top. Bake as regular cornbread.

Mexican Corn Bread II

Cousin-Dorthea Stewart Mayo Hatten - Morganfield, KY

1/2 c. self-rising flour
1/2 c. plain flour
1 c. self-rising meal
2 eggs
1/4 c. sugar
1/4 c. oil
1 c. cream style corn
2 T onion
2 hot peppers, chopped
1 slice cheese broken into small pieces
1 green pepper, chopped

Mix flour, meal, sugar, onion, peppers, and cheese. Then add eggs, oil, and corn. Stir well and bake in 8 or 9 inch skillet for 30 minutes or until done. 350°.

Mom's Corn Bread

(Martha Hylton Stuart)
Sister-Mary Nelson - Greenup, KY

2 1/2 c. white cornmeal
1/2 c. flour
dash of salt
thick buttermilk (mix enough to make a batter)
pinch of soda (pinch=what you can pick up between
thumb and first 3 fingers)

Mix well, pour into hot greased iron skillet, or bread pan and bake at 500° until brown and crusty.

Quick Corn Bread

Cousin-Madison Adkins - Defiance, OH

2 c. self-rising corn meal
1/2 c. self-rising flour
1 T sugar
1 T melted shortening
1 c. milk

Stir ingredients until well blended. Heat round iron skillet, (if you don't have one–any skillet will do). Add 1 T shortening making sure it coats sides and bottom. Turn batter into skillet, and bake about 45 minutes in 400° oven-or until crust is golden brown. Turn out on rack to cool.

Muffins

Apple Muffins

Cousin-James E. Hilton - Frankfort, KY

1 1/4 c. oil
2 c. sugar
3 eggs
3 c. flour
2 tsp. vanilla
1 tsp. salt
1 tsp. soda
1 c. chopped nuts
1 c. coconut
2 c. chopped apples

Cream oil and sugar, then beat in eggs. Add vanilla. Sift in flour, salt, and soda. Fold in nuts, coconut, and then apples. Drop batter in muffin tins. Bake 350° for 20-30 minutes. Makes approximately 3-1/2 dozen.

Spiced Apple Muffins

Cousin-Alma Stewart Webb - St. Clair Shores, MI

2 c. flour
1/2 c. sugar
4 tsp. baking powder
1/2 tsp. salt
1/2 tsp. cinnamon
1 egg, beaten
1 c. milk
1/4 c. melted butter
2 c. chopped apples

2 T sugar
1/2 tsp. cinnamon

Beat egg and combine milk and melted butter. Add dry ingredients. Mix thoroughly and fold in apples. Fill muffin cups half full, sprinkle tops with mixture of sugar and cinnamon,. Bake at 425° for about 20 minutes.

Bran Muffins

Cousin-Alma Stewart Webb - St. Clair Shores, MI

2 c. Nabisco 100% bran cereal
4 c. All Bran cereal
2 c. boiling water
4 eggs
1 c. margarine
2 c. sugar
1 tsp. salt
1 qt. buttermilk
5 c. flour
5 tsp. baking soda
Raisins (optional)

Combine first three ingredients. Blend in remaining ingredients. Drop batter in muffin tins. Bake at 375° for 30 minutes. Will keep in refrigerator 6 weeks.

Do-Ahead Bran Muffins

Cousin-Anne Hilton Short - Forestville, MD

1/2 c. butter or margarine, melted
1 c. firmly packed brown sugar
1/2 c. unsulfured molasses
4 eggs, lightly beaten
2 c. milk
2 c. whole bran cereal
1 c. unprocessed bran flakes
1 box (12 Oz.) pitted prunes, diced
1 c. all purpose flour
1 c. whole wheat flour
4 tsp. baking powder
1 tsp. salt
1 tsp. cinnamon
1/4 c. chopped natural almonds
2 T sesame seed

In large bowl whisk butter or margarine, brown sugar and molasses until smooth. Beat in eggs and milk. Stir in cereal, bran flakes and prunes. In medium bowl combine flours, baking powder, salt and cinnamon. Add to liquid ingredients; stir until moistened. (Can be made ahead. Refrigerate in a covered glass container up to 2 weeks.) Preheat oven to 400°. Grease 32 (or desired quantity) 2 1/2 inch muffin pan cups. Spoon batter into prepared cups, filling each about three quarters full. Sprinkle with almonds and sesame seed. Bake 20 to 25 minutes and transfer to wire rack. Makes 32 muffins.

Honey-Corn Muffins

Niece-Sandy Nelson Perrine - Greenup, KY

1-3/4 c. all-purpose flour
3/4 c. white cornmeal
1/4 c. sugar
1 T baking powder
1 tsp. baking soda
1 tsp. salt
1/2 c. milk
1/4 c. fresh orange juice
1/4 c. (1/2 stick) butter, melted
1/4 c. honey
1 egg

Preheat oven to 350°. Grease muffin cups. Combine dry ingredients in bowl. Blend milk, melted butter, honey, juice and egg in small bowl. Add to dry ingredients, stirring until smooth; do not overmix. Divide batter among the muffin cups, bake 15 minutes or until golden brown and serve immediately with butter. Makes 16.

Pumpkin Muffins

Cousin-Randa Jane Murphy - Lucasville, OH

3/4 c. brown sugar
1/4 c. molasses
1/2 c. soft butter
1 egg
1/4 c. chopped pecans
1 c. pumpkin
1 tsp. soda
1/4 tsp. salt
1 3/4 c. flour

Cream sugar, molasses, and butter; add egg and pumpkin and blend well. Mix flour, soda and salt; beat this mixture into pumpkin batter. Fold in chopped pecans. Fill well greased muffin tins about 1/2 full. Bake 375° for 20 minutes. (Mini-muffin tins about 10 minutes). Doubled, this recipe makes 1 dozen regular and 2 dozen mini-muffins. Good for breakfast!

Raisin Bran Muffins

Cousin-Mae Pennington Fellows - Albuquerque, NM

1 (15 oz.) box Raisin Bran
5 c. flour
3 c. sugar
4 eggs
1 qt. buttermilk
5 tsp. soda
2 tsp. salt
1 c. oil
1/2 c. raisins (optional)

Mix real well in large bowl. Store in refrigerator (covered) Keeps 3 weeks. (Bake fresh or bake and freeze). Bake at 400° for 15 minutes.

Six Week Bran Muffins

Cousin-Faye Hilton - Frankfort, KY

6 c. Kellog's All Bran
2 c. boiling water
1 c. corn oil
3 c. sugar
4 eggs
1 qt. buttermilk
3/4 lb. seeded raisins (approx.)
1 c. chopped nuts (optional)
2 1/2 c. unsifted whole wheat flour
2 1/2 c. all purpose flour
4 tsp. soda
2 tsp. salt

Pour boiling water over bran in large mixing bowl and let stand to be added last. In another large bowl, mix flour, sugar, soda and salt. Beat eggs, stir in buttermilk and oil and add to flour mix. Stir in raisins and nuts. Mix bran into this mixture. Put in tight covered container and store in refrigerator until ready to bake. Grease muffin tins and fill 3/4 full. Bake at 375° for approx. 20 min. Batter will keep up to six weeks stored in frig. Do not stir batter when you get ready to bake.

Quick Breads

Fresh Apple Nut Bread

Niece-Sandy Nelson Perrine - Greenup, KY

1/4 c. (1/2 stick) butter, room temperature
1 c. packed light brown sugar
2 eggs
3 c. unsifted flour
2 c. peeled grated apple
3/4 c. chopped nuts
1-1/2 tsp. baking soda
1 tsp. powder
1 tsp. grated lemon peel
1 tsp. salt
1 tsp. cinnamon
1/4 tsp. grated fresh nutmeg
3/4 c. buttermilk

Preheat oven to 350°. Grease and flour a 9 x 5 inch loaf pan. Cream butter and sugar in medium bowl. Beat in eggs. Combine next 9 ingredients in separate bowl and blend into creamed mixture alternately with buttermilk. Turn into pan and bake until toothpick inserted in center comes out clean, about 1 hour. Cool 10 minutes, remove from pan and cool on wire rack. Dust with confectioners sugar.

Apricot Bread

Niece-Freda Keeney - Greenup, KY

1 c. boiling water
1-1/2 c. (1 pkg.) dried apricots
1/2 tsp. baking soda
1 c. granulated sugar
2 eggs
2 3/4 c. all-purpose flour
3 tsp. baking powder

Pour boiling water over the apricots and let stand just until tender, don't oversoak them. Drain off and reserve water. (If you don't have 1 c. add water to make 1 c.) Roughly chop apricots. Pour liquid into a large bowl, add soda, sugar, and eggs and mix well. Then add apricots, flour, baking powder. Mix again. Divide dough into two well-greased and floured loaf pans (9 x 5 x 3). Bake in preheated oven 350° for about 45 minutes or until done.

Banana Bread

Sister-Glennis Stuart Liles - Greenup, KY

1-3/4 c. sifted all-purpose flour
2 tsp. baking powder
1/4 tsp. baking soda
1/2 tsp. salt
1/3 c. shortening
2/3 c. sugar
2 eggs, well beaten
1 c. mashed, ripe bananas (2-3)

Sift together flour, baking powder, soda, and salt. Cream shortening and sugar. Add eggs and beat well. Add flour mixture alternately with bananas. Bake at 350° for 1 hour and 10 min., (or until done) in 9 x 5 x 3 loaf pan. Makes one loaf. Recipe can be doubled.

Banana Nut Bread

Cousin-Alma Stewart Webb - St. Clair Shores, MI

1 c. sugar (or 3/4 c. honey)
1/4 c. Crisco
2 eggs
1-1/2 c. mashed ripe bananas
3/4 tsp. soda
1/2 tsp. salt
2 c. flour
1/2 c. nuts chopped

Cream shortening and sugar together. Add eggs and beat well. Add soda to mashed bananas and add to creamed mixture. Add flour and salt, mix well. Add nuts, grease pans. Bake in 325° oven 1 hour and 15 minutes. Makes 2 breads (2" x 7-5/8" pans).

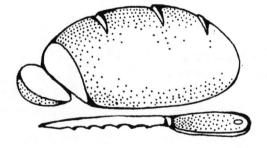

Cranberry Bread

Niece-Shirley Stuart - Greenup, KY

3 c. all-purpose flour
1 tsp. soda
1 tsp. baking powder
1 tsp. salt
2 eggs
1 c. granulated sugar
1/4 c. melted butter
1 1/4 c. milk
1 1/4 c. raw cranberries, roughly chopped
3/4 c. chopped walnuts or pecans

Sift flour with soda, baking powder and salt. In mixing bowl beat eggs, add sugar and blend. Stir in melted butter and milk. Stir in flour and fold in cranberries and nuts. Do not beat. Spread dough in a well greased 10 x 5 inch loaf pan. Bake in preheated oven 55-60 min. Let stand in tin for a few minutes before turning out on rack to cool. When cool wrap in plastic or foil and let sit overnight or at least a day before cutting. Store in refrigerator.

Kentucky Bourbon-Fruit Loaf

Brother-in-law-Herbert (Whitey) Liles - Greenup, KY

3 c. flour
1 T baking powder
1/2 tsp. baking soda
1/2 tsp. salt
3/4 tsp. allspice
4 T butter
1/2 c. dark molasses
1/2 c. sugar
2 eggs
1/2 c. Kentucky bourbon
1/2 c. strong coffee (use 2 tsp. instant coffee granules for
                    1/2 c. boiling water).
1-1/2 c. glace diced fruit and peel

Sift together flour, baking powder, soda, salt, and allspice; set aside. In mixing bowl, cream butter, molasses and sugar. Beat in eggs. Stir in bourbon and coffee. Add dry ingredients; stir in just until moistened. Fold in glace fruit and peel. Pour into greased 9-by-5-by 3 inch loaf pan. Bake in 350° oven about 1 hour, until inserted toothpick comes out clean. Let cool in pan for 10 minutes. Remove from pan to cool completely on wire rack. Makes 1 loaf.

Herbed Beer Bread

Cousin-Betsy Shultz - Portsmouth, OH

Preheat oven to 325°F

3 c. self-rising flour
3 T granulated sugar
1 T dried Italian herbs (or 1 tsp. each of oregano, basil, thyme)
12 oz. beer at room temperature
1/2 c. parmesan cheese, grated
1 T shortening
3 T cornmeal
2 T soft butter

In large mixing bowl, combine the flour, sugar, cheese and dried herbs. Mix well. Stir in the room temperature beer until batter is stiff. Grease loaf pan with the shortening and sprinkle bottom and sides with cornmeal. Pour batter into pan. Bake at 325° for 65 minutes. Brush loaf with softened butter and sprinkle with cornmeal. Turn out on rack to cool. This recipe also makes an interesting pizza crust.

Pumpkin Bread

Niece-Sandy Nelson Perrine - Greenup, KY

3 c. sugar
4 eggs, beaten
1 c. salad oil
1-1/2 tsp. salt
1 tsp. cinnamon
1 tsp. nutmeg
2/3 c. water
2 c. canned pumpkin
3-1/2 c. flour
2 tsp. soda

Mix sugar, eggs, oil, salt, cinnamon, nutmeg, and water in a bowl. Add pumpkin and mix well. Stir in flour and soda. Place in two well-greased loaf pans. Bake at 350° for 1 hour.

Zucchini Bread I

Cousin-Norma Jean Pennington Darnell - Greenup, KY

3 eggs
2 c. sugar
1 c. oil
3 c. flour
1 tsp. soda
1 tsp. salt
1/2 tsp. baking powder
2 tsp. cinnamon
2 c. grated zucchini (peeled and seeded)
3 tsp. vanilla
1/2 c. chopped pecans or walnuts

Mix together egg, sugar, and oil. Then add all the remaining ingredients and mix together. Grease and flour two large or three small loaf pans. Pour batter into pans and bake one hour at 350°. This bread freezes well, or the zucchini may be grated and frozen until you wish to make the bread.

Glaze:
1 c. powdered sugar
Add enough lemon juice to make paste and pour over hot bread.

Zucchini Bread II

Cousin-Faye Hilton - Frankfort, KY

1 c. cooking oil
3 eggs, beaten
2 tsp. vanilla
2 c. all purpose flour
1 c. whole wheat flour
1 c. brown sugar
1 c. granulated sugar
1 tsp. soda
1 tsp. baking powder
1 tsp. salt
2 tsp. gr. cinnamon
1 tsp. nutmeg
1/2 tsp. pumpkin pie spice
2 c. grated zucchini (unpeeled)
1/2 c. chopped nuts, raisins, and/or pineapple (optional)

Grease and flour 2 large loaf pans. Mix oil, eggs, vanilla, and sugars; combine five dry ingredients and add to egg mixture. Add zucchini, nuts, raisins or pineapple. Mix thoroughly. Bake at 350° for approx. 1 hour. Yields 2 large loaves. (I use 1 c. nuts and no raisins, or pineapple)

Zucchini Bread III

Cousin-Beverly Stewart - Winter Haven , FL

3 eggs
1/4 tsp. baking powder
2 c. sugar
3 c. flour
1 c. coarsely chopped nuts
1 c. vegetable oil
3 tsp. ground cinnamon
3 tsp. vanilla
1 tsp. salt
2 c. zucchini (raw, grated)
1 tsp. baking powder

Beat eggs till light and foamy. Add sugar, oil, zucchini and vanilla and mix lightly but well. Combine flour, salt, soda, baking powder and cinnamon and add to egg, zucchini mixture. Stir until well blended. Add nuts and pour into two large loaf pans. Bake at 350° for 1 hour. Cool on rack.

Popovers

Nephew-Tony Abdon - Greenup, KY

2 eggs, beaten
1 c. milk
1 T melted shortening
1 c. sifted all-purpose flour
1/2 tsp. salt

Combine the eggs, milk and shortening, then add the flour and salt and beat with rotary beater until the batter is smooth and free of lumps. Pour into hot oiled custard cups or muffin pans, filling 1/2 full. Bake 15 minutes at 425°, then reduce the oven temp. to 350° and bake 20 minutes longer. Add 1/4 c. grated sharp cheddar cheese, if desired. 8-12 servings.

Yeast Breads

Buns, Orange Blossom (from frozen dough)

Niece-Regina Nelson Stout - Greenup, KY

5-1/2 to 6-1/2 c. unsifted flour
3/4 c. sugar
1 tsp. salt
3 pkgs. active dry yeast
1/2 c. softened butter or margarine
1 c. very warm water (120-130° F)
3 eggs
Melted butter or margarine
Orange Sugar (Recipe follows)

In a large bowl thoroughly mix 1 1/4 c. flour, sugar, salt and undissolved active dry yeast. Add softened butter. Gradually add water to dry ingredients and beat 2 minutes at medium speed of electric mixer, scraping bowl occasionally. Add eggs and 1/4 c. flour. Beat at high speed 2 minutes, scraping bowl occasionally. Stir in enough additional flour to make a soft dough. Turn out on lightly floured board; knead until smooth and elastic, about 8 to 10 minutes. Divide dough into 3 equal portions. Divide each portion into 8 equal pieces; form each piece into a small ball. Dip each ball into melted butter then coat with an equal part of the prepared Orange Sugar. Place in a greased 8" round cake pan. Cover pan tightly with plastic wrap, then with aluminum foil place in freezer. Repeat with remaining pieces of dough and coating. Keep frozen up to 4 weeks.

Remove from freezer. Let stand, covered loosely with plastic wrap at room temperature until fully thawed, about 3 hours. Let rise in a warm place, free from a draft, until more than doubled in bulk, about 2 hours and 15 minutes. Bake at 350° for 25-30 min. or until done. Remove from pans and cool on wire racks.

Orange Sugar: Mix together 1 c. sugar and 2 T grated orange peel. Makes 2 dozen buns.

Cinnamon Leaf Coffee Ring

Cousin-Ginny Belle Smith - Lucasville, OH

2 c. milk
2 pkg. dry yeast
3/4 c. shortening
1/4 c. margarine
1/2 c. sugar
2 tsp. salt
4 egg yolks or 2 eggs beaten
6 c. flour

Cool milk to warm; sprinkle the yeast over the top, let stand to soften. Cream shortening and butter, add sugar and salt. Cream until light and fluffy. Add eggs, yeast, milk and enough flour to make soft dough. Knead until smooth and elastic on lightly floured board. Place in greased bowl, cover and let rise until double. (1 hr.) Roll dough thin, cut into rounds, with a biscuit cutter. Dip each round into melted butter (1 cup) then in cinnamon and sugar mixture (2 tsp. of cinnamon to 2 cups of sugar). Stand up in well buttered ring molds until full. Let rise until light (1 hour.) Bake in 350° oven about 25 minutes. Cool slightly before turning out. Makes 20-25 servings. Make plain rolls out of left over dough.

Swedish Coffee Ring with Almond Filling

Cousin-Randa Jane Murphy - Lucasville, OH

1 pkg. active dry yeast
1/4 c. warm water
3/4 c lukewarm milk (scalded, then cooled)
1/4 c. sugar
1/4 c. margarine or butter, softened
1 egg
1/2 tsp. ground cardamon
1/2 tsp. salt
3-1/4 to 3-1/2 c. all-purpose flour

Dissolve yeast in warm water in large bowl. Stir in milk, sugar, margarine, egg, cardamon, salt and 2 cups of flour. Beat until smooth. Stir in enough remaining flour to make dough easy to handle.

Turn dough onto lightly floured surface; knead until smooth and elastic, about 5 minutes. Place in greased bowl; then turn greased side up. Cover; let rise in warm place until double, 1 to 1-1/2 hours. (Dough is ready if indentation remains when touched). Prepare almond filling.

Almond Filling
Mix 1 cup almond paste, 1/4 cup packed brown sugar and 1/4 cup margarine or butter, softened, until smooth.

Punch down dough. Roll into rectangle, 15 x 9 inches, on lightly floured surface. Spread with filling. Roll up tightly, beginning at 15 inch side. Pinch edge of dough into roll to seal well. Stretch into a ring on lightly greased cookie sheet. Pinch ends together. With scissors, make cuts 2/3 of the way through the ring at 1 inch intervals. Turn each section on its side. Let rise until double in bulk, 40 to 50 minutes. Heat oven to 350°. Bake until golden brown, 25 to 30 minutes. (If coffee ring browns too quickly, cover loosely with aluminum foil). Spread ring with glaze; garnish with nuts and cherries if desired.

Dill Bread

Cousin-Joseph Hilton Hunt - Hamilton, OH

1 c. creamed cottage cheese
2 T sugar
1 T minced onion
1 T butter
2 tsp. dill weed
1 tsp. salt
1/4 tsp. soda
1 egg
1 pkg. active dry yeast
1/4 c. warm water
2 to 2-1/4 c. flour

Heat cottage cheese until lukewarm and add the next 7 ingredients. Mix the yeast and water; add to mixture. Add flour to form a stiff dough. Let rise in a round casserole or 2 small loaf pans (40 minutes). Bake at 350° for 45 minutes. Spread with butter and coarse salt on top while still hot.

Buttermilk Doughnuts

Niece-Lori Ann Stuart - Greenup, KY

1 pkg. dry yeast
1/2 c. warm water (105-115°)
1/2 c. buttermilk
3 T shortening, melted
3 T sugar
2-1/2 to 3 c. self-rising flour
vegetable oil
2-1/2 c. sifted powdered sugar
1/4 c. milk

Dissolve yeast in warm water in a large mixing bowl; let stand 5 minutes. Add buttermilk, shortening, sugar, and 1-1/2 c. flour, stirring well. Add enough remaining flour to make a soft dough.

Turn out onto a floured surface; knead several times. Roll dough to 1/2-inch thickness, and cut with a 2 1/2-inch doughnut cutter. Place doughnuts on lightly floured surface. Cover and let rise in warm place (85°), free from drafts, 45 minutes or until doubled in bulk.

Heat 2 to 3 inches of oil to 375°: drop in 4 or 5 doughnuts at a time. Cook about 2 minutes or until golden brown, turning once. Drain well on paper towels.

Combine powdered sugar and milk; stir until smooth. Dip each doughnut in glaze while warm; allow excess glaze to drip off. Cool on wire racks or serve warm. Yield: 14 doughnuts.

Oatmeal Yeast Loaves

Cousin-William Everett Holbrook - Greenup, KY

1 c. quick-cooking oats
2 c. boiling water
1/2 c. molasses
1/3 c. butter or margarine
2-1/2 tsp. salt
2 pkgs. dry yeast
1/3 c. warm water (105-115°)
5 1/2 to 6 c. all-purpose flour

Combine oats and boiling water in large mixing bowl; let stand about 20 minutes. Add molasses, butter, and salt, stirring until butter melts.

Dissolve yeast in warm water; let stand for 5 minutes. Stir yeast mixture and 2 cups flour into oats mixture; mix well. Gradually stir remaining flour into batter. (Dough will be soft.)

Turn dough out onto a well floured surface, and knead about 5 minutes or until smooth and elastic. Place dough in greased bowl, turning to grease top. Cover and let rise in a warm place (85°), free from drafts, 1 hour or until doubled in bulk.

Punch dough down, and divide in half; shape each half into a loaf. Placed in two greased 8 x 4 x 3 inch loafpans.

Cover and let rise in a warm place (85°), free from drafts, 1 hour or until doubled in bulk. Bake at 350° for 30 minutes or until sound hollow when tapped. Yield: 2 loaves.

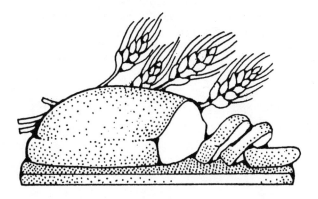

Whole Wheat Pita Rounds

Niece-Shirley Stuart - Greenup, KY

1 pkg. dry yeast
1 c. warm water (105-115°)
1 T sugar
1 1/2 c. all-purpose flour
1/2 tsp. salt
1 1/2 c. whole wheat flour

Dissolve yeast in warm water in a large mixing bowl; add sugar and let stand 5 minutes. Add all-purpose flour and salt; beat at low speed with an electric mixer until smooth. Gradually stir in whole wheat flour.

Turn dough out onto a floured surface; knead 3 minutes until smooth and elastic. Cover dough and let rest 10 minutes. Divide dough into 6 equal portions; shape each portion into a 5-inch circle. Place circles on lightly greased baking sheets. Bake at 450° for 8 to 10 minutes. Cut in half with scissors. Yield: 12 bread rounds. If bread round is to be filled with sandwich filling, make pocket in bread with a small sharp knife from cut side of round.

Hot Rolls I

Cousin-William Everett Holbrook - Greenup, KY

2 pkg. dry yeast
1 c. lukewarm water
1 tsp. sugar
1 c. cooking oil
1 c. scalded milk
1/2 c. sugar
1/2 T salt
2 eggs, beaten
6 c. flour (about)

Sprinkle the dry yeast and the tsp. sugar over the lukewarm water; set aside. Put the oil, sugar and salt in a large bowl. Pour in the scalded milk and stir until all of the ingredients are dissolved. Cool to lukewarm. Stir yeast mixture and the eggs into the lukewarm mixture. Add about 6 c. flour (give or take a little) in 2 additions: mixing first with a wooden spoon and then by hand until you have a soft dough which is easy to handle. Have dough as soft as possible-almost sticky. Turn out on lightly floured board and knead till smooth and elastic.

Grease a large bowl the size you mixed the dough in. Place dough in bowl. Let dough rise for 1 hour or more until the dough is near the top of the bowl. Punch down dough. Work dough until it isn't dry. Grease a large baking sheet with cooking oil. Pinch off dough about the size of a small biscuit. Form into a round ball by turning around and around in your hand until it is round and smooth. (Might take some practice.) Place on baking sheet, with a very small space between rolls.

Let rise until double in size. 1 hour or more. Place in preheated 375° oven. Bake until golden brown, about 20 minutes. Melt about 1/2 stick of butter in a small pan. Remove rolls from oven. Brush rolls with the melted butter while still hot. Note: This recipe should make about 2 dozen medium size rolls.

Hot Rolls II

Cousin- Edna Stewart Duncan - Huntington, WV

1 c. shortening
3/4 c. sugar
1 c. cold water
2 pkgs. yeast
3 tsp. lemon juice
1 c. boiling water
2 eggs
1 1/2 tsp. salt
6 c. flour

Melt shortening in boiling water. Blend in cold water, sugar, salt, yeast, and beaten eggs. Add 3 cups flour, beating well with a mixer. Add lemon juice and remaining flour. Let raise until double. Make into rolls or keep in refrigerator and cover with double wax paper and damp tea towel. Remove as needed. To make clover leaf rolls, put 3 small balls of dough in greased muffin tin. Let rise until double in bulk. Bake at 350° for 15 to 20 minutes.

Hot Rolls III

Cousin-Brian Hotopp - Columbus, OH

These have a light texture and buttery flavor. They almost melt in your mouth. They do have to be refrigerated overnight.

*2 eggs
1 c. hot water
1 c. cold water
1 stick margarine
1/2 c. sugar
1 pkg. yeast
7 c. flour*

Beat eggs in small bowl and set aside. Pour hot (boiling) water over margarine and stir until margarine is melted. Add sugar to margarine and mix well. Dissolve yeast in mixture and add cold water. Add eggs and mix well. Add flour, a few cups at a time and mix thoroughly, using hands if necessary. Cover and refrigerate overnight.

Roll dough onto floured surface and cut with biscuit cutter. Dip each roll in melted butter and place in cake pan. Cover rolls and let rise in warm place until doubled in size. Bake at 375° for about 5 minutes or until golden brown.

Ice Box Rolls

Daughter-Jane Stuart Juergensmeyer - Gainesville, FL

*2 c. boiling water
1/2 c. sugar
1 tsp. salt
1 scant teacup lard
2 eggs
2 cakes of yeast
1/4 c. warm water
1 tsp. sugar
8 c. flour*

Dissolve yeast and 1 tsp. sugar together in warm water; dissolve 1/2 c. sugar, lard and salt in boiling water; cool. Combine the two mixtures together. Add eggs, and 4 c. flour and beat well. Add 4 more c. flour and beat. Cover and store in refrigerator. Let rise at room temperature until double in bulk before baking.

Out of this World Rolls

Cousin-Mae Pennington Fellows - Albuquerque, NM

*2 pkgs. yeast
1/2 c. warm water*

*3 eggs-well beaten
1/2 c. shortening
1/2 c. sugar
1 c. warm water
1 tsp. salt
4-1/2 c. flour divided*

Dissolve yeast in1/2 c. warm water in a large bowl: Beat eggs well and add to dissolved yeast. Add other ingredients to 2-1/2 c. flour, beat well, add rest of flour, cover and let rise. Punch down and refrigerate over night. Shape and let stand 3 hours. Roll like jelly roll (I spread this with melted butter before I roll). Cut thin and place in muffin tins. Bake at 400° for 12 to 15 minutes.

Potato Rolls

Sister-in-law-Betty Stuart - Greenup, KY

*8 c. flour
2 eggs
1 c. shortening (Spry or Crisco)
1 c. (heaping) mashed potatoes
1 c. potato water
1 c. warm water
1 cake of yeast
1-1/2 tsp. salt
1/4 c. sugar*

Sift dry ingredients into large crock or bowl. Add eggs, shortening, water and potatoes. Knead thoroughly. Cover with damp cloth, put in ice box or refrigerator overnight. Next day take out of the refrigerator and turn over in greased bowl. Shape into rolls. Let set at least 1-1/2 to 3 hours at room temperature before baking. 2-1/2 dozen of delicious cloverleaf rolls. Dough will keep several days in refrigerator.

Yeast Rolls

Cousin-Ramona Adkins - Defiance, OH

2 oz. sugar
3 oz. fat
1 pkg. dry yeast
2 eggs, beaten
1-1/2 tsp. salt
2/3 qt. scalded milk
1/2 c. luke warm water
2 lb.-6 oz. flour

Put sugar, salt, and shortening in bowl, add hot milk. Mix on low speed. Cool to luke warm. Mix yeast, water and eggs with all above at med. speed, until blended. Add flour to make a moderately soft dough. Mix on low speed until smooth and satiny. Let rise in warm place until double in size. Punch down, let rise again. Form into rolls and bake 15-25 minutes at 400°.

Sally Lunn

Niece-Ruth Nelson - Greenup, KY

This recipe was brought over from England with the early settlers.

1 c. lukewarm milk
1 pkg. yeast
1/2 c. softened butter or oil
1/3 c. sugar
1/2 tsp. salt
3 eggs
3-1/2 c. flour

Dissolve yeast in milk in a mixing bowl. Let stand for five minutes. Add butter, sugar, salt, and eggs, and beat with a strong rotary beater or electric mixer. Gradually adding 3-1/2 c. flour. Leave the mixture in the bowl and let rise until very light and about double in size. Spoon into a buttered 10-inch angel cake pan or Turk's head pan or 2 dozen, 2-inch muffin pans. Let rise about 1 hour. Bake 50 minutes at 350° in a large pan or 20 minutes at 425° in muffin pans.

Freezer White Bread

Brother-in-law-Herbert (Whitey) Liles - Greenup, KY

12-1/2 to 13-1/2 c. unsifted flour
1/2 c sugar
2 T salt
2/3 c. instant nonfat dry milk solids
4 pkgs. active dry yeast
1/4 c. softened butter or margarine
4 c. very warm water (120-130°F)

In a large bowl thoroughly mix 4 c. flour, sugar, salt, dry milk solids, and undissolved active dry yeast. Add butter. Gradually add water to dry ingredients and beat 2 minutes at medium speed of electric mixer, scraping bowl occasionally. Add 1 1/2 c. flour. Beat at high speed 2 minutes, scraping bowl occasionally. Stir in enough additional flour to make a stiff dough. Turn out onto lightly floured board; knead until smooth and elastic, about 15 minutes. Cover with a towel; let rest 15 minutes.

Divide dough into 4 equal parts. Form each piece into a smooth round ball. Flatten each ball into a mound 6 inches in diameter. Place on greased baking sheets. Cover with plastic wrap. Freeze unto firm. Transfer to plastic bags. Freeze up to 4 weeks.

Remove from freezer; place on ungreased baking sheets. Cover; let stand at room temperature until fully thawed, about 4 hours. Shape each ball into loaves. Place in greased 8 1/2 x 4 1/2 x 2 1/2" loaf pans. Let rise in warm place, free from draft, until doubled in bulk, about 1 1/2 hours. Bake at 350° about 35 minutes, or until done. Remove from pans and cool on wire racks.

*For round loaves: Let thawed dough rise on ungreased baking sheets until doubled, about 1 hour. Bake as above. Makes 4 loaves.

Other Breads

Dumplings

Cousin-William E. Holbrook - Greenup, KY

3 eggs
Ball of butter (size of a small egg)
1/2 c. milk
3 c. self-rising flour

Combine all ingredients and mix well. Make dumplings any size you wish. Drop in boiling broth, and cover tightly-do not remove lid for 15 minutes. This may be used with chickens, tomatoes or blackberries.

Lemon Bread

Cousin-Loretta Benner-Lucasville, OH

1-1/2 c. sugar
6 T margarine
3 eggs
1 T lemon extract
1 medium lemon peel, grated
1/2 c. milk
1-1/2 c. flour
1-1/2 tsp. baking powder
1/4 tsp. salt
3 T fresh lemon juice

Cream 1 cup of the sugar and margarine. Add eggs, extract, lemon peel, and milk. Beat in flour, baking powder, and salt. Pour into greased and floured 9 inch loaf pan. Bake at 350 degrees for 30 to 40 minutes.

Combine lemon juice and 1/2 cup of sugar. Remove bread from oven and top with mixture. Return to oven for 10 minutes. Cool for 30 minutes and remove from pan.

Indian Fry Bread

Niece-Betty Baird - Wadestown, WV

3 to 3-1/2 c. flour
1/2 tsp. salt
1 T baking powder
1 T. shortening
1 c. warm water
Oil for frying

In a large bowl, combine the first four ingredients. Add water, a small amount at a time, blending dough until it is soft but not sticky, about 5 minutes (too much stirring makes it tough). Cover and let rest 30 minutes.

Heat oil (2-3 inches deep) in heavy skillet to 370°. Pull off 2-inch pieces of dough and stretch them into flat rounds (like small pizza crusts). Ease the dough rounds carefully into hot oil. Dough sinks, then slowly rises. When bubbles begin turn dough gently and fry other side until lightly browned. Total cooking time per piece is 3-5 minutes. Drain on paper towels or paper bags and serve hot. Yield 12-4 inch breads.

This bread can be served many ways: sweetened with honey or sugar and cinnamon sprinkled on, or topped with hot salsa, ground beef, tomatoes and lettuce, or a rich guacamole. The variety is endless.

French Toast

Niece-Melissa Liles - Greenup, KY

3 eggs (or 6 yolks) beaten slightly
1/2 tsp. salt
1 tsp. sugar
1 c. milk
6-8 slices bread
fat for frying

Combine eggs, salt, sugar, and milk in shallow dish. Dip bread in egg mixture to moisten. Brown on one side on well oiled griddle or skillet. Turn and brown other side. Add fat as necessary to prevent sticking. Serve with butter and syrup, honey, or any fruit spread. 2-4 servings.

Buckwheat Pancakes

Nephew-John D. Baird - Wadestown, WV

3/4 c. unbleached flour
1/2 c. buckwheat flour
2 T sugar
1 T baking powder
1/2 tsp. salt
1 egg
1 c. and 2 T milk
3 T butter or margarine, melted

In bowl, sift flours, sugar, salt and baking powder. In another bowl, beat eggs, milk and butter. Add all at once to the flour mixture; mix just until moist (batter will be lumpy). Cover and let stand 6 hours at room temperature, or refrigerate over night. This will make fluffier pancakes.

Preheat griddle to 400°, or until a few drops of water sprinkled on the hot griddle dance about. Brush griddle with oil. Stir before baking. Use a scant 1/4 c. for each pancake. Bake until edges are slightly dry, then turn to brown other side. Makes 12 pancakes.

Serve with maple syrup and butter. Tip: Keep pancakes warm by placing them on a plate with a colander turned upside down over them. Set in warm place. Heat stays in, steam escapes.

German Pancakes

Cousin-Beverly Jane Benner Murphy - Lucasville, OH

4 eggs
1/2 c. plain flour
1/2 tsp. salt
1/2 c. milk
2 T melted butter
powdered sugar
maple syrup

Butter a 9-inch heavy skillet. Put eggs in blender. Cover and process until light yellow. Add remaining ingredients. Process until smooth. Pour all of the batter into the skillet. Bake in preheated oven at 450° for 10 minutes. Reduce heat to 350° and bake until browned. Dust with powdered sugar. Serve immediately with maple syrup.

Good with sausage. Toward the end of baking it puffs up and "crawls"up the sides of the pan. Very pretty for company. It tastes like a combination french toast and pancakes.

Bugs Bunny Bread

Cousin-Loretta Benner-Lucasville, OH

1 c. sugar or packed brown sugar
2/3 c. salad oil
2 eggs
1 tsp. cinnamon
3/4 tsp. nutmeg
1/4 tsp. salt
1 tsp. baking soda
1-2/3 c. whole wheat or graham flour
1-1/2 c. carrots, finely grated
1/2 c. raisins
1/2 c. chopped nuts

Preheat oven to 350 degrees. Cream sugar with oil. Add eggs and cream well. Sift together dry ingredients and add to creamed ingredients. Blend well. Add carrots and mix well. Stir in raisins and nuts. Pour batter into a greased standard loaf pan. Bake in 350 degree oven for 1 hour.

Cakes and Frostings

Cakes

Fresh Apple Cake I
Fresh Apple Cake II
Fresh Apple Cake III
Apple Nut Cake
Applesauce Cake I
Applesauce Cake II
Applesauce Cake III
Applesauce Cake IV
Applesauce Jam Cake
Kentucky Stack Cake
Old-Fashioned Stack Cake
Apple Filling for Stack Cake
Old Fashioned Dried Apple Stack Cake I
Old Fashioned Dried Apple Stack Cake II
Banana Split Cake
Blackberry Cake I
Blackberry Cake II
Jerry's Chocolate Upside Down Cake
Old Fashioned Blackberry Cake
Easy Blackberry Cake
Kentucky Butter Cake
Carrot Cake
Buttermilk-Brown Sugar Cheesecake
Easy Cheese Cake
Chocolate and Cherry Ring
Chocolate Praline Layer Cake
Date Cake
Duncan Turtle Cake
Faye's Favorite Chocolate Cake
Funnel Cakes
New Mexico Chocolate Sheet Cake
Texas Chocolate Cake
White Chocolate Cake
Coconut Cake
Rave Coconut Cake
Chess Squares
Chess Cake
Cinnamon Coffee Cake
Maude's Coffee Cake
Eggless, Butterless, Milkless, Cake
Candied Fruit Cake

Poor Man's Fruit Cake
Pork Fruit Cake
Grandma's Soft Gingerbread
Old Fashioned Molasses Cake (Gingerbread)
Gum Drop Cake
Jelly Roll
Oatmeal Cake
Orange Slices Fruit Cake
Orange Special
Pineapple Cake
Pineapple Deluxe Cake
Pineapple Nut Cake
Poppy Seed Cake I
Poppy Seed Cake II
Pound Cake
Nut Pound Cake
Queen Elizabeth II Cake
7 Up Cake
Sno-ball Cake
Mom's Old Fashioned Spice Cake
Strawberry Cake
Three Minute Cake
Texas Pecan Cake
Texas Sheet Cake
Southern Yam Cake
Mother's Yellow Cake
"You're Lucky If You Have Any Left" Cake

Frostings

Basic Fluffy Frosting
Orange Frosting
Chocolate Frosting
Strawberry Frosting
Banana Frosting
Caramel Frosting
Chocolate Glaze
Cooked Cake Frosting
Fluffy Cream Cheese Frosting
Nougatine Frosting
Quick Fudge Frosting

The loving family

Hickory Nut Cake

Wife-Naomi Deane Norris Stuart - W-Hollow, KY
3/4 c. butter
1/2 c. sugar
1 c. top milk
6 egg whites
3/4 tsp. salt
4 tsp. baking powder
1 c. hickory nuts
1/2 tsp . vanilla
3 c. flour

Method:
Cream butter and sugar. Flour nuts with 1/4 c. of the flour. Add milk and flour alternately. Add nuts, fold in beaten whites and flavoring. Bake in layers 20 to 30 minutes. In tube pan bake 1 hour at 350°. When cool ice as you wish or sprinkle with powdered sugar (I do).

On this very spot where I am using this typewriter, my mother and father used to sit around a table in their kitchen. Four of their seven children, for two were dead and one was born later, sat with them. Here we planned and talked and laughed. Only we didn't have an open fireplace. We had a big cookstove we called a wood range. It burned wood like a fireplace, and heat danced above its flat top like sunlight over a tin roof on a midsummer afternoon. Dad used to cut the stovewood for this range, and I carried armfuls inside the kitchen and put them inside the woodbox. In the mornings while Mom got breakfast, I used to go to the kitchen long before daylight and sit on the woodbox close to the stove while the kitchen got warm. But after the stove got really hot, we couldn't stay in this kitchen, no matter if it was twenty below outside, unless we raised a window to let the heat out.

Naomi and I rebuilt the fireplace and chimney in the old living room after we began housekeeping here. We figured that where this hearth stands is a great tradition of family life around the open fire. At least twenty families have lived here in the century and a half this house has stood. I can remember eight of these families myself. We estimated that six or seven thousand people, young and old, have sat before a blazing winter fire here and laughed, talked, joked, ate, and lived life joyously and fully in the years that have passed.

Before we tore down the old stone chimney, made by Eric Brickey, a Stonemason of another century, the elements had eroded many of these large stones until they were so thin there was danger of the chimney falling. heat escaping from this chimney melted the snow for a radius of twenty feet around. This frightened us, so we tore it down and replaced it with one made of bricks. But this was not breaking any old tradition, for the stone chimney had replaced an even earlier one made of sticks and mud. Sam Brickley, the bricklayer who made our new chimney, was a grandson of Old Eric, who had built the stone chimney and fireplace almost a hundred years before.

I wish the doors had been shut for each family in the century and a half past, and we could open them to look in on evenings of long ago when a man with buckskin moccasins on his feet and a coonskin cap on his head stood before the wood fire in a fireplace built of clay and sticks. I wish we could see his wife and their young children, the long rifle hanging to a joist and a powder horn on the wall. Captain George Naylor Davis (1781-1847) belonged to that time. He trained a company of men near here and took them by boat down the Ohio and Mississippi to help Andrew Jackson in the Battle of New Orleans. Later he served on Andrew Jackson's staff, for the General took a fancy to him. Now Captian George Naylor Davis lies buried in Brick Union's rural churchyard, which is six miles from here. There were no roads then, no schools, no work but hunting, fishing, clearing of land, building, and trading furs with Indians.

Then, like turning the pages of a book, I would like to see each family that shared this fireplace up until the present. I myself can remember back to 1915. Eric Brickey made the big chimney and fireplace so large it took a mule to pull a backstick for it. It took several men to roll one over the floor to get it in behind the andirons. Sam Brickey told us that his grandfather, Eric Brickey, called his stone chimneys, so many of which he built in this area, his "living monuments." Sam, in turn, called our new brick chimney one of his "living monuments." His living monument, too, would pass away when another age developed new chimney materials. But the tradition of the open fire would not pass away if we could do anything to keep it alive.

If we could close the kitchen doors to perpetuate what took place before our fireplace tonight, here is what we would pass along to some future inhabitants of this house.

It was after dinner, and we were drying the dishes. Naomi had already brought extra wood for the fire and filled the brass kettle that stands in the corner. I stopped drying long enough to put an extra sick of wood on the grate.

Naomi joined Jane in a Christmas carol, and while we finished the dishes and the flames leaped up through the wood in our kitchen fireplace, we sang "Silent Night." Christmas was a week or two off, but its spirit always precedes it. I remembered that this same song was sung before this same fireplace in the years from 1915 to 1918. And I am sure others sang it here long before then.

We sang "God Rest Ye Merry, Gentlemen" as we sat before the fire. Naomi got up to find a nutcracker, and I went to the woodshed to fetch a peck of hickory nuts and the two bricks which we keep for this purpose. I laid them on the hearth. Naomi was going to bake a hickory-nut cake, and we had to have the kernels. Jane used one of the bricks while I used the other to crack the hickory nuts. We put them in Naomi's lap, and she took the kernels from the nuts. We then threw the nuts, clean of their kernels, into the blazing fire.

We worked slowly cracking our thin-shelled hickory nuts. Naomi, Jane, and I had gathered them in October from a tall hickory tree that grows about a hundred yards up the valley at the edge of the pine grove. We had gathered ourselves plenty for the long winter but had left enough for our squirrels. Now, by the time we had filled the crock with hickory-nut kernels, we had cracked a peck. We had sung all the Christmas carols we knew, including some we didn't know too well. Jane had recited "The Night Before Christmas" without halt. We had each recited a poem. Then Jane popped corn for herself and her mother, and we finished with an evening cup of tea and a piece of angel-food cake.

That was all, except for the talk and the gaiety and love that I will not try to put down here.

Now Jane and Naomi are fast asleep. I have been sitting here thinking about life in front of this fireplace over the century and a half. The fire in the fireplace is now a bed of embers.

Jesse Stuart, *The Year of My Rebirth*, (New York: McGraw-Hill Book Company, Inc. 1956), p. 318-320.

41

Cakes

Fresh Apple Cake I

Cousin-Rae Anne Hilton - Frankfort, KY

1-1/2 c. veg. oil
2 eggs
2 c. sugar
2 T vanilla
3 c. flour
1 tsp. soda
1/2 tsp. salt
1 tsp. cinnamon
3 c. diced apples
1 c. nuts

Cream oil and sugar. Beat in eggs and then add vanilla. Sift in flour, soda, salt, and cinnamon. Add nuts and fold in apples. Pour batter into bundt pan and bake for 1 hour at 350°.

Fresh Apple Cake II

Cousin-Ginny Belle Smith - Lucasville, OH

3 eggs
1-1/2 c. oil
2 c. sugar
2 tsp. vanilla
3 c. sifted flour
1 tsp. baking soda
1 tsp. cinnamon
1/4 tsp. salt
3 c. chopped apples
1 c. walnuts

Mix first four ingredients on high speed for 3 min.

Add dry ingredients slowly.

Fold in apples and nuts. Pour into a greased and floured tube pan. Bake at 350° for 1 hour and 15 min.

Topping:
1 c. light brown sugar
1/4 c. milk
1 stick butter

Boil for 3 min.

Pour over cake while hot from the oven. Let cool in pan with topping on it for about 1/2 hour.

Fresh Apple Cake III

Cousin-Claudine Dyke - Ashland, KY

1 c. oil
3 eggs
2 c. sugar
1 tsp. vanilla
4 c. chopped apples
1 c. chopped nuts (walnuts or pecans)
3 c. flour
1 tsp. baking powder
1 tsp. soda
1 tsp. salt
1 tsp. cinnamon
1 tsp. nutmeg
1 tsp. cloves

Mix oil, eggs, and vanilla. Sift dry ingredients together, add to oil and egg mixture. Mix well. Fold in apples and nuts. Bake in tube pan at 350° 1 hour and 15 minutes. Remove from pan while warm and add glaze.

Glaze:
1/2 stick butter
1/2 tsp. vanilla
1/2 c. brown sugar
2 T milk

Boil 1 minute and pour over cake.

Apple Nut Cake

Cousin-Norma Jean Pennington Darnell - Greenup, KY

1 c. oil
3 eggs
2 c. sugar
1 tsp. vanilla
3 c. plain flour
1 tsp. salt
1 tsp. soda
1 tsp. cinnamon
1 tsp. nutmeg
1 tsp. cloves
3 c. apples diced
1 c. nuts

Mix oil, eggs, sugar, vanilla. Sift dry ingredients, blend with first mixture. Add apples and nuts. Pour into greased wax lined tube pan. Place in a cold oven and bake at 350° for 1 hour and 10 minutes.

Glaze:
1/2 stick margarine
1/2 tsp. vanilla
2 T milk

Boil mixture 1 minute and spread on cake.

Applesauce Cake I

Cousin-Phyllis Hilton Parker - Portsmouth, OH

1 stick of margarine
1 c. white sugar
1 c. applesauce, unsweetened
2 c. flour
1/2 c. chopped nuts
1 tsp. baking soda
1 tsp. cinnamon
1/2 tsp. cloves
1 c. raisins

Grease and flour 9 x 13 x 2 inch baking dish or pan. Cream margarine and sugar together, add applesauce, blend well. Sift flour, soda, and spices gradually into the creamed mixture. Blend. Stir in raisins and nuts. Spread batter evenly over the pan. Bake at 350° for about 40 minutes. Cake can be served hot or cold and requires no icing.

Applesauce Cake II

Cousin-Karen Hotopp Steele - Dayton, OH

Gary's (my husbands) Grandma Drew made applesauce every fall. This was a favorite recipe.

1 c. sugar
1/2 c. lard
1 c. unsweetened applesauce
1-3/4 c. flour
1 egg
2 T cocoa
1 tsp. soda
1/2 tsp. cloves
1/2 tsp. allspice
1/2 tsp. cinnamon
1/2 c. nuts and/or raisins

Thoroughly mix all ingredients. Pour into small cake pan or loaf pan that has been greased and floured. Sprinkle top with cinnamon and sugar if desired. Bake at 350° until cake tests done.

For a different flavor, omit the cocoa.

Applesauce Cake III

Cousin-Rosalie Stewart - Ravenswood, WV

4 eggs
2 c. sugar
2 c. flour
1 can applesauce
1 can black walnuts
1 lb. English walnuts
1 tsp. cloves
2 tsp. cinnamon
1/2 box raisins
1/2 lb. butter
2 tsp. soda

Preheat oven to 350°. Add 1 cup of the flour to nuts and raisins. Add soda and spices to applesauce. Cream shortening and sugar; add eggs. Then add applesauce mixture and remaining flour, nuts and raisins. Bake approximately 40 min.

Applesauce Cake IV

Cousin-Ruth Stewart Walters - Ceredo, WV

1/2 c. soft shortening
2 c. sugar
1 very large egg
1-1/2 c. applesauce
2-1/2 c. flour
1-1/2 tsp. soda
1-1/2 tsp. salt
3/4 tsp. cinnamon
1/4 tsp. cloves
1/4 tsp. allspice
1/2 c. water
1/2 c. seeded raisins, cut up
1/2 c. walnuts, cut up

Grease and flour 9 x 13 in. pan. Preheat oven to 350°. Cream together shortening and sugar until fluffy. Beat in egg thoroughly then add applesauce. In separate bowl sift together flour, soda, salt, cinnamon, cloves, and allspice. Stir alternately with water into applesauce mixture. Mix well then add raisins and walnuts. Bake for 45-50 minutes. For a decorative effect sift confectioners sugar through a paper doily onto top of cake.

Applesauce Jam Cake

Cousin-Margaret Terry Hatten - Huntington, WV

1 c. shortening
3 c. brown sugar
2 eggs
2 c. applesauce
1 c. jam
1 tsp. salt
2 tsp. cinnamon
1 tsp. cloves
2 tsp. soda
4 c. flour

Cream shortening, sugar, and eggs together. Dissolve soda in applesauce and add salt, cinnamon, and cloves. Stir until well mixed. Add jam and blend well, then add flour and mix well. A cup of raisins and a cup of nuts can be added is desired. Bake for 2 hours at 350°. (Bakes better in tube pan.)

Kentucky Stack Cake or Kentucky Pioneer Washday Cake

Cousin-Essie Hilton Rowland - Chillicothe, OH
Cousin-Alma Stewart Webb - St. Clair Shores, MI

1 c. sorghum
1 c. margarine
1 c. sugar
4 c. sifted flour
2 tsp. baking powder
1/2 tsp. cloves
1/2 tsp. salt
1/4 c. milk
1/2 tsp. soda
4 lg. eggs

Cream sorghum, margarine, and sugar till well blended. Sift dry ingredients together. Add to creamed mixture alternately with egg-milk liquid. Stir only till smooth. Divide batter into 6 equal amounts about 1 cup batter to each. Spread batter into well-greased 9" cake pans. (Makes 6 layers). Bake at 350° for 12 to 15 minutes. Stack layers with applesauce, sweetened and spiced to suit taste. (Dried apples, cooked to a thick sauce and seasoned with cloves made the filling for stack cakes of old.)

44

Old-Fashioned Stack Cake

Sister-Sophie Stuart Keeney, -Greenup, KY

1 c. firmly packed brown sugar
1 c. shortening
1 c. molasses
1 c. buttermilk
2 eggs beaten
1 tsp. soda
1 tsp. ground ginger
dash of salt
5-1/2 c. all purpose flour
6-2/3 c. dried apples or substitute apple butter (approx.)

Combine sugar, shortening and molasses; beat until smooth. Add buttermilk, eggs, soda, ginger, and salt; mix well. Add flour, about 1 cup at a time, beating after each addition just until blended. (Do not overbeat.) Divide dough into 10 portions, and place each on a greased baking sheet; pat or roll into 10 in. circles. Bake at 350° for 5-7 minutes. Carefully remove to cooling rack. Stack the layers, spreading about 2/3 c. dried apples or apple butter between each. Spoon about a mound of apple butter or dried apples on top of cake. Garnish with dried apples if desires. Yield one 10 in. Cake.

Apple Filling for Dried Apple Stack Cake

Sister-Sophie Stuart Keeney - Greenup, KY

1 lb. dried apples
1 c. brown sugar
1/2 c. white vinegar
2 tsp. cinnamon
1/2 tsp. cloves
1/2 tsp. allspice

Wash apples, cover with water and cook until tender. Mash thoroughly. Add other ingredients. Cool before spreading between layers.

Old Fashioned Dried Apple Stack Cake I

Cousin-Essie Hilton Rowland - Chillicothe, OH

Cream together:
1/2 c. shortening
1/2 c. molasses
Add 1 well beaten egg and 1 tsp. vanilla.

Sift together:
3-1/2 c. flour
1/2 tsp. soda
1 tsp. ginger
2 tsp. baking powder
1/2 tsp. salt
1/2 c. sugar

Add sifted mixture to creamed mixture alternately with 1/2 c. buttermilk. Roll on a floured board to a thickness of a pie crust. Cut out disc with a scalloped pie pan (as many as the dough will make.) Bake on lightly greased cookie sheet. Bake in a moderately hot oven 12-15 minutes. Make a thick sauce with about 3 cups of dried cooked apples, sweetened and spiced to suit taste. (Cinnamon or cloves are good.) Stack layers with the dried apple sauce on each layer.

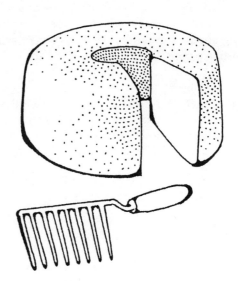

Old Fashioned Dried Apple Stack Cake II

Cousin-Loretta Adkins Benner - Lucasville, OH

4-1/2 c. flour
1 tsp. soda
2 tsp. baking powder
3 tsp. ginger
1/2 tsp. salt
1 c. butter or margarine
1 c. light brown sugar, packed
3/4 c. molasses
2 eggs
3/4 c. sour milk
2 tsp. vanilla

Mix batter. Dough must be stiff. Chill dough 2 or 3 hours or over night in the refrigerator. Divide dough into about 10 equal balls. Press each ball out as flat as possible into a well greased and lightly floured round layer cake pan. Bake at 375° for about 12 minutes or until lightly browned.

You will need at least 1/2 gallon of cooked dried apples that have been sweetened. Add apple pie spice or cinnamon to suit your taste. Make sure apples have been cooked down so that no water is standing on them. They should be thick and cooled if possible. As the cake layers get done, place on cake plate and top each layer with the cooked dried apples. Add as many layers as you want. When you have as many layers as you want, spread remaining apples around the out-side of cake as if you were frosting a cake. Do not put apples on the top of the last layer.

My grandmother, Mary Hylton Johnson made this cake without a recipe, handing it down to my mother, Martha Johnson Adkins. My mother also made it without a recipe. It became a traditional cake at our Thanksgiving dinner each year.

Banana Split Cake

Niece-Kathy Abdon - Greenup, KY

2 c. graham cracker crumbs
1 stick butter

Melt butter and mix with crumbs, press into bottom of 9 x 13 pan.

1 stick butter
1 box confectioners sugar
2 eggs

Mix and beat well (about 15 minutes): spread over crust.

Top sugar mixture with *1 lg. can crushed pineapple (well drained) and 1 lg. sliced banana.*

Cover with 1 lg. bowl of Cool Whip. Sprinkle with nuts and cherries.

Blackberry Cake I

Cousin-Rosalie Stewart - Ravenswood, WV

2/3 c. butter or margarine
2 c. sugar
3 c. flour (all purpose)
2 c. blackberries (juice and all)
3 eggs
1/2 tsp. cinnamon
1/2 tsp. cloves
1/2 tsp. nutmeg
2 tsp. soda (dissolved in 1/2 cup water)

Cream butter and sugar; add eggs one at a time and beat well after each addition. Add water and soda, then add flour and spices. Add berries and juice last. Add nuts if desired. Bake in preheated oven at 350° about 35 minutes or until done.

Blackberry Cake II

Cousin-Margaret Terry Waller - Ceredo, WV

1 c. shortening
2 c. white sugar
1 T soda dissolved in 1 c. of buttermilk
1 c. blackberries
1 tsp. cloves
1 tsp. cinnamon
1 tsp. nutmeg
1 tsp. salt
3 eggs
3 c. flour

Cream shortening and sugar. Add eggs, soda, buttermilk, and blackberries. Sift flour with salt and spices, add to creamed mixture. Bake in tube pan for about 1 hour at 350°.

Jerry's Chocolate Upside Down Cake

Sister - Glennis Stuart Liles - Greenup, KY

3/4 c. sugar
1 c. flour
3 T cocoa
1/2 c. milk
4 T melted margarine
1 tsp. vanilla
(No eggs)

Preheat oven to 350 degrees. Combine sugar, flour and cocoa. Add milk, margarine, vanilla, and beat well. Pour into a 8" X 9" pan. Pour syrup over batter and bake 30 to 35 minutes. Do not over bake. The size of the pan determines exact baking time.

SYRUP

3/4 c. white sugar
1/2 c. brown sugar
2 T cocoa
1 c. milk
1 T margarine

Combine white and brown sugar with cocoa. Add milk, margarine, and stir until mixed.

Old Fashioned Blackberry Cake

Cousin-Beatrice Kay Stewart Stevens - Huntington, WV

2 c. sugar
3/4 c. butter or margarine
3 eggs
4 T buttermilk
3 T coffee (liquid)
1 c. blackberries
1 tsp. soda
1 tsp. baking powder
1 tsp. cinnamon
2 c. flour
1 tsp. cloves
1 tsp. nutmeg
1 tsp. vanilla

Cream together softened butter and sugar. Beat eggs and berries well and add to creamed mixture. Stir in buttermilk, coffee, and vanilla. Mix dry ingredients together, blending spices well. Add dry mixture to batter and beat well, about 2 minutes. Bake in 350° oven for 35-40 minutes. Top with your favorite glaze or delicious served plain.

Easy Blackberry Cake

Cousin-Connie Frazier Stewart - Kenova, WV

1 box spice cake mix
1/2 c. Crisco oil
2 or 3 eggs
1 can blackberry pie filling (Thank You)

Mix first 3 ingredients well. Fold in berries. Bake in 9 x 13 in. pan until center springs back. Frost after cool with sour cream frosting.

Kentucky Butter Cake

Niece-Barbara Keeney Oney - Raceland, KY

3 c. flour
1 tsp. baking powder
1 tsp. salt
1/2 tsp. baking soda
1 c. butter
2 c. sugar
4 eggs
1 c. buttermilk
2 tsp. vanilla

Sift together, flour, baking powder, salt, and soda. Cream butter and gradually add sugar. Cream well. Add eggs one at a time, cream each before adding another. Combine buttermilk and vanilla: add sifted ingredients to creamed mixture alternately with buttermilk, beginning and ending with dry ingredients. Blend well after each addition. Grease a 10 inch tube pan on the bottom. Pour in batter and bake 60-65 minutes at 350° or until cake springs back. Run a spatula around the edge and stem of pan, then prick the cake with a fork and pour this hot butter sauce over it.

1 c. sugar
1/4 c. water
1/2 c. butter
1 T vanilla

Combine sugar, water, and butter in saucepan. Heat until butter is melted, but do not boil. Add vanilla.

Carrot Cake

Sister-Mary Nelson - Greenup, KY

3 c. plain flour
2 c. grated carrots
1 c. crushed pineapple
1-1/2 c. corn oil
3 tsp. soda
2 T lemon extract
3 c. sugar
1 c. nuts
1 c. raisins
3 unbeaten eggs
1-1/2 tsp. cinnamon

Mix well. Bake in 350° oven for 1 hour in bundt pan.

Glaze for Cake

1 c. sugar
1/2 c. buttermilk
1/2 tsp. soda
2 T butter
2 tsp. lemon extract

Boil 3 minutes and pour over warm cake.

Buttermilk-Brown Sugar Cheesecake

Niece-Sandy Nelson Perrine - Greenup, RY

1 (8 oz.) pkg. cream cheese at room temperature
2 eggs, beaten
3/4 c. firmly packed light brown sugar
1/4 c. buttermilk
2 T Amaretto liquor
1 tsp. vanilla
1 unbaked 9" graham cracker pie shell
1/3 c. lightly toasted slivered almonds
1/4 tsp. cinnamon

Preheat oven to 350°. Combine first 6 ingredients in a blender until creamy, about 1 minute. Pour into pie shell, top with almonds and cinnamon. Bake until lightly browned, about 30 minutes. Cool. Cover and refrigerate until set. Serve chilled. 8 servings.

Easy Cheese Cake

Cousin-Melinda Shultz Arrick - Lucasville, OH

3 (8 oz pkgs.) cream cheese, softened
1 c. + 3 T sugar, divided
4 eggs
2 tsp. vanilla extract
graham cracker crust
1 (8 oz.) carton sour cream
Fresh strawberries

Combine cream cheese and 1 c. sugar; beat until smooth and creamy. Add eggs and vanilla; blend well. Pour filling into a 10 in. spring form pan lined with graham cracker crust. Bake at 350° for 1 hour or slightly firm around the edges. Combine sour cream and 3 T sugar; spread over cheese cake, bake 10 minutes. Let cool completely. Remove cake from pan and chill. Garnish with strawberries.

Graham Cracker Crust

1-1/2 c. graham cracker crumbs
1/2 tsp. ground cinnamon
1/2 c. sugar
1/2 c. melted butter

Combine all ingredients and press into bottom of a 10 in. spring form pan.

Chocolate and Cherry Ring

Cousin-Geraldine Holbrook - Greenup, KY

2 c. all purpose flour
3/4 c. sugar
1 tsp. baking soda
1 tsp. ground cinnamon
1/8 tsp. salt
2 eggs, beaten
1/2 c. Crisco oil
2 tsp. vanilla
1 (21 oz.) can cherry pie filling
1 c. semisweet chocolate pieces
1 c. chopped walnuts
powdered sugar

In a large mixing bowl stir together flour, sugar, baking soda, cinnamon, and salt. In another bowl combine eggs, oil and vanilla; add to flour mixture, mix well. Stir in cherry

pie filling, chocolate pieces, and nuts. Turn mixture into a greased and floured 10 inch fluted tube pan. Bake in a 350° oven for 1 hour. Cool in pan on a wire rack for 15 minutes. Remove from pan and cool. Sift powdered sugar atop.

Chocolate Praline Layer Cake

Sister-in-law-Lucille Norris - Greenup, KY

1/2 c. butter
1/4 c. whipping cream
1 c. firmly packed brown sugar
3/4 c. coarsely chopped pecans
1 pkg. (pudding included) devil's food cake mix
1-1/4 c. water
1/3 c. oil
3 eggs

Heat oven to 325°. In small heavy saucepan, combine whipping cream, butter and brown sugar. Cook over low heat just until butter is melted, stirring occasionally. Pour into two 8" or 9" round cake pans; sprinkle evenly with chopped pecans. In large bowl, combine cake mix, water, oil and eggs at low speed until moistened; beat 2 minutes at high speed. Carefully spoon batter over pecan mixture. Bake at 325° for 35 to 40 minutes or until cake springs back. Cool 5 minutes. Remove from pans and cool completely.

Topping:
1-3/4 c. whipping cream
1/4 c. powdered sugar
1/4 tsp. vanilla

In small bowl, beat whipping cream until soft peaks form. Blend in powdered sugar and vanilla; beat until stiff peaks form. To assemble cake, place one layer on serving plate, praline side up; spread top with half of whipping cream. Top with second layer, praline side up, and top with remaining whipped cream. Garnish with whole pecans and chocolate curls. Store in refrigerator covered.

Date Cake

Cousin-Ethel Hilton Porter - Ashland, KY

1 c. water
1 c. chopped pitted dates
1 tsp. baking soda
1/3 c. softened butter
1 c. sugar
1 egg
1 tsp. vanilla
1-1/2 c. flour
1 tsp. baking powder
1/2 tsp. salt
1/2 c. chopped walnuts

Pour the boiling water over dates and baking soda. Allow to stand while mixing the cake batter. Cream butter with sugar until very smooth and creamy. Add the unbeaten egg and vanilla and beat well.

Sift together flour, baking powder, and salt. Mix with the creamed mixture until well blended. Stir in walnuts and the date mixture. Pour into a greased and floured 13 x 9 x 2 in. pan. Bake in moderately hot oven, 375° for 35 minutes. Remove from pan and cool. Frost if desired. 15 servings.

Duncan Turtle Cake

Cousin-Ruth Stewart Walters - Ceredo, WV

1 pkg. Duncan Hines German Choc. cake mix
1-1/3 c. water
1/3 c. evaporated milk
3 eggs
3/4 c. margarine

Blend and beat 2 min. Pour 1/2 batter into a greased and floured 9 x 13 in. pan. Bake 15 min. at 350°. While this is baking melt 14 oz. pkg. Kraft Caramels (unwrap in advance) with 1/3 c. plus 2 T evaporated milk over low heat. Pour over cake as soon as removed from oven; sprinkle 12 oz. pkg. choc. chips and 1 c. chopped pecans. Top with remaining batter. Bake 25-30 min. or longer. Good served with ice cream or cool whip.

Faye's Favorite Chocolate Cake

Cousin-Ruth Stewart Walters - Ceredo, WV

Mix together in large bowl:
2 c. sugar
2 c. self-rising flour

In a saucepan bring to a boil:
1 stick margarine
1 T cocoa
1/2 c. cooking oil
1 c. hot water
pinch of salt

Pour cocoa mixture over flour and sugar mixture, mix well and add: 2 eggs, 1/2 c. buttermilk, 1 tsp. vanilla. Batter will be thin. Pour into 9 x 13 in. pan. Bake at 350° for 30 minutes.

Icing:
In saucepan mix 1 stick margarine, 4 T cocoa, 6 T buttermilk. Bring to a boil and gradually add 1 box powdered sugar. Mix well and pour over cake while hot. You may add 1 can angel flaked coconut and 1/2 c. nuts.

Funnel Cakes

Cousin-Loretta Benner-Lucasville, OH

2 eggs, beaten
1 1/2 c. milk
2 c. sifted flour
1 tsp. baking powder
1/2 tsp. salt
2 c. cooking oil for frying

Mix eggs and milk. Mix dry ingredients and add to egg mixture. Beat smooth. Test batter in funnel. If too thick, add milk. If too thin, add flour.

Heat cooking oil to 360 degrees in 8 in. skillet. Cover the funnel bottom with left index finger. Put 1/3 cup of batter into funnel at a time. Release batter over oil in spiral motion, rings touching. Fry until golden brown, turning carefully. Drain on paper towel. Sprinkle with powdered sugar from a sifter. May be eaten as a finger food or served on a plate with maple syrup and butter.

New Mexico Chocolate Sheet Cake

Cousin-Mae Pennington Fellows - Albuquerque, NM

2 c. flour
2 c. sugar
1/2 lb. oleo
1 c. water
3 rounded T cocoa
2 eggs
1/2 c. buttermilk
1 tsp. vanilla
1/2 tsp. salt
1 tsp. soda

Place flour and sugar in a large bowl, don't sift. Boil oleo, water, and cocoa. Add sugar and flour to cocoa mixture then add remaining ingredients. Beat well. Bake at 425° for 25 minutes in 11 x 17 in. pan.

Frosting:
1/4 lb. oleo
3 T cocoa
1/4 c. milk
1 lb. powdered sugar
1 tsp. vanilla
1/2 c. broken nuts

Combine first three ingredients, then add remaining ingredients. Beat well. Frost while hot. This is a moist cake and freezes well.

Texas Chocolate Cake

Sister-in-law-Betty Stuart - Greenup, KY

2 c. flour (sifted)
2 c. sugar
1 stick margarine
1/2 c. Crisco
1 tsp. soda
1 tsp. vanilla
4 T cocoa
1 c. water
1/2 c. buttermilk
2 eggs

Add sugar to flour, sift and set aside. Put margarine, Crisco, cocoa and water in saucepan and boil. Pour while hot over flour and sugar mixture in big pan, beat well.

In cup, mix buttermilk and soda, add 1 tsp. vanilla, add eggs last and mix. Blend together flour and buttermilk mixtures. Place in a long baking pan, after it has been greased and floured. Bake at 350° for 35-40 minutes. Ice cake while warm.

Icing:
1 stick oleo
4 T cocoa
6 T buttermilk

Mix and bring to a boil. Add gradually 1 box confectioner's sugar. Set off stove, beat in 1 tsp. vanilla, 1 c. chopped pecans. Spread while warm.

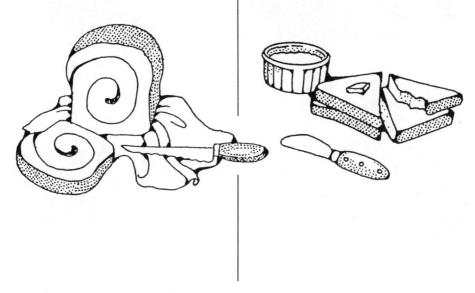

White Chocolate Cake

Cousin-Loretta Adkins Benner - Lucasville, OH

1/4 lb. white chocolate (melt over hot water)
1 c. butter or margarine
2 c. sugar
4 eggs
1 tsp. vanilla
dash of salt
2-1/2 c. cake flour
1 tsp. baking powder (sift with flour)
1 c. buttermilk
1 c. chopped pecans
1 c. angel flaked coconut

Cream butter, sugar, chocolate. Add eggs, one at a time, then add vanilla, salt, flour, baking powder, and buttermilk. Stir in the nuts and coconut. Bake at 350° for 30 minutes (layers), 75 minutes in a tube pan. (Grease and flour pan)

Icing
2 c. white sugar
2 sticks butter or margarine
1 tsp. vanilla
dash of salt
1 small can condensed milk

Combine all ingredients and let stand for 1 hour. Cook (Stirring occasionally) until a soft ball forms when dropped in cold water. Remove from heat and beat until creamy. Spread on cake.

This is my favorite cake. It is especially good for the Easter season. I generally sprinkle some coconut on the top and add a few colored jelly beans as a decoration.

Coconut Cake

Sister-in-law-Lucille Norris - Greenup, KY

12 oz. frozen coconut-unsweetened
(can use sweetened if can't find unsweetened)
12 oz. sour cream
2 c. conf. sugar
Mix and refrigerate overnight or 12 hours.

Bake Duncan Hines Yellow Butter Cake mix in 2-8" pans. Cool and split cake into 4 layers. Put filling between 3 layers. Frost outside with cool whip mix. Cover and refrigerate for 5 days. Enjoy!

Rave Coconut Cake

Sister-Mary Nelson - Greenup, KY

1 pkg. yellow cake mix (2 layer size)
1 pkg. Jello Brand vanilla instant pudding and pie filling
1-1/3 c. water
4 eggs
1/4 c. oil
2 c. Bakers Angel Flake Coconut
1 c. chopped walnuts

Blend cake and pudding mix, eggs, water and oil, beat 4 minutes. Stir in coconut and walnuts and pour into 3 greased and floured pans (9" layer pans). Bake at 350° for 35 min. cool 15 min., fill and frost with cream frosting.

Coconut Cream Cheese Frosting

4 T butter
2 c. coconut
1 pkg. cream cheese
2 T milk
3-1/2 c. confectioner's sugar
1 T vanilla

Melt 2 T butter, add coconut stirring it constantly over low heat until golden brown, spread on paper to cool. Cream 2 T butter with cream cheese, add milk and sugar alternately, beating well. Add vanilla and stir in 1-3/4 c. of the coconut and spread on top and sides of cake layers. Sprinkle with the browned coconut.

Chess Squares

Cousin-Frances Hilton Hunt - Bloomfield, KY

1 box yellow cake mix
1 stick soft oleo
1 egg
1 box conf. sugar
8 oz. cream cheese
3 eggs

Mix first 3 ingredients and press on bottom of pan. Mix last 3 ingredients until smooth. Pour over cake mixture and bake at 350° for 30-35 minutes. Cut into squares.

Chess Cake

Cousin-Connie Frazier Stewart - Kenova, WV

Bottom:
1 stick margarine
1 egg
1 box cake mix (lemon or orange)

Mix together and press in 9 x 13 pan

Top:
1 box confectioners sugar
3 eggs
1 lg. cream cheese
1 tsp. vanilla

Pour on top and bake for 45-50 minutes.

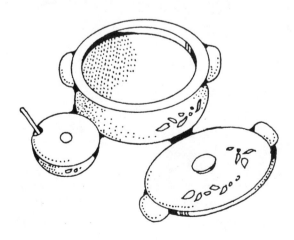

Cinnamon Coffee Cake

Cousin-Karen Hotopp Steele - Dayton, OH

3/4 c. sugar
1 T lard (heaping)
1 egg
2 c. flour
1 c. sour milk
1/2 tsp. soda
1 tsp. salt
1 tsp. baking powder
cinnamon and sugar

Thoroughly mix all ingredients. Pour into small cake pan or loaf pan that has been greased and floured. Sprinkle top with cinnamon and sugar. Bake at 350° until tests done. (20-30 minutes)

This recipe came from my husband's Grandmother.

Maude's Coffee Cake

Cousin-Beverly Jane Benner Murphy - Lucasville, OH

2 c. sugar (1 brown and 1 white)
2 eggs
1 stick butter
1 c. cold coffee
2 c. flour
2 tsp. baking powder
1 tsp. baking soda
1 c. applesauce
1/4 tsp. cinnamon
1/4 tsp. cloves
1/4 tsp. allspice
1/2 tsp. salt
1 tsp. vanilla

Mix all ingredients. Bake at 325° until done. This makes a very moist cake that does not need icing. However, it is very good with cream cheese icing. I often substitute applebutter for the applesauce and leave out the cinnamon.

Eggless, Butterless, Milkless Cake

Cousin-Margaret Terry Waller - Ceredo, WV

Put into a saucepan the following ingredients. Boil for 3 minutes, then cool.

1 c. brown sugar
1 c. cold water
2 c. raisins
1/3 c. shortening
1/4 tsp. salt
1/2 tsp. cloves
1/4 tsp. grated nutmeg
1 tsp. cinnamon

When cool, add 2 cups flour into which has been sifted and 1/2 tsp. of baking powder. Add 1 tsp. of soda dissolved in a little hot water. Add 3/4 cup of nut meats. Bake about 45 minutes in slow oven at 350°.

This recipe was handed down to me and dates back to the days of World War I when eggs, butter, and milk were scarce.

Candied Fruit Cake

Wife-Naomi Deane Norris Stuart - W-Hollow, KY

1-1/2 lb. pitted dates
1 lb. whole candied cherries
1 lb. candied pineapple
2 lbs. pecans
4 eggs
2 tsp. baking powder
2 c. flour
1 c. sugar
1/2 tsp. salt

Mix flour, baking powder, and salt. Add to all fruits. Mix. Beat eggs, add sugar. Mix and pour over fruit mixture. Mix. Add pecans and mix well, (I use hands) until everything is moist. Line pans with greased brown paper. Bake at 275°—Mold 1-1/4 hours, loaf 1-1/2 hours. Place a pan of water in the bottom of the oven while baking.

Poor Mans Fruit Cake

Cousin-Florence Stuart Wolfe - East Liverpool, OH

1 lb. raisins
1 c. cold water
2 c. sugar
4 c. flour
1 c. nuts
1 tsp. cinnamon
1 tsp. allspice
1 tsp. baking soda in hot water
1/2 c. shortening

Cook raisins in 2 cups of water for 15 min., then add cold water. Cool. Mix together sugar, flour, and other remaining ingredients. Pour raisins with liquid in flour mixture, mixing well. Bake at 350° for approximately 50-60 minutes in two 5 x 8 loaf pans.

Pork Fruit Cake

Cousin-Lola Hilton - Moraine, OH

1 lb. pork sausage (bulk)
1 box raisins
1 box currants
1 c. brewed coffee black
2-1/2 c. brown sugar light
1/2 lb. candied fruit
1-1/2 c. nut meats
1 tsp. soda
1 tsp. cloves
1 tsp. cinnamon
3 c. flour

Mix all ingredients. Bake time 1-1/2 hours at 250-300°. Makes 2 loaf pans or one large round pan. I put rum on mine and age for a while. This cake does not dry out.

Grandma's Soft Gingerbread

Niece-Carrol Keeney Abdon - Greenup, KY

1 c. sorghum molasses
1/2 c. butter or shortening
1/2 c. milk (sour)
2 eggs
2 c. flour
1-1/2 tsp. soda
2 tsp. ginger
1/2 tsp. salt

Put butter and molasses over medium heat and bring to a boil. Remove and add soda then beat well. When cool add milk and well beaten eggs. Add dry ingredients sifted together and mix well. Bake in well greased and floured cake pan at 350° for 40 minutes. Serve warm or cold. Very good served with whipped cream or fresh apple sauce.

Old Fashioned Molasses Cake (Gingerbread)

Niece-Nancy Sue Darby Lake - Berea, KY

1/2 c. sugar
1/2 c. butter and lard mixed
1 egg (large)
1 c. molasses
2-1/2 c. sifted flour
1-1/2 tsp. soda
1 tsp. cinnamon
1 tsp. ginger
1/2 tsp. cloves
1/2 tsp. salt
1 c. hot water

Cream shortening and sugar. Add beaten egg, molasses, then dry ingredients which have been sifted together. Add hot water and beat until smooth. The batter is soft and makes a fine textured cake. Bake in greased shallow pan for 35 minutes in a moderate (350°) oven. Delicious served warm with dab of sweetened whipped cream on top!

Gum Drop Cake

Cousin-Essie Hilton Rowland - Chillicothe, OH

1 lb. colored gumdrops (no black) cut in pieces
1 c. chopped nuts
1 c. margarine
1 lb. raisins
2 c. sugar
1-1/2 c. applesauce
1 tsp. vanilla
2 eggs
4 c. flour
2 T baking powder
1 tsp. soda
1-1/2 tsp. sour milk
1 tsp. cinnamon
1/4 tsp. cloves
1/4 tsp. nutmeg
1/4 tsp. salt

Dissolve soda in sour milk. Sift dry ingredients but keep enough flour to roll gumdrops and raisins. Add balance. Bake 1-1/2 hours in slow oven (250°). Makes 2 cakes or 1 tube cake and one 8" x 8" square cake.

Jelly Roll

Cousin-Mary Belle Johnson - Portsmouth, OH

Mix together:
6 eggs
1 tsp. soda
1 tsp. lemon or vanilla flavoring (depending on choice of
jelly)
2 c. all purpose flour
6 T milk
1-1/2 c. sugar
2 tsp. cream of tartar

Spread dough thinly in very large pan. Bake at 350° until done. Turn out on moistened cloth. Spread with jelly of choice. Roll while hot. Must be very thin to roll properly but good anyway.

Oatmeal Cake

Cousin-Beverly Stewart - Winter Haven, FL

Mix together and let stand 20 minutes.
1 c. oats (old fashioned)
1-1/4 c. boiling water

Cream together:
1/2 c. margarine (1 stick)
2 eggs
1 c. brown sugar
1 c. white sugar

Sift together:
1-1/2 c. flour
1 tsp. cinnamon
1 tsp. soda
1/2 tsp. salt

Combine all ingredients and pour into a 13 x 9 in. pan and bake at 350° for 30 minutes.

Icing for Oatmeal Cake

1 c. brown sugar
2 T milk
6 T butter or margarine
1 can coconut

Combine above ingredients and spread on cake. Put cake under broiler and brown the coconut. Be careful as this will brown quickly.

Orange Slices Fruit Cake

Cousin-Goldie Adkins - East Liverpool, OH

2-1/2 c. flour
4 eggs
2 c. sugar
1 c. butter and oleo mixed
1 tsp. soda in 1 c. buttermilk
1 lb. orange slices (cut up)
2 c. coconut
1/2 lb. dates
2 c. pecans or walnuts

Combine first 5 ingredients and blend well with mixer. Dredge fruits and nuts in extra cup flour and add to mix. Bake in greased and floured angel food pan at 300° for 2 hours.

Topping:
I c. orange juice
2 c. powdered sugar

Spoon over cake when hot but not all at once. Leave in pan over night.

Orange Special

Cousin-Katherine Hilton - Ashland, KY

1 c. margarine
1 c. sugar
2 eggs
1 c. sour cream
2 c. flour
1 tsp. soda
Rind of 2 oranges (grated)
1/2 c. nuts (ground) either pecan or walnuts

Cream sugar and margarine. Add eggs, sour cream, sifted flour, and baking soda. Blend well using mixer for last minute-careful not to overbeat. Fold in grated orange rind and nuts. Bake in tube pan at 350° for 1 hour.

Glaze:
Combine juice of 1-1/2 oranges (3/4 cup) with 2/3 cup of sugar. Heat slowly about 20 min., stir occasionally. Spoon over cake while cake is still hot. Let soak in. This makes it the elegant cake it is.

Pineapple Cake

Cousin-Katherine Stewart Martin - Racine, WS

Bake Jiffy Cake (white or yellow) in 9 x 12 in. pan.

Mix well:
1 pkg. instant vanilla pudding
2 c. milk
8 oz. creamed cheese (softened)

Spread on cooled cake. Spread 1 can drained, crushed pineapple. Top with whipped cream and nuts. Refrigerate for 24 hours.

Pineapple Deluxe Cake

Cousin-Anna Laura Adkins - Ceredo, WV

1 box yellow cake mix
1 (20 oz.) can of crushed pineapple
1 lg. box instant vanilla pudding
2 pkgs. Dream Whip

Use sheet cake pan. Bake cake as directed on box. When cake is done, while still hot, make slits in cake with sharp knife. Spread crushed pineapple on cake while hot. Mix pudding as directed on box and spread over pineapple. Mix Dream Whip as directed on packet and spread over pudding. Chill in refrigerator until ready to serve.

Pineapple Nut Cake

Cousin-Lola Hilton - Moraine, OH

2 c. flour
2 eggs
1/4 tsp. salt
2 c. sugar
2 tsp. soda
1 tsp. vanilla
1 c. broken English walnuts
1 can (20 oz.) crushed pineapple with juice

Mix by hand, no mixer. Preheat oven to 350° and bake in 9 x 13" cake pan 40 to 50 minutes, and cool.

Icing for Cake:
1 (8 oz.) cream cheese
1-1/2 c. powdered sugar
1 stick margarine
1 tsp. vanilla

Mix well with mixer and spread on cake.

Poppy Seed Cake I

Cousin-Scott W. Stewart - Kenova, WV

1 box yellow cake mix
4 eggs
1-1/4 c. water
1/2 c. oil
1 pkg. (sm.) instant banana pudding
1/4 c. poppy seeds

Put all ingredients in mixing bowl and beat well. Pour batter into well greased and floured bundt pan. Bake at 350° for 45 minutes.

Poppy Seed Cake II

Cousin-Marie Pennington Hardymon - Greenup, KY

1 box white, yellow, or lemon cake mix
1 box instant coconut or lemon pudding mix
1 c. water
4 eggs
1/2 c. oil
4 T poppy seeds

Mix together dry ingredients, add water and oil. Add 1 egg at a time, beat well after each. Pour into well greased and floured bundt pan. Bake for 45 minutes at 350°. Cool for 15 minutes before removing from pan.

Pound Cake

Cousin-Marie Pennington Hardymon - Greenup, KY

2 sticks butter
1/2 c. Crisco
3 c. sugar
5 eggs
1 tsp. coconut flavoring
1 tsp. vanilla-butternut flavoring
1 tsp. rum flavoring
3 c. plain flour
1/2 tsp. salt
1/2 tsp. baking powder
1 c. milk

Cream butter, Crisco, sugar; add one egg at a time and beat well. Add flavoring. Add dry ingredients alternately with milk. Mix well. Bake 1-1/2 hours at 325°.

Glaze:
1 c. sugar
1/2 c. water
1 tsp. almond extract

Melt sugar in water slowly: add almond extract. Make holes in top of cake and pour on. Use lemon juice instead of water and omit almond, if you like lemon.

Nut Pound Cake

Cousin-Ruth Stewart Walters - Ceredo, WV

3-1/2 c. all-purpose flour
2 tsp. baking powder
1 tsp. salt
1-1/2 c. shortening
2 c. sugar
6 eggs
1-1/2 tsp. rum extract
1 c. milk
4 coarsely chopped black walnuts or pecans

Preheat oven to 300°. Lightly grease bottom and sides of a 10 in. tube pan. Line with brown paper; grease paper. Sift flour, baking powder and salt together; set aside. Put shortening into a large mixing bowl. Gradually add sugar, beat at med. speed, until light and fluffy. Add eggs, one at a time, beating well after each addition. Blend in rum extract, blend in flour mixture in fourths, alternately, with milk, beginning and ending with flour mixture. Fold in nuts. Spoon batter into prepared pan, spreading evenly. Bake at 300° for 1 hour 50 minutes to 2 hours or until a tooth pick inserted near center comes out clean. Let cake cool in pan on wire rack for 30 min. Turn out onto rack. Gently remove paper. Invert cake again and cool cake completely. Wrap in aluminum foil or plastic wrap. To serve, cut into thin slices. Top with whipped cream or ice cream, if desired.

Queen Elizabeth II Cake

Wife-Naomi Deane Norris Stuart - W-Hollow, KY

Pour 1 c. boiling water over 1 c. chopped dates and 1 tsp. soda. Let stand and mix the following:

1 c. sugar
1 c. margarine (I use butter)
1 beaten egg
1 tsp. vanilla
1-1/2 c. flour
1 tsp. baking powder
1/2 c. chopped nuts
1 tsp. salt

Add to date mixture. Bake in 9" x 12" pan for 35 minutes at 350°.

Icing:
5 T brown sugar
5 T cream
2 T butter

Boil 3 minutes and spread on cool cake. Cover with 1 can coconut and chopped nuts. (I mix nuts and coconut with icing and spread over cake with fork.)

7 Up Cake

Cousin-Lola Hilton - Moraine, OH

1 box yellow cake mix
1 box pineapple or vanilla instant pudding
3/4 c. oil
4 eggs

Mix well. Then add 10 oz. 7 Up. Beat well. Bake in greased and floured pan (13 x 9 x 2") 40 minutes at 350°.

Icing
3 eggs beaten
1-1/2 c. sugar
1 T flour
1 stick margarine
1 c. crushed pineapple (undrained)
1 small can coconut

Cook eggs, sugar, flour, and margarine until thick over medium heat. Add the pineapple and coconut and pour over cake when it comes out of oven.

Sno-Ball Cake

Cousin-Pat Stewart - Ravenswood, WV

1 prepared Angel food cake
2 envelopes of Dream Whip
1 pkg. unflavored jello, prepared
1 can coconut
1 can crushed pineapple

Whip Dream Whip. Tear angle food cake in small pieces. Mix pineapple and jello together, add Dream Whip. Make a layer of cake, pour over 1/2 of Dream Whip mixture, then another layer of cake and pour over remaining Dream Whip. Sprinkle coconut over all of cake.

Mom's Old Fashioned Spice Cake

Cousin-Ruth Helen Stewart Smith - Ceredo, WV

1 tsp. soda
1 tsp. salt
4 tsp. cloves
4 tsp. cinnamon
2-1/2 c. sugar
2-1/2 c. buttermilk
flour
1 c. shortening

Glaze:
1/2 c. buttermilk
1/2 tsp. soda
1 c. sugar
1 stick butter
1/2 tsp vanilla

Mix soda, salt, cloves, cinnamon, and sugar. Then add buttermilk. Add enough flour to make a stiff dough. Fold in melted shortening. Do not use mixer. Bake at 350°. Mix glaze ingredients together in sauce pan and cook for 2 minutes. Pour on warm cake. Let cool and serve.

Strawberry Cake

Cousin-Marie Hilton Ellington - Ashland, KY

1 box white cake mix
1 box strawberry jello
4 eggs
1 c. Wesson oil
1/4 c. hot water
1 sm. box frozen strawberries

Put all ingredients in large mixing bowl. Beat 4 minutes on medium speed. Bake at 350° in greased and floured 13 x 8" pan for 45 minutes.

Frosting:
1/2 box powdered sugar
1/4 stick butter or margarine
1/4 c. frozen strawberries, drained (about 1/4 sm. box)

Cream above ingredients and spread on cooled cake.

Three Minute Cake

Sister-in-law-Laura Avanelle Norris Callihan
Greenup, KY

1 c. sugar
1/2 c. butter
1 egg
1/2 c. milk
1/2 c. cocoa
1/2 tsp. salt
1-1/2 c. sifted flour
1 tsp. soda
1/2 c. boiling water
1 tsp. vanilla

Put in a bowl in order given. Beat 3 minutes. Bake slowly. This is a good old recipe. I've used it since 1945.

Texas Pecan Cake

Cousin-Melinda Shultz Arrick - Lucasville, OH

2 c. butter or margarine softened
2 c. sugar
6 eggs
4 c. all-purpose flour, divided
1-1/2 tsp. baking powder
1-(2 Oz.) bottle lemon extract
4 c. chopped pecans
2-1/2 c. golden raisins

Cream butter in a large mixing bowl; gradually add sugar, beating until light & fluffy. Add eggs, one at a time, beating well after each addition. Combine 3-1/2 c. flour and baking powder; gradually add to creamed mixture alternating with lemon extract, beginning and ending with flour mixture. Beat well after each addition (batter will be thick). Dredge pecans and raisins in remaining 1/2 c. of flour; stir into batter. Spoon batter into a greased and floured 10 inch tube pan. Bake at 325° for 1 hour and 30 minutes or until cake tests done. Cool in pan 15 minutes; remove, and let cool completely before serving. Yield: 1 (10 in.) cake.

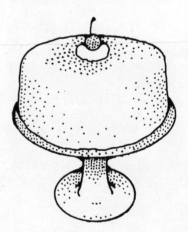

Texas Sheet Cake

Cousin-Donna Stewart Broscious - Ravenswood, WV

Bring to a boil:
*2 sticks of oleo
1 c. water
4 T cocoa*

Cream together:
*2 eggs
1/2 c. sour cream*

Add:
*2 c. flour
1/2 tsp. salt
2 c. sugar
1 tsp. soda*

Mix all together and bake on greased and floured cookie sheet at 350° for 20 minutes.

Icing:
*1 stick of butter
6 T milk
4 T cocoa*

Bring to boil. Add 1 lb. box confectioners sugar.

Southern Yam Cake

Cousin-Anne Hilton Short - Forestville, MD

*2 c. sugar
1 c. margarine or butter, softened
1-1/2 tsp. vanilla
5 eggs
16 oz. can cut yams, drained
3 c. self-rising, all-purpose, or unbleached flour
2 tsp. cinnamon
1/2 tsp. soda
1/2 tsp. nutmeg
1 c. chopped pecans
1 c. raisins
8-1/4 oz. can crushed pineapple, well drained
15-3/4 oz. can ready-to-spread coconut pecan frosting*

Heat oven to 325°. Grease and flour 10 inch tube pan. In large bowl, cream sugar, margarine, and vanilla until light and fluffy. Add eggs, one at a time, beating well after each. Cut up yams; add to creamed mixture, beating until well mixed. Lightly spoon flour into measuring cup; level off. Add flour and cinnamon, soda, and nutmeg; mix well. By hand, fold in pecans, raisins and drained pineapple. Spoon batter into prepared pan; spread evenly. Bake at 325° for 60 to 70 minutes or until toothpick inserted in center comes out clean. Cool upright in pan 10 min. Invert onto serving plate. Cool completely. In medium saucepan, heat frosting over medium heat just until melted, stirring constantly. Spoon over cooled cake allowing some to run down the sides. Makes 16 servings.

Mother's Yellow Cake

(Myrtle Norris)
*Sister-in-law-Laura Avanelle Norris Callihan
Greenup, KY*

*3/4 c. butter or 1-1/2 stick margarine
2 c. sugar
2 or 3 eggs
1-1/4 c. milk
3 c. flour
3 tsp. baking powder
salt
1 tsp. vanilla*

Cream butter and sugar, add eggs. Alternate milk and combined dry ingredients. Bake at 350° until toothpick comes out clean.

61

"You're Lucky If You Have Any Left" Cake

Cousin-Dorothy Holbrook, Greenup, KY

Crust:
2 sticks margarine
2 c. plain flour
1 c. pecans—chopped fine

Mix and press into a 9" x 13" in. greased pan. Bake until lightly brown (about 20 minutes) in a 350° oven. Cool.

Second layer:
1 c. powdered sugar
1 (9 oz.) carton Cool Whip
1 lg. pkg. cream cheese

Mix together and spread on cool crust.

Third layer:
3 pkgs. instant pudding mix (any flavor)
4-1/2 c. cold milk

Beat until pudding is set and spread on top of second layer.

Fourth layer:
Spread a 9 oz. carton of Cool Whip over the pudding and sprinkle with finely chopped pecans. Refrigerate for several hours and keep refrigerated.

Basic Fluffy Frosting

Cousin-Thelma Edwards - Ceredo, WV

Blend 1 stick Miracle Margarine with dash of salt and 1 tsp. vanilla. Add 3 cups sifted confectioner's sugar alternately with 1/4 c. of cream, beating until light and fluffy.

Orange Frosting:
Substitute 1 tsp. grated orange rind and 1/4 c. orange juice for vanilla and cream.

Chocolate Frosting:
Add 1/3 c. cocoa.

Strawberry Frosting:
Substitute 1/4 c. mashed strawberries for cream.

Banana Frosting:
Substitute 1/4 c. mashed bananas for cream.

Caramel Frosting

Cousin-Judy Castle - Huntington, WV

1/2 c. butter
1 c. brown sugar
1/4 c. powdered milk
2 c. confectioner's sugar
1 tsp. vanilla

Melt butter, add brown sugar; let bubble 2 minutes, stirring. Add 1/4 c. water and powdered milk; bring to a boil. Remove from heat; beat in confectioner's sugar. Add vanilla.

Chocolate Glaze

Cousin-Margaret Booth - Ceredo, WV

Melt together 2 T butter and 2 squares unsweetened chocolate. Beat in 2 T boiling water, 1 c. confectioner's sugar, dash salt, and 1/4 tsp. vanilla extract.

Cooked Cake Frosting

Cousin-Mary Beth Stewart Martin- Racine, WS

3 T flour
1 c. milk

Cook in double boiler until thick, then let cool.

1 c. butter
1 c. sugar
1 tsp. vanilla

Cream butter, sugar, and vanilla. When cooked part is cooled add the rest and beat till well blended.

Fluffy Cream Cheese Frosting

Cousin-Bonnie Dominiak - Chula Vista, CA

1 (3 oz.) pkg. cream cheese, softened
1/4 c. plus 2 T margarine, softened
1 T orange juice or whipping cream
1 tsp. vanilla
1-3/4 c. sifted powdered sugar

Beat cream cheese and margarine until fluffy; add orange juice and vanilla, and mix well. Gradually add powdered sugar, mixing until light and fluffy. Makes about 1 c.

Nougatine Frosting

Cousin-Helen Jobe - Ceredo, WV

2 egg whites, unbeaten
1-1/2 c. sugar
4 T water
2 T light corn syrup
2 T honey
1/4 tsp. cream of tartar
1/8 tsp. salt
1/2 tsp. vanilla
1/2 c. chopped walnuts
2 T candied cherries, cut in small pieces

Put first 7 ingredients in top of double boiler and mix thoroughly. Place over rapidly boiling water and beat constantly with rotary egg beater until mixture will hold a peak (7 minutes). Remove from hot water, add vanilla and beat until thick enough to spread. To 1/3 of icing add walnuts and cherries and spread between the layers. Spread plain frosting on top and sides of cake. Makes enough frosting for top and sides of two 8-inch layers.

Quick Fudge Frosting

Cousin-Wanda Lee Maynard - Huntington, WV

Sift 2 c. confectioner's sugar and 1/4 c. cocoa. Add 1/8 tsp. salt. Heat 1/4 c. undiluted evaporated milk and 2 T butter. Add to first mixture with 1 tsp. vanilla extract. Beat until smooth.

Candy and Cookies

Candy

Kentucky Bourbon Balls
Caramel Corn I
Caramel Corn II
Cracker Jack Style Caramel Corn
Ding Bats (Date Balls)
Divinity
No Cook Fondant
Fudge Candy
Chocolate Marshmallow Fudge
Dee's Fudge Candy
Five-minute Fudge
Mom's Fudge
Old Fashioned Fudge
Peanut Butter Fudge
Kentucky Cream Candy
Molasses Candy
Molasses Popcorn Balls
Peanut Brittle
Spiced Pecans
Randa's Sea Foam Snow Candy
Spiced Nuts
Texas Toffee Bars

Cookies

Brownies
Applesauce Brownies
Iowa Brownies

Butter Pecan Turtle Cookies
Chocolate Chip Bars
Chocolate Oatmeal Cookies
Christmas Fruit Cake Cookies
Cupcakes in a Cone
Honey Jumbles
Crisp Honey Cookies
Kentucky Puffs
Lemon Crackers
Grandma Stuart's Famous Lemon Pillows
Lemon Squares
Melissa's Favorite Cookies
Molasses Cookies I
Molasses Cookies II
Molasses—peanut Cookies
Mom's Molasses Cookies
Mother's Molasses Cookies
Old Fashioned Molasses Cookies
No Bake Cookies I
No Bake Cookies II
No Bake Oatmeal Cookies
Old Fashioned Oatmeal Cookies
Peanut butter Cookies
Queen Anne's Lace
Russian Tea Cakes
Shortbread Fans
Snickerdoodles
Star Cookies
Old Fashioned Sugar Cookies
Surfer Squares

Jesse Stuart

I think Deane is more magic than a dream.
She loves wild music in the wind at night;
She loves the music of a mountain stream-
She sees cold glistening beauty in starlight.
Deane is more stately than an ash in April
And straighter than a mountain valley pine;
She is more sprightly than a young jonquil,
Her dark-brown hair is like the curled love-vine.
Her beauty fills the pockets of my brain;
Her image is embedded in my heart!
She's filled with song, the old and new refrain
She's hummed until they have become a part-
I cannot speak a tribute for her hair;
I cannot tell the magic of her eyes;
I cannot write a sentence to compare-
I wish I could before her beauty dies.

* Stuart, Jesse, *Album of Destiny*, (New York: E. P. Dutton & Co., Inc., 1944), p. 41.

Candy

Kentucky Bourbon Balls

Niece-Betty S. Baird - Wadestown, WV

1/2 stick margarine
2 lbs. powdered sugar
3 or 4 jiggers of Kentucky Bourbon
Pecans (halves)
Dipping chocolate

Use first three ingredients to make fondant and form balls around pecans (which may be soaked in bourbon first.) Dip in dipping chocolate. Store in closed containers.

Caramel Corn I

*Sister-in-law-Laura Avanelle Norris Callihan
Greenup, KY*

1/2 c. butter
1/2 c. dark Karo syrup
1 c. brown sugar
1/2 tsp. soda

Combine above ingredients in saucepan, bring to boil. Pour over 5 qts. of popped corn. Stir well. Bake at 350° for 45 minutes. Stir while in oven every 10 minutes. Makes large roaster full.

Caramel Corn II

Niece-Martha Stuart Wheeler - Knoxville, TN

Pop enough corn to make 16 cups of popped corn. Mix together:
2 c. brown sugar
1/2 lb. butter
1/2 c. light Karo syrup
Boil 5 minutes, remove from heat, add:

1 tsp. vanilla
1 tsp. salt
1 tsp. baking soda

Blend and pour over popped corn, mixing well. Bake at 250° for 1 hour. Remove from oven every 15 minutes and stir from the bottom. When finished spread on waxed paper and cool.

Cracker Jacks, Style Caramel Corn

Cousin-Al Lester - Kenova, WV

2 gal. popped corn
2 c. brown sugar
2 sticks oleo
1/2 c. white syrup
1/2 tsp. baking soda

In large saucepan melt oleo, syrup and sugar, let boil one minute. Remove from heat, add baking soda. Place corn in large baking pan and pour mixture over it. Bake at 225° for 1 hour. Stir about every 15 min. Add peanuts when you stir last time. (Can omit nuts.)

Ding Bats (Date Balls)

Cousin-Wally Hall - Frankfort, KY

1 c. dates, chopped
1/2 c. butter
1 egg, beaten
1 c. sugar
1 T vanilla
1 c. walnuts, chopped
2 c. Rice Krispies
coconut, Angel Flake

Cook first four ingredients till thick. Then mix in vanilla, walnuts and Rice Krispies. Make into balls and roll in coconut.

Divinity

Cousin-Rena Stewart - Magee, MS

Good divinity requires heavy beating. The 2-temperature method here lessens the chore.

1/2 c. Karo red label syrup
2-1/2 c. sugar
1/4 tsp. salt
1/2 c. water
2 egg whites
1 tsp. vanilla
1 c. coarsely chopped nuts (Optional)

Combine corn syrup, sugar, salt and water in saucepan. Cook over medium heat, stirring constantly, until sugar is dissolved. Cook, without stirring, to firm ball stage (248°) or until a small amount of syrup forms a firm ball which does not flatten when dropped into very cold water. Just before syrup reaches 248°, beat egg whites with electric mixer or rotary beater until stiff but not dry. Pour about one-half of the syrup slowly over egg whites, beating constantly. Cook the remainder of the syrup to soft crack stage (272°) or until a small amount of syrup separates into threads which are hard but not brittle when dropped into very cold water. Add syrup slowly to the first mixture, beating constantly. Continue beating until mixture holds its shape. If mixture becomes too heavy for beater, continue beating with a wooden spoon. Add vanilla and nuts. Drop from tip of spoon onto waxed paper. Makes about 1-1/4 lbs.

No Cook Fondant

Niece-Jennifer Stuart - Greenup, KY

Make a dozen different candies with this basic no cook fondant. Let the kids mold it.

1/3 c. soft margarine
1/3 c. Karo red label syrup
1/2 tsp. salt
1 tsp. vanilla
4-1/2 c. sifted confectioners sugar

Blend margarine, corn syrup, salt and vanilla in large mixing bowl. Add sifted confectioners sugar all at once. Mix all together—first with a spoon and then with hands knead in dry ingredients. Turn onto board and continue kneading until mixture is well blended and smooth. Makes about 1-1/3 pounds candy. Store in a cool place. Flavor and shape may be varied as follows:

No Cook Fondant Variations

Mint Patties: Substitute 1 teaspoon peppermint or wintergreen flavoring for vanilla. Tint to desired color, using green vegetable coloring for wintergreen and red coloring for peppermint. Shape into balls; or roll thin and cut into any shape desired.

Orange or lemon creams: Substitute 2 teaspoons orange extract or 1 teaspoon lemon extract for vanilla. Tint to a delicious orange or yellow using vegetable coloring. Shape as above.

Almond diamonds: Substitute 1 tsp. almond extract for vanilla. Add 1/2 c. coarsely chopped blanched and toasted almonds. Roll out or pat to 1/2 inch thickness. Cut into diamonds.

Candied fruit squares: If desired, rum, or rum extract may be substituted for vanilla. Add 1/2 c. finely chopped mixed candied fruit. Roll; cut into squares.

Mocha logs: Add 2 teaspoons powdered instant coffee. Shape into small rolls about 1/2 inch in diameter and 2 inches long. Roll in chocolate candy cake decorations.

Fudge Candy

Cousin-Mary Belle Johnson - Portsmouth, OH

1-1/2 to 2 sqs. bitter chocolate
1/4 tsp. salt
2 c. granulated sugar
2 T butter
2 tsp. corn syrup
3/4 c. evaporated milk
1/2 tsp. vanilla

Melt chocolate over low heat in saucepan to be used. Add sugar mixing thoroughly, then add syrup, salt and butter. Mix until well blended, add milk and stir until sugar dissolves. Boil to soft ball stage (235°F) to make soft ball test. Allow fudge to fall in small drops in teacup of cold water. If drops can be formed in balls that hold their shape, candy is done. Otherwise continue cooking. Remove from heat, add flavoring, cool thoroughly (can set pan in ice water) not stirring until hand can be held on bottom of pan. Beat vigorously 4 to 6 minutes, add peanut butter or nuts, or whatever. Turn into a buttered pan quickly after candy turns opaque and softens. Cut in squares. For marshmallowy fudge add 1 cup marshmallow, cut in bits when ready to pour. Also increase chocolate.

Chocolate Marshmallow Fudge

Niece-Martha "Marty" Abdon - Greenup, KY

5 c. sugar
2 sticks butter (chop up)
1 can cream

Mix the above mixture together and let come to a boil. Boil and stir for 9 minutes. Remove from heat: Add 2 small pkgs. choc. chips, 1 pint marshmallow cream and nuts if desired. Beat together until thick. Pour into greased 9 x 13 pan. Cut into squares when cool. Very good and creamy.

Dee's Fudge Candy

Cousin-Rosalie Stewart - Ravenswood, WV

1st step:
Grease pan and put aside.

3 pkg. chocolate chips
1 cube oleo
1 (8 oz.) jar marshmallow cream
1 T vanilla

Put aside in large bowl.

2nd step:
1 lg. can milk
4-1/2 c. sugar

Cook 10 minutes at rolling boil.

3rd step:
Pour step 2 over step 1 and beat until chocolate chips are melted. Add nuts. Pour in greased pan. Let stand 24 hours before cutting.

Five-Minute Fudge

Nephew-Gene Darby - Greenup, KY

2/3 c. Carnation milk
1-2/3 c. sugar
1/2 tsp. salt
1/2 c. chopped pecans
1-1/2 c. miniature marshmallows
1-1/2 c. chocolate chips
1 tsp. vanilla
1 stick butter

Mix Carnation, sugar, and salt in a saucepan. Cook over low heat for 5 minutes, stirring constantly. Remove from heat. Quickly mix in butter, vanilla, marshmallows, chocolate chips, and nuts and stir well. Spread into 8 x 8 greased baking dish and refrigerate. Cut into squares. (Never fails!)

Mom's Fudge

Cousin-Brian Lester - Kenova, WV

4-1/2 c. sugar
1 c. evaporated milk
1/2 lb. margarine
1 lg. pkg. chocolate chips
1 (7 oz.) jar of marshmallow creme

Combine sugar, milk, and margarine in pan and cook over med. heat. After mixture begins to boil, cook for 9 min. stirring constantly. Remove from heat and pour over pkg. of chocolate chips and jar of marshmallow cream. I have this already in a large saucepan. When choc. chips and marshmallow cream are dissolved you may add nuts if desired. Quickly pour into 9 x 13 buttered pan. When cool enough to cut, store in air tight container. If fudge is allowed to get too cold it will not cut well. You may use 18 oz. jar of Jif peanut butter instead of choc. chips for peanut butter fudge.

Old Fashioned Fudge

Cousin-Pat Stewart - Ravenswood, WV

2 c. of sugar
2 T cocoa heapened

Mix well.

Add 1 T Karo syrup (white) and 1 can carnation milk. Cook to soft ball. Add vanilla and beat.

Peanut Butter Fudge

Cousins-David and Thomas Adkins, Lucasville, OH

3 c. sugar
1 c. milk
1/2 stick margarine
1 c. peanut butter
1 tsp. vanilla

Combine sugar, milk, and margarine and boil until it forms a soft ball in a glass of water. Take off heat and add peanut butter and vanilla. Beat until it becomes creamy. Turn into a well buttered pan. Nuts may be added or crunchy peanut butter may be used.

Kentucky Cream Candy

Cousin-Judy Castle - Huntington, WV

3 c. sugar
1 c. water
1 stick margarine

Combine and stir until sugar dissolves. Do not stir after mixture starts to boil. Boil to 265°. Pour on marble slab or hard cool surface. As edges cool, push toward center once. When cool enough to handle, pull with buttered hands. (Cool hands with damp cloth). Pull and fold over in a half twist. When pulling is completed, cut into pieces with scissors.

Molasses Candy

Sister-Glennis Liles - Greenup, KY

Boil for 10 minutes 1 cup of molasses, 2 cups of sugar, 1 T of vinegar, and butter about the size of a hickory nut. Then cool it enough to pull. Why bother to tell you how to pull molasses candy; everybody knows that. Break in pieces by tapping with a knife.

Molasses Popcorn Balls

Niece-Martha "Marty" Abdon - Greenup, KY

1 c. molasses
1 c. sugar
1 T butter or margarine
4 qts. unsalted popped corn

Combine molasses, sugar and butter in a 2 qt. saucepan. Place over low heat and stir until sugar is dissolved. Cook over medium heat, until syrup, when dropped in very cold water, seperates into threads which are hard but not brittle. Pour syrup over popped corn, stirring to coat each kernel. When cool enough to handle, shape into balls with lightly buttered hands. Wrap each ball in wax paper.

Yields: about 2 dozen balls.

Peanut Brittle (2 lbs.)

Cousin-Margaret Booth - Ceredo, WV

2 c. sugar
1 c. light corn syrup
1/4 c. water
2 c. raw peanuts (Spanish, unsalted)
1 tsp. baking soda
1 tsp. salt
1 tsp. vinegar

Combine the sugar, corn syrup, and water in a saucepan and cook to soft-ball stage. Add peanuts and cook to hard crack stage. Remove from heat and add soda, salt and vinegar. Stir well and pour into a buttered, chilled cookie pan. Cool and break in pieces.

Spiced Pecans

Niece-Connie Keeney - Greenup, KY

1 egg
2 T water
2 c. (1/2 lb. pecan halves)
1 tsp ground cinnamon
1/2 c. sugar
3/4 tsp. salt
1/4 tsp. ground cloves
1/4 tsp. ground nutmeg

Beat egg and water with a fork in a medium bowl until well blended. Stir in pecans, mix until coated. Remove nuts from bowl with a fork and arrange in an 8-in. square baking pan.

Mix sugar, cinnamon, salt, cloves and nutmeg in a small bowl. Sprinkle over nuts in pan, toss gently until thoroughly coated. Spread coated nuts on ungreased cookie sheet.

Bake in slow oven (300°), shake pan several times during baking, 25 minutes, or until golden (watch carefully).

Cool nuts on cookie sheet. Store in metal tin with tight-fitting cover. Suggestion variation: for spiced orange walnuts, substitute 2 cups walnut halves for the pecans and 1/2 tsp. grated orange rind for spices in the recipe above.

IMPORTANT: Soak pan immediately.

Randa's Sea Foam

Cousin-Randa Jane Murphy - Lucasville, OH

3 c. sugar
3/4 c. white syrup
3/4 c. water

Boil to soft ball stage.

Mix:
1 small package of strawberry jello or any flavor
2 egg whites

Beat until stiff. Gradually add syrup mixture a little at at time. Beat until very stiff. Spoon onto waxed paper and let harden.

Snow Candy

Niece-Eileen McCarten Nelson - Greenup, KY

Many Mother's and Grandmother's in my family have made this candy for children on snowy January afternoons. The candy recipe, which was to be poured in a greased pan, came from Pickerton's Wisdom, published in East Hampton, Mass. in 1893.

1 pan of newly fallen snow
2 c. brown sugar
1/2 c. butter
4 T. molasses
2 T water
2 T vinegar

Boil sugar, butter, molasses, water and vinegar in a large pot until the candy reaches the hard crack stage on a candy thermometer or when a thread of candy cracks when it is drizzled into a glass of cold water. Immediately remove the candy from the heat. Pour thin ribbons of candy over the pans of snow. The candy will harden and melt the snow. Crack the ribbons of candy into pieces and give them to your children.

Spiced Nuts

Cousins-David and Thomas Adkins - Lucasville, OH

1 c. sugar
2 T cinnamon
1/2 T cloves
1/2 tsp nutmeg
1/4 tsp. salt
1/4 c. water
1 lb. shelled English walnuts

Combine sugar, spices, salt and water. Cook to soft ball stage. Stir in nuts with a wooden spoon. Stir until nuts become sugary. Spread on waxed paper. Store in a can or canister.

Texas Toffee Bars

Sister-in-law-Lucille Norris - Greenup, KY

1/2 c. sugar
2 sticks butter
1 c. chopped nuts

Boil 2 minutes. Spoon over graham crackers, separated on buttered cookie sheet. Bake 12 minutes until bubbly at 325°. Cool only slightly. Remove from sheet and put on rack.

Cookies

Brownies

Cousin-Teresa Hilton - Frankfort, KY

2 (1 oz.) unsweetened squares of chocolate
1/2 c. margarine = 1 stick
1 c. sugar
2 eggs
1 tsp. vanilla
1/2 c. flour (sifted)
1/2 c. chopped pecans

Cream margarine and add sugar and eggs, beat well. Melt chocolate and blend in with vanilla, flour, and nuts. Bake in greased 8 x 8 x 2 pan at 325° for 35 minutes.

Icing:
Cream 1/4 stick butter, 1/2 square melted chocolate,1-1/2 c. XX sugar, 1/2 tsp vanilla, and 1 T milk. Mix well and spread on brownies when cool.

Applesauce Brownies

Cousin-Mary Beth Stewart Martin - Racine, WS

1/2 c. butter
2 (1 oz.) squares unsweetened chocolate
3/4 c. sugar
2 eggs, beaten
3/4 c. applesauce
1-1/4 tsp. vanilla
1 c. flour
1/2 tsp. baking powder
1/4 tsp. baking soda
1/4 tsp. salt

Nut Topping:
2 T sugar
1/4 c. chopped nuts
1/2 c. semisweet chocolate pieces

Melt together butter and chocolate. Add rest of ingredients and mix well. Pour brownie mixture into greased 8 x 8 pan. Mix topping ingredients, sprinkle over batter. Bake at 350° for 30-35 minutes. Cool and cut in squares.

Iowa Brownies

Cousins-David and Thomas Adkins - Lucasville, OH

1/2 c. soft margarine
1 (16 oz.) can choc. syrup
1 c. flour
1 c. sugar
4 eggs
1 c. chopped nuts

Cream margarine and sugar, slowly add syrup; then add eggs one at a time. Add flour. Beat until well blended and add nuts. Turn onto a greased sheet pan 9 x 13. Bake 350° for 25 minutes.

Topping:
3/4 c. margarine
1/3 c. milk
1-1/2 c. sugar
1/2 c. chocolate bits

Combine 1st three ingredients in saucepan. Bring to a boil and boil 1 minute, remove from heat. Add choc. bits and stir until melted. Quickly spread on warm brownies. Topping will be runny but will harden.

Butter Pecan Turtle Cookies

Niece-Martha "Marty" Abdon - Greenup, KY

Crust:
2 c. all-purpose flour
1 c. firmly packed brown sugar
1/2 c. butter, softened
1-1/2 c. pecan halves

Topping:
2/3 c. butter
1/2 c. firmly packed brown sugar
1/2 to 3/4 c. semisweet choc. chips

Crust: Preheat oven to 350°F. In large mixer bowl combine flour, brown sugar and butter; beat at medium speed 2 to 3 minutes. Press into ungreased 13 x 9" baking pan. Pat pecan halves evenly into unbaked crusts.

Topping: In small heavy saucepan combine butter and brown sugar. Cook over medium heat until mixture begins to boil. Boil 1 minute, stirring constantly. Pour over crust. Bake in center of oven 18 to 22 minutes, or until topping is bubbly and crust is light golden brown. Remove from oven. Sprinkle on chocolate chips; do not spread. Cool on wire racks. Cut into bars. Makes about 3-1/2 dozen.

Chocolate Chip Bars

Niece-Kathy Abdon - Greenup, KY

1/3 c. shortening
1/2 c. butter (1 stick)
1/2 c. granulated sugar
1/2 c. brown sugar (packed)
1 egg
1 tsp. vanilla
1-1/2 c. flour
1/2 tsp. baking soda
1/2 tsp. salt
1/2 c. chopped nuts
1 pkg. semi-sweet chocolate pieces

Heat oven to 375°. Mix shortening, butter, both sugars, egg and vanilla well. Stir in remaining ingredients. Spread in ungreased, oblong pan (9 x 13 x 2). Bake 20-25 minutes, cool, cut into bars. Makes 32.

Chocolate Oatmeal Cookies

Niece-Jerri Oney - Raceland, KY

2 c. sugar
1/4 c. cocoa
1/2 c. milk
1 stick butter
1 tsp. vanilla
1/2 c. peanut butter
3 c. quick oats

Mix sugar, cocoa, milk and butter in saucepan. Boil one minute. Remove from heat, add peanut butter, vanilla, and oats. Stir and drop by teaspoon on wax paper. Cool and serve.

Christmas Fruit Cake Cookies

Cousin-Faye Hilton - Frankfort, KY

1-3/4 c. sugar
1/2 c. shortening
3 eggs
3 c. flour
1 tsp. cinnamon
1/2 tsp. nutmeg
1/2 tsp. cloves
1/2 tsp. salt
1 lb. chopped dates
1/2 lb. chopped candied cherries
1/2 lb. chopped candied pineapple
1/2 lb. chopped pecans
1 T. vanilla
1/2 tsp. soda dissolved in 1/4 c. water

Cream sugar and butter. Add eggs, one at a time, beating after each addition. Mix sifted flour and spices and add 3/4 cup of the flour to nut, fruit mix and mix well. Add vanilla, then the fruit flour mixture. Add the remaining flour mixture, and last, the soda and water mix. Drop by tsp. full on greased cookie sheet—bake at 350° about 12 minutes. Best if not baked too brown.

Cupcakes in a Cone

Cousin-Kevin Travis Murphy - Lucasville, OH

Mix up a box of your favorite cake mix according to box instructions. Place cup ice cream cones in cup cake pans and fill 3/4 full of batter. Bake at 350° until done, about 1/2 hour. When cool frost with your favorite frosting and top with a cherry. The whole thing is edible. No messy cup cake papers.

Honey Jumbles (1893)

Niece-Betty Stuart Darby Baird - Wadestown, WV

1 c. molasses
2 1/3 c. honey
1/2 c. shortening
5 tsp. soda
6 tsp. cream of tartar
1 tsp. salt
1 c. sugar
1 c. buttermilk
3 eggs
9 to 9-1/2 c. flour (dough should be rather stiff)

Cream molasses, honey, sugar and shortening. Add slightly beaten eggs and buttermilk. Mix soda, salt, cream of tartar and flour. Mix flour mixture into honey-molasses mixture. Mix well—may have to use hands. Drop by teaspoonfuls on cookie sheet. Bake at 400° for 7 minutes or until brown. Makes approximately 16 dozen cookies.

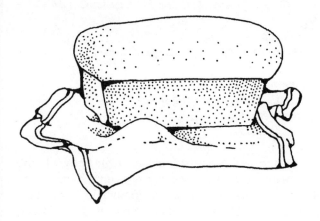

Crisp Honey Cookies

Niece-Betty Stuart Darby Baird - Wadestown, WV

5 c. sifted flour
3 tsp. baking powder
1/4 tsp. soda
1/4 tsp. (scant) salt
1 c. shortening
1 c. brown sugar
2 eggs, beaten
1 c. honey
3/4 c. nuts, if desired

Sift together flour, baking powder, soda and salt. Cream shortening and sugar; add eggs and mix well. Mix in honey. Add flour mixture to creamed mixture. Form into rolls (about 3). Chill. Cut in 1/4 inch slices. Bake on ungreased cookie sheet 400° for 7 minutes. Makes about 9 dozen.

Kentucky Puffs

Cousin-Mary Catherine Stewart Martin - Racine, WS

Boil one pint of milk with a pound of butter, stir them into 3 quarters of a pound of flour and let cool. Then add nine eggs.(yolks and whites, to be beaten separately and whites to be added last) Fill cup or tins half full and bake. When done, sprinkle with white sugar while hot. Very nice with tea.

Lemon Crackers

Cousin-Ginny Belle Smith - Lucasville, OH

2-1/2 c. sugar
1 c. shortening (half lard and half butter)
2 eggs
1 T lemon oil
2 T baking ammonia (drug store)
1 pint sweet milk
Approx. 8 c. flour

Dissolve the ammonia in the milk the night before. In the A.M. cream the sugar, shortening, eggs until creamy. Add the lemon oil and milk. Mix. Add enough flour to make a stiff dough. Chill for 4 hours or more. Roll on floured board, medium thin. Sprinkle with sugar, press in. Cut into cracker shapes. Prick with fork. Bake at 350° for 10 minutes til bottoms are browned on a greased cookie sheet.

Grandma Stuart's Famous Lemon Pillows

Cousin-Ila Shanks - Zelienople, PA

How well I remember them. They were so delicious and they really weren't pillows-they were cookies. We, the grandchildren, called them pillows because that's what we thought they looked like.

Grandma Clara Stuart was Mrs. James Stuart. Grandpa James Stuart and Jesse's father, Mitchell Stuart, were brothers. My mother, Florence Stuart Wolfe, was a daughter of James and Clara Stuart.

5 tsp. (1/2 oz.) baking ammonia
1 c. milk
1/2 c. shortening
1-1/4 c. sugar
5 c. flour (about)
2 eggs, beaten
1/4 tsp. salt
1/2 tsp. oil of lemon

Dissolve baking ammonia (available in drugstores) in milk at least 1/2 hour before using. Cream sugar and shortening together until fluffy. Add beaten eggs and mix well. Add part of flour and the salt alternately with the milk mixture and oil of lemon. Mix well, adding flour just until dough is easy to handle. Divide dough into several parts. Roll dough on lightly floured surface until 1/4 inch thickness. Cut with square cookie cutter. Place cookies about 2" apart, on lightly greased baking sheet. Bake in preheated oven (375°) for 8-10 minutes or until lightly browned. Remove to wire rack to cool. Yields 2-3 dozen cookies.

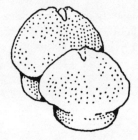

Lemon Squares

Wife-Naomi Deane Norris Stuart - W-Hollow, KY

1 c. flour
1/2 c. butter
1/4 c. confectioners sugar
2 eggs
1 c. sugar
1/2 tsp. baking powder
1/4 tsp. salt
2 T lemon juice

Heat oven to 350° (mod.). Measure flour by dipping method or by sifting flour. Mix flour, butter and confectioners sugar thoroughly. Press evenly in square pan 8 x 8 x 2. Bake 20 minutes. Beat rest of ingredients together, and pour over crust. Bake 20-25 minutes more. Do not overbake.

Melissa's Favorite Cookies

Cousin-Faye Stewart Lester - Kenova, WV

1-1/2 sticks margarine
1-1/2 c. graham cracker crumbs
1 can Eagle brand sweetened condensed milk
1 large pkg. semi-sweet chocolate chips
1 can (3-1/2 oz.) flaked coconut (use more if desired)
1 c. chopped pecans

In 9 x 13 in. baking pan, melt margarine, remove from heat. Sprinkle crumbs over margarine. Pour condensed milk evenly over crumbs. Top with chocolate chips, coconut and pecans, press down gently. Bake at 350° for 25 min. or until golden brown. Cool. Cut into bars.

Molasses Cookies I

Cousin-Teresa Hilton - Frankfort, KY

3/4 c. soft shortening
1 c. brown sugar
1 egg
1/4 c. molasses
2-1/4 c. flour
2 tsp. baking soda
1/4 tsp. salt
1/2 tsp. cloves
1 tsp. cinnamon
1 tsp. ginger

Mix first four ingredients. Then gradually sift in flour, soda, salt, and spices. Chill and then roll into balls. Dip top of balls in sugar and put on ungreased cookie sheet. Sprinkle tops lightly with water. Bake 10-12 minutes at 350°.

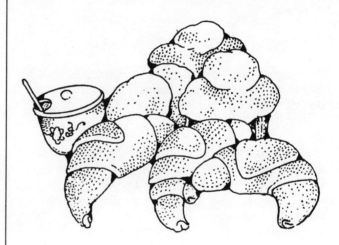

Molasses Cookies II

Niece-Jean Keeney Lush - Bowling Green, KY

Molasses was always available.

Mix together:
1/3 c. soft shortening
1 c. brown sugar
1-1/2 c. dark molasses

Stir in:
1/2 c. cold water

Sift together and stir in:
6 c. sifted all purpose flour
1 tsp. salt
1 tsp. allspice
1 tsp. ginger
1 tsp. cloves
1 tsp. cinnamon
1 c. nuts
1 c. raisins

Stir in 2 tsp. soda dissolved in 3 T cold water

Chill dough, usually overnight. Next morning roll out 1/2 inch thick. With 2-1/2 in. cutter cut four dozen cookies. Bake 350° for 15-18 minutes.

Note:
We always had these and this is not the recipe mother used. She has the recipe and it does not contain nuts or raisins. I keep these for Jim in the freezer. They are his favorite. Special note: Dough very thick and hard to handle.

Molasses-Peanut Cookies

Cousin-Anne Hilton Short - Forestville, MD

2-1/2 c. all purpose flour
2 tsp. baking powder
1/4 tsp. baking soda
3/4 c. butter or margarine, at room temperature
1/2 c. granulated sugar
2/3 c. light molasses
1/2 c. chunky peanut butter
1 lg. egg
For garnish: 1 c. coarsely chopped unsalted roasted peanuts

Mix flour, baking powder, and baking soda. In a large bowl, beat butter and sugar with electric mixer until fluffy. Beat in molasses, peanut butter and egg. With mixer on low speed gradually beat in flour mixture just until blended. Wrap dough and chill 1 hour or until firm enough to shape. Heat oven to 350°. Form dough into 1 inch balls. Dip half of each ball into the chopped nuts. Place nut sides up 2 inches apart on ungreased cookie sheets. Bake 10 to 12 minutes until lightly browned. Cool on cookie sheet 1 minute before removing to rack to cool completely. Store tightly covered. Makes 60.

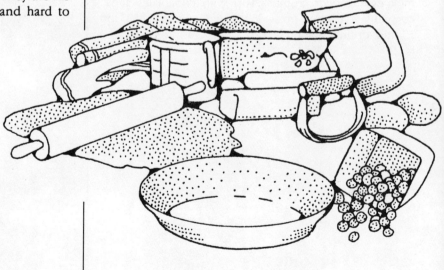

Mom's Molasses Cookies

Cousin-Ginny Belle Smith - Lucasville, OH

3/4 c. molasses
3/4 c. sour milk
3/4 c. lard and butter, melted
1 tsp. ginger
1/2 tsp. soda
2 tsp. baking powder
3-1/2 c. all-purpose flour
1/2 tsp. salt
1-1/2 tsp. cinnamon
1 tsp. vanilla
1 egg
1/3 c. brown sugar
1/2 tsp. nutmeg

Cream shortening, beat in sugar, molasses and egg. Sift together flour, soda, and baking powder. Add milk, shortening, cinnamon, ginger, salt and flour. Chill thoroughly. Add just enough flour to roll on lightly floured board. Roll 1/8 inch thick. Bake in 350° oven for 12 minutes. Keep in covered tin.

* My mother used to have these baking when I came home from school. Oh! How good with a glass of milk.

Mother's Molasses Cookies

Cousin-Essie Hilton Rowland - Chillicothe, OH

1 c. medium dark molasses
1 c. brown sugar
1 c. butter
1/2 tsp. ginger
1 tsp. baking soda
1/4 c. hot water
1 tsp. cinnamon
1/2 tsp. nutmeg
1 tsp. baking powder
approx. 5 c. flour
2 eggs

Combine molasses, brown sugar, butter and ginger. Bring to boil in saucepan. Cool. Add eggs, (well beaten). Dissolve soda in hot water and add to mixture. Sift rest of spices and baking powder with 2-1/2 cups flour and add to mixture. Add balance of flour till dough is stiff enough to roll. Chill. Roll into 1/8 inch thickness and cut with cookie cutter. Place on greased baking sheet and bake in 375° oven for 12 minutes.

Old Fashioned Molasses Cookies

Sister-Sophie Stuart Keeney - Greenup, KY

1-1/2 c. molasses
2/3 c. shortening
3 tsp. baking soda
1/2 c. sugar
1/2 c. hot water

Stir above ingredients together until they foam, then add:
flour (about 5 cups)
1 tsp. ginger
1/2 tsp. cinnamon
1/2 tsp. nutmeg
salt

Roll out on board; cut with cookie cutter. Bake on greased baking sheet 375° for 10 minutes. Makes about 5 dozen cookies.

No Bake Cookies I

Cousin-Pat Stewart - Ravenswood, WV

3 c. oats
2 c. sugar
1 stick oleo
1/3 c. cocoa
1/2 c. milk
1 tsp. vanilla
2 T peanut butter

Boil sugar, butter, milk, cocoa for 3 or 4 minutes. Then add peanut butter, vanilla and oats. Spread on waxed paper by spoon.

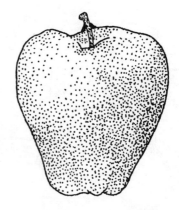

No Bake Cookies II

Cousin-Donna Stewart Broscious - Ravenswood, WV

2 c. sugar
1 stick oleo
1/2 c. milk
4 T peanut butter
1/2 c. nuts or coconut
1 tsp. vanilla
1/4 to 1/2 cup cocoa
3 c. dry oats

Mix sugar, cocoa, and milk. Bring to a boil. Boil for 3 minutes then remove from heat. Add peanut butter, nuts or coconut, if desired, and vanilla. Add oats, mix and drop on waxed paper. Cool.

No Bake Oatmeal Cookies

Cousin-Janet Stewart Mayo - Kenova WV

Combine:
2 c. sugar
3 T cocoa
1/2 stick margarine
1/2 c. milk

Bring to hard boil and boil for one minute. Remove from heat and add at once;

2-1/2 c. minute oats
1/2 c. peanut butter
1/2 tsp. vanilla

Mix and drop by spoon on wax paper quickly. To make plain peanut butter, leave out cocoa.

Old Fashioned Oatmeal Cookies

Cousins-David and Thomas Adkins - Lucasville, OH

1 c. raisins
1 c. water
3/4 c. shortening
1-1/2 c. sugar
2 eggs
1 tsp. vanilla
2-1/2 c. all-purpose flour
1 tsp. soda
1 tsp. salt
1 tsp. cinnamon
1/2 tsp. baking powder
1/2 tsp. cloves
2 c oats, uncooked
1/2 c. chopped nuts.

Simmer raisins, and water over med. heat until raisins are plump about 15 minutes. Drain raisins, reserve liquid and add enough water to make 1/2 c. Mix thoroughly sugar, eggs, and vanilla. Stir in liquid. Blend remaining ingredients. Drop dough by rounded tsp.about 2 inches apart. Bake 8 to 10 minutes on ungreased cookie sheet. (Bake until light brown.)

Peanut Butter Cookies

Cousin-Mary Arnold - Hillsboro, OH

1 c. crisco
1 c. peanut butter
1 c. white sugar
1 c. brown sugar
1 tsp. salt
2-1/2 c. flour
2 tsp. soda
2 eggs, beaten
1/2 c. milk

Roll into balls and put on greased cookie sheet and press with fork. Bake 375° for 12-15 min.

Queen Anne's Lace
Cousin-Randa Jane Murphy - Lucasville, OH

Pick medium-sized clusters of the white flowers call Queen Anne's Lace (wild carrot) that grows in pastures and fencerows around North Eastern Ky. Wash and pat dry. Dip in pancake batter. Deep fry until lightly browned. Dust with Powdered sugar. Tastes like the old-fashioned anise used to flavor Christmas cookies. Serve while warm. Delicious!

Russian Tea Cakes
Niece-Phyllis Tejeda - Xenia, OH

1 c. butter
1 c. powdered sugar
2-1/2 c. flour
2 tsp. vanilla
1 c. chopped nuts
dash of salt

Cream together butter, sugar, salt, and vanilla. Stir in flour and nuts. Roll into one inch balls and place on greased baking sheet. Bake at 350° for 12-15 minutes. Roll in powdered sugar while warm and again when cool.

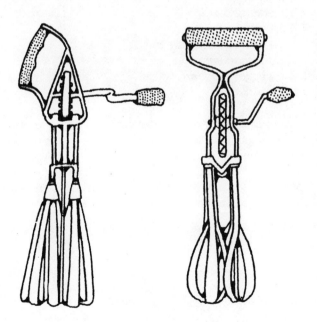

Shortbread Fans
Niece-Lori Ann Stuart - Greenup, KY

One of these crisp buttery cookies makes an elegant addition to any ice-cream dessert. For an interesting variation, combine 1/4 c. finely chopped peanuts, pecans, or walnuts with the other ingredients before kneading.

Makes 32 fans.

1 c. butter or margarine, softened
1/2 c. light brown sugar
2 c. unsifted all-purpose flour
1/4 tsp. salt
1 tsp. vanilla extract
1/2 tsp. almond flavoring

In a medium bowl, combine all ingredients. Stir together until well combined. Knead into a ball. Preheat oven to 300°.

Divide shortbread dough into four balls. On ungreased cookie sheets, with a lightly floured rolling pin, roll each ball into a 7-inch round.

Trim edges of shortbread rounds evenly with a knife or pastry wheel. Score each round into 8 wedges. If desired, flute outside edge of dough with the tines of a fork and score centers of fans with a pastry wheel or knife to make designs.

Bake 20 minutes or until centers are firm and edges have just started to color. Remove tray from oven. Immediately cut through dough on scored line. Let cool 5 minutes; remove to cooling rack. Cool completely and store in an airtight container.

Snickerdoodles

Cousin-Cristi Arnold - Hillsboro, OH

Makes about 3 dozen small cookies

1/2 c. (1 stick) soft butter or margarine
1/4 c. confectioners sugar
1 tsp. vanilla
1 c. sifted enriched flour
1/2 c. finely chopped nuts
2 T granulated sugar
2 tsp. cinnamon

Preheat oven to very low (275°). Place butter or margarine in mixing bowl. Blend in conf. sugar and vanilla. Add the flour, a little at a time, and mix well. Stir in the nuts. Mix the granulated sugar and cinnamon on a piece of waxed paper. Shape the dough into small balls. A tablespoon will help to make balls of the same size. Roll cookie balls in the sugar-cinnamon mixture and place on an ungreased cookie sheet, 1 inch apart. Bake about 30 minutes. When cookies are done, they will be round balls, slightly soft on top. Remove cookies from the oven. Use spatula to lift cookies to the cooling rack or paper towels.

Star Cookies

Nephew-Gene Darby - Greenup, KY

These are my favorite Christmas cookies.

Mix:
3 c. flour
2 tsp. baking powder
1/2 tsp. salt

Cream together:
1-1/2 c. sugar
1/2 c. butter
1/2 c. shortening
2 eggs
1 tsp. vanilla
1 T milk

Gradually add dry ingredients to cream mixture. Roll and cut with star shaped cutter. Bake in preheated 375° oven for 10-12 minutes. Decorate or frost as you like.

Old Fashioned Sugar Cookies

Cousin-William E. Holbrook - Greenup, KY

2-1/4 c. sifted flour
1/4 tsp. salt
2 tsp. baking powder
1 c. sugar
2 eggs, beaten
1/2 tsp. vanilla
1 T milk
1/2 c. butter or oleo

Sift flour, salt and baking powder together. Cream butter and sugar together. Add eggs and vanilla. Add to sifted ingredients and milk. Roll out and cut (roll very thin (1/16") for crisp cookies.) Sprinkle with sugar and bake on lightly greased cookie sheet for 5-7 minutes at 425°. Makes about 2-1/2 dozen.

Surfer Squares

Cousin-Mary Catherine Stewart Martin - Racine, WS

1 c. butterscotch pieces
1/4 c. granulated brown sugar
1/4 c. butter
1 egg
3/4 c. flour
1 tsp. baking powder
1/4 tsp salt
1 c. semi-sweet chocolate bits
1 c. mini marshmallows
1/2 c. chopped walnuts
1 tsp. vanilla

In med. saucepan, melt butterscotch pieces, granulated brown sugar and butter over med. heat, stirring constantly. Remove from heat. Add egg, beat well. Add flour, baking powder and salt. Stir in remaining ingredients. Spread in a greased 8" square pan and bake 350° for 20 to 25 min. Cool and cut in squares.

Canning and Freezing

Pickles and Relish

Bread and Butter Pickles
Gaythel's Dill Pickles
Ginger Pickles
Pickled Corn
Corn Relish
Mom's Corn Relish
Quick, Old-Fashioned Corn Relish
"Apple" Cucumber Rings
Charlie's Hot Tomato Kraut
Kraut Relish
Pickled Peppers (in crock)
Hot Peppers
Pickled Mushrooms
Pickled Okra
Hot Sweet Relish
Zucchini Rind Pickles
Watermelon Rind Pickles

Jelly and Semi-soft Spreads

Apple Butter
Aunt Viola Hilton's Sweet Apple Preserves
Sweet Cherry-Orange (freezer jam)
Cider-Sage Jelly
Cider and Spice Jelly

Cinnamon Rum Plum Conserve
Fruit Cup (freezer jam)
Frozen Fruit Jam
Ginger Marmalade
Kiwi Fruit Jam (freezer-no cook)
Orange and Spice Jelly
Frozen Fresh Peach Jam
Peach-Blueberry (freezer jam)
Peach Honey
Pepper Jelly
Raspberry-Pear (freezer jam)
Rhubarb Jam
Rhubarb Marmalade
Strawberry Preserves
Strawberry-Peach (freezer jam)
Winter Jam

Other Canned and Frozen Foods

Apple Pie Filling (canned)
Canned Peaches
Tasty Peach Pie Filling (canned)
Chili Sauce
Honey Plums
Pimientos (freezer)
Zucchini Pineapple
Taco Sauce

Preservation of Food

Sister– Mary Stuart Nelson

Most of what I remember as a girl growing up in the Stuart family is the way we preserved our food. We had no plastics, refrigeration, or freezers. We did own a cellar and a smoke house for storing food.

We dug our potatoes and spread them to dry. After drying, we filled the bin of the cellar, and the remainder we holed up in the garden. Next we scooped the dirt to make a round hole which we filled with dry leaves from the woods. We added potatoes, covered them with more leaves, then covered the leaves with dirt. This made a large potato hill. In winter, we made a small hole in the side where we reached our hands through to get the potatoes, then we covered the hole with a piece of tin. We also preserved apples and turnips in this manner.

We picked winter apples by hand from the trees, wrapped them in paper, and placed them in barrels to be covered by hay in the barn loft to keep them from freezing. We peeled early apples, sliced them, and spread them in the hot summer sun for drying. Then we stored them in a jar or a bag to be used for dried apple stack cakes or fried pies. We also made and canned apple sauce by peeling, coring, or slicing the apples and cooking them. If needed, we ran them through a sieve and, while hot, sealed them in glass canning jars with a rubber band and zinc lid. We also used apple sauce to make apple butter, which we cooked outside over an open fire in a large brass kettle. We added sugar and cinnamon along with several pennies that scraped the bottom of the kettle to keep it from scorching, stirred it with a long handled wooden spoon, and sealed it in glass jars or stone jars, sealing the lid to the top of the jar with hot sealing wax. We also sulphured apples for frying. With a small metal utensil called a corer, we removed the core and placed a layer of apples in a barrel or a jar where we made a hole in the center and burned a pan of sulphur. We covered this to hold the sulphur in the apples. After this layer was done, we added another layer of apples for the same process until the container was filled.

We placed late cabbage head down in a long dirt trench in the garden and covered them with dirt, leaving the roots above the soil for pulling. When removed, they were bleached white and were very sweet. After the cabbage was cut, we made it into kraut by placing a layer of shredded cabbage and a layer of coarse salt in a large stone churn and beating it until the brine covered the

Mary Stuart

cabbage. When the container was full, we weighted it by placing plates on top of the jar and tucking a white cloth neatly around the cabbage. We used a large rock, washed and wrapped in a white cloth to hold the cabbage in the brine. Using this method, we also made salt pickles, pickled beans, pickled corn, and mustard kraut.

Beans were another vegetable we preserved. We strung, broke, and scalded them, then put them in glass canning jars to which a teaspoon of salt and water were added to fill the jar. We sealed the jars tightly and placed them in a wash tub with wood or lids placed in the bottom to avoid breakage and cooked them over an open fire outside. These we stored in the cellar. We also preserved beans by

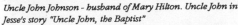
Uncle John Johnson - husband of Mary Hilton. Uncle John in Jesse's story "Uncle John, the Baptist"

Mitchell Stuart, Jesse's father check's Jesse's flock of sheep on Seaton Ridge.

stringing them on a long piece of twine and hanging them to dry. This process was called "leather britches." Later we soaked the beans in water overnight and cooked them with a large piece of pork.

Wild blackberries, strawberries, wild grapes, wild crab apples, peaches, and other fruits made the cellar canning. We made juices into jellies and jams by the boiling method on the old wood cook stove. The cellar was always filled.

Small cucumbers we made into sweet pickles, the large ones into dill or salt pickles, and mixture of all the garden left overs made up the sweet relish that was eaten with brown or white soup beans. We saved small cabbages growing on the stalks after the large heads were cut by putting them in relish.

We cured pork in the smoke house by smoking it with a mixture of wood to give it flavor. We hung it from the rafters, but later in the spring before the weather was warm, we washed it in borax water and buried it in a large box of wheat bran. Before storing, we put it in white muslin sacks. Pork was plentiful all summer. We used scraps of meat to make lye soap for the family wash. We made the soap in a large iron kettle over an open fire, cooled it, and cut it into blocks or bars.

We got raw milk from the cows morning and night and separated it in the cellar with a cream separator. The cream we sold for extra money as well as the eggs from the hens. This gave money for sugar, coffee, soda, salt, etc. The skimmed milk we fed to the pigs, but we used some to churn in the old churn and dash for buttermilk and country butter. This buttermilk made good wholesome cornbread in the oven of the old wood cook stove. We lowered the sweet milk for drinking in the well until the water came to the lid of the bucket. It was as cold as the well water.

We cut dried pumpkins or made them into pumpkin butter by the same process as apples or peach butter.

It was nice to sit around the open wood fire and pop corn in a wire popper or parch it by using butter in an iron skillet stirring it while it turned to a golden brown.

We made cornbread on an open fire in a skillet that had legs and a lid. We poured the cornbread dough into the greased skillet, placed the lid on top, then covered the lid with live coals. This was good on the quilting days in the winter along with the cold sweet milk for lunch.

I would take nothing for these memories, and I am proud to be a member of the Stuart family.

Jesse Stuart and baby sister Glennis (5 yrs. old)

Corner of Martha and Mitchell Stuart's cellar

Between high hills, my Love, we have our shack,
A growing garden, hives for honeybees;
We have our cattle, barn and bins and stack,
And we have blooming flowers and shrubs and trees.
We have steep mountain slopes of growing grain,
Tobacco, corn, potatoes, cane and wheat;
Our loamy land will yield if we get rain. . .
Should we have drouth, we must expect defeat.
We'll pick wild huckleberries from the ridges,
And wild blackberries from the the dogwoods' shade,
And wild strawberries from the south-hill ledges
To can and store before our crops are made.
We must be ready when this season passes
With cans of fruit, with bulging barn and bins,
With sorghum made, with bright full jelly glasses
To face the coming snows and icy winds.

*Stuart, Jesse, *Album of Destiny*, (New York: E. P. Dutton & Co., Inc., 1944), p. 94.

Pickles and Relish

Bread and Butter Pickles

Cousin-Ethel Stewart Terry - Ceredo, WV

25-30 medium size cucumbers
8 large white onions
2 large sweet peppers
1/2 c. salt
5 c. cider vinegar
5 c. sugar (2-1/2 lbs.)
2 T mustard seed
5 tsp. tumeric
1/2 tsp. cloves

Wash cucumbers and slice as thin as possible. Chop onions and peppers. Combine with cucumbers and salt. Let stand 3 hours (can stand overnight). Drain. Combine vinegar, sugar, and spices in large kettle. Bring to boil. Add drained cucumbers; heat thoroughly but do not boil. Pack while hot into sterilized jars and seal. Let stand about six weeks before using.

Gaythel's Dill Pickles

Cousin-Loretta Benner - Lucasville, OH

Wash freshly gathered cucumbers and arrange in quart canning jars. Into each jar add:

1 small hot pepper
1 tsp. dill seed
1/2 tsp. alum
1 grape leaf
1 clove of garlic

Combine the following ingredients, heat to a boil and pour over pickles and seal.

7 quarts of water
1-3/4 c. coarse salt
1 c. vinegar
1 tsp. cream of tartar

(If liquid remains, save in refrigerator until cucumbers are gathered again.)

Ginger Pickles

Cousin-Dorothy Holbrook - Greenup, KY

1 gallon cucumbers
handful of salt
4 T alum
1 T ginger

Syrup:
3 lbs. sugar
1 qt. vinegar
3 cinnamon sticks
2 T celery seed

Soak cucumbers, sliced thin, with salt, in hot water, enough to cover cucumbers. Let stand for four days.

Drain and boil in fresh water with alum for 10 minutes.

Drain and boil in fresh water with ginger for 10 min; drain. Combine ingredients for syrup and pour over cucumbers. Boil 15 minutes. While hot put in jars. Note: 2-1/4 cups of sugar equals 1 lb.

Pickled Corn

Sister-Glennis Stuart Liles - Greenup, KY

Cook corn on the cob and cut it off. Place corn in a pillow case and put bag in a crock. Cover bag with a solution of:

1 gallon water
1 c. coarse salt
3/4 c vinegar

Weight down and allow to ferment. Skim as necessary. Can in glass jars if desired after fermentation. This is very good with soup beans, fried potatoes and corn bread.

(Original) Corn Relish

Sister-Glennis Stuart Liles - Greenup, KY

4 red peppers; chopped
4 green peppers; chopped
1/2 gallon raw corn; cut off
2 c. chopped onion
1-1/2 c. sugar
1 qt. vinegar
1-1/2 tsp. salt
1 T dry mustard
1 T celery seed
4 T flour
1-1/2 tsp. tumeric

Cook all ingredients, except flour, for 15 minutes. Mix flour with enough cold water to make a paste and add to corn mixture. Cook 5 min; stirring constantly to prevent sticking. Ladle into jars and seal. Process 15 min. in boiling water. Makes 6 pts.

I never really liked corn relish until I ate some at Greenbo Lodge. I experimented three summers before I came up with a recipe that tasted like theirs.

Mom's Corn Relish

Nephew-Roy Abdon - Greenup, KY

10 c. fresh corn
10 c. finely chopped cabbage
5 lg. onions, ground fine
5 sm. red peppers, ground
3 c. sugar
1/2 gallon vinegar
3 T salt
4 T mustard seed
1 T celery seed

Cook everything together one-half hour and seal in sterilized jars.

Quick, Old-Fashioned Corn Relish

Niece-Sandy Nelson Perrine - Greenup, KY

*Keeps indefinitely in the refrigerator.
*Makes 1 2/3 cups.

1/2 c. cider vinegar
1/3 c. sugar
1 tsp. salt
1/2 tsp. celery seed
1/4 tsp. mustard seed
1/4 tsp. hot pepper sauce

1-1/2 c. cooked corn (16 oz. can) drained
2 T chopped green bell pepper
1 T chopped pimento
1 T minced white or green onion

Combine first 6 ingredients in saucepan and bring it to a boil. Cook 2 minutes; remove from heat and cool. Place remaining ingredients in a medium bowl. Add cooled mixture and blend slightly. Chill and cover.

"Apple" Cucumber Rings (4 days)

Sister-Sophie Stuart Keeney - Greenup, KY

Day 1: 2 gal. ripe cucumber, peeled, seeded, sliced 1/4" rings. Cover with mixture of and soak 24 hours:
2 c. pickling lime
8-9 qts. water

Day 2: Pour off mixture and rinse. Cover with ice water (and a little salt) for 3 hours. Drain, simmer 2 hours in:
1 c. vinegar
2 bottles red food coloring
1 T alum
water to cover

Drain, discard water, rinse. Make solution of:
2 c. vinegar
2 c. water
10 c. sugar
8 sticks cinnamon
1 pkg. Brach's Red Hot's (Cinnamon Candies)

Heat solution for 30 minutes. Pour over pickles. (add water to make enough to cover, if needed).

Day 3: Drain solution, heat it to boiling and pour back over pickles.

Day 4: Drain solution, heat it to boiling. Pack rings in jars (sterilized pints or half pints). Pour solution over and seal (more boiling water may be added if needed.)

Charlie's Hot Tomato Kraut

Niece-Betty Stuart Baird - Wadestown, WV

hot peppers
onions
salt

Equal parts of:
green tomatoes
sweet peppers (mix green and red for color)
cabbage

Chop and measure the above vegetables, add four chopped onions for each quart of vegetables. Add chopped hot peppers, depending on hotness desired. Mix all thoroughly and place in stone jar. Add 1 c. salt per gallon of vegetables. Add enough cold water to bring brine over top of vegetables. Let kraut ferment to desired taste. When it suites your taste put in sterilized jars and seal.

Kraut Relish

Cousin-Joyce (Jimmie) Carter McKinney - Scarbro, WV

2 c. chopped canned sauerkraut
2 T coarsely snipped scallions
1 small red tomato; cut in pieces
1/4 c. minced green pepper
salt and pepper to taste

In bowl mix kraut, scallions, tomato and green pepper. Add salt and pepper. Refrigerate overnight. Makes three cups. Keeps well. I serve with turkey.

Pickled Peppers (in crock)

Niece-Betty Stuart Baird - Wadestown, KY

green and red sweet peppers
salt
chopped cabbage
vinegar
1 c. brown sugar

Select firm well shaped peppers. Wash and cut off tops (reserve). Remove seeds. Soak over night in salt water. Then fill with cabbage seasoned with salt. Replace tops and sew on with heavy thread and long needle. Boil enough vinegar to cover, pour brown sugar over peppers. Leave over night and drain vinegar. Heat it to boiling and pour back over peppers. Repeat twice. (Three mornings in all.) Keep crock covered, in a cool place.

Hot Peppers

Brother-in-law-H. C. (Whitey) Liles - Greenup, KY

peppers
sauer kraut
sprig of dill or 1 tsp. dill seed
1 T coarse salt
brine of: 1/2 part white vinegar
*   1/2 part water*

Wash peppers, cut off tops and remove seeds, wash again. Drain sauer kraut, then stuff into each pepper. Pack in jars, add dill and salt. Then make brine of vinegar and water, bring to boil. Pour boiling hot into hot jars then seal. Process hot water bath for 5 minutes. Before serving slice crosswise if desired.

Pickled Mushrooms

Sister-in-law- Lucille Norris - Greenup, KY

2 c. mushrooms (small)
1 tsp. sea salt
1 bay leaf
1 clove garlic (minced)
cider vinegar (to cover 3/4 to 1 c. mushrooms)
1 tsp. fennel seed

Sprinkle salt over mushrooms. Heat vinegar and fennel. When mixture simmers, add mushrooms, bay leaf, and garlic. Simmer 5 minutes. Pour in sterilized jar. Makes 1 pint.

Nice to serve with meat instead of relish or pickles.

Pickled Okra

Cousin-Helen Shultz - Portsmouth, OH

Hot peppers (1 for each jar)
Garlic (1 clove for each jar)
3-1/2 lb small okra pods
Dillseeds (1 tsp. for each jar)
1 pt. white vinegar
4 c. water
1/3 c. salt

Place hot pepper and garlic clove in hot sterilized pint jars. Remove part of stem from each okra pod. Pack okra into jars. Add dill seeds. Combine vinegar, water and salt in saucepan; bring to a boil and then simmer about 5 minutes. Pour over okra. Adjust lids and process in boiling water bath at simmering temperature for 10 minutes (have water boiling hot at start). Let pickles stand several weeks before opening. Approx. 4-5 pints.

Hot Sweet Relish

Cousin-Dorothy Holbrook - Greenup, KY

1 peck green tomatoes
1/2 c. pickling salt
1 qt. hot banana peppers
8 lg. sweet green or red peppers (or mixed)
2-1/2 lbs. onions
3 c. sugar
4-1/2 c. vinegar
1/2 box mixed pickling spice (tied in cheesecloth)

First, grind tomatoes and sprinkle with pickling salt. Let stand while grinding peppers and onions. Then drain well. Add all ingredients. Cook slowly. Stirring occasionally for about 30 minutes. Put in sterilized jars and seal.

A word of caution: use rubber gloves while grinding the hot peppers and keep away from eyes.

Zucchini Pickles

Sister-Mary Stuart Nelson - Greenup, KY

4 qts. zucchini
6 onions, sliced
2 lg. peppers (red or green)
5 c. sugar
1 T tumeric
2 T mustard seed
1-1/2 tsp. celery seed
3 c. vinegar (white)
1/4 to 1/2 c. coarse salt

Dissolve salt and enough water to cover first three ingredients and let stand 3 hours. Drain thoroughly. Mix in other ingredients. Bring to a boil, add drained squash, onions, and peppers then bring to a boil. Pack in jars and seal.

Watermelon Rind Pickles

Cousin-Dorothy Holbrook - Greenup, KY

4 qts. prepared watermelon rind
3 T slaked lime or 1 c. salt
2 qts. cold water
2 T whole cloves
3 sticks cinnamon
2 pieces of ginger root
8 c. sugar
1 lemon, thinly sliced
1 qt. white vinegar
1 qt. water

To prepare watermelon rind—trim dark skin and pink flesh from thick watermelon rind; cut in 1-inch pieces or as wanted. Dissolve lime or salt in 2 qts.water. Pour over rind. If needed add more water to cover rind. Let stand 2 hours if lime is used, or 6 hours if salt if used. Drain, rinse and cover rind with cold water. Cook until just tender, drain. Tie spices in cheesecloth bag. Combine spices with remaining ingredients and simmer ten minutes. Add watermelon rind and simmer until clear. Add boiling water if syrup becomes too thick before rind is clear. Remove spice bag. Pack boiling hot, into sterilized canning jars. Leaving 1/8 inch head space. Yield: about 7 pints. Note: If lime is used pickles will be crisper.

Jelly and Semi-soft Spreads

Apple Butter

Cousin-Grace Carter - Sophie, WV

11 c. applesauce
6 c. sugar
1/2 c vinegar (go light)
1/2 to 3/4 c. cinnamon candy

Boil 1/2 hour on top of stove. Makes 7 pints. Pour in sterilized jars and seal.

Aunt Viola Hilton's Sweet Apple Preserves

Sister-Glennis Stuart Liles - Greenup, KY

apples
sugar
cinnamon (optional)

Take sweet apples (or apples that won't cook up), pare and core them, cut in cubes or irregular-shaped pieces of small size. Weigh the fruit, lay it in a crock, cover it with its own weight in granulated sugar, and let it stand for forty-eight hours. Then drain off the liquid into a preserving pan, bring it to boil; add the apples, and let them boil slowly, without stirring, until they become transparent. Pour into jars and seal. Preserves may be flavored with cinnamon if desired.

Sweet Cherry-Orange (Freezer Jam)

Cousin-Bob Hall - Huntington, WV

1-3/4 c. prepared fruit (about 1-1/4 lb. fully ripe sweet cherries and 1 medium orange
4 c. (1-3/4 lb.) sugar
1/4 c. fresh lemon juice
1 pouch Certo Fruit Pectin

First prepare the fruit. Pit and grind cherries. Measure 1-1/2 cups into large bowl or pan. Grate the rind from the orange, measure 1/2 tsp. Section orange, removing membrane; dice the sections and measure 1/4 cup. Add orange rind and sections to cherries.

Then make the jam. Thoroughly mix sugar into fruit; let stand 10 minutes. Add lemon juice to fruit pectin in small bowl. Stir into fruit. Continue stirring 3 minutes. (A few sugar crystals will remain.) Ladle quickly into scalded containers, filling to within 1/2 inch of tops. Cover at once with tight lids. Let stand at room temperature 24 hours; then store in freezer. Small amounts may be covered and stored in refrigerator up to 3 weeks. Makes about 4-3/4 cups or about 6 (8 fl. oz.) containers.

Cider-Sage Jelly

Cousin-Wanda Lee Maynard - Huntington, WV

1/2 c. boiling water
3 T dried sage, or 6 T fresh sage
1-1/2 c. cider
3-3/4 c. sugar
yellow food coloring
1/2 c. liquid pectin

Pour boiling water over sage. Cover and let stand 15 minutes. Strain. Add more water if needed to make 1/2 cup. Add cider and sugar. Heat to boiling. Add few drops of coloring. Add Pectin, stirring constantly. Boil hard for one minute. Skim, and pour into hot sterilized jars. Seal. Makes 4-1/2 pint jars.

Sage may be replace with any other herb desired

Cider and Spice Jelly

Cousin-Rena Stewart - Magee, MS

4 c. cider (or apple juice)
1 (1-3/4 oz.) pkg. powdered fruit pectin
6-1/2 c. sugar
1 tsp. ground cinnamon
1/4 tsp. ground nutmeg
1/8 tsp. ground cloves

In a 10-qt. kettle combine cider and pectin. Bring to a full rolling boil (a boil that cannot be stirred down). Add remaining ingredients, stirring frequently. Boil hard for one minute, stirring constantly. Remove from heat. Skim off foam with metal spoon. Ladle quickly into hot sterilized 1/2 pt. jars, leaving a 1/4 inch headspace. Seal, using lids or paraffin. Makes 7 half-pints.

Cinnamon Rum Plum Conserve

Niece-Nancy Sue Darby Lake, Berea, KY

4 (16 oz.) cans plums, undrained
3 c. sugar
1 c. raisins
4 (3 inch) cinnamon sticks
1-1/2 c. coarsely chopped walnuts
1/3 c. dark rum

Drain plums, reserving 2 cups juice in a large, heavy saucepan or Dutch oven. Carefully remove skin and pits from plums; set aside plums in a medium bowl. Add sugar, raisins, and cinnamon sticks to reserved 2 cups juice. Bring to a boil, stirring frequently until sugar dissolves. Boil gently, uncovered, until the mixture registers 250° on a candy thermometer (do not stir). Add reserved plums; bring to a boil. Boil gently, stirring constantly, 15 minutes or until mixture thickens. Remove from heat, and remove cinnamon sticks. Stir in walnuts and rum.

Quickly ladle conserve into hot sterilized jars, leaving 1/4 inch headspace. Cover at once with metal lids, and screw bands tight. Process in boiling water bath 15 minutes. Yield: 9 half-pints.

Fruit Cup (Freezer Jam)

Cousin-Betty Ruth Walker - Huntington, WV

2-1/2 c. prepared fruit (about 1 pt. fully ripe strawberries, 1/4 medium ripe pineapple, 2 medium oranges and about 1/2 lb. fully ripe pears)
4-1/2 c. (2 lb.) sugar
3/4 c. water
1 box Sure-Jell Fruit Pectin

First prepare the fruit. Stem and thoroughly crush one layer at a time; about 3/4 c. strawberries. Peel, core and finely chop or grind 3/4 c. pineapple. Peel and section oranges; remove all membrane and seeds and crush thoroughly; measure 1/2 c. Peel, core and finely chop or grind 1/2 c. pears. Combine measured fruits in large bowl or pan.

Then make the jam. Thoroughly mix sugar into fruit; let stand 10 minutes. Mix water and fruit pectin in small saucepan. Bring to a full boil and boil 1 minute, stirring constantly. Stir into fruit. Continue stirring 3 minutes. (A few sugar crystals will remain.) Ladle quickly into scalded containers, filling to within 1/2 inch of tops. Cover at once with tight lids. Let stand at room temperature 24 hours; then store in freezer. Small amounts may be covered and stored in refrigerator up to 3 weeks. Makes about 5-1/2 cups or about 7 (8 fl. oz.) containers.

Frozen Fruit Jam

Cousin-Thelma Edwards - Ceredo WV

4 c. sugar
1-1/2 c. orange juice
4 (16 oz.) pkgs. frozen strawberries

Combine sugar and orange juice in a large, heavy saucepan or Dutch oven. Bring to a boil over medium heat, stirring constantly until sugar dissolves. Boil gently, uncovered, until candy thermometer registers 250°. Do not stir.

Add fruit and boil gently, stirring constantly, until the candy thermometer reaches 212°. Remove from heat.

Quickly ladle jam into hot, sterilized jars, leaving 1/4-inch headspace. Cover at once with metal lids, and screw bands tight; process in boiling-water bath 15 minutes. Yield: 7 half-pints.

Ginger Marmalade

Cousin-Betty Stuart - Kenova, WV

1-1/2 c. chopped, peeled fresh ginger
2 c. water
2 T lemon juice
3 c. sugar
1-3 oz. packet liquid pectin

Combine in large heavy saucepan, ginger, water, and lemon juice. Bring to boiling. Reduce heat and cook until ginger is tender—about 30 minutes.

Stir sugar into ginger mixture. Return to boiling; add pectin. Boil rapidly, stirring one minute. Remove from heat.

Pour marmalade into 4 dry sterilized jars, leaving 1/2 inch headspace at top. Put on lids and tighten. Process in boiling-water bath for 10 minutes. Makes 4-1/2 pint jars (4 cups.)

Kiwifruit Jam (Freezer, No Cook)

Niece-Betty Stuart Darby Baird - Wadestown, WV

1-3/4 c. mashed peeled kiwi (6 or 7)
4 c. sugar
1 tsp. grated lemon peel
2 T lemon juice
1 pouch (3 oz.) liquid fruit pectin (not powdered)
5 freezer bags (pint size)

Have kiwi at room temperature and put into bowl. Add sugar and stir thoroughly. Let stand 10 minutes. Put lemon peel, lemon juice and pectin into small bowl; stir well. Stir into fruit and continue stirring 3 minutes. (A few sugar crystals will remain.) Immediately divide jam evenly in bags (about 1 cup in each); seal. Let stand at room temperature 24 hours to set. Store bags in freezer. When ready to use, remove jam from bag, stir, and serve. This kitchen-tested recipe makes 4-1/2 cups jam.

Orange and Spice Jelly

Cousin-Connie Stewart - Ceredo, WV

2 c. orange juice (about 5 med. oranges)
1/3 c. lemon juice (about 2 med. lemons)
2/3 c. water
1 pkg. (1-3/4 oz.) powdered pectin
2 T orange peel, finely chopped
1 tsp. whole allspice
1/2 tsp. whole cloves
4 stick cinnamon 2" long
3-1/2 c. sugar

Mix orange juice, lemon juice, and water in a large saucepan. Stir in pectin. Tie loosely in a cheese cloth bag, orange peel, allspice, cloves, and cinnamon and add to fruit mixture.

Place on high heat and, stirring constantly, bring to a full rolling boil that cannot be stirred down. Add sugar, continue stirring and heat again to a full rolling boil. Boil hard one minute.

Remove from heat. Remove spice bag and skim off foam. Pour immediately into hot sterilized jars and seal. Makes 4—8 oz. glasses.

Frozen Fresh Peach Jam

Cousin-Mary Belle Johnson - Portsmouth, OH

4 c. crushed fresh peaches
1/4 c. lemon juice (Real Lemon may be used)
1 pkg. powdered pectin
1/2 c. light corn syrup
5-1/2 c. sugar

Use dry clean jars with tight fitting lids. Prepare crushed peaches, add lemon juice in 4 qt. kettle. Slowly add pectin. Let stand for 20 minutes, stirring every 5 minutes. Add syrup, then sugar blending well after each addition. Place over low heat until warm to touch, do not allow mixture to become hot. Pour into jars leaving 1/2" space at top. Cover jars at once. Let set until jelled. Store in freezer until ready to use, keep in refrigerator after opening. Really good as a sauce for ice cream.

Peach—Blueberry (Freezer Jam)

Cousin-Helen Jobe - Ceredo, WV

1-3/4 c. prepared fruit
(about 1/2 pint fully ripe blueberries and
1 lb. fully ripe peaches)
4 cups (1-3/4 lb) sugar
2 T fresh lemon juice
1 pouch Certo fruit pectin

First prepare fruit. Finely chop or grind blueberries. Measure 1/2 c. into large bowl or pan. Peel, pit and finely chop or grind peaches. Measure 1-1/4 c. and add to blueberries.

Then make the jam. Thoroughly mix sugar into fruit.; let stand 10 minutes. Add lemon juice to fruit pectin in small bowl. Stir into fruit. Continue stirring 3 minutes. (A few sugar crystals will remain.) Ladle quickly into scalded containers, filling to within 1/2 inch of tops. Cover at once with tight lids. Let stand at room temperature 24 hours; then store in freezer. Small amounts may be covered and stored in refrigerator up to 3 weeks. Makes about 4 cups or about 5 (8 fl. oz.) containers.

Peach Honey

Niece-Eileen McCarten Nelson - Greenup, KY

Whole washed peaches
sugar

Put your peaches in the largest pot you own. Cover them with water and simmer the peaches an hour or so until the peaches are quite mushy and the liquid looks syrupy. Sieve the peaches through a jelly bag. Measure peach juice and discard peaches.

Pour measured peach juice into a large pot. Add two cups of sugar to every cup of peach juice that you have. Set the pot over low heat and bring to a boil, stirring the peach honey constantly. Simmer honey about thirty minutes. The honey should look like warm syrup when it is finished. Seal the honey in hot sterilized jars. Use peach honey on biscuits, waffles, pancakes, etc. The honey also works well as a ham glaze.

Pepper Jelly

Cousin-Joyce (Jimmie) Carter McKinney - Scarbro, WV

2 c. chopped sweet peppers
1 c. chopped hot peppers
2 sm. or 1 lg. jar red chopped pimientos
1-1/2 c. white vinegar
7 c. sugar
1 tsp. red food coloring (or green)
1 bottle liquid fruit pectin (Sure-Jell will not work.)

Combine peppers, pimientos and vinegar, boil 6 minutes. Add sugar and boil another 6 minutes. Add food coloring and pectin, boil and stir three minutes. Pour into hot jars and seal. Makes 4 pints. Very good spread on cream cheese and crackers (Ritz) also on sliced pork.

Pepper Jelly
(Approx. 11 pints)

Cousin-Joyce (Jimmie) Carter McKinney - Scarbro, WV

6 c. chopped sweet peppers
2 c. chopped hot peppers
2 lg. jars chopped pimientos
4 c. white vinegar
21 c. sugar
2 tsp. red or green food coloring
4 bottles fruit pectin

Boil peppers, pimientos and vinegar 15 minutes. Add sugar and boil 15 minutes. Add food coloring and pectin—boil and stir 7 minutes. Pour into hot jars and seal.

Raspberry—Pear
(Freezer Jam)

Cousin-Judy Castle - Huntington, WV

3-3/4 c. prepared fruit (about 3 pt. fully ripe red raspberries and about 1-1/2 lb. fully ripe pears.)
1 T fresh lemon juice
3 c. sugar
1 box Sure-Jell light fruit pectin

First prepare the fruit. Thoroughly crush, one layer at a time, about 3 pints red raspberries. Measure 2 cups into large bowl or pan. Peel, core and finely chop 1-3/4 c. pears. Add to raspberries. Add lemon juice.

Then make the jam. Measure sugar. Combine pectin with 1/4 cup of the sugar. Gradually add pectin mixture to fruit, stirring vigorously. Set aside for 30 minutes, stirring frequently. Gradually stir in sugar until dissolved. Ladle quickly into scalded containers, filling to within 1/2 inch of tops. Cover at once with tight lids. Let stand at room temperature overnight; then store in freezer. Small amounts may be covered and stored in refrigerator up to 3 weeks. Makes 5-1/2 cups or about 7 (8 fl. oz.) containers.

Rhubarb Jam

Cousin-Mae Pennington Fellows - Albuquerque, NM

1 lb. or 1 pkg. frozen rhubarb
1 (8 oz.) can crushed pineapple
3-1/4 c. sugar
3 oz. pkg. raspberry jello

Bring rhubarb, pineapple and sugar to a boil. Boil 12 minutes. Add jello, stir until dissolved, put in jars. Keep in refrigerator. Real good.

Rhubarb Marmalade
Cousin-Margaret Booth - Ceredo, WV

1 (8-oz.) orange
1 (4-oz.) lemon
4 lbs. frozen cut rhubarb, thawed
1 (15-oz.) package golden raisins
10 c. sugar

Cut away half of peel from orange and entire peel from lemon using a vegetable peeler (be careful to avoid pith) Thinly slice peel, and set aside. Cut away and discard remaining peel and pith from orange and lemon. Section fruit, working over a bowl to collect juices. Discard seeds and tough membrane. Chop pulp in bowl.

Place reserved peel, chopped pulp with juice, rhubarb, raisins, and sugar in a large, heavy saucepan or Dutch oven. Stir well. Bring to a boil, stirring constantly. Boil gently, stirring frequently, until candy thermometer registers 220° (about 15 minutes).

Ladle marmalade into hot sterilized jars, leaving 1/4 inch headspace. Cover with metal lids, and screw bands tight. Process in boiling-water bath 10 minutes. Yield: about 13 half-pints.

Strawberry Preserves
Wife-Naomi Deane Norris Stuart - W-Hollow, KY

2 pt. sugar
2 pt. berries
1/2 stalk rhubarb

Mix 1 pt. berries and 1 pt. sugar. Bring to boil, then add the other pint of berries and sugar, with the rhubarb. Boil for 15 minutes.

Strawberry—Peach (Freezer Jam)
Cousin-Bonnie Dominiak - Chula Vista, CA

3-1/2 c. prepared fruit (about 1 pint. fully ripe strawberries and 1-1/2 lb. fully ripe peaches)
3 c. (1-1/4 lb.) sugar
1 box Sure-Jell light fruit pectin

First prepare the fruit. Stem and thoroughly crush, one layer at a time, about 2 cups strawberries into large bowl or pan. Peel, pit, and grind or finely chop 1-1/2 cups peaches. Add to strawberries.

Then make the jam. Measure sugar. Combine pectin with 1/4 c. of the sugar. Gradually add pectin mixture to fruit, stirring vigorously. Set aside for 30 min., stirring frequently. Stir in sugar until dissolved. Ladle quickly into scalded containers, filling to within 1/2 inch of tops. Cover at once with tight lids. Let stand at room temperature overnight; then store in freezer. Small amounts may be covered and stored in refrigerator up to 3 weeks. Makes 5 cups or about 6 (8 fl. oz.) containers.

Winter Jam
Cousin-Wally Hall - Frankfort, KY

3 c. cranberries
1 c. apples, diced
1 lemon (juice and grated rind)
1 c. crushed pineapple-1-1/2 c. water
1 c. sugar

Cook cranberries and apples in water until they are clear and tender. Add the pineapple, lemon and sugar. Mix well and boil the mixture rapidly until it is thick and clear.

Pour hot jam into sterilized jars and seal.

Other Canned And Frozen Foods

Apple Pie Filling (Canned)
Cousin-Shirley Stewart - Ceredo, WV

4 c. sugar
1 c. cornstarch
1 tsp. salt
3 tsp. cinnamon
1 tsp. nutmeg (optional)
10 c. water
sliced apples, enough to fill 7 qt. jars

Mix ingredients and cook until thick. Stirring as necessary to prevent burning.

Divide mixture evenly among 7 sterilized jars, keeping about 3/4 c. reserved for later use.

Put thinly sliced apples in jars, pressing them down until covered with mixture. Add reserved mixture as needed.

Seal and process in pressure canner 15 minutes at 10 lbs. pressure.

Canned Peaches
Niece-Phyllis Tejeda Xenia, OH

One of my best memories of Uncle Jesse and Aunt Dean is from the times I stopped to visit, usually without permission from Mother, on my way home from the school bus stop. I had to pass their house and just couldn't resist the urge to visit . There was always a treat to share. My favorite was cookies and home canned peaches.

peaches
sugar

Wash jars, rinsing well with hot water. Into each jar put 2/3 cup sugar. Peel fruit and pack jar. Complete filling with hot water as needed. Seal and place in hot water bath. Process 8 min. after water comes to a boil. Remove and set jars upright to cool. Sugar may take several days to dissolve completely.

Tasty Peach Pie Filling (Canned)
Cousin-Dottie Hatten - Morganfield, KY

11 lbs. peaches (24 c. sliced)
8 c. water
1 T Sour Salt (citric acid)
1 c. water
6 c. sugar
1 c. cornstarch
1 tsp. allspice
1/2 tsp. cinnamon
1/2 tsp. nutmeg
1/4 tsp. cardamom (optional)
1 tsp. almond extract

Peel and slice peaches into the 8 cups water and sour salt to prevent darkening. Drain and rinse. Combine sliced peaches with water and 2 cups of the sugar. Cook until heated through. In a bowl mix together the remaining 4 cups sugar, cornstarch and spices. Add to peaches along with the almond extract. Reheat just to the boiling point. Pack in hot, sterilized quart jars leaving 1/4-inch headspace. Adjust lids. Process in boiling water bath 15 minutes. Makes 5 quarts.

Chili Sauce
Cousin-Jimmie Stewart - Catlettsburg, KY

6 lbs. tomatoes, peeled, cored and quartered
1 lb. onions (5 med.) chopped
3/4 lb. green peppers (3 med.) chopped
3 c. vinegar
1 c. honey
1 T dry mustard

Combine all ingredients in a 8 qt. saucepan. Boil gently, stirring frequently, for 3 hours, or until mixture is reduced to half volume. Pour sauce, while hot, into sterilized jars. Adjust lids and process in boiling water bath 15 minutes. Yield: 4-5 pints. NOTE: Make sure tomatoes are still firm. Do not use overripe ones.

Honey Plums

Cousin-Linda Spence - Huntington, WV

6 lbs. red plums
2 c. honey

Wash and stem plums and pack in hot sterilized 1-qt. jars. Combine 6 c. water with the honey and bring to boil. Fill jars to 1/2" from top with the mixture. Seal and process in water bath 20 minutes. Remove from canner and cool on rack in draft free place. Serve as dessert. Makes about 5 quarts.

Pimientos

Cousin-Brenda Marcum - Kenova, WV

Let sweet peppers ripen on the vine to a rich, deep red. To skin the peppers, assemble them on a broiler pan and turn the broiler on high. With the peppers 2 to 3 inches from the heating element, the skins will begin to bubble and blacken in a few minutes. Watch the peppers carefully, turning them so they char evenly; the idea is to separate the skin from the flesh, which will become tender as it roasts.

As soon as peppers are roasted, wrap them in a tea towel or put them in a paper bag. After they have cooled 15 to 20 minutes, pick off the flakes of skin. Rinse them in cold water to remove stubborn spots and cut away any remaining spots. Split each pepper lengthwise, pull out seeds and ribs and cut off the stem end. Lay peppers on a baking sheet and place in freezer for a few hours until they are solid. Then place in plastic freezer bags for storage in freezer. These frozen pimientos are just as versatile as the kind you buy in a jar.

Zucchini Pineapple (Pineapple Substitute)

Cousin-June Haney - Huntington, WV

16 c. peeled, seeded, shredded zucchini
1-1/2 c. lemon juice (commercial kind)
46 oz. unsweetened pineapple juice
1-3/4 c. very mild flavored honey

Combine all ingredients in an 8 qt. pot. Bring to a boil. Lower heat and simmer for 20 minutes, stirring frequently. Strain the pulp, reserving liquid. Divide the pulp evenly between 8 pt. sterilized jars. Pour in liquid, dividing it between the jars. Seal. Process 30 minutes in boiling water bath. Yield: 8 pts. or 4 qts.

Taco Sauce

Cousin-Scott Stewart - Ceredo, WV

3 c. chopped, peeled tomatoes
4 jalapeno peppers (2 green, 2 yellow) seeded and chopped
3/4 c. onion
3 garlic cloves, minced
1/2 c. vinegar

Combine all ingredients and bring to a boil in saucepan. Cover and simmer 5 minutes. Pour immediately into hot sterilized pint jars. Use all the liquid, dividing it equally among the jars. Leave 1/2 inch. Slide a rubber spatula (or something else nonmetallic) along the inside surface of the glass to release air bubbles. Adjust lids and process for 20 minutes in a boiling water bath. Yield: 2 pints.

Desserts

Desserts and Sauces

Apple Pizza
Banana Cream Torte
Blackberry Cobbler
Fresh Blackberry Cobbler
Blackberry Dumplings
Easy Blackberry Pudding
Blueberry Dumplings (or Raspberry)
Grandma Stuart's Bread Pudding
Susan's Bread Pudding
Old-Fashioned Bread Pudding
Cherry Blossom Dessert
Cherry Crisp
Cherry Delight
Cherry Squares
Chocolate Delight Dessert
Quick Fruit Cobbler
Patchwork Cobbler
Royal Fruit Cups
Lemon Delight
Peach Cobbler
Easy Peach Cobbler
Pistachio Pudding Dessert
Plum Pudding With Brandy Butter
Strawberry Jello
Strawberry-Rhubarb Bars
Sweet Potato Cobbler
Trifle
West Virginia Orange Whip

Frozen Desserts and Ice Cream

Frozen Fruit Pudding
Kiwi Ice
Frozen Lemon Cream Pie
Popsicles
All-American Ice Cream
Chocolate Fudge Ice Cream

Citrus Sherbert
Rich Coffee Ice Cream
French Ice Cream
Lemon Velvet
Old-Fashioned Frozen Custard
Easy Homemade Ice Cream with Oreo Cookies
Plum Ice Cream
Strawberry Ice Cream
Texas Cookies and Cream
Snow Ice Cream
Vanilla Ice Milk
Basic Vanilla Ice Cream and Variations
Country Style Vanilla Ice Cream
Homemade Ice Cream Cones
Ice Cream Drinks
    Strawberry Ice Cream Soda
    Taffy Ice Cream Frosted
    French Velvet
Ice Cream Filled Nut Roll
Ice Cream Watermelon Wedges
Ice Cream-Sandwich Cookies
Tortoni

Sauces and Toppings

Apricot Rum Sauce
Butterscotch Sauce
Chocolate Sauce
Custard Sauce
Foamy Sauce
Fruit Sauce
Hard Sauce
Hot Fudge Sauce
Lemon Sauce
Peach Sauce
Raspberry Sauce
Strawberry-Orange Sauce
Vanilla Sauce

Jesse Stuart

Dried apple stack cake at the home of Betty Stuart and John Baird

Mitchell Stuart (Jesse's father)

103

Desserts and Sauces

Apple Pizza

Niece-Barbara Keeney Oney - Raceland, KY

Pastry for double crust pie
7 c. unpared apple slices
1-1/2 T lemon juice
1 c. sugar
1 tsp. cinnamon
1/4 tsp. nutmeg
3/4 c. flour
1/2 c. sugar
1/2 c. butter

Roll pastry on lightly floured surface until it fits 14" pizza pan. Place in pan and finish the edge. Overlap apple slices in circular pattern to within 3/4" of the outside. Sprinkle with lemon juice. Mix 1/2 c. sugar, cinnamon, nutmeg, and sprinkle over apples. Combine flour and 1/2 c. sugar; cut in butter until crumbly and sprinkle over apple slices. Bake at 450° for 20-25 minutes.

Banana Cream Torte

Cousin-Katherine Stewart Martin - Racine, WS

24 graham crackers, finely rolled in crumbs
1/3 c. softened butter
2 T sugar

Blend well. Take out 4 to 5 T crumbs mixture to sprinkle over top of pudding. Press remaining crumb mixture firmly against sides and bottom of well buttered spring form torte pan.

Filling:
2 pkgs. vanilla pudding
2 bananas
3 egg whites
6 T sugar

Prepare pudding according to directions on pkg. Cool and pour into crumb lined pan. Slice bananas over top of pudding. Beat egg whites stiff, but not dry. Add sugar gradually. Spread meringue on top of bananas. Sprinkle remaining crumbs on top of meringue. Bake 20 minutes in oven at 350°. Chill overnight before removing from pan. (If you have no other use for the 3 egg yolks, they may be added to the pudding.)

Blackberry Cobbler

Cousin-Ken Smith Jr. - Portsmouth, OH

4 c. fresh blackberries
1-1/2 c. sugar
6 T butter
2-1/2 c. flour
2 tsp. baking powder
1/2 tsp. salt
1 c. milk

Place fresh blackberries in buttered (13" x 9") baking dish. In large mixing bowl, cream together butter and sugar. Add the next three ingredients alternately with milk. Pour this mixture over blackberries and spread evenly.

In a separate mixing bowl mix together:
2 c. sugar
1/2 tsp. salt
2 T corn starch

Pour this mixture over batter mixture and spread evenly. Then pour 2 cups hot water on top of cobbler. Bake at 375° for one hour.

Fresh Blackberry Cobbler

Niece-Hilde Darby - Greenup, KY

Crust:
2-2/3 c. self-rising flour
a little milk
4 T sugar
1 stick butter (or 1-1/2 st. whipped margarine)

Filling:
2 qts. blackberries, washed and drained
1-3/4 c. sugar
1 tsp. cinnamon
1/4 c. flour
1 stick butter

Mix flour and sugar. With pastry blender, cut butter in until pieces are very small. Add milk, a little at a time and mix well. With wooden spoon, beat dough about 20 strokes. Take 2/3 of dough and roll out on well-floured wax paper. Place into 9 x 13 in. cake pan. Preheat oven to 450°.

Mix blackberries with sugar mixture and place on dough. Dot with butter. Roll out remaining third of dough, cut into strips and place on top of berries diagonally in two layers, forming diamonds. Bake 15 minutes on 450°, reduce heat to 350° and bake 20 to 30 minutes or more. Serve warm with ice cream, or cold.

Blackberry Dumplings

Sister-Sophie Stuart Keeney - Greenup, KY

Part 1
3 pints ripe blackberries
3/4 c. water
1 c. sugar
1-1/2 T butter

Combine in pan and let set while fixing part 2.

Part 2
2 c. flour (sifted)
3 T sugar
1 tsp. salt
1 egg
3-1/2 tsp. baking powder
milk

Sift the flour, sugar, salt, and baking powder into mixing bowl. Add egg, mix well, and then add enough milk to make a stiff batter.

Now, place part 1 on stove and bring to a boil. Add drops of dumpling batter, a spoonful at a time, into the boiling mixture. Cover with lid and cook for 15-20 minutes. Can be served with cream or ice cream. Use other berries if desired.

Easy Blackberry Pudding

Niece-Ruth Nelson - Greenup, KY

2 c. sugar
3/4 c. butter
2 c. sifted flour
1/2 c. boiling water
1 tsp. salt
2 tsp. baking powder
1 c. milk
2 c. blackberries

Cream 1 c. sugar and the butter together. Add the flour, baking powder, salt, milk, and mix well. Then pour blackberries on top, then pour 1 c. sugar and the 1/2 c. boiling water. Bake in moderate oven at 350°, until top is golden brown. Will take about 50 minutes.

Blueberry Dumplings (or Raspberry)

Niece-Ruth Nelson - Greenup, KY

1 can (15 oz.) blueberries (or raspberries)
sugar to taste
2 tsp. quick cooking tapioca
dash salt
1 c. biscuit mix
2 T butter, melted
1/4 c. milk
cinnamon

In skillet mix berries, sugar to taste, tapioca and salt. Let stand while preparing biscuit dough. Make dough with biscuit mix, 1 T sugar, butter and milk. Heat berries to boiling, reduce heat and drop dough from tablespoon onto mixture. Sprinkle with cinnamon. Cover and cook over very low heat about 20 minutes. Serve warm, with cream if desired. Four servings.

Grandma Stuart's Bread Pudding

Niece-Nancy Sue Darby Lake - Berea, KY

4 c. dry bread
1/2 c. seedless raisins, washed
2 c. scalded milk
2 well-beaten eggs
1/2 c. sugar
1/2 tsp. salt
1 tsp. cinnamon
1/2 tsp. nutmeg
1 tsp. vanilla

Pinch the bread into small pieces and mix with raisins. Add scalded milk to beaten eggs, sugar, salt, cinnamon, nutmeg and vanilla; beat well. Place bread and raisins into a well greased 1-1/2 qt. casserole. Pour eggs and milk mixture over bread and raisins. Bake at 350° for about one hour.

Grandma (Martha Hilton Stuart) used biscuits instead of light bread-if there were any left after Gene and I raided the warming closet of the old kitchen stove. Those breakfast biscuits were even better after the long walk from Plum Grove School. Bread pudding didn't last long, especially if there was molasses or honey or dip for topping.

Susan's Bread Pudding

Cousin-Susan Shultz Arnold - Portsmouth, OH

3 c. dry bread cubes
3 c. milk, scalded
3/4 c. sugar
1 T butter
1/4 tsp. salt
4 slightly beaten eggs
1 tsp. vanilla
1/2 c. seedless raisins

Soak bread in milk 5 minutes. Add sugar, butter and salt. Pour slowly over eggs; add vanilla and mix well. Pour into a greased 1-1/2 qt. baking dish. Bake in a pan of hot water at 350° until firm, about 1 hour. Add seedless raisins before baking if desired. Serve with lemon sauce.

Lemon Sauce
1/2 c. sugar
1 T cornstarch
dash of salt
dash nutmeg
1 c. boiling water
2 T butter
1-1/2 T lemon juice

Mix sugar, cornstarch, salt and nutmeg; gradually add boiling water and cook over low heat until thick and clear. Add butter and lemon juice, blend thoroughly.

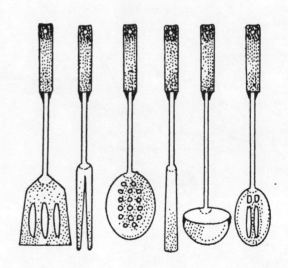

Old-Fashioned Bread Pudding

Nephew-Tony Abdon - Greenup, KY

Heat to scalding:
2 c. milk
4 c. bread crumbs

Cool, pour over:
1/4 c. butter, melted
1/2 c. sugar
2 eggs, slightly beaten
1/4 tsp. salt
1/2 c. seeded raisins
1 tsp. cinnamon or nutmeg

Pour into buttered 1-1/2 qt. casserole (7-1/2"). Bake until silver knife inserted in pudding comes out clean. Serve warm, with or without cream.

Temp: 350°
Time: Bake 40 to 45 min.
Amount: 6 servings.

Cherry Blossom Dessert

Cousin-Grace Carter - Sophie, WV

Sift:
1-1/2 c. flour
1 tsp. salt
1/2 tsp. soda

Blend in:
1 c. packed brown sugar
3/4 c. quick oats

Cut in:
1/2 c. shortening

Press half of oatmeal mixture into bottom of pan (ungreased). Spread 1 can of cherry pie mix. Cover with remaining oatmeal mixture. Press down gently with spoon. Bake at 350° for 25-30 min.

Cherry Crisp

Niece-Jerry Oney - Raceland, KY

Preheat oven to 450°. Pour one 21 ounce can of cherry pie filling in a baking dish. Combine 3/4 cup all-purpose flour, 3 T brown sugar, and 1/4 tsp. cinnamon. Add 6 T butter. Mix till crumbly. Sprinkle over cherry filling. Bake 15 minutes. Reduce heat to 375° and bake 10 more minutes. Serve with whipped cream.

Cherry Delight

Cousin-Anna Laura Adkins - Ceredo, WV

2 packets dream whip
2 (8 oz.) pkgs. cream cheese
2 c. sugar-granulated or powdered
2 lg. cans cherry pie filling
Graham cracker crust

In sheet pan mix:

2-1/2 c. graham cracker crumbs
1 stick melted butter
3 T sugar

Mix with fork and press around sides and bottom of pan and bake 5 minutes; let cool.

Mix dream whip as directed on packet, cream cheese and sugar and whip until smooth. Pour into pie crust and spread cherry pie filling on top. Let chill.

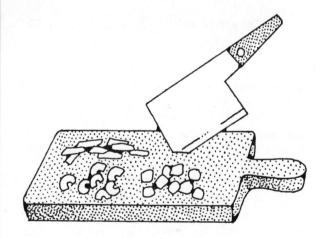

Cherry Squares

Cousin-Beverly Stewart - Winter Haven, FL

Pastry-Make this first

1 c. flour
1/3 c. butter softened
3 T powdered sugar

Mix and spread in 8" sq. pan. Bake for 25 minutes at 350°.

Combine the following:
1 tsp. vanilla
1/2 c. maraschino cherries; cut up
1 c. sugar
1/4 tsp. salt
3/4 c. chopped nuts
1/4 c. flour
1/2 c. coconut
2 eggs
1/2 tsp. baking powder

Spread on baked dough and bake an additional 25 minutes at 350°. Cut in squares.

Chocolate Delight Dessert

Cousin-Faye Stewart Lester - Kenova, WV

Crust:
1 c. plain flour
1 stick of margarine (softened)
1 c. chopped pecans

Cream together and press in 9 x 13 in. pan. Bake at 375° for 20 min.

Filling:
1 c. powdered sugar
1 (8 oz.) cream cheese (room temp.)
1 c. Cool Whip
1 large instant choc. Pudding

Mix sugar and cheese together and add cool whip. Blend well and spread over crust (cooled). Make pudding according to instructions and spread over cheese mixture. Cover pudding mixture with cool whip. Then sprinkle with chopped nuts (pecans). Refrigerate for 4 hours before serving.

Quick Fruit Cobbler

Cousin-June Stewart Haney - Huntington, WV
Cousin-Anna Laura Adkins - Ceredo, WV

1 c. self-rising flour
1 c. granulated sugar
1 stick melted butter or margarine
1 c. water or milk
1 or 2 lg. cans peaches or fruit desired

In sheet pan (13" x 9"), melt 1 stick of butter. Mix flour, sugar, and water to make a batter. Pour over melted butter. Add fruit on top of batter. Bake at 400° for 30 minutes or until golden brown.

Patchwork Cobbler

Cousin-William Everett Holbrook - Greenup, KY

3 c. flour
1 c. sugar
pinch salt
1 c. oil
1 c. buttermilk
4 T flour
3 c. sugar
1 qt. fresh or frozen blackberries

Using 3 c. flour, 1 c. sugar, salt, oil, and buttermilk, prepare a biscuit dough.

Divide in half. Press one half into bottom and up sides of 9 x 13 in. baking dish.

Sprinkle 2 T of flour on top of dough and 1-1/2 c. sugar.

Next add as many blackberries as you like at least one qt. and spread evenly. Top with 2 T of flour and another 1-1/2 cups of sugar.

Take T of the remaining dough with some flour and press out into pieces. Add pieces lapping and over lapping until they cover the berries in a patchwork pattern. This makes a crunchy crust. Bake in 350° oven 1 hr.

Royal Fruit Cups

Niece-Barbara Keeney Oney - Raceland, KY

1/2 c. mayonnaise
1 T lemon juice
2 tsp. sugar
1 c. cubed fresh pineapple
1 cantaloupe, peeled and cubed
1/2 c. seedless grapes
1 c. fresh strawberries halved
2 bananas sliced
1 c. cubed watermelon
1 medium peach, peeled and cubed
1 c. miniature marshmallows
lettuce leaves
cottage cheese
maraschino cherries

Combine mayonnaise, lemon juice, and sugar; stir well and set aside. Combine the next 7 ingredients; add marshmallows. Toss gently. Spoon fruit into lettuce lined sherbert or champagne glasses and top each with a spoonful of cottage cheese. Spoon mayonnaise mixture over each; top with a cherry. Yield 6-8 servings.

Lemon Delight

Cousin-Norma Jean (Pennington) Darnell - Greenup, KY

First Layer:
1 stick of margarine melted
4 T sugar
2 c. graham cracker crumbs

Press in bottom of a 9 x 13 in. pan.

Second Layer:
1 c. Cool Whip
1 c. powdered sugar
1 (8 oz.) pkg. soft cream cheese

Mix together. Spread over 1st layer

Third Layer:
2 pkgs. instant lemon pudding
3 c. milk

Fourth Layer:
Spread with cool whip.

Keep in refrigerator.

Peach Cobbler

Cousin-Ethel Stewart Terry - Ceredo, WV

1 c. sugar
1 c. milk
1 c. flour
1 can of peaches with juice (large can)
1 stick of butter

Melt butter in pan. Mix sugar and flour together then add milk. Pour batter into pan with melted butter. Pour peaches on top of batter. Ingredients will blend together while baking. Bake at 350° until brown.

Easy Peach Cobbler

Cousin-Linda Ellington - Ashland, KY

Melt 1/2 stick butter or margarine in 14" x 8" cake pan.

Mix:

1 c. sifted all-purpose flour
1/2 c. sugar
1/2 tsp. nutmeg
2 tsp. baking powder

Add: 3/4 c. milk

Pour this batter over the melted butter. Then pour a large can of peaches over the batter. Sprinkle brown sugar on top. Bake at 400° for 35-40 minutes or until brown on top. Can be served with ice cream or cool whip.

Pistachio Pudding Dessert

Cousin-Goldie Adkins - East Liverpool, OH

1st layer:
Melt in pan 1-1/2 c. oleo. Mix together 1-1/2 c. flour, 3 tsp. sugar, and 1/2 c. finely chopped nuts. Press or pour mixture into pan. Bake for 25-35 minutes at 350°. Cool completely.

2nd layer:
1 c. powdered sugar, 1 c. cool whip; 1 (8 oz.) cream cheese (soft). Mix with mixer. Spread on cooled crust.

3rd layer:
3 small pkgs. Pistachio Pudding (Instant), 4 c. milk. Mix until stiff. Spread on second layer, and put 1/2 c. cool whip on top and sprinkle with nuts. You may use vanilla or chocolate pudding instead if you wish.

Plum Pudding With Brandy Butter

Niece-Nancy Sue Darby Lake - Berea, KY

1/2 lb. ground suet
grated rind and juice of 1 orange and 1 lemon
1/4 c. brandy
2 T rum
2 eggs, slightly beaten
3/4 c. finely chopped, peeled tart apple
2/3 c. brown sugar, packed
2/3 c. preserved ginger, chopped
1-2/3 c. golden raisins
1-2/3 c. dark raisins
1-1/4 c. chopped mixed candied peel
4 c. soft stale bread crumbs
1-1/4 c. unsifted flour
1 tsp. cinnamon
1/2 tsp. nutmeg
1/4 tsp. nutmeg
1/4 tsp. mace

Mix ingredients in order given, sifting flour and spices together before adding. Press firmly in 2 greased 1 qt. pudding molds. Cover tightly and steam 3 hours, or until done. Serve with Brandy Butter. Makes 12-16 servings.

Brandy Butter:
Beat 1 c. soft butter with 1 c. confectioner's sugar until blended. Gradually beat in 6-8 T brandy.

Strawberry Jello

Cousin-Phyllis Hilton Parker - Portsmouth, OH

1 large pkg. strawberry jello
1 can crushed pineapple (15 oz.)
1 pkg. frozen strawberries
3 bananas
1 pt. sour cream

Dissolve strawberry jello in 2 cups of boiling water. Use strawberry juice (from thawed pkg. of strawberries) and pineapple juice (from can of crushed pineapples) with enough water to make 2 cups of cold liquid. Combine. Add 1 can drained pineapples, 1 pkg. drained thawed strawberries and 3 mashed bananas. Put 1/2 fruity jello in 9 x 13 in. dish. Allow to set. (Leave other 1/2 out of the refrigerator.) Spread 1 pint sour cream on set jello and add second half of jello. Allow to set. Cut in squares to serve.

Strawberry-Rhubarb Bars

Cousin-Katherine Stewart Martin - Racine, WS

1 c. flour
1 tsp. baking powder
1/4 tsp. salt
1/4 c. butter or oleo
1 egg
1 T milk
2 c. rhubarb, cut fine
1 pkg. strawberry jello
1/4 c. butter
1 c. sugar
1/2 c. flour

Sift together flour, baking powder, and salt. Cut in the butter. Add egg, mixed with milk. Spread in greased 9 x 9 in. pan. Cover with rhubarb and sprinkle with dry jello. Combine butter, sugar, and flour and sprinkle evenly over all. Bake at 375° for 40 minutes. Serve with whipped cream. (1-1/2 recipe may be used in a 9 x 13 in. pan.)

Sweet Potato Cobbler

Cousin-Mary Belle Johnson - Portsmouth, OH

Pastry for double crust 9" pie
3 c. sliced cooked sweet potatoes (reserve liquid)
1 c. sugar
butter or margarine
1 tsp. ground nutmeg
1/2 tsp. ground cinnamon
1-1/2 c. water (that potatoes were cooked in)

Roll 2/3 of pastry and place in bottom of ungreased 8" square baking pan. Combine sweet potatoes and sugar; put on pie crust. Dot with butter and sprinkle with cinnamon and nutmeg. Pour water over mixture. Roll out remaining pastry and cut in strips; layer strips across in a lattice pattern. Bake in 350° oven for 45-60 minutes.

Trifle

Cousin-Cindy Arnold - Hillsboro, OH

1 pkg. Jelly rolls
2 pkgs. vanilla instant pudding
1 pkg. black raspberry jello
1 box cool whip

Make jello with one cup hot water, cool. Slice jelly rolls and put in bottom of dish. Add jello and let it cool in refrigerator. Then add vanilla pudding and cool whip on top.

West Virginia Orange Whip

Cousin-Katherine Hilton - Ashland, KY

1 (9 oz.) cool whip
1 (3 oz.) orange jello (dry)
1 small cottage cheese
1 small can crushed pineapple (drained)
1 small can mandarin oranges (drained)

Mix cool whip and jello. Add other ingredients and mix. Chill well and serve.

Frozen Desserts and Ice Cream

Frozen Fruit Pudding

Niece-Amber Wheeler - Knoxville, TN

1 can (1 lb.) fruit cocktail
1 pkg. lime (or lemon) pudding and pie filling
3/4 c. sugar
1 egg
1 envelope whipped topping mix (prepared as directed) or
1/2 pint heavy cream (whipped)
1/2 c. chopped pecans

Drain fruit, reserving liquid. Add enough water to liquid to make 2-1/4 c. Combine pudding, sugar and 1/4 c. fruit liquid in a saucepan. Add egg and blend well. Stir in remaining liquid. Cook stirring constantly, over medium heat until mixture comes to a boil. Chill 1 hour. Blend prepared topping into pudding mixture. Add fruit and nuts. Pour into an 8" x 4" loaf pan and freeze. Place in refrigerator 30 minutes before serving. Serves 6.

Kiwi Ice

Niece-Lori Ann Stuart - Greenup, KY

Light, fresh, and very pretty. Looks great in clear glass bowls.

4 kiwi fruit (reserve a perfect slice for each serving)
5 T fresh lemon or lime juice
1/4 T grated rind
1 c. water
1/2 c. sugar
1/2 c. light corn syrup

Puree fruit, juice, and rind in blender. Cook water, sugar, and corn syrup until sugar dissolves. Mix it all together and pour into a shallow pan. Put it in the freezer for 1-1/2 hours. Take it out and beat it till it's light and fluffy, then back to the freezer for at least 2 hours more. Garnish with slices of fresh fruit. Another garnish would be fresh mint sprigs or pineapple slices. Serves 4.

Frozen Lemon Cream Pie

Niece-Shirley Stuart - Greenup, KY

1 (9 inch) graham cracker crumb crust
3 eggs, separated
1/2 c. plus 2 T sugar
1/4 c. (ReaLemon) lemon juice
1 c. (1/2 pt.) whipping cream, whipped

In large bowl, beat egg yolks and 1/2 c. sugar until light and add ReaLemon. In small bowl, beat egg whites to soft peaks, gradually add remaining sugar. Beat to stiff peaks. Fold egg whites into lemon mixture, gradually fold in whipped cream. Spoon into crust. Freeze 3 hours or until firm.

Serve with Raspberry Sauce.

Popsicles

Cousin-Kevin Travis Murphy - Lucasville, OH

1 small pkg. jello
2 c. cold water
2 c. hot water
1 pkg. kool-aid
1 c. sugar

Dissolve jello, sugar, and kool-aid in hot water. Stir in cold water. Freeze.

All-American Ice Cream

Sister-Mary Stuart Nelson - Greenup, KY

Ice cream was originally made from just cream, a sweetener, and flavoring. This recipe uses sweetened condensed milk, a product that has been in American kitchens since before the Civil War, to give sweetened and smooth texture to the ice cream. You can make All-American Vanilla, Chocolate, Strawberry, Blueberry, Peach, or Peanut Butter ice cream from this recipe.

Makes 1-1/2 qts.

1 14-oz. can sweetened condensed milk (NOT evaporated milk)
3 c. half-and-half
1 T vanilla extract (for other flavors see variations below)

Chill the container of an ice-cream maker or a 9 x 13 inch baking pan in the freezer.

Combine all ingredients in the chilled container of ice-cream maker and process according to manufacturer's directions.

Variations:

Chocolate: Melt 2 squares (1 oz size) unsweetened or semi-sweet chocolate. Stir into vanilla ice-cream ingredients and process.

Strawberry, Blueberry, or Peach: Add 1 cup fruit puree to vanilla ice-cream ingredients when they have processed for about half the time.

Peanut Butter: Add 1/2 c. chunky peanut butter to vanilla ice-cream ingredients and process.

Chocolate Fudge Ice Cream

Nephew-Scott Darby Lake - Berea, KY

2 (14 oz.) cans sweetened condensed milk
2 (4 oz.) packages chocolate instant pudding mix
2 quarts milk

Combine all ingredients in a large bowl; stir well. Pour mixture into freezer can of a 5-quart hand-turned or electric freezer. Freeze according to manufacturer's instructions. Serve immediately. Yield: about 1 gallon.

Citrus Sherbert

Niece-Nancy Sue Darby Lake - Berea, KY

1 qt. milk
3 c. orange juice
2 c. sugar
1 c. half-and-half
1/2 c. lemon juice

Combine all ingredients in a large bowl; stir well. Pour mixture into freezer can of a 5-qt. hand-turned or electric freezer. Freeze according to manufacturer's instructions. Let ripen a least 1 hour. Yield: 1 gallon.

Rich Coffee Ice Cream

Niece-Betty Stuart Baird - Wadestown, WV

In 1898, Mrs. Lincoln of the Boston Cooking School prepared a booklet, Frosty Fancies, for the White Mountain Freezer Company, manufacturers of hand-crank ice cream freezers. The booklet included this recipe—

1 T instant coffee granules
1/3 c. boiling water
4 c. light cream
4 eggs; slightly beaten
1 c. sugar
1 tsp. vanilla

Dissolve coffee granules in boiling water; set aside. In a large saucepan combine cream, eggs, and sugar. Cook and stir over medium heat till mixture coats metal spoon. Remove from heat; stir in coffee and vanilla. Cool; chill. Freeze in 4-qt. ice cream freezer according to manufacturer's directions. Makes about 2 qts.

French Ice Cream

Brother-In-Law-Herbert (Whitey) Liles - Greenup,KY

Eggs give French ice cream a golden color and added richness. Our variations of this creamy treat include Fudge, Coffee, Mocha, Rum Raisin, Pistachio, and Amaretto ice creams. Makes 1-1/2 qts.

1 c. half-and-half
1/2 vanilla bean
3 eggs
3/4 c. granulated sugar
2 c. heavy cream
dash salt

In a small heavy saucepan, over low heat, warm half-and-half until bubbles appear around the edges. Split the vanilla bean and add to the half-and-half while it is heating.

In a medium bowl, with electric beater, beat eggs until thick and fluffy. Gradually beat in sugar. Pour scalded half-and-half and 1 cup of heavy cream over eggs and beat with a wire whisk until well combined. Set aside with vanilla bean still in the mixture, until cool. Chill container of ice-cream maker.

In medium bowl with electric beaters, beat remaining cream just until soft peaks form. Remove vanilla bean from custard. Fold custard into whipped cream.

Pour mixture into container of ice-cream maker and process according to manufacturer's directions.

Variations:
Fudge: Add 3 squares (1 oz.size) unsweetened chocolate to half-and-half and heat until chocolate is melted.

Coffee: Stir 3 T instant coffee into hot half-and-half

Mocha: Melt 1 square unsweetened chocolate in half-and-half as it heats. Stir 1-1/2 T instant coffee into mixture when chocolate is melted.

Rum Raisin: Soak 1/2 c. raisins in 1/4 c. dark rum for 1 hour. Fold into soft ice cream as soon as it has finished processing.

Pistachio: Add 1 tsp. almond flavoring and a few drops green food coloring to cream mixture before processing. Fold 1/2 c. chopped pistachios into soft ice cream as soon as it has finished processing.

Amaretto: Fold 1/2 c. Amaretto into cream mixture before processing and fold 1/2 c. chopped toasted almonds into soft ice cream as soon as it has finished processing.

Lemon Velvet

Niece-Theresa Darby - Normantown, WV

4 c. sugar
juice of 8 lemons
5 half-pint cartons whipping cream
1 T lemon extract
milk

Mix the sugar and lemon juice, then add the whipping cream, lemon extract and enough milk to fill a 4-5 quart old-fashioned ice cream freezer. Freeze for about 30 minutes.

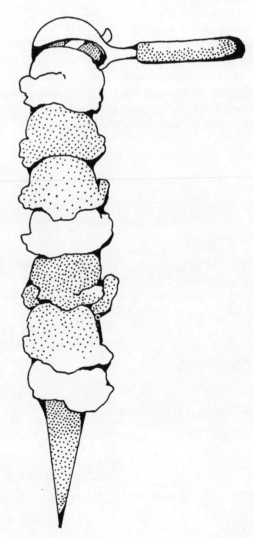

Old-fashioned Frozen Custard

Brother-in-law-Herbert (Whitey) Liles - Greenup, KY

1-1/2 c. milk
3/4 c. sugar
2 egg yolks, slightly beaten
3 tsp. vanilla extract
2 c. heavy or light cream
Few drops food coloring as desired

Heat milk until very hot, but do not boil. Add sugar and stir until dissolved. Cool slightly and slowly pour mixture over the beaten egg yolks, stirring constantly. Place mixture in a double boiler and cook, stirring constantly until mixture coats the spoon.

Remove from heat and chill thoroughly in the refrigerator. Add vanilla, cream, food coloring and other flavorings* and pour into ice-cream freezer container. Freeze according to directions supplied by the manufacturer of the appliance.

*Flavor variations: Coffee: Add two teaspoons of instant coffee to mixture at the same time the vanilla is added.

Chocolate: Mix four teaspoons cocoa powder with sugar before adding to milk.

Fresh fruit: Puree one cup of fresh fruit in a blender. Reduce vanilla to one teaspoon or omit. Use food coloring to complement color of fruit. Fold in fruit puree just before adding cream.

Chopped nuts, candies, coconut, or pieces of cookies should be added during the last few minutes of churning. Carefully clear ice or brine from container top. Remove paddle and container and swirl ingredients into the still-soft ice cream. Churn until mixture is hard. After ice cream is sufficiently churned, it may be stored in the freezer for additional hardening.

Easy Homemade Ice Cream with OREO Cookies

Nephew-Samuel Darby - Normantown, WV

Makes about 1-1/2 quarts

*3 egg yolks
1 (14 oz.) can Eagle Brand Sweetened Condensed Milk.(NOT evaporated milk)
4 tsp. vanilla extract
1 c. coarsely crushed OREO Chocolate Sandwich Cookies (about 12 cookies)
2 c. (1 pint) whipping cream, whipped (do not use whipped topping)*

In large bowl, beat egg yolks; stir in Eagle Brand and vanilla. Fold in cookies and whipped cream. Pour into aluminum foil-lined 9 x 5 inch loaf pan or other 2 quart container. Cover; freeze 6 hours or until firm. Scoop ice cream from pan or peel off foil and slice. Return leftovers to freezer.

Plum Ice Cream

Niece-Nancy Sue Darby Lake - Berea, KY

*2 eggs
1 c. sugar
2 c. pureed ripe plums
4 c. heavy cream
1 T vanilla*

In medium-sized saucepan, combine eggs, sugar and plums. Cook, stirring occasionally, over moderate heat, until mixture thickens. Remove from heat.

Pour plum mixture into large bowl; cool 10 minutes. Stir in heavy cream and vanilla. Chill 2 hours. Follow directions for basic ice cream and let harden 2 hours after freezing. Makes 1 quart.

Strawberry Ice Cream

Nephew-Michael Drew Lake - Berea, KY

5 eggs
2 c. sugar
1 (1.4 oz.) envelope whipped topping mix
1 (12 oz.) can strawberry-flavored soda
1-1/2 T vanilla extract
1 qt. plus 3-1/2 c. half-and-half
2 c. fresh strawberries, coarsely chopped

Beat eggs; gradually add sugar, beating until thick and lemon colored. Add whipped topping mix; stir until smooth. Stir in remaining ingredients.

Pour mixture into freezer can of a 5-qt. hand-turned or electric freezer. Freeze according to manufacturer's instructions. Let ripen at least 1 hour. Yield: 5 qts.

Texas Cookies And Cream

Brother-in-law-Herbert (Whitey) Liles - Greenup, KY

1 can Eagle Brand condensed milk
7 eggs
2 c. sugar
2 pts. milk
1 qt. half-and-half
2 T vanilla extract
1 bag OREO cookies, chopped

Mix together the Eagle Brand, eggs, sugar, milk, half-and-half and vanilla extract. Freeze, either in hand-cranked or automatic ice cream maker. When finished, blend in the chopped-up cookies and freeze again.

Snow Ice Cream

Cousin-Kevin Travis Murphy - Lucasville, OH

2 lg. eggs
1-1/2 c. sugar
1/2 tsp. salt

Beat the above mixture until it is thickened and a lemon color.

Add:
1/4 c. cream or evaporated milk
1 T vanilla
3 gallons light snow

Beat in a little at a time.

Vanilla Ice Milk

Niece-Melissa Liles - Greenup, KY

2 (14 oz.) cans sweetened condensed milk
2 c. half-and-half
1/4 c. sugar
1 egg, beaten
1 T vanilla extract
6 c. milk

Combine first 5 ingredients in a large bowl; stir well. Stir in milk.

Pour mixture into freezer can of a 5-qt. hand-turned or electric freezer. Freeze according to manufacturer's instructions. Let ripen at least 1 hour. Yield: 1 gallon.

Basic Vanilla Ice Cream, and Variations

Niece-Betty Baird - Wadestown, WV

2 eggs
1 c. sugar
3 c. milk, divided
3 c. heavy cream
1 T vanilla

1. In large saucepan, combine eggs, sugar and 2 cups milk. With rotary beater, beat mixture until well blended. Cook over medium heat, stirring constantly, until mixture thickens and coats a metal spoon (do not boil).

2. Pour custard mixture into large bowl; cool 10 minutes. Stir in remaining 1 c. milk, heavy cream and vanilla. Chill in refrigerator 2 hours.

3. Wash ice cream can, dasher and cover in hot sudsy water. Rinse under hottest tap water; dry thoroughly. Chill can.

4. Pour chilled ice cream mixture into ice cream freezer can (no more than 2/3 full—ice cream needs room to expand). Place can in freezer bucket; put dasher and lid in place; fit the motor or crank unit into the lid and fasten to bucket, following manufacturer's directions.

5. For electric models start motor by plugging in unit and let run 2 minutes before packing ice and salt. On hand crank models start churning after packing ice and salt.

6. Fill bottom of bucket with 2 inches crushed ice; cover with 1/4 c. rock salt. Continue to layer ice and salt in same proportions to 1 inch below rim of bucket. (For gallon freezer, you will need approximately 16 cups crushed ice and 2-1/2 c. rock salt.) Add 1 c. cold water to start ice melting.

7. Freeze following manufacturer's directions, adding more crushed ice and rock salt to keep bucket filled. Freezing time will vary with type of machine.

8. Allow ice cream to churn until motor begins to slow or seems to stall, or when hand model becomes difficult to turn. Keep drain opening clear during cranking. If it becomes clogged, free it with a pencil. To prevent motor damage on electric model, unplug as soon as motor slows down.

9. Remove motor or hand crank. Wipe ice and salt off can lid. Remove lid and dasher. If desired, add ingredients for ice cream variations as specified in following recipes.

With large spoon, push ice cream down in can; cover with aluminum foil or waxed paper; replace lid and plug hole in lid with cork.

10. To "ripen" ice cream, drain water from bucket. Repack bucket with 4 parts crushed ice to 1 part rock salt; let harden 2 hours before serving. Or spoon soft ice cream into plastic freezer containers, leaving 1/2 inch at top to allow for expansion; cover and freeze.
Makes 2 quarts.

Variations:
Double Chocolate-Chocolate Chip Ice Cream
1 recipe Basic Vanilla Ice Cream
2 sqs. (2 oz.) unsweetened chocolate, melted
1 c. mini-chocolate chips
2 tsp. peppermint flavoring (optional)

Prepare Basic Vanilla Ice Cream adding melted chocolate at the end of Step 1. Stir mini-chocolate chips and peppermint flavoring, if using, into soft churned Basic Vanilla Ice Cream (Step 9). Let harden 2 hours. Makes 2 qts.

Peach Praline Ice Cream
1 c. pecans
1/2 c. firmly packed light brown sugar
2 T butter
1 recipe Basic Vanilla Ice Cream
1-1/2 c. peeled, pitted and chopped ripe peaches.

In medium-sized saucepan, combine pecans, brown sugar and butter. Cook over moderate heat, stirring occasionally for 5 minutes. Pour mixture out onto cookie sheet; let harden then chop coarsely.

Prepare Basic Vanilla Ice Cream. Fold pecan praline and peaches into soft churned ice cream (Step 9). Let harden 2 hours. Makes 2 qts.

Pistachio Ice Cream
1 recipe Basic Vanilla Ice Cream
2 tsp. almond extract
1/2 c. blanched chopped pistachios
Green food coloring

Prepare Basic Vanilla Ice Cream, adding almond extract with vanilla at Step 2.

Stir pistachios and food coloring, if desired, into soft-churned ice cream (Step 9). Let harden 2 hours. Makes 2 quarts.

Country Style Vanilla Ice Cream

Cousin-Ruth Stewart Walters - Ceredo, WV

4 eggs
2-1/3 c. sugar
4 c. milk
4 c. whipping cream
2-1/2 T vanilla
1/4 tsp.salt

In large mixing bowl: beat eggs until foamy, gradually add sugar; beat until thickened. Add milk, cream, vanilla and salt. Mix thoroughly. Chill; churn freeze. Makes 4 qts.

Homemade Ice-Cream Cones

Cousin-Betsy Shultz - Portsmouth, OH

No special equipment is needed to make these home-made ice-cream cones. Just bake chocolate or vanilla batter on cookie sheets, roll around cardboard cones, cool, and fill with your favorite homemade ice cream. Makes 8 cones.

1/2 c. unsifted all-purpose flour
1/4 c. sifted brown sugar
dash salt
1/4 c. vegetable oil
2 egg whites
1 T water
1 tsp. vanilla extract

For chocolate cones add:
2 T unsweetened cocoa
1/2 T water

Cut eight 7-inch rounds from oaktag or thin flexible cardboard. Roll into cones with a 2-inch opening at top. Tape securely. Set aside. Preheat oven to 350°.

Sift together flour, brown sugar, and salt into a medium bowl. In a small bowl or measuring cup combine oil, egg whites, water, and vanilla. If making chocolate cones, stir cocoa into oil before adding other moist ingredients and the additional 1/2 T water.

Add moist ingredients to dry ingredients and stir until smooth. Lightly grease two nonstick cookie sheets. Pour 1-1/2 T of batter into the center of one cookie sheet. Spread batter to make a 6-1/2 inch round. Bake 5 to 6 minutes or until edges have just started to brown and center of cookie is firm. Watch cookies carefully. If they are under-baked they will not be crisp; if over-baked, they will not roll nicely.

Loosen cookie from tray and carefully roll around a prepared cone. Lay, open side down, on a cooling rack. Cool completely, but don't remove paper cone. You may spread the batter for a second cookie and put it in the oven on a separate rack 3 minutes after the first cookie goes in. Do not remove two cookies from the oven at the same time because one may harden while you are rolling the other.

Store cones in a tight container with paper cones still inside until ready to use. To fill, remove paper cones and scoop ice cream into cookie cone. Fill gently; these cones are not as strong as commercially purchased cones.

Ice Cream Drinks

Cousin-Katherine Hilton - Ashland, KY

French Velvet
2 heaping tsp. quick chocolate flavored mix
1/2 c. milk
1/4 c light cream
dash of cinnamon

Stir briskly until blended. Serve with a cinnamon stick stirrer.

Strawberry Ice Cream Soda
1 c. crushed strawberries
4 tsp. sugar
carbonated water
1 pint strawberry ice cream
2 c. milk

Mix together strawberries and sugar; put into four 12-oz. glasses. Fill each glass 1/2 full with carbonated water. Add ice cream; stir. Fill to top with milk. Garnish with plump red strawberry.

Taffy Ice Cream Frosted
2 T unsulphured molasses
milk
1 scoop coffee ice cream
carbonated water

Put unsulphured molasses in 12-oz. glass; fill half full with milk. Add ice cream, and beat with electric beater. Pour into tall glass.

Ice Cream Filled, Nut Roll

Niece-Ellen Keeney Douglas - Lexington, KY

Dip almonds in chocolate to garnish this elegant dessert.

1/2 c. cake flour (not self-rising)
2/3 c. unsweetened cocoa, divided plus some for dusting
1 tsp. baking powder
1/4 tsp. salt
4 eggs, separated, at room temperature
3/4 c, sugar, divided
2 pints coffee ice cream, slightly softened
2 tsp. instant coffee powder
1/4 c. confectioner's sugar

1-1/2 c. heavy cream
2 squares (1 oz. each) semisweet chocolate
1 T vegetable shortening
8 whole unblanched almonds

Preheat oven to 375°. Grease 15 x 10 x 1 inch jelly-roll pan; line bottom with wax paper. Set aside. On wax paper sift together flour, 1/3 cup cocoa, baking powder and salt. Set aside. In small bowl of electric mixer, beat egg whites at high speed until foamy white and double in volume. Beat in 1/4 c. sugar, 1 T at a time, until meringue stands in soft peaks.

In large bowl of electric mixer, beat egg yolks with 1/2 c. sugar until thick and lemon color. Lower speed to medium and add flour-cocoa mixture, beating until batter is smooth.

Whisk a small amount of the meringue into cocoa batter, then fold remaining meringue into mixture until no streaks remain. Spread batter evenly into prepared pan. Bake 12 to 15 minutes or until cake springs back when lightly pressed with fingertip,

While cake is baking, tear off a large sheet of foil and cover with paper towels. With small sieve, dust paper towels generously with extra cocoa. With sharp knife, loosen cake around pan edges; invert immediately onto prepared paper towels; peel off wax paper.

Starting at short end, roll up cake, foil and paper towel together. Place roll, seam side down on wire rack; cool completely. Unroll cake carefully. Spread evenly with ice cream. Using foil as a lifter, reroll cake—this time without foil or paper towel inside. Place roll seam side down, on chilled serving plate; place in freezer.

In small bowl of electric mixer, combine coffee powder, confectioner's sugar and remaining 1/3 c. cocoa. At low speed, gradually beat in heavy cream until mixture is smooth. Beat at high speed until firm peaks form. Remove 1/2 c. and place in pastry bag fitted with small star-tipped tube; set aside.

Spread coffee cream over roll. Pipe reserved coffee cream down center of cake; return to freezer.

In small saucepan over low heat, melt semisweet chocolate with shortening; stir to combine. Dip ends of almonds into chocolate mixture; place on plate; set in refrigerator or freezer to firm up.

With back of spoon, drizzle remaining chocolate over roll in zig-zag fashion. Place chocolate covered almonds down center of roll. Freeze until firm. Makes 8 to 12 servings.

Ice Cream Watermelon Wedges

Cousin-Anne Hilton Short - Forestville, MD

3/4 c. "M & M's" Plain Chocolate candies
2 T butter or margarine, melted
Green food coloring
1 pkg. (7 oz.) coconut
1/2 gallon strawberry, pink peppermint or other pink ice cream

Separate the dark brown and the green candies. Cut these in half; set aside. Chop remaining candies and place in freezer. Combine butter and food coloring in a large bowl. Toss in 2 cups coconut, stirring until uniformly colored. Line a 10-inch baking pan with foil. Press green coconut around the edges of the pan about 1 inch up. Spoon half the ice cream into bottom of pan. Sprinkle with the chopped candies then top with the remaining ice cream. Press green candies around the edge of the ice cream, then sprinkle the remaining coconut around the edge. Press the brown candies in the center. Cover and freeze until firm. To serve, lift from pan by the foil; cut into wedges. Makes 8 to 10 servings.

Ice Cream Sandwich Cookies

Cousin-Marie Hilton Ellington - Ashland, KY

It's easy to make your own ice-cream sandwiches with these chocolate sugar cookies. The dough may be cut into rounds or oblong, or chilled in a roll and sliced like an icebox cookie. Crumbled cookies make a delicious stir-in for vanilla or mint ice cream.

Makes 24 round or 16 oblong cookies.

1/2 c. butter, softened
2/3 c. granulated sugar
1 egg
2 tsp. vanilla
1/3 c. cocoa
1-3/4 c. unsifted all-purpose flour
3/4 tsp. salt
1/2 tsp. baking powder
1/4 c. milk
Additional granulated sugar (optional)

In a medium bowl, cream together butter, sugar, egg, and vanilla until smooth.

Sift together cocoa, flour, salt, and baking powder, onto waxed paper. Add dry ingredients to butter mixture alternately with milk until well combined.

Divide dough in half; roll one half to make a 10 x 10 inch rectangle about 1/8 inch thick. Cut into 5 x 2-1/2 in. rectangles or cut out 3-inch rounds with a cookie cutter. Or, form dough into a roll, 3 inches in diameter. Wrap tightly and refrigerate 2 hours or until firm.

To bake cookies, preheat oven to 350°. Arrange cut cookies on a lightly greased cookie sheet or slice icebox cookies 1/8 inch thick and arrange on cookie sheet. Brush tops with water; if desired, sprinkle with granulated sugar. Bake 12 to 15 minutes or until centers are firm. Cool completely.

Tortoni

Cousin-Mary Catherine Stewart Martin - Racine, WS

1 (14 oz.) can Eagle Brand Sweetened Condensed
Milk.(Not evaporated milk)
3 egg yolks, beaten
1/4 c. light rum
2 tsp. vanilla extract
2/3 c. coconut macaroon crumbs (about 5 macaroons)
1/2 to 3/4 c. slivered almonds, toasted
1/3 to 1/2 c. chopped maraschino cherries
2 c. (1 pint) whipping cream

In a large bowl, combine all ingredients except whipping
cream. Mix well. Fold in whipping cream. Fill 2-1/2 inch
foil cups; cover, freeze 6 hours or until firm. Garnish as
desired. Return the ones left over to freezer. Makes 1-1/2
to 2 dozen.

Sauce And Toppings
(for ice cream and desserts)

Apricot Rum Sauce

1/4 c. packed light brown sugar
1/2 c. water
2-in. piece ginger root, peeled
2 cinnamon sticks
2 cans (16 oz. each) apricot halves, drained
1/4 c. raisins
1/4 c. rum
1 tsp. lime juice
2 pints vanilla ice milk

In saucepan stir sugar in water over medium heat until
dissolved. Add ginger and cinnamon. Bring to a boil; boil
1 minute. Remove from heat; stir in apricots, raisins, rum
and lime juice. Cool; chill at least 3 hours. Remove ginger
and cinnamon before spooning over individual servings
of ice milk. Makes 8 servings (about 3 cups).

Butterscotch Sauce

Butterscotch sauce makes a perfect topping for baked
apples, crepes, fritters, dumplings, and—of course—ice
cream.

Makes 1-1/4 cups.

1/4 c. butter or margarine
3/4 c firmly packed brown sugar
2 T light corn syrup
1/2 c. half-and-half
1 tsp. vanilla extract

In a small heavy saucepan, melt butter. Stir in brown
sugar, corn syrup, and half-and-half.

Cook 1 minute over low heat, stirring constantly, until
sugar is dissolved. Remove from heat and stir in vanilla.
Cool to room temperature. Sauce may be stored in refrigerator for several days. Mixture will separate during storage; stir before serving.

Chocolate Sauce

2 sqs. unsweetened chocolate
3/4 c. milk
1/4 tsp. salt
1-1/2 c. sugar
3 T light corn syrup
2 T butter
1 tsp. vanilla

Melt chocolate and combine with milk, over low heat.
Beat until smooth and add salt, sugar, and corn syrup.
Cook, stirring occasionally about 2-3 minutes. Add butter
and vanilla.

Custard Sauce

Scald 1-1/2 c. milk in top of double boiler over simmering
water. Mix 1/8 tsp. salt, 3 egg yolks, and 3 T sugar. Stir in
small amount of hot milk, put back in double boiler and
cook, stirring, until thickened. Cool and flavor sauce with
vanilla or almond.

Foamy Sauce

In double boiler, cream 1 c. confectioner's sugar and 1/2 c. soft butter or margarine. Add 2 egg yolks, beaten. Cook over simmering water, stirring, until thickened. Fold in 2 stiffly beaten egg whites and 1 T of brandy or rum. Serve warm. Serves 4-6.

Fruit Sauce

Sister-Glennis Stuart Liles - Greenup, KY

1/2 c. sugar
1/4 c. honey
2 c. water
1/2 c. figs
1/2 c. walnuts
1/2 c. candied cherries
1/2 T brandy or 3/4 tsp. cinnamon

Mix sugar, honey and water in a saucepan and cook over medium heat for 10 minutes. Stir occasionally until mixture comes to a boil.

Meanwhile, cut dates and figs in quarters; chop walnuts and cherries (not too fine); add fruit, nuts and cinnamon to sugar syrup and cook 2 minutes longer. Give it a stir now and then to prevent fruit from sticking to bottom of pan. Makes 1 pint of sauce that can be served hot or cold over ice cream. You'll notice this sauce thickens somewhat on standing.

Hard Sauce

Cream 1/2 c. soft butter with 1-1/2 c. sifted confectioner's sugar until light and fluffy. Add 1 tsp. vanilla or 2 T rum or brandy. Chill. Serves 8-10.

Hot Fudge Sauce

Cousin-Kevin Travis Murphy - Lucasville, OH

1-1/2 c. sugar
1-1/2 c. brown sugar
3/4 c. cocoa
1/4 c. flour
2 tsp. vanilla
1/4 tsp. salt
1 can evaporated milk
1 c. water
2 T butter

Mix in saucepan. Cook on medium until sauce starts to bubble. Will keep in refrigerator for 4 months.

Lemon Sauce

In saucepan, mix 1/2 c. sugar, 1/8 tsp. salt, 2 T cornstarch. Gradually stir in 1 c. boiling water. Cook, stirring, until thickened. Remove from heat; stir in 2 T butter, juice 1 lemon and 1 tsp. grated rind. Serve warm. Makes 1-3/4 c.

Peach Sauce

1 (8 oz.) can sliced peaches in unsweetened syrup, drained
1 T sugar
1 T margarine
1 (8 oz.) carton plain low-fat yogurt

Place peaches in container of an electric blender. Process until smooth, set aside.

Cook sugar and margarine in a small saucepan over low heat until sugar melts. Stir in yogurt and reserved peaches; cook just until hot. (Do not boil.) Serve warm or chilled over ice milk or fresh fruit. Yield: about 1-1/2 c.

Raspberry Sauce

Reserve 2/3 c. syrup from 1 (10 oz.) package thawed frozen red raspberries. In small saucepan, combine syrup, 1/4 c. red currant jelly a 1 T cornstarch. Cook and stir until slightly thickened and clear. Cool. Add raspberries.

Strawberry-Orange Sauce

This sauce is also luscious over fresh poached peaches.

2 T sugar
2 tsp. cornstarch
1 tsp. grated orange rind
1 pkg. (10 oz.) quick-thaw strawberries, slightly thawed

In medium-size saucepan, combine sugar, cornstarch, and orange rind.

In food processor or blender container, puree strawberries until smooth. Gradually stir into mixture in saucepan.

Bring slowly to boiling over low heat, stirring constantly, until mixture is thickened and translucent. Remove from heat; cool. Refrigerate until cold. Makes 1 c.

Vanilla Sauce

In small saucepan, mix 1/2 c. sugar and 1 T cornstarch. Stir in 1 c. boiling water. Simmer 5 minutes. Stir in 2 T butter and 1 tsp. vanilla. Add a dash salt. Serve warm. Makes 1-1/4 c.

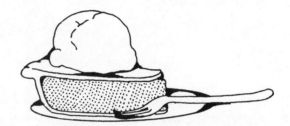

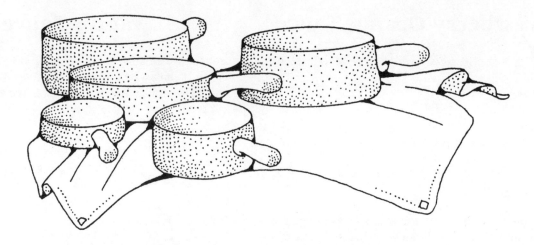

Aunt Viola Wright Hilton, wife of Martin Hilton

Jesse's mother, Martha Hilton Stuart

Eggs and Cheeses

Eggs and Egg Dishes

Bacon and Egg Pie
Baked Eggs
Brunch Eggs
Deviled Eggs
Egg Casserole
Egg and Potato Skillet Supper
Egg in a Nest
Eggaroni
Cheese Omelet
Pickled Hard-cooked Eggs with Beets
Scotch Eggs
Scrambled Eggs
Stuffed Eggs

Cheese

My Real Cheese and Macaroni
Corn Cheese Bake
Cheese Fondue
Cheese Pie
Cheese Souffle I
Cheese Souffle II
Cheese Tomato Dish
Kentucky Hot Brown
Welsh Rarebit

Jesse and Deane's kitchen

Jesse and Deane's kitchen

126

Jerry B. (Mongrel Mettle) Jesse and Rusty

Sugarlump

Usually I was first up, slipping out the back door to watch dawn find its way into W-Hollow. There was always special light filtering in pointing out this tree and that, the split-rail fence, and finally Jesse and Deane's lovely home. At that moment, sound carried across the leaves and grass like over water and I could hear the distant crows awake and tell of the morning.

After the light, after a few moments of watching and listening, I'd return, again through the back way and into the kitchen where I'd find Deane at the refrigerator getting slices of sugarmelon for the wild near-pet groundhog, Sugarlump. The kitchen table was already set for breakfast, and the coffee was already hot.

Deane and I talked, drank coffee, and watched Sugarlump stand on her back legs and hold the melon in her front legs; she looked almost like a child in a fur coat.

Soon Jesse and Joy were up, coming into the kitchen one at a time, and there was talk and more talk and the sweet odor of orange juice, coffee, bacon, eggs, and always fresh fruit.

Eggs were anyway you wanted them and Jesse's favorite was poached, surrounded with corned beef hash.

There was always after-breakfast coffee (Deane mixed half decaf and half straight). Jesse lit up his King Edward or Swisher Sweet cigar, Joy and Deane a cigarette, and I a pipe. Smoke filled the room like blue conversation. We talked of the Reds' game, writing, how the world was going and where it had been, our travels, and how many babies Sugarlump had had this season.

Meals in W-Hollow were always events exciting as life itself. A memorable breakfast, like dawn, sun, birds, wind, and Sugarlump, made a good world better.

Lee Pennington

127

Eggs and Egg Dishes

Bacon and Egg Pie

Cousin-Judy Castle - Huntington, WV

pastry for one 9" crust pie
1/2 lb. bacon
5 eggs, unbeaten
2 eggs, beaten
1 c. milk or light cream
1 tsp. nutmeg
1 T flour
1/2 tsp. salt
1/2 tsp. pepper

Line pie pan with pastry. Fry bacon until crisp, drain, and crumble over bottom of the unbaked pie shell. Break the five eggs, one at a time, on top of the bacon, spacing them evenly around the pie. Mix the two beaten eggs with remaining ingredients and pour over the bacon and eggs. Bake at 400° for 15 minutes. Reduce heat to 325° and bake 30 minutes longer or until knife inserted in the center comes out clean. Serve hot or cold, cut in wedges. Very good with sliced tomatoes.

Baked Eggs

Sister-in-law-Lucille Norris - Greenup, KY

8 slices stale bread (remove crust and cube)
1-1/2 c. sharp cheddar cheese
6 lg. eggs
2-1/2 c. milk
1 T brown sugar
1/2 tsp. salt
1/2 tsp.dry mustard
add pepper as you wish
1 green onion minced
brown and serve sausage

Mix all ingredients except sausage. Pour into greased 9 x 13 Pyrex dish. Let set in icebox for 24 hours. Bake uncovered for 1 hr. at 300°. Lay sausage on top while baking.

Brunch Eggs

Cousin-Margaret Booth - Ceredo, WV

3 doz. eggs
1/4 c. milk
2 cans cream of mushroom soup, undiluted
1/2 c. sherry
1 lg. can mushrooms, drained
1/4 lb. butter
1/2 lb. cheddar cheese, grated
paprika

Beat the eggs in a bowl and stir in the milk. Heat the soup in a saucepan and stir until smooth. Add sherry and mushrooms. Scramble eggs mixture in butter in a skillet just until soft. Place half the eggs in a casserole and add half the soup mixture. Add half the cheese and repeat layers. Sprinkle with paprika. Bake at 300° for about 1 hour.

Deviled Eggs

Niece-Ellen Keeney Douglas - Lexington, KY

6 hard cooked eggs
1/2 tsp salt
1/2 tsp. dry mustard
1/4 tsp. pepper
3 T mayonnaise

Cut peeled eggs lengthwise into halves. Slip out yolks and mash with fork. Mix in salt, mustard, pepper and mayonnaise. Fill whites with egg yolk mixture. Arrange eggs on serving plate. Sprinkle paprika over eggs. Cover and refrigerate.

Egg Casserole

Cousin-Wally Hall - Frankfort, KY

8 hard-cooked eggs, chopped
1-1/2 c. diced celery
1 tsp. minced onion
1/2 tsp. salt
2/3 c. mayonnaise
1 c. grated sharp American cheese
1 c. crushed potato chips

Combine all ingredients except cheese and potato chips and toss lightly. Turn into 4 individual casseroles and sprinkle with cheese and potato chips. Bake at 375° for 25 minutes. 4 servings.

Egg and Potato Skillet Supper

Cousin-Bob Hall - Huntington, WV

1/4 c butter
4 med. potatoes, cooked and sliced (about 3 c.)
1 med. onion, sliced
1 T snipped parsley or parsley flakes
1/2 tsp. paprika
8 eggs
1/2 c. milk
1 tsp. salt
1/4 tsp. pepper

In large fry pan, over med. heat, melt butter. Add potatoes, onion, paprika and parsley. Cook, stirring occasionally, until potatoes begin to brown and onion is tender (5-7 minutes). Reduce heat. Meanwhile, beat eggs, milk, salt and pepper together with a fork. Pour egg mixture over potato mixture. As eggs begin to set, gently draw pancake turner completely across bottom and sides of skillet, forming large soft curds. Continue until eggs are thickened, but do not stir constantly. Cook until eggs are thickened throughout but still moist.

Egg in a Nest

Cousin-Kevin Travis Murphy - Lucasville, OH

slice of bread
egg
oil
salt and pepper

Cut a hole in the center of a slice of bread with a biscuit cutter. Heat skillet with enough cooking oil to cover the bottom. Place bread slice in skillet. Break an egg and drop in the hole in the center of the bread slice. Add salt and pepper. Fry until done turning once to brown the other side.

Eggaroni

Cousin-Helen Jobe - Ceredo, WV

2 T butter
2 T flour
2 c. milk
9 hard cooked eggs
3 eggs, beaten
2 c. cooked elbow macaroni (1/2 of 7 oz. pkg.)
1/2 c. chopped celery
1/4 c. chopped onion
1 tsp. salt
3/4 tsp. marjoram
1/8 tsp. pepper

Melt butter in large saucepan. Blend in flour and cook until mixture is smooth. Stir in milk, all at once. Heat to boiling, stirring constantly. Reserve 4 slices from center of hard-cooked eggs. Stir chopped eggs and all remaining ingredients in milk mixture. Pour into greased 1-1/2 qt. casserole. Bake in 350° oven 35-40 minutes. Garnish with reserved egg slices. Serve hot.

Cheese Omelet

Cousin-Wanda Lee Maynard - Huntington, WV

2 eggs
1 T water
salt and pepper
1 T butter
1 c. grated cheese

Whisk the eggs with a fork until mixed but not frothy. Stir in water and seasonings. Melt butter in an omelet pan. Add the egg mixture and cook rapidly, stirring with a fork. Bring some of the cooked mixture to the center, allowing the uncooked egg to come in contact with the pan. When the top is almost set add the grated cheese. When cheese is melted and the underside of the omelet is golden brown, fold the omelet and turn it onto a plate. Serve immediately.

Pickled Hard-cooked eggs with Beets

Cousin-Loretta Adkins Benner - Lucasville, OH

16 oz. can of small whole red beets
1/2 tsp. salt
2 T sugar
6-8 hard-cooked eggs, peeled
1/2 c. white vinegar
1/2 c. water
1 T mixed pickling spices

Drain liquid from beets into a saucepan. Add vinegar, water, salt, spices, and sugar. Heat to boiling then simmer 5 minutes. Place eggs in a bowl or glass jar. Place beets on top of eggs. Pour liquid over all, cover and refrigerate at least 2 days before serving.

Scotch Eggs

Cousin-Rena Stewart - Magee, MS

4 eggs, hard-cooked
little flour
salt and pepper
12 oz. sausage meat
1 egg, beaten
3 T dry bread crumbs
deep fat or oil for frying

When eggs are cool, coat each in a little seasoned flour. Divide the sausage into four equal parts and press into squares on a floured board. Wrap a square of sausage around each egg and seal edges. Mix beaten egg and bread crumbs and coat eggs. Fry in deep fat until golden brown. Cool. Cut in half to serve.

Scrambled Eggs

Cousin-Betty Ruth Walker - Huntington, WV

4 eggs
salt and pepper
2 T milk or light cream
2 T butter

Beat the eggs with milk, add salt and pepper. Melt butter in skillet over low heat. Pour in the eggs and stir lightly until just set. Serve hot.

Stuffed Eggs

Cousin-Thelma Edwards - Ceredo, WV

6 hard-boiled eggs
2 cucumber pickles, chopped fine
4 slices crisp-fried bacon, crumbled
1 T prepared mustard
2 T mayonnaise
salt and pepper to taste
paprika (optional)

Peel hard-cooked eggs and slice lengthwise. Gently remove yolks into bowl. Mash yolks and mix with other ingredients. Spoon mixture into white halves. Sprinkle lightly with paprika if desired.

Cheese

My Real Cheese and Macaroni

Cousin-Katherine Hilton - Ashland, KY

white sauce
1 pt. milk
cheese
8 oz. macaroni
bread crumbs
bacon (optional)

Make a basic white sauce-adding milk, put cheese (cut up) into sauce and stir until melted and smooth.

Cook macaroni (Al-dente') and drain. Pour into baking dish with sauce, cover with fine bread crumbs and a slice or two of bacon (opt.) Bake around 20 minutes at 300° or low heat.

Corn Cheese Bake

Cousin-Marie Pennington Hardymon - Greenup, KY

1/3 c. flour
1 (16 oz.) can cream style corn
1 (16 oz.) can whole kernel corn, drained
1 (3 oz.) pkg. cream cheese, cubed
1/2 c. Swiss cheese, shredded
1/2 tsp. onion salt

Stir flour into cream style corn; add cheese and salt; heat and stir until cheese melts. Stir in remaining ingredients. Bake, uncovered, 30-35 min. at 400°.

Cheese Fondue

Cousin-Betty Stewart - Kenova, WV

3 T butter or margarine
3 T flour
1/2 tsp. garlic salt
1/2 tsp. salt
dash of white pepper
dash of nutmeg
2-1/2 c. milk
1 lb. Swiss process cheese, shredded
1 tsp. Worcestershire sauce
dash of hot sauce
French bread-cut in 1" cubes

Melt butter in a fondue pot over med. heat. Stir in the flour, garlic salt, salt, pepper and nutmeg. Stir in the milk and cook, stirring constantly, until smooth and slightly thickened. Add the cheese, a small amount at a time, and cook over low heat, stirring until cheese is melted. Stir in remaining ingredients except bread. Spear cube of bread with fondue fork and twirl bread in cheese mixture until coated. Cool slightly and eat.

Cheese Pie

Cousin-Linda Spence - Huntington, WV

3 eggs, well beaten
1/2 tsp. salt
1/2 c. evaporated milk
1 c. grated sharp cheese
1-9" unbaked pie shell

Combine eggs, salt, milk and cheese and pour into pie shell. Bake at 325°-350° for about 30 minutes or until crust is done. Serve hot. Serves 6.

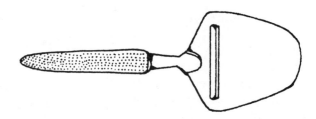

Cheese Souffle I

Wife-Naomi Deane Norris Stuart - W-Hollow, KY

8 slices buttered bread;cut in squares (crust removed)
1/2 lb. Old English cheese cut in sqs.
2 c. milk
1 tsp. dry mustard
3 eggs
1 tsp. salt and pepper (each)
paprika

Beat milk and eggs together. Add mustard, salt and pepper. Pour over bread and cheese mixture into baking dish. Let stand overnight or 2 days in refrigerator. Place dish in a pan of water and bake at 325° for 60 minutes. Sprinkle with paprika.

Cheese Souffle II

Cousin-Brenda Marcum - Kenova, WV

10 slices day-old bread
3/4 lb. New York State cheese, grated
4 beaten eggs
1/2 tsp. Worcestershire sauce
2-1/2 c. milk
1 T grated onion
1 tsp. salt
1/2 tsp. dry mustard
dash of cayenne pepper

Trim the crust from the bread, then place alternate layers of bread and cheese in a baking dish. Mix remaining ingredients and pour over bread and cheese. Bake at 325° for 40 minutes or until set. May be prepared ahead and kept in refrigerator until time for baking. 8 servings.

Cheese-Tomato Dish

Cousin-Jimmie Stewart - Catlettsburg, KY

8 oz. elbow macaroni
2 T butter
1 can tomato soup
1 sm. can tomato sauce
1 c. chopped Velveeta cheese
1 c. chopped mozzarella cheese
4 slices American cheese
salt and pepper to taste

Cook macaroni according to package directions, then drain and place in a greased casserole. Stir in butter until melted. Mix in tomato sauce and soup. Stir in the chopped cheeses, salt and pepper, mixing thoroughly. Lay the cheese slices on top. Bake at 350° for 30 minutes. 4-6 servings.

Kentucky Hot Brown

Cousin-Steve Stewart - Ceredo, WV

1 slice toast
2 oz. sliced turkey
2 oz. sliced ham
5 oz. cheese sauce
1 slice tomato
2 slices crisp bacon

Toast bread and place in center of plate. Stack turkey and ham on top of toast, then ladle cheese on top. Place tomato on top of sauce, criss-cross bacon and bake at 350° 10-15 minutes or until cheese bubbles.

Welsh Rarebit

Cousin-Brian Lester - Jacksonville, FL

1/4 c. butter
8 c. shredded sharp cheddar cheese
2 tsp. Worcestershire sauce
1 tsp. dry mustard
dash of cayenne pepper
1 c. light cream
4 eggs, slightly beaten

Melt butter in top of double boiler. Add the cheese and heat, stirring occasionally until cheese melts. Add Worcestershire sauce, mustard and pepper. Combine cream and eggs and stir into cheese mixture. Cook until thick, stirring frequently. Keep warm. Serve on buttered toast or buttered English muffins.

Fish and Seafood

Fried Bass
Fried Catfish
Baked Crab Meat and Shrimp
Crab Cakes
Fish-Five Ways to Cook
Baked Fish—Crumb Topped
Fish—Fried in Deep Fat
Hush Puppies
Linguine With Clam Sauce
Lobster Tails—Citrus Buttered
Oyster Bake
Oyster Corn Bake
Oyster—Pan Roasted
Salmon Stuffed Tomatoes
Salmon Loaf

Salmon Patties
Seafood Casserole
Seafood Gumbo
Scalloped Oysters
Simple Salmon Skillet Supper
Shrimp and Wild Rice
Shrimp Cocktail
Shrimp Mold
Tartar Sauce
Tuna Casserole
Tuna Fish Casserole
Tuna Noodle Casserole
Tuna Pepper Casserole
Tuna Potato Casserole

Jesse's grandfather - Mitchell Stuart

Elegy for Mitch Stuart

I.
O clansman, weep!
Mitch Stuart's dead!
Old age took him
At home in bed.
No Van Horn put
A bullet through
Mitch Stuart's head.

One war was not enough for him.
He gathered in his clan;
And warring in the black-oak hills,
They fought it man to man.
And old gin-drinking Mitch
He thinned the Van Horn clan.

II.
When old Mitch Stuart
Heard the brass band
On a parade day
Play "Dixie Land,"

On his lame leg
And hickory cane
He would step out
And march again.

His nineteen children
Dared not bother
On parade day
Their marching father.

134

His hickory cane,
His clumsy feet;
Would pop pop on
The home-town street.

But not again
His hickory cane
And clumsy feet
Will pop pop on
The home-town street.

III.

O thunder, pound your drums!
Pound, pound your drums! your big bass-drums!
For old Mitch Stuart comes . . .
His ox cart comes.

O lightning, cut the sky!
Old Mitch is coming to lie.

O oxen, roll your wheels!
O roll your wheels . . . your muddy wheels!
Under the rain's white spikes of steel
They haul old Mitch.

IV.

For him they pray
No lofty prayer;
The little crowd
Gathered there . . .
For him they sing
No songs of folly,

But by his grave
Six soldiers kneel
And over it fire
A farewell volley.

V.

Over his chestnutoak
Flies the wood crane,
Chestnutoak roots have grooved
His mortal brain.

Blue dreamer with ears deaf
To falling rain;
Blue dreamer with eyes blurred
To flying crane,

Do you dream you will rise again?

Blackberry briars are white with bloom
Where old Mitch Stuart lies;
Jarflies are singing at his tomb
Under the Blaine Creek skies.

VI.

If on his slab were carved
Something beside his name
And dates and regiment,
I know old Mitch would want
His epitaph to be:

Here lies old Mitch Stuart
With a bottle and a gun;
He's a-drinkin' and a-fightin' still;
He's got 'em on the run.
His feet are to the east,
His head is to the west . . .
No Van Horn's left to hit
The heat in his clay breast.

Old Mitch's a-fightin' still,
He's got 'em on the run . . .
One hand is on his bottle,
The other on his gun.

Jesse Stuart, *Kentucky is My Land*, (Ashland, Kentucky: The Jesse Stuart Foundation, 1987), pp. 30-33.

Fish and Seafood

Fried Bass

Nephew-Ron Wheeler - Knoxville, TN

2 lbs. bass, well cleaned
lemon juice
1/2 c. cornmeal
1/2 c. flour
1 tsp. salt
1/4 tsp. pepper

Squeeze lemon juice on bass slices. Combine cornmeal, flour salt and pepper, then roll the bass in cornmeal mixture. Fry in 2-inch deep shortening until brown. Drain.

Fried Catfish

Nephew-Stacy Nelson - Greenup, KY

2 lb. dressed catfish
salt to taste
2 c. buttermilk
2 c. cornmeal
1 lb. shortening

Cut catfish into serving pieces and sprinkle with salt. Dip catfish pieces in buttermilk and roll in cornmeal. Fry in hot shortening in heavy skillet until brown. Drain on paper towels. Serves 4.

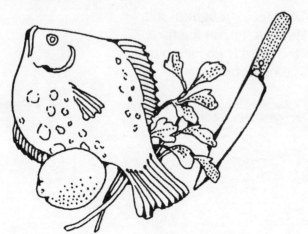

Baked Crab Meat and Shrimp

Cousin-Ila Shanks - Zelienople, PA

1 med. sized green pepper, diced
1 med. sized onion, minced
1 c. chopped celery
1-6-1/2 oz. can crab meat, flaked
1 (5-3/4 oz.) can shrimp, drained
1/2 tsp. salt
1/8 tsp. Worcestershire sauce
1 c. salad oil
1 c. buttered bread crumbs

Combine ingredients, except crumbs. Place in individual sea shells or in a greased casserole and sprinkle with buttered crumbs. Bake in moderate oven (350°) for 30 minutes.

Crab Cakes

Nephew-James Stephen Stuart - Greenup, KY

1 tsp. minced onion
2 tsp. finely chopped celery
butter
3 T flour
3/4 c. milk
2 eggs, beaten
1/2 tsp. Worcestershire sauce
1 c. crab meat
1/2 c. soft bread crumbs
paprika
salad oil

Saute the onion and celery in butter. Melt 3 T butter in saucepan and blend in flour. Add the milk, gradually and cook until thick, stirring constantly. Cool and add onion, celery, 1 egg and Worcestershire sauce. Mix, then fold in crab meat. Chill and mold into oblong cakes. Roll in remaining egg and cover with bread crumbs. Sprinkle with paprika, then chill until ready to use. Deep fry in hot oil until brown on both sides. Serve with tartar sauce. Makes 4 servings.

136

Fish—Five Ways to Cook

Sister-Glennis Liles - Greenup, KY

1. Grilling—Use fish at least 1" thick. Place approximately 6 inches from coals. Baste often.

2. Frying—At 350° fry with oil. Use 5/8" thick fillets, or small whole fish. Dip fish in flour or meal. Fry one to three minutes on each side or until brown.

3. Baking—Seasoned melted fat, sauce or topping should be brushed on fish to keep moist. Bake at 350°.

4. Broiling—Use at least 1" thick fish, 3 to 4 inches from heat. Baste often with melted fat, oil, or basting sauce.

5. Steaming—Place 2" of seasoned liquid (water) in a deep pot equipped with wire rack. Bring water to a boil, place fish on rack, cover tightly and steam 5-10 minutes.

Note: Fish is done when it flakes easily with a fork.

Baked Fish—Crumb Topped

Sister-Glennis Liles - Greenup, KY

1 lb. fish fillets (Orange Roughy very good)
melted butter or margarine
1/4 c. fine dry bread crumbs
1 T chopped parsley
1/8 tsp. each salt, pepper and paprika
lemon wedges

Cut fillets into serving pieces. Coat on all sides in about 3 T melted butter. Place in baking dish. Combine bread crumbs, parsley, seasoning and 1 T melted butter. Sprinkle crumb mixture over fillets. Bake 450° for 8-10 minutes or until fish flakes easily when tested with a fork. Serve with lemon wedges. Makes 4 servings.

Fish—Fried In Deep Fat

Brother-in-law-Herbert (Whitey) Liles - Greenup, KY

3 lbs. fish fillets
1 lemon
1-1/2 pts. oil
buttermilk (enough to cover fish)
2 c. pancake mix
2-1/2 c. club soda
flour

Soak fish fillets in just enough buttermilk to cover. Slice one lemon on top, cover and refrigerate 2-3 hours. Heat oil in 2-1/2 qt. saucepan. Drain fish, cut in small pieces and dredge in flour.

In another bowl combine pancake mix and club soda to give consistency of buttermilk. Dip floured fish into batter—let excess drip off into bowl. Deep fry 4 minutes each side. Keep warm in 250° oven until all are fried.

Hush Puppies

Brother-in-law-Herbert(Whitey) Liles - Greenup, KY

2 c. self-rising corn meal mix
1 med. onion, chopped
1 c. milk
1 egg, well beaten

Combine corn meal mix and onion, and mix well. Stir in milk and egg. Drop by rounded teaspoonfuls in deep hot fat where fish have been fried. Cook 1-1/2 to 2 minutes, turning once. Remove from fat and drain. Makes about 3 dozen hush puppies.

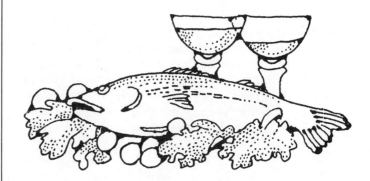

Linguine with Clam Sauce

Niece-Anne Liles O'Hare - Ashland, KY

2 T margarine
1/2 c. olive oil
1 med. container mushrooms, chopped
chopped scallions to taste
fresh or pureed garlic
1 or 2 cans minced clams
oregano, basil, parsley, coarse pepper (to taste)
1/2 c. sour cream
1 egg
cooked pasta

Heat margarine and olive oil in a skillet. Add mushrooms, scallions and garlic. Saute for a few minutes. Add clams, saving the juice. After clam mixture has cooked about 10 minutes add juice, oregano, basil, parsley and pepper. Simmer for several minutes. Mix sour cream with egg and add to sauce. Heat sauce and serve over pasta.

Lobster Tails—Citrus Buttered

Nephew-James Stephen Stuart - Greenup, KY

4-6 (8 oz.) frozen lobster tails
1/4 c butter or margarine, melted
2 tsp. lemon juice
1/2 tsp. grated orange peel
1/4 tsp. salt
dash ground ginger
dash paprika
lemon wedges

With a sharp knife cut through center of hard top shell of partially thawed lobster tails. Cut through meat, but not through under shell. Spread open, butterfly style, so lobster meat is on top. Place tails on broiler pan, shell side down. Combine melted butter, lemon juice, orange peel, salt, ginger and paprika. Brush over meat. Broil 4 inches from heat till meat loses its translucency and can be flaked easily when tested with a fork, about 17-20 minutes. Loosen meat from shell by inserting fork between shell and meat. Serve with lemon wedges. Makes 4 servings.

Oyster Bake

Niece-Lori Ann Stuart - Greenup, KY

1-1/2 pts. oysters or 2 (12 oz.) cans frozen oysters, thawed
1/2 of 3-1/2 oz. can french-fried onions
2 T snipped parsley
2 T grated Parmesan cheese
2 T butter or margarine
salt and pepper

Drain oysters, sprinkle with salt and pepper. Arrange in buttered 8 x 1-1/2" round baking pan. Cover oysters with onions, parsley and cheese. Dot with butter. Bake at 450° till browned, about 8-10 minutes. Makes 4 servings.

Oyster Corn Bake

Sister-in-law-Laura Avenelle Norris Callihan Greenup, KY

2 cans (10 oz.) frozen condensed oyster stew
1 can cream style corn (1 lb. 1 oz.)
1 can whole kernel corn, drained (same)
1-1/4 c. crushed cracker crumbs
1 egg, beaten
1/2 tsp. salt
dash seasoned pepper
2 T butter melted
1/2 c. cracker crumbs
2 T pimento, chopped
1/4 c. onion, chopped
1 tsp. ground sage

Thaw oyster stew, (hot water) 10 minutes. Combine stew, corns, cracker crumbs, egg, seasonings, pimento and onion. Pour into greased 2 qt. casserole. Combine melted butter and 1/4 c. cracker crumbs, sprinkle on top. Bake 350°, for 1 hour or till knife comes out clean. Serves 8 to 10.

Oysters—Pan Roasted

Cousin-Judy Castle - Huntington, WV

1 pt. small oysters
1/4 c. butter, melted
1-3 oz. can sliced mushrooms, drained
1/4 c. dry red wine
1/4 c. snipped parsley
1/2 tsp. salt
toast points

Drain oysters. Arrange in a 11 x 7 x 1-1/2" baking dish. Combine butter, mushrooms, wine, parsley, salt and dash of pepper. Pour over oysters. Bake at 400° till edges of oysters begin to curb, about 10 minutes. Serve over toast points. Makes 4 servings.

Salmon Stuffed Tomatoes

Niece-Martha Stuart Wheeler - Knoxville, TN

1 (15-1/2 oz.) can red salmon
1 c. diced celery
2 T chopped sweet pickle
1 T chopped green pepper
1 tsp. chopped fresh chives
1/2 c. mayonnaise
2 T lemon juice
tomatoes

Drain salmon, and remove skin and bones; flake salmon with a fork. Add celery, sweet pickle, green pepper, and chives; mix well. Combine mayonnaise and lemon juice; add to salmon, stirring well. Chill 2-3 hours. Trim stem end of tomatoes and slice wedges to top end of tomato, being careful not to cut all the way. Tomato will open like a flower. Stuff with a mound of salmon mixture. Good for a light summer meal.

Salmon Loaf

Niece-Shirley Stuart - Greenup, KY

1 (1 lb.) can salmon
1 egg, beaten
2 c. soft bread crumbs
1/2 c. milk
2 T parsley, minced
2 T chopped onion
1 tsp. salt
pepper to taste
2 T butter
2 T lemon juice
1/2 green pepper, chopped
1 stalk celery, chopped

Drain salmon and flake. Add bread crumbs and remaining ingredients. Mix well. Turn into greased loaf pan. Smooth top of loaf and bake 40 minutes in 375° oven or until firm to the touch in the center.

Salmon Patties

Niece-Jennifer Stuart - Greenup, KY

1 can salmon
1/2 c. soft bread crumbs (or enough flour to hold ingredients together.)
1 egg, beaten
1/8 tsp. salt
1/8 tsp. pepper
minced onion (optional)

Flake salmon and remove small bones. Mix salmon with other ingredients and fry in hot fat until golden brown. Minced onion may be added before frying, if desired.

Seafood Casserole

Niece-Anne Liles O'Hare - Ashland, KY

6 slices white bread
1 lb. scallops
1 can crab meat or lobster meat
3 eggs
2 c. milk
1/4 c. butter or margarine
1/4 tsp. dry mustard
6 slices American cheese
salt to taste

Remove crusts from bread and place in an oiled oblong casserole. Cut scallops in bite-size pieces and parboil in small amount of water 5 minutes. Drain. To casserole add scallops, slivers of cheese, melted butter, and crab or lobster. Beat eggs and combine with milk. Add salt and mustard and pour mixture over seafood. Refrigerate overnight. Bake at 350° for 1 hour. Serves 4.

Seafood Gumbo

Nephew-John O'Hare - Ashland, KY

2 T flour
2 T veg. oil
1 c. coarsely chopped onions
1/3 c. coarsely chopped green pepper
1 tsp. minced fresh garlic
1 c. crushed tomatoes
1 c. water
2 bay leaves
1 tsp thyme
1 tsp. salt
1/4 tsp. black pepper
1/4 tsp. white pepper
1/8 tsp. cayenne pepper
2 pkgs. (10 oz. each) frozen cut okra
1 lb. med. shrimp, shelled and deveined
1 pt. oysters in their liquid (24)
1 can (6-1/2 oz.) crabmeat, cartilage removed, can juices reserved
2 c. hot cooked rice

In 4 qt. saucepot, whisk together the flour and oil. Heat over med. heat, stirring occasionally, until mixture is a rich, deep brown, about 45 minutes. This is called a roux.

Add onions, green pepper and garlic; cook and stir 5 minutes. Add tomatoes with their liquid, water, bay leaf, thyme, salt and the three peppers. Cook, stirring occasionally, 30 minutes. Add okra; bring to a boil. Add shrimp and oysters; heat 5 to 10 minutes just until shrimp turn pink. Stir in crabmeat and reserved juices from can. Heat. Serve over hot cooked rice. Makes about 2-1/2 qts. or 10 servings.

Scalloped Oysters

Cousin-Marie Hilton Ellington - Ashland, KY

2 c. Pepperidge Farm Stuffing (I use 1/2 cornbread stuffing)
1 pint oysters (drain and reserve liquid)
1/2 tsp. salt
1/2 tsp. pepper
1/2 stick margarine (cut into 1/4" slices)
2 c. milk (scalded)

Sprinkle 1/2 stuffing on the bottom of a greased 2 qt. casserole. Place a layer of oysters, salt and pepper over the stuffing. Dot with margarine. Repeat with another layer of stuffing, oysters, salt and pepper. Top with a layer of stuffing dotted with margarine. Pour the reserved liquid from the oysters over the stuffing. Then, pour the milk over the casserole. Use more if you think the casserole will be too dry. Bake at 350° for about 45 minutes, or until the milk bubbles through the top.

Simple Salmon Skillet Supper

Cousin-Katherine Hilton - Ashland, KY

potatoes
shortening
1 lg. onion, diced
salt and pepper
1 can salmon (drained)

Start a pan of potatoes to fry in any shortening and add 1 large onion (diced), salt and pepper. When nearly done add 1 can of salmon (drained.) Finish frying to brown. Serve hot. (I call this Strikers Special.)

Shrimp and Wild Rice
Niece-Anne Liles O'Hare - Ashland, KY

1/2 c. thinly sliced onion
1/4 c. thinly sliced green pepper
1/2 c. fresh mushrooms, sliced thin
1/4 c. butter
1 T Worcestershire sauce
A few drops Tabasco
2 c. cooked wild rice
1 lb. cooked and shelled shrimp
2 T. flour
2 T. butter
2 c. chicken broth

Saute the onion, green peppers and mushrooms in butter until soft. Add the seasonings, rice and shrimp to the vegetables. In a separate saucepan, melt butter and blend in flour. Add chicken broth slowly and stir constantly until the sauce is smooth; add to the shrimp mixture. Place in a buttered casserole and bake at 300° until thoroughly heated.

Shrimp Cocktail
Nephew-Aaron Wheeler - Knoxville, TN

1/4 c. lemon juice
1/4 c. salad oil
1/4 tsp. seafood seasoning
1/2 tsp. seasoned salt
3/4 c. chili sauce
1 T. horseradish
2 T chopped onion
2 lbs. cleaned cooked shrimp

Combine all ingredients except shrimp and blend well. Place shrimp in refrigerator container, then pour sauce over shrimp. Cover and refrigerate 24 hrs., stirring occasionally. Serve in cocktail glasses.

Shrimp Mold
Niece-Ellen Keeney Douglas - Lexington, KY

1 (10-3/4 oz.) can tomato soup, undiluted
1 8 oz. pkg. cream cheese
1 envelope (1 T) Knox unflavored gelatin
1/4 c. cold water
1 c. mayonnaise
2 tsp. lemon juice
1/2 tsp. salt
1/2 c. chopped celery
1/2 c. chopped green pepper
1 T finely chopped onion
1 (4-1/2 oz.) can small shrimp-drained and rinsed

Combine soup and cheese, cook over low heat, stirring constantly, until cheese melts. Sprinkle gelatin in cold water, stirring well. Add gelatin to hot soup mixture-cool. Fold in mayonnaise, salt and lemon juice. Refrigerate until slightly thickened, add celery, green pepper, shrimp, and onion to soup mixture stirring to mix. Pour into lightly greased 4 cup mold. Refrigerate until firm.

Tartar Sauce
Niece-Jennifer Stuart - Greenup, KY

1 c. mayonnaise
1 T grated onion
1 T minced dill pickle
1 tsp. chopped parsley
1 tsp. chopped pimiento

Combine all ingredients in a bowl and cover. Chill for several hours. Serve with seafood.

Tuna Casserole
Niece-Kathy Abdon - Greenup, KY

1 can tuna
1 can celery soup
1/2 c. grated cheese
2 T chopped onion
1 c. cooked noodles
1/2 green pepper, chopped

Flake tuna, add remaining items. Bake at 350° for 30 minutes.

Tuna Fish Casserole
Niece-Martha Deane Callihan North - Champaigne, IL

2 cans tuna
sliced potatoes (raw)
sliced onions
salt and pepper to taste
catsup

Layer potatoes 1/4 inch deep in greased casserole dish. Layer onions, then tuna, salt and pepper. Cover with catsup. Cover casserole and bake one hour at 350.

Tuna Noodle Casserole
Cousin-Anne Hilton Short - Forestville, MD

1 pkg. (8 oz.) wide egg noodles
3 T butter or margarine
1/4 lb. mushrooms, sliced
1/2 c. chopped onion
1/3 c. chopped green pepper
1/3 c. coarsely chopped celery
3 T flour
2 c. milk
1 c. chicken broth
1/4 tsp. salt
1/4 tsp. freshly ground pepper
2 cans (7 oz. each) tuna, drained
1 c. crushed potato chips

Preheat oven to 350°. Grease a 2 qt. casserole. In saucepan cook noodles according to pkg. directions. In medium skillet melt butter or margarine over medium heat. Add mushrooms, onion, green pepper and celery. Saute about 5 min., stirring occasionally. Stir in flour until smooth: cook about five minutes stirring frequently. Gradually add milk and chicken broth, stirring until smooth. Add salt and pepper. Simmer 10 minutes, stirring occasionally. In large bowl, combine noodles, sauce and tuna; toss well. Spoon into prepared casserole. Sprinkle top with crushed potato chips. Bake 30 min. Let stand 10 minutes before serving. Makes 6 servings.

Tuna-Pepper Casserole
Niece-Amber Wheeler - Knoxville, TN

2 med. green peppers
1 can (about 7 oz.) tuna, drained and flaked
1 can condensed cream of mushroom soup
1/4 c. milk
3 T chopped pimientos
3 T chopped green stuffed olives
3 T prepared tartar sauce
4 slices American cheese, halved
1/2 c. buttered bread crumbs

Halve peppers and take out seeds. Cook peppers in water 15 minutes, drain. Slice into 1/2" wide strips. Place in a 6 c. shallow baking dish. Mix tuna with soup, milk, pimientos, olives and tarter sauce in bowl. Spoon half over pepper strips. Top with half the cheese. Repeat. Sprinkle with buttered bread crumbs. Bake in 350° oven 25 minutes or until bubbly. Makes 4 servings.

Tuna and Potato Casserole
Niece-Melissa Liles - Greenup, KY

4 c sliced pared potatoes
2 T butter or margarine
1 T fat or oil
4 T flour
2 c. milk
1 med. onion, minced
3/4 tsp. salt
1/8 tsp. pepper
1 T minced parsley
1-7 oz. can tuna

Cook the sliced potatoes in boiling salted water about 10 minutes, drain. Melt butter and fat, stir in flour; then add milk, onion, salt and pepper. Cook, while stirring, until smooth and thickened. Add parsley. Arrange potatoes and tuna in alternate layers in baking dish, pour sauce over all and bake at 350° for 45 minutes. Salmon may be substituted for the tuna.

142

Fruits and Fruit Salads

Ambrosia Salad
Apple Pizza
Baked Apples
Applesauce
Rich Cherry Salad
Fruit Casserole
Fruit Dip
Fruit Pizza
Fruit Salad I
Fruit Salad II

Creamy Fruit Salad
Papaws
Spiced Peaches
Baked Pineapple
Frozen Pineapple-Cranberry Salad
Scalloped Pineapple
Rhubarb
Seven-Up Salad
Strawberry Dressing
24 Hour Salad

When we had our family reunions at Aunt Mary and Uncle John Johnson's, their son Lonnie (Bill) would roll watermelons from the springhouse after dinner.

Eating watermelon after dinner at family reunion, Martha Hilton Stuart extreme right

144

Mother - *Martha Hylton Stuart when she was young*

Jesse and his mother, Martha Hylton Stuart

When I was walking in the big earth room
One April when the trees were white with bloom,
I dreamed of fruit the slender twigs would bear.
The apple tree was maker of a dream . . .
An apple coming through such slender stem!
And when my mother came, I stood beside her.
She was the tree and I was fruit born of her.

*Stuart, Jesse, *Album of Destiny*, (New York: E. P. Dutton & Co., Inc., 1944), p.93.

Fruits and Fruit Salads

Ambrosia Salad

Cousin-Valerie Hilton Kerr - Ashland, KY

Drain well -
1 lg. can fruit cocktail mix
2 lg. cans pineapple chunks
2 sm. cans mandarin oranges
1 can tropical fruit mix
1 jar maraschino cherries

Mix in -
1 sm. can of coconut
bag miniature marshmallows

Add -
1 sm. carton of sour cream

Chill before serving. Optional: Add 1 sliced banana right before serving.

I am submitting this recipe because I remember my mother making it for the Hilton-Stuart reunion each year during Labor Day weekend.

Apple Pizza

Niece-Martha Stuart Wheeler - Knoxville, TN

Prepare pastry for 2 crust pie. Roll out and line a large pizza pan. Pare and slice 5-6 medium cooking apples. Arrange sliced apples over crust. Combine: 1/2 c. sugar, 1 tsp. cinnamon and sprinkle over apples. Combine: 1/2 c. sugar, 3/4 c. flour, 1 stick butter, until crumbly, then sprinkle over apples. Bake at 450° for 20 minutes.

Baked Apples

Nephew-Tony Abdon - Greenup, KY

These glazed apples can be served warm with ice-cream on the side.

6 lg. red cooking or baking apples
1/4 c. sugar
1/2 c. water or unsweetened apple juice
2 T butter or margarine, softened
2 T light brown sugar
1/2 tsp. ground cinnamon
2 T dried currants
1 T sliced almonds

Core apples through the stem ends, being careful not to go through the bottom. Make opening about 1 inch in diameter to accommodate the filling. Pare the top of each apple a third of the way down; reserve peel. Place apples in 12 x 8 inch baking dish.

Combine peel, sugar, and water; heat to boiling. Boil over low heat 10 min. Discard peel. Stir lemon juice into syrup. Pour syrup around top (peeled part) of apples and into dish.

In cup or small bowl, combine butter, brown sugar, and cinnamon. Fill cavity of each apple with some currants and almonds. Top each with some butter mixture.

Bake apples 45-60 minutes or until apples are tender, basting occasionally with syrup. Serve warm or chilled.

Applesauce

Nephew-Tony Abdon - Greenup, KY

Wash, pare, core, and slice about 8 tart apples. Place in saucepan. Add water (1 c. to 1 qt. apples). Simmer until apples are tender. Stir in 1/2 c. sugar, dash of salt, 1 tsp. lemon juice, 1/8 tsp. cinnamon or nutmeg. Taste, add more sugar if desired. Cook 1 min. more. Serve cold. Elegant topped with whipped cream or ice cream.

Rich Cherry Salad

Cousin-Frances Hilton Hunt - Bloomfield, KY

1-1/2 c. condensed milk
1 lg. cool whip
1 lg. can crushed pineapple, drained
1 can cherry pie filling

Mix condensed milk and cool whip. Add fruit, chill and serve. May be frozen.

Fruit Casserole

Sister-in-law-Lucille Norris - Greenup, KY

1 can pineapple
1 can peaches
1 can pears
1 can apricots
1/2 c. brown sugar
2 T cornstarch
2 c. juice (from fruit)
1 stick butter
1/2 c. pecans
1 tsp. curry powder
1 sm. jar maraschino cherries

Boil juice, sugar, curry, cornstarch and butter until creamy. Add fruit and nuts and bake 45 minutes at 350°.

Fruit Dip

Cousin-Margaret Terry Waller - Ceredo, WV

8 oz. cream cheese
1/2 c. confectioner's sugar
1 egg, beaten
1/2 tsp. vanilla

Blend ingredients together. Let set for about one hour. This is really good with sliced apples.

Fruit Pizza

Cousin-Katherine Hilton - Ashland, KY

Cookie shell pastry:

1 c. unsifted flour
1/2 tsp. salt
1 T sugar
6 T butter or oleo
1 egg yolk
1 T water
4 1/2 tsp. lemon juice or rum

Combine first four ingredients. In a separate bowl, beat together remaining three ingredients. Then add them to first mixture and blend with a fork. Shape into a ball and chill. Roll out 1/4" thick and fit into large pizza pan. Bake at 350° until lightly brown. Cool

Pizza Topping:
1 pkg. (8 oz.) cream cheese
1 c. granulated sugar

Mix together and spread on cooled crust. Spread, in alternate layers over cream cheese, 3 cans of different fruit pie filling. Top with glaze.

Glaze:
1/2 c. powdered sugar
1 T milk
Combine and mix well.

Fruit Salad I

Cousin-Lynn Hunt Newton - Hamilton, OH

2 cans (14 oz. each) chunk pineapple
1 (14 oz.) can mixed chunk fruit
1 can (14 oz.) pears
1 can (14 oz.) peaches
1 1/2 cups fresh or frozen strawberries
2 bananas
3 fresh oranges, peeled and cut.

Drain liquid from all cans of fruit into bowl. Cook together 1 small pkg. vanilla pudding, 1 small pkg. tapioca pudding and liquid from fruits. Add 4 T orange juice. Cool completely. Add to fruit and toss.

Fruit Salad II

Cousin-Katherine Stewart Martin - Racine, WS

1 lg. can fruit cock tail (undrained)
1 lg. can pineapple chunks (undrained)
1 lg. can mandarin orange slices (drained)
1 pkg. Jello Lemon Pie mix (instant)
1 pkg. vanilla pie mix (instant)

Stir first three ingredients together, then combine together both pie mixes. Pour over the fruit mixture (dry) and stir.

Creamy Fruit Salad

Cousin-Katherine Stewart Martin - Racine, WS

1 can (8 3/4 oz.) fruit cocktail, drained
2 bananas, peeled and sliced crosswise
1 small unpared apple, diced
1/2 c. seedless green grapes, halved
5 maraschino cherries, halved
1/4 c. miniature marshmallows
1/2 cup whipping cream (whipped)
Strawberries

In a large bowl, combine fruit cocktail, and all fruit except strawberries. Fold in whipped cream and marshmallows; refrigerate. Just before serving, garnish with strawberries. 4 to 6 servings.

Papaws

Sister-Glennis Stuart Liles - Greenup, KY

The papaw is best when soft enough to yield to slight pressure of the thumb. Wash and chill thoroughly. It may be eaten as is or cut into quarters or wedge shaped pieces, seeds removed, and served with wedges of lemon or lime, or with salt or sugar. Delicious combined with orange sections.

Spiced Peaches

Sister-Glennis Stuart Liles - Greenup, KY

2 (29 oz.) cans cling peach halves
1 1/3 c. sugar
1 c. vinegar
4 cinnamon sticks
2 tsp. whole cloves

Drain peaches, reserve syrup. Combine peach syrup, vinegar, cinnamon sticks and cloves in a saucepan. Bring to a boil, simmer 10 minutes. Pour over peach halves; let cool. Store in refrigerator. Makes 4 pints.

Baked Pineapple

Cousin-Rea Anne Hilton - Frankfort, KY
Cousin-Norma Jean Pennington Darnell - Greenup, KY

2 lg. cans pineapple chunks (drained)
1 c. sugar
1/2 c. flour

Mix sugar and flour with pineapple and put into baking dish. Melt 1 stick of butter. Crush 1 stack Ritz crackers. Place crackers on top of pineapple mixture. Pour melted butter over crackers. Bake at 350° uncovered for 35 to 40 minutes.

Frozen Pineapple-Cranberry Salad

Cousin-Fred Hilton - Ashland, KY

1 can (20 oz.) crushed pineapple
1 can (16 oz.) whole berry cranberry sauce
1 c. dairy sour cream
1/4 c. coarsley chopped pecans
Crisp salad greens

Drain pineapple. Combine pineapple, cranberry sauce, sour cream, and pecans. Pour into 8 inch square pan or loaf pan. Freeze for several hours or overnight. To serve, remove from freezer 45 minutes before cutting into squares or slices. Serve on salad greens. Serves 8.

Scalloped Pineapple

Sister-in-law-Lucille Norris - Greenup, KY

1 c. margarine
2 c. sugar
4 eggs, beaten
1/4 c. milk
4 c. white bread cubes
1 (20 oz.) can crushed pineapple

Cream together margarine, sugar & eggs. Add remaining ingredients and mix well. Place in buttered oblong pan and bake at 375° for 15 minutes and then 350° for 1 hour. Serves 6-8.

Rhubarb

Sister-Glennis Stuart Liles - Greenup, KY

Early spring rhubarb has light pink stalks and light leaves. The rhubarb which comes later has dark reddish green to green stalks with deep green foliage. The stalks of good rhubarb are fresh and crisp, not flabby.

To prepare: Before cooking rhubarb, trim the ends, remove the leaves, and wash it thoroughly. Do not peel unless the stalks are tough or stringy, as you get better color. Because of its high water content, rhubarb requires little water in cooking.

To make rhubarb sauce use:
1-1/2 lbs. rhubarb
1/2 c. water
1/8 tsp. salt
2/3 c. sugar

Combine all ingredients in a sauce pan; cover and simmer about 10 minutes. This sauce is good as a breakfast fruit or as dessert with or without whipped cream.

Seven-Up Salad

Cousin-Margaret Terry Waller - Ceredo, WV

1 lg. pkg. cream cheese
1 sm. can crushed pineapple
1 tsp. sugar
1 tsp. vanilla
1/2 c. chopped pecans
1 pkg. lemon jello (lime can be used)
1 c. boiling water
12 ozs. 7-Up

Dissolve jello in boiling water, mix cheese and beat well until smooth. Stir in pineapple, sugar, vanilla, and nuts. Add 7-Up and blend well. If lemon jello is used, you may want to add a few drops of green food coloring for color.

Strawberry Dressing

Cousin-Alma Martin - Racine, WS

1 pkg. (10 oz.) frozen strawberries, thawed, drained and crushed.
2/3 c. mayonnaise
1 carton (8 oz.) strawberry-flavored yogurt

Combine first 2 ingredients; fold in yogurt. Cover and chill 1 hour. Serve over honeydew wedges and strawberries. Garnish with mint. Makes 2 1/3 cups.

24 Hour Salad

Cousin-Joyce (Jimmie) Carter McKinney - Scarbro, WV

1 lg. can crushed pineapple
1/2 lb. miniature marshmallows
1/4 lb. chopped pecans
1/2 c. sugar
1/4 tsp. salt
1 1/2 c. sweet milk
6 eggs, well beaten
2 T vinegar
3 T flour
1 pt. whipping cream

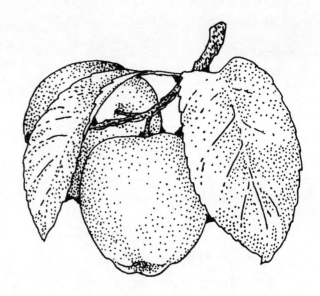

Heat milk slowly while mixing eggs, sugar, salt, flour and vinegar. Take out enough milk to mix egg mixture thin enough to pour in hot milk. Cook like custard. Remove from heat and cool. Add pineapple, pecans and marshmallows and chill. When cold, add whipped cream and let set in refrigerator for 24 hours.

Mother made this once a year at Christmas from the time I was small. I make it now at Christmas, but take a short-cut, use cool whip instead of whipping cream.

Grits, Hominy, Pasta, and Rice

Cheese Grits
Garlic Grits (meat free)
Grits and Turkey Casserole
Grits with Rosemary and Grapes
Hominy, Homemade with Homemade Lye
Corn Meal Mush I
Corn Meal Mush II
Asparagus Pasta
Manicotti Cheese Bake
Noodle-Vegetable Casserole
Green Noodle Casserole

Cheddar Garden Pasta
Baked Rice with Spinach and Cheese
Golden Rice and Cheese
Rice Casserole
Fried Rice with Meat and Vegetables
Mushroom Rice
Old Fashion Rice Pudding
Rice Pilaf
Pizza Rice
Spanish Rice

Emmett and Myrtle Spence Norris - Naomi Deane's parents

L to R. Naomi Deane Stuart and her sister Nancy Curry with dogs. Jerry B. and Rusty (Mongrel Mettle)

152

Jesse and Naomi Deane Stuart World War II

Jesse and a favorite cousin Mary Belle Johnson slip away for a chat during a family gathering

Grits, Hominy, Pasta, and Rice

Cheese Grits

Cousin-Mahala Hilton - Frankfort, KY

1 c. grits
1 c. sharp cheese, grated
1 roll garlic cheese, chopped
1/2 stick margarine
1 T Worcestershire sauce
Salt to taste
Red pepper (Optional)

Cook grits according to package. When done, add butter, cheese and Worcestershire sauce. Stir until melted. Pour into greased casserole dish. Bake 350° for 30 minutes.

Garlic Grits (Meat Free)

Cousin-Alma Stewart Webb - St. Clair Shores, MI

Add 1-1/2 c. minute grits to 3 c. water

Cook as on package. In a cup, combine 1 stick margarine, 1/2 to 1 roll garlic cheese, pinch of salt, and 2 eggs; beat well. Fill to 1 cup level with milk (more milk may be used if a less firm custard is desired). Add to grits mixture and put in greased casserole. Cover with cornflakes or cheese Ritz crumbs and bake at 350° for 40 minutes.

Grits and Turkey Casserole

Niece- Rebecca Sue Callihan - Lexington, KY

1 c. quick grits
4 c. turkey or chicken stock
2 c. cooked turkey or chicken, cut into small pieces
1 c. garlic-herb cheese (such as Boursin), Montrachet or soft goat cheese
1/3 c. sliced sun-dried tomatoes
2 T chopped fresh basil
1 c. cooked chopped or sliced collards or turnip greens

Preheat oven to 350°. Cook grits according to package directions, substituting turkey or chicken stock for the water. In a casserole, mix grits with remaining ingredients and bake until heated through, about 20 minutes. Serves 4.

Grits with Rosemary and Grapes

Niece-Regina Nelson Stout - Greenup, KY

5 c. turkey or chicken stock, boiling
1 c. grits
1-2 T rosemary, chopped or whole
1 c. grapes, preferably scuppernongs or muscadines, halved and seeded
1 T butter
Salt
Freshly ground black pepper
1 c. pecan halves, toasted

Bring stock to boil and add grits, rosemary and grapes. Cook 30 minutes, until thick. Add butter, salt and pepper to taste. Add pecans and serve. Serves 4.

Hominy, Homemade with Homemade Lye

Niece-Betty Stuart Darby Baird-Wadestown, WV

First you make the lye:
Put hardwood ashes into a bucket or any container (not aluminum or tin) with holes in the bottom. Pour water over the ashes and catch drippings that run out of the holes. Again, do not use tin or aluminum. A wooden, glass, or pottery container is good. Be careful not to get this liquid on your skin. It is very strong! Next: Select about 12-15 good ears of corn (dry). The best corn is white, large flat grains, but any good white or yellow corn can be used. Shell the corn and discard any grains that are damaged or not fully developed. Place the lye in a large iron kettle over an outside fire. Add water. Make it 1/3 lye; 2/3rds water, and add the corn. Bring it to a boil and cook until the grains begin to swell and the outer skin begins to crack off the corn (probably 15-30 minutes). Wash the grains thoroughly in running water and rub off the husks. Be sure to wash off all husks and all of the lye. Rinse the corn several times. Put the corn back in a kettle and continue to cook it until it is tender. It is now ready to use. It is good cooked with dried beans or fired in bacon grease, with sliced green onion added.

Corn Meal Mush I

Sister-Sophie Stuart Keeney - Greenup, KY

Put 2 quarts of water into a clean dinner pot or stew pan. Cover and let it become boiling hot. Then add 1 T of salt. Use yellow or white cornmeal; take a handful of the meal with the left hand and a pudding stick or large spoon in the right. Stir the hot water around and by degrees let the meal fall in. Continue to stir and add meal until it is as thick as you can stir easily. When it is sufficiently cooked, approximately 1/2 hour, it will bubble or puff up. this is eaten cold or hot, with milk or butter and syrup or meat and gravy the same as you would serve potatoes or rice.

This recipe surely brings back memories. When we were young we had mush for breakfast and what we didn't eat came right back to the table the next meal as fried mush. Mom didn't let her mush go to the hogs.

Corn Meal Mush II

Cousin-Essie Hilton Rowland - Chillicothe, OH

1 c. corn meal
1 tsp. salt
3 c. boiling water
1 c. cold water

Mix corn meal with the cold water and then gradually add to salted, rapidly boiling water, stirring constantly. Bring to a full rolling boil while stirring and keep over fire about 3 minutes or until thickened.

For fried mush, turn into lightly greased bread pan; cover while hot to prevent crust forming. When cold, slice and fry in hot fat. Serve with butter and syrup.

For corn meal scrapple: Prepare above recipe and add 1-1/2 cups chopped peanuts to mush right after taking it from stove. Then follow same procedure as for fried mush. When cold, dip the slices in flour and brown in hot fat.

Asparagus Pasta

Cousin-Nancy Fannin - Kenova, WV

1 lb. asparagus
6 T olive oil
1 clove garlic, minced
1 lb. pasta (fettucini or spiral)
1/2 c. ham, cut in small pieces
3/4 c. tomato, diced and seeded
1/2 c. white chicken meat, diced
8 black olives, pitted and sliced
2 T wine vinegar
Salt
Pepper, freshly ground

Wash, peel and blanch asparagus. Drain and cool immediately. Cut each spear into 1 inch pieces. Heat olive oil; cook garlic in oil one minute, then pour into large heat-proof bowl. Cook pasta in boiling water 10 minutes. Drain. Combine pasta with olive oil. Add asparagus, ham, tomato, chicken, olives and vinegar. Season with salt and pepper to taste. Serve room temperature or cold. 4-6 servings.

155

Manicotti-Cheese Bake

Sister-in-law-Betty Stuart - Greenup, KY

1/2 lb. ground beef
1/2 c. minced onion
1/4 c. chopped green pepper
2/3 c. tomato paste
2 c. water
1-1/2 tsp. salt
1/2 tsp. pepper
1 tsp. sugar
1-1/2 tsp. Italian seasoning
1 pkg. small manicotti shells
2 c. Ricotta cheese
1 c. shredded Mozzarella cheese

Saute ground beef, onion, and green pepper for 10 minutes and drain fat. Add tomato paste, water, salt, pepper, sugar, and seasoning and simmer 15 minutes. Parboil manicotti in 4 c. salted water for 4 minutes, then drain on paper towels. Combine the cheeses and fill the manicotti shells. Place the shells in a greased casserole and cover with ground beef sauce. Bake at 350° for 20-30 minutes. Serves 4.

Noodle-Vegetable Casserole

Cousin-June Haney - Huntington, WV

2 T diced red or green pepper
3 T butter
4 T flour
Mustard to taste
3 c. milk
8 oz. grated American cheese
8 oz. medium noodles, cooked
1 (no. 2) can peas, drained
1 (no. 2) can shoestring carrots, drained
3/4 tsp. salt
Dash of pepper

Saute red or green pepper lightly in butter, then blend in flour. Add mustard and stir in milk gradually. Cook and stir until thick. Reserve a small amount of cheese for topping and add remaining cheese to sauce. Place noodles, peas, carrots, and seasonings in a buttered casserole and add cheese sauce. Toss to mix. Top with cheese. Bake at 350° for 30 minutes. Serves 6.

Green Noodles Casserole

Niece-Martha Stuart Wheeler - Knoxville, TN

3 c. green noodles
3/4 tsp. hot sauce
1/4 c. butter
1/4 c. flour
1 tsp. salt
2-1/2 c. milk
1 c. diced sharp cheddar cheese
1/4 c. grated Parmesean cheese
1 (4 oz.) can pimento
3 hard-cooked eggs, sliced

Cook noodles according to package directions, adding 1/4 tsp. hot sauce to the water. Drain and rinse. Melt the butter in a saucepan and stir in flour, salt and remaining hot sauce. Add milk and stir over medium heat until smooth and slightly thickened. Add the cheeses and stir until melted. Add the pimiento and noodles and mix. Pour into 1-1/2 qt. casserole. Bake at 350° for about 25 minutes. Top with eggs and cook for 5 minutes longer. 6-8 servings.

Cheddar Garden Pasta

Niece-Shirley Stuart - Greenup, KY

1 lb. carrots, diagonally sliced
1 T butter
1/2 tsp. dried basil
1 can cream of celery soup
1/3 c. milk
1/2 c. shredded cheddar cheese
2-1/2 c. cooked corkscrew macaroni

In covered saucepan, in 1/2" of boiling water, cook carrots until tender; drain. In saucepan heat butter. Add basil. Stir in soup, milk, and cheese. Heat, stirring constantly until cheese melts. Add carrots and pasta; toss to coat. Heat. Serves 6.

Baked Rice with Spinach and Cheese

Cousin-June Haney - Huntington, WV

1 (10 oz.) pkg. frozen spinach
1 c. cooked rice
1 c. shredded sharp cheese
2 slightly beaten eggs
2 T butter
1/3 c. milk
2 T chopped onion
1/2 tsp. Worcestershie sauce
1 tsp. salt

Cook spinach according to pkg. directions and drain. Blend all ingredients together and pour into a greased 1-quart casserole. Bake at 350° for 25 minutes or until inserted knife comes out clean. Serves 6.

Golden Rice and Cheese

Niece-Melissa Liles - Greenup, KY

2 c. cooked rice
3 c. shredded carrots
2 c. grated cheese
2 eggs, beaten
1-1/2 tsp. salt
2 T onion flakes
1/2 c. milk

Combine all ingredients and toss to mix well. Place in a buttered casserole. Bake at 350° for 35-40 minutes. 6 servings.

Rice Casserole

Cousin-Marie Pennington Hardymon - Greenup, KY

1/2 stick margarine
1 med. onion, chopped
1 can beef bouillon
1 can beef consume'
1 can rice
1 (4 oz.) can mushrooms

Wash rice; saute onion in butter; add rice. Mix in other ingredients. Pour into greased casserole. Bake for 45 minutes at 350°.

Fried Rice with Meat and Vegetables

Niece-Martha Stuart Wheeler - Knoxville, TN

Cook 1 c. rice or have ready 3 c. leftover rice
4 T. cooking oil
1/4 to 1/2 lb. any cooked or raw meat, cut into thin strips.
3 cloves garlic, minced
1 lg. onion, chopped coarsley
1 tsp. salt
1/4 tsp. pepper
1 T soy sauce

Heat oil in large skillet. Add remaining ingredients except rice. Stir fry until meat is tender and hot, about 1-2 minutes.

Add:
3 c. cooked rice
Stir fry 5 minutes, add: 1 c. leftover or frozen vegetables. Stir well into rice meat mixture. Just before serving, add: 2 eggs, beaten. Over medium heat, stir carefully through rice until eggs are cooked. Serve piping hot with green salad.

Mushroom Rice

Niece-Shirley Stuart - Greenup KY

1 c. uncooked regular rice
2 (4 oz.) cans sliced mushrooms (undrained) or 1 pkg. fresh mushrooms
1 can beef broth
1/8 tsp. garlic powder
1/8 tsp. seasoned pepper
1/2 c. melted butter
2 T sherry cooking wine

Combine all ingredients and bake uncovered for 1 hour in 350° oven.

Old Fashioned Rice Pudding

Niece-Nancy Sue Darby Lake - Berea, KY

2 eggs. beaten
1 1/3 c. milk
1/4 c. sugar
1 T butter or margarine, softened
1 tsp. vanilla
1/8 tsp. salt
2 c. cooked rice
1/3 c. raisins
1/2 tsp. grated lemon rind
1 tsp. lemon juice
3 T soft breadcrumbs
1 T butter margarine

Combine eggs, milk, sugar, butter, vanilla and salt. Mix well. Stir in rice, raisins, lemon rind and juice. Spoon into a lightly greased 1-quart baking dish. Combine breadcrumbs and butter; sprinkle breadcrumbs on top, bake at 325° for 40-45 minutes or until set. Serves 4-6.

Rice Pilaf

Niece-Regina Nelson Stout - Greenup, KY

2 T butter
1/3 c. chopped onion
1/4 c. chopped green pepper

Saute until onion takes on transparent appearance.

Add: 2 c. uncooked long grain rice. Stir well. Add: 4 c. chicken broth

Bring to boil, cover and simmer on low for 15 minutes. Add 1 c. frozen peas (do not thaw) and 1 (2. oz.) pkg. slivered almonds. Fold in gently. Cook additional 5 minutes. Serves 8.

Pizza Rice

Cousin-Beverly Jane Benner Murphy - Lucasville, OH

2 c. enriched long grain rice
(cooked according to pkg. directions).
DO NOT USE MINUTE RICE.

Add to cooked rice:
2 (10-1/2 oz.) cans pizza sauce
1 (15 oz.) can tomato sauce
Oregano and garlic salt to taste
1 lb. sausage, fried and drained
1 green pepper, chopped
1 onion, chopped
2 sm. or 1 lg. can mushrooms, drained

Mix together well:
1 pkg. pepperoni, sliced thin
1 lg. pkg. shredded Mozzarella cheese
Parmesan cheese, grated

In a 13" x 9" pan and a small casserole dish (to freeze for later), make a layer of the rice mixture. Top with pepperoni, Mozzarella and Parmesan. Then another layer of the rice mixture, etc. End with cheese and top with green pepper rings. Bake 45 minutes at 350°.

Spanish Rice

Sister-Sophie Stuart Keeny - Greenup, KY

3/4 c. rice
5 T fat
5 c. water
2 onions, chopped
2 c. tomatoes
1/2 c. chopped green pepper or pimientos
Salt, pepper, paprika

Fry the rice in fat until brown. Add water and boil until soft. Drain. Saute the onion in a little fat; mix with tomatoes and chopped peppers or pimientos and add to the rice. Add seasoning and place in a greased casserole. Bake at 350°. This dish makes a good one-dish meal.

Make Ahead or Make Your Own

General

Bacon Bits
Biscuit Mix
Butter
Chili Powder
Cottage Cheese
Dog Biscuits
Gravy Measures
Herbs
Herb Salt
Almost Kaluha
Kiwifruit Daiquiri
Lemon Pepper
Mead-Honey Wine
Homemade Pasta
Salt Substitute
Seasoned Salt
Apple Pie Spices
Homemade Maple Syrup
Sweetened Condensed Milk
White Sauce
Uncle Vernon Kendall's Dandelion Wine
Wine, Grape
Whiskey, Moonshine
Yogurt

Liqueurs You Can Make at Home

Basic Sugar Syrup I
Basic Sugar Syrup II
Anise Liqueur
Apple Cinnamon Cream Liqueur
Cherry Bounce
Chocolate Liqueur
Coffee Liqueur
Creme De Menthe
Daiquiri Liqueur
Orange Liqueur
Raspberry Liqueur
Strawberry Liqueur
Coffee Flavored Liqueur

Pickling Spices

Mixed Pickling Spices
Dill Pickling Spices
Curried Pickling Spices
Pickling Spice II

Just For Fun

Jared's Best Mud Pie
Play Dough

Uncle James Stewart - Mitchell's brother

James Stewart, Mitchell's brother with granddaughter Thelma.

L to R. Front row - Nephew Gene Darby, cousin Doc Copley, Jesse, daughter Jane, 2nd row - Cousin Clara Stuart Copley, parents - Martha and Mitchell Stuart and Uncle Joe Stuart (Mitchell's brother)

Uncle Marion Stewart and his wife, Mary Ann (Mitchell Stuart's sister) Uncle Marion was Uncle Mel in Jesse's writings.

Bacon Bits

Cousin-Judy Castle - Huntington, WV

Fry bacon until very crisp. Drain thoroughly between layers of paper towels; crumble into bits and store in a jar. Keeps long time. Use on salads and soups.

Biscuit Mix

Cousin-Margaret Booth - Ceredo, WV

4 c. unbleached white flour
2/3 c. instant nonfat dry milk
1 tsp. salt
3 T baking powder
1/2 c. vegetable shortening

Sift together dry ingredients. Then blend in shortening. Put in covered container and store in refrigerator until needed. To make biscuits use: 1/4 c. water to each cup of mix. Roll out on floured board to 1/2 inch thick. Cut out biscuits and place on greased cookie sheet. Bake in 425° oven 10-15 minutes. Each cup of mix makes about 6 small biscuits.

Butter

Cousin-Bonnie Dominiak - Chula Vista, CA

2 c. cold whipping cream
1/4 tsp. salt
10 drops yellow food coloring

In large mixing bowl, beat cream 8-10 minutes (decrease speed last few minutes) until liquid separates out. Drain, rinse with cold water. Work in food coloring and salt.

Chili Powder

Cousin-Wally Hall - Frankfort, KY

1 c. dried chili peppers or 3/4 c. crushed hot red pepper flakes
1/2 c. ground cumin
2 T garlic powder
1 T oregano
1 T cayenne pepper, or more to taste

Remove stems and most of the seeds from the chili peppers, shread coarsley. Put all ingredients in a blender or food processor container and whirl until powdered. Let powder settle before taking off lid.

Cottage Cheese

Cousin-Helen Jobe - Ceredo, WV

To make cottage cheese, simply heat a quart of milk in a heavy utensil or a double boiler. Certified raw milk is best. When the milk is warm, add one tablespoon of lemon juice. Stir it and keep the heat low. When the milk curdles, remove the pan from the stove. Now pour the entire quart into a muslin bag or cheesecloth and allow it to drain.

You can make cottage cheese from yogurt. This is perhaps the simplest method and the result is tangy and delicious. Simply pour homemade yogurt into your cheese bag and let it drain for an hour or two. This drained yogurt can be used in recipes for dips, spreads, sauces and dressings, when you want a thicker consistency than an ordinary yogurt. To make yogurt cream cheese, you would allow the yogurt to drain overnight. For a sharper cheese, use yogurt that is several days old. Add a little kelp or salt. This cheese may be used plain or mixed with mixed green onions, chives, caraway seeds, pimentoes, olives, or crushed pineapple to make delicious tantalizing spreads and sandwich fillings.

Dog Biscuits

Cousin-Bob Hall - Huntington, WV

1 pkg. active dry yeast
1 c. warm chicken broth
2 T molasses
1-3/4 to 2 c. all-purpose flour
1-1/2 c. whole wheat flour
1 c.cracked wheat
1/2 c. cornmeal
1/2 c. nonfat dry powdered milk
2 tsp. garlic powder
1 egg, beaten
1 T milk

Dissolve yeast in 1/4 c. warm water. Stir in broth and molasses. Add 1 c. of the all-purpose flour, the whole wheat flour, cracked wheat, corn meal, dry milk, garlic and 2 tsp. salt. Mix well. On floured surface, knead in remaining flour. Roll out, 1/2 of dough at a time, to 3/8 inch thickness. Cut into desired shapes. Place on ungreased baking sheets. Brush tops with mixture of egg and milk. Repeat with remaining dough. Bake in 300 degree oven for 45 minutes. Turn oven off; let dry overnight in oven. Makes 42-48 biscuits.

Gravy Measures

Cousin-June Haney - Huntington, WV

Here's what to measure for the amount of gravy you want:

To make

1 cup:	2 cups:	3 cups:	4 cups:
2 T fat	4 T fat	6 T fat	8 T fat
2 T flour	4 T. Flour	6 T Flour	6 T Flour
1 c. water	2 c. water	3 c. water	4 c. water

Now follow these three simple steps:

1. Tip roasting pan enough to let drippings flow into one corner. As fat rises to top pour off into a bowl, but leave brown bits in pan. Follow measurements above for fat, flour, and water needed.

2. Measure fat into pan, then blend in flour, stirring and cooking just until mixture bubbles. Stir in measured water, keeping pan over low heat all the time so mixture doesn't spatter or scorch.

3. Continue cooking, scraping baked on juices from bottom and sides of pan as you stir, until gravy thickens and boils 1 minute. Season to taste; darken with a bit of bottled gravy coloring, if you wish.

Herbs

Cousin-Helen Shultz - Portsmouth, OH

Herbs bring out the best in foods, enhancing the flavor of almost every dish. The best way to learn about cooking with herbs is to try our recipes that call for only a single herb, so you become familiar with its taste. Then begin mixing the herb with others. Remember that it's best to avoid combining two strong herbs such as sage and rosemary. When you use a strong and a delicate herb in the same dish, keep the most aromatic herb to a minimum so the more delicate one doesn't become over powered.

Fresh herbs can be substituted for dry herbs in most recipes. The rule to remember when substituting is 1 T fresh herbs to 1 tsp. of the dried, or 3 to 1. Because fresh herbs lose their flavor when cooked for any length of time, it is best to add them to the pot a few minutes before the dish is done, unless it's a simmering stew or soup.

When using fresh herbs, gather from the garden as you need them. Wash in cold water and discard any bad leaves. They will keep fresh and crisp for several days in sealed plastic bags or containers in your refrigerator. Chop small amounts as you need them.

Experiment to find flavors and quantities you enjoy. Begin with small amounts and increase as necessary for the flavor you enjoy. The degree of seasoning is a matter of personal preference. Sometimes a simple change in the seasonings creates an entirely new dish.

To preserve herbs for winter use, the most aromatic herbs, like thyme, rosemary, winter savory, sage, and bay seem to dry with almost as much flavor as they have when fresh. Freezing is the alternative to drying for the more delicate herbs such as parsley, chives, and basil. They can be frozen in small bunches in plastic bags or containers and cut off and chopped as needed. Or you can pre-chop the herbs, pack them in plastic containers, and spoon out the amount required.

Basil is best known for its use with tomatoes. It can be sprinkled over sliced tomatoes with an oil and vinegar dressing, or used to make homemade tomato or pizza sauce.

Bay leaves are very pungent and only 1/2 to 1 leaf is needed to flavor a medium sized stew. It adds flavor to soup stock, stews, or casserole.

Chives are one of the best known herbs and are a mild onion substitute. An appetizing spread can be made by adding chopped chives to cream cheese. Chives and sour cream as a topping for baked potatoes is the best known usage.

Dill is an easily grown annual plant which is used in relishes, fish sauces, or in making dill pickles. It is known as dill weed before the seed heads form.

Lemon Balm has lemon scented leaves which gives a lemon- mint flavor to soups, pudding, or cookies. It also gives added flavor in iced tea or fruit drinks.

Marjoram is sweeter and milder flavored than oregano. It makes an ordinary vegetable have a special flavor. Particulary green salads, bean dishes, or tomatoes. It is also good with dishes such as meat loaf, stew, or scrambled eggs.

Mint is a traditional American beverage ingredient. Orange or pineapple mint, regular mint, and lemon balm is a good combination for iced tea. Chopped mint leaves are good on peas, carrots, potatoes, and fish. Mint sauce with leg of lamb is an old favorite.

Oregano is most commonly associated with spaghetti sauce or pizza. It can also be a flavorful addition to beef or lamb stews, salads, or tomato juice. The addition of oregano to bland vegetables like zucchini makes it come alive.

Parsley is thought of by many as a garnish only. Due to its high vitamin C content, it should be added to foods whenever possible. Sprinkle it over boiled and buttered potatoes, fresh broiled fish, or meats and vegetables. Parsley is a basic ingredient of fine herbs which usually consists of a balen of parsley, chervil, tarrogon, and chives.

Parsley is also used for bouquet garni. This is sprigs of fresh herbs tied in a bunch or in cheese cloth and immersed in soup or stew while it is cooking. Parsley, bay leaf, and thyme are basic for bouquet garni, but any other herb may be added.

Rosemary is a very versatile herb. Either rub into or sprinkle on lamb, chicken, or pork before roasting. Rosemary leaves add sweeter flavor to fruit ades or punch. Fry small boiled potatoes in butter with rosemary leaves for a tasty and crunchy dish. Use sparingly at first because it has a pungent flavor.

Sage leaves added to poultry stuffing give it its characteristic flavor. Sage is a strong flavored herb and very aromatic. It can be used in sausage, liver, and cheese.

Savory is both a perennial and annual herb. Both savories are good used in hot or cold bean dishes, lentils, meats, or in poultry stuffing.

Tarragon is one of the most widely used herbs and is best known for use in sea food and chicken specialties. When used with fish it seems to remove most of the fishy taste.

Thyme is an easily grown perennial which adds flavor to clam or fish chowder. It is also good in stuffings for poultry or breast of lamb. For lamb shish-kabob, mix some oil, Worcestershire sauce, and thyme, and marinate lamb cubes for a few hours before broiling over the grill.

A sprig of rosemary or tarragon placed in the cavity of a chicken before roasting adds a subtle flavor to the chicken. A tablespoon of finely chopped lemon balm or lemon thyme leaves to the batter of lemon tea bread or pound cake enhances the zest of the lemon. One bay leaf in the soup kettle gives a new dimension to the entire pot. Fresh chopped parsley or sweet basil sprinkled over scrambled eggs or tomatoes add eye appeal as well as flavor.

Herb Salt
Cousin-Wanda Lee Maynard - Huntington, WV

1 c salt
1/2 c. fresh, chopped parsley
1/2 c. fresh chives in small snips
1/2 c. fresh, chopped basil

Mix all ingredients in a bowl for 5 minutes with your fingertips, bruising herb leaves, and rubbing salt into the herbs. Pour onto a shallow tray and let dry until brittle. Store in a shaker-top bottle and use it on a variety of foods. Very good on cottage cheese.

164

Almost Kaluha
Sister-in-law-Laura Avanelle Norris Callihan
Greenup, KY

3 c. water
3 c. sugar
10 tsp. instant coffee
4 tsp. vanilla
1 qt. vodka

Simmer water, sugar, and coffee covered for 1 hour. Cool, add vanilla and vodka - store in covered container for 30 days. Tumble once in a while so it won't crystalize.

Kiwifruit Daiquiri
Niece-Betty Stuart Darby Baird - Wadestown, WV

1 California kiwifruit, pared and sliced
2 or 3 tsp. sugar
1 T lime juice
1 or 2 oz. rum
1 drop green food color (optional)
8 ice cubes, crushed
2 California kiwifruit slices

Combine all ingredients except kiwifruit slices in blender container; blend unto smooth. Garnish edge of each glass with kiwifruit slice. Makes 2 servings.

Variation: Rum may be omitted.

Lemon Pepper
Cousin-Dottie Hatten - Morganfield, WV

3 T dried lemon peel
1/4 c. salt
1/4 c. coarsely ground black pepper
2 T garlic powder
1 T sugar (optional)

Powder the lemon peel in a mortar and pestle or blender. Combine lemon powder with remaining ingredients and use on steaks, lamb, pork chops, potatoes, or tomato juice.

Mead-Honey Wine
Nephew-Sam Darby - Normantown, WV

Ingredients (for one gallon):
3 lb. honey
3-1/2 qts. water
4 tsp. nutrient
2 tsp. citric acid
1/4 tsp. tannin
1/2 tsp. wine yeast
campden tablets

Equipment:
2 gal. plastic bucket
5 ft. of siphon hose
2 (1 gal.) glass jugs
airlock & cork
wooden spoon and 5 wine bottles and corks

Wash your plastic bucket and rinse it with campdon solution (8 tablets dissolved in 1 pt. water). Pour 1 gal. water barely warm to touch, in bucket and stir in 3 lbs. of honey. Add tannin, nutrient, citric acid and yeast, stir thoroughly and cover with a clean cloth. At room temp. fermentation should begin in a few hours and a foamy "head" will appear. Stir your brew each day until the "head" disappears, (usually in 2 to 3 days at room temp.)

Wash a gal. jug and rinse it with campden solution. Siphon the wine into the jug being careful not to disturb the sediment which has already formed on the bottom of the bucket. Fit the airlock, filled 1/3 full of campdon sol. into the drilled cork and place it in the jug. Store your wine away from strong light at a temp. of 60-70° for several months while it stops working and begins to clear. Add campden solution to the airlock if it evaporates.

When the wine looks fairly clear you will observe a good deal of the sediment. It is time to siphon the wine into the second gallon jug, leaving the sediment behind. Top the jug up with water if it is not full and replace airlock.

When your wine is stable and clear and has shown no activity for several months, it may be bottled. There are specific clearing agents which can can be added to a wine that remains hazy, but generally time and patience is the best medicine.

Have clean wine bottles which have been rinsed with campden solution ready, as well as corks which have been soaked in campden solution for two hours. Fill the bottles with the siphon to within 1 in. of the bottom of the cork. Insert corks with a corker and leave bottles upright for a day or two to observe that the corks stay seated. Store bottles on sides at 50°, if possible. Try to avoid storage where temperature changes frequently. Wait for several months or longer before using.

Homemade Pasta (Basic Recipe)

Cousin-Shirley Stewart - Ceredo, WV

2-1/3 c. all-purpose flour
2 egg whites
1 whole egg
1/4 c. water

In large bowl place 2 c. of the flour. Combine egg whites, whole egg, and water; add to flour and mix well. Sprinkle kneading surface with remaining flour. Turn dough out and knead for 8-10 minutes or until smooth and elastic. Cover; let rest 10 minutes. Divide dough into thirds. On lightly floured surface, roll each piece to a rectangle about 15 x 12 inches. If dough becomes too elastic, cover and let rest 5 more minutes. Using sharp knife, cut dough into strips of desired width. Lift and shake noodles to separate. Cook fresh pasta in large amount of boiling salted water for 5 minutes, Drain.

To store pasta, wrap with a clear plastic wrap or place in airtight container and refrigerate. Cook within 2 or 3 days. Makes about 1 lb. uncooked pasta. For Fettuccini: cut pasta dough into 1/4 inch-wide strips. For Linguini: cut pasta dough into 1/8 inch-wide strips. For Lasagna: cut pasta dough into 3 inch-wide strips.

Salt Substitute

Nephew-Walter Stuart (Ted) Keeney - Greenup, KY

1 T garlic powder
1/2 tsp. cayenne pepper
1 tsp. ground basil
1 tsp. ground marjoram
1 tsp. ground thyme
1 tsp. ground parsley
1 tsp. ground savory
1 tsp. ground mace
1 tsp. onion powder
1 tsp. black pepper
1 tsp. ground sage

Combine seasonings; pour into a salt shaker. Use in place of salt.

Seasoned Salt

Niece-Connie Keeney - Greenup, KY

3/4 c. salt
1 T coarsley ground black pepper
2 T dried parsley flakes, finely crushed
2 T onion powder
1/2 tsp. garlic powder

Combine ingredients. Use with steaks, chops, salads, soups or hot vegetables.

Apple Pie Spices

Cousin-Virgie Litchfield - Ceredo, WV

Use to complement dried apples in desserts, casseroles, or sauces. Freshly ground spices work the best, but you can substitute those already ground.

1/2 c freshly ground cinnamon
1 T freshly grated nutmeg
1 T freshly grated allspice
1 tsp. freshly ground cloves
1/2 tsp. freshly grated ginger

Blend spices to a powder using a blender or by hand. Store in an air-tight container with the following instructions: Use 1-1/4 tsp. apple pie spices to each 3 cups dried, sliced apples.

Homemade Maple Syrup

Cousin-Connie Stewart - Ceredo, WV

2 c. sugar
2 c. water
1 tsp. maple flavoring

Combine all in a saucepan. Bring to a boil and boil 5 minutes. Bottle: refrigerate. Makes 2-1/2 cups.

Sweetened Condensed Milk

Cousin-Frances Hilton Hunt - Bloomfield, KY

1 c. instant dry milk
2/3 c. sugar
1/3 c. boiling water
3 T melted oleo

Combine ingredients in electric blender. Process until smooth. Makes 1-1/4 cups. Recipe can be used in salads and desserts that call for sweetened condensed milk.

White Sauce

Niece-Melissa Liles - Greenup, KY

2 T butter or margarine
2 T flour
1/2 tsp. salt
1/8 tsp. pepper
2 c. milk

Uses: Cream soups, chowders, casseroles

Have flour, salt, and pepper measured and ready. Melt butter or margarine over low heat in small saucepan. Watch it, for it should just melt, not bubble and turn brown. (We like a wooden spoon for stirring).

Stir flour, salt and pepper quickly into melted butter, then cook, stirring all the time, just until it bubbles and is rich and buttery.

Stir in milk slowly. (This helps to keep sauce from lumping). Continue cooking and stirring from bottom of pan until sauce thickens and boils 1 minute.

Uncle Vernon Kendall's Dandelion Wine

Sister-in-law-Laura Avanelle Norris Callihan Greenup, KY

3 lemons, cut up
9 lbs. sugar
3 lbs. golden raisins
3 gal. water
1 qt. blossoms
1 cake yeast

Let water come to a boil with lemons, sugar and blossoms. Simmer for 20 minutes. Cool to luke warm; crumble in yeast. Let set 7 days, stir twice a day. Strain and add scalded raisins. Let set 5 weeks; stir once a day. Strain and bottle.

Cut off yellow blossoms only, can be stored in quart jar and refrigerated until you have enough. This is a good sipping wine.

Wine, Grape

Cousin-Scott Stewart - Ceredo, WV

1 qt. pure unsweetened grape juice
5 c. sugar
1/2 T dry yeast
25 kernels field corn (dry)
1 med. apple, coared, unpeeled and cut in chunks

Combine juice, sugar and yeast. Put apple and corn in a jug, then juice, yeast and sugar mixture. Put a balloon on for a cap with a rubber band. Place in a warm place for 5-7 weeks. Strain and bottle.

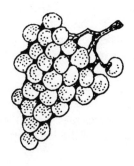

Whiskey (Moonshine)

Cousin-Faye Stewart Lester - Kenova, WV

1. Place shelled, whole corn in a container with a hole in the bottom. Cover with warm water and place a hot cloth over it. Add more water from time to time as it drains. Keep in a warm place until corn has 2 inch sprouts.

2. Dry corn and grind it into meal. Add boiling water and let stand in a warm place to ferment. This is called mash. Yeast may be added, 1/2 lb. per 50 gallons of mash, to speed up fermentation. Let mash stand until it quits working (bubbling). It is in the beer stage, and it is sour.

3. A special cooker, consisting of a top and bottom should be used to run off the whiskey. Put mash inside and paste the top on with "red dog chop" or some other paste so that if the fire gets too hot and pressure builds up the top will blow off. This prevents an explosion which might wreck the still.

4. A copper pipe or arm projects over to one side in the top of the cooker. This arm tapers down from 4-5 inch diameter to the same diameter as the worm which is usually one to one and a quarter inch. For the worm use a 20 ft. copper pipe and fill it with sand and stop up ends. This prevents the pipe from kinking when it is bent. Wrap the pipe around a post making it into a spiral. Take out sand and clean the pipe, attach firmly to the arm at one end. Run the worm through a barrel that can be kept full of cold running water, running the water in at the top and out an opening at the bottom. Place the bottom end of the worm in a container to catch the run-off.

5. Put a fire under the cooker. This causes the spirit to rise in vapor along with the steam. It goes into the arm and then the worm where the cold water causes condensation and the liquid is caught in the container at the end.

6. The first run-off is impure and weak and must be redistilled to rid it of impurities and water. Clean cooker before second run-off. The first will be too strong, but toward the last it will be weak, going from about 200 proof to 10 proof, but when mixed together it should be around 100 proof.

7. To test for right proof use a small glass vial. When the vial is tilted, small bubbles rise. When they set half above and half below the top of the liquid, then it is the right proof.

8. Filter through charcoal and the shine is ready for consumption.

Yogurt

Cousin-Nancy Fannin - Kenova, WV

1 qt. 2 % fat or skim milk, divided
1/2 c. instant nonfat dry milk
3 T plain yogurt, room temperature

Combine 1 c. milk and nonfat dry milk in a small bowl, stir until dry milk is dissolved. Pour remaining milk into saucepan; stir in dry milk mixture. Heat slowly over low heat to 190° to 210°. Remove from heat and cool to 110°. Remove protein film from top of milk and discard. Stir yogurt until smooth. Stir about 1/3 c. warm milk mixture into yogurt until well combined; then add yogurt mixture to milk in saucepan; mix well. Pour into large container or individual containers, leaving about 1/2 inch space at top. Cover; incubate 3 to 4 hours at a constant temperature of about 110°. Do not disturb. After 3 hours, gently shake to see if it is firm. If not, let stand 1 hour more and check again. Refrigerate at least 6 hours before serving. Yield: approximately 1 qt. Note: For whole milk yogurt, do not add dry milk. Follow directions given above.

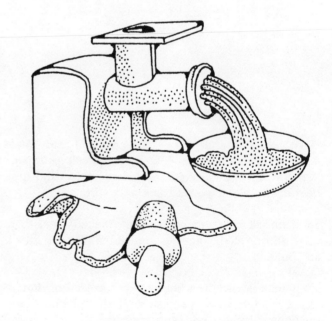

Liqueurs You Can Make At Home

Nephew-John Baird - Wadestown, WV

Liqueurs and cordials (the names are interchangable) are increasing in popularity and consumption today. They can be a pleasant after-dinner drink, or an elegant ingredient to add to desserts or to combine with fresh fruits. They are easy to make at home, with no special equipment needed, and a small amount makes a unique gift to close friends and relatives. (Cordials can definitely not be made for sale). The three basic ingredients are the alcohol base (usually vodka or sometimes brandy or rum), sugar for sweetness (either as a syrup or in granular form), and the flavor you choose. For fruit liqueurs, a white-sugar syrup is used; while for chocolate and coffee flavors, brown sugar is substituted for part of the white. All the ingredients except the spirits, are found in the supermarket. Keep the liqueurs in a cool, dark place (a kitchen cabinet or even the basement) to mellow and age. For gift-giving, there are myriad decorative bottles sold in gift, variety and department stores. If the bottles have cork stoppers, brush the corks and around the necks of the bottles with melted paraffin to prevent evaporation. For serving at home, you may wish to display your liqueur in your best crystal cordial bottle

Basic Sugar Syrup #1

Makes 3-3/4 c.
1 lemon
3 c. granulated sugar
2 c. water

Pare very thinly the bright-colored rind from the lemon (no white). Blot peel on paper toweling to remove any excess oil. Combine sugar, water and peel in a large saucepan; heat to boiling, stirring often. Lower heat, simmer for 5 minutes. Strain syrup into a glass container and cool to room temperature before preparing liqueurs.

Basic Sugar Syrup #2

Makes 3-1/2 c.
1-1/2 c. firmly packed brown sugar
1 c. granulated sugar
2 c. water

Combine brown and granulated sugars and water in a large saucepan. Heat to boiling, stirring often. Lower heat; simmer for 5 minutes. Pour syrup into a glass container and cool to room temperature before preparing liqueurs.

Anise Liqueur

Makes about 1-1/4 pts.
1-1/3 c. vodka
1-1/4 c. basic sugar syrup #1
2 tsp. vanilla
1 tsp. anise extract
yellow food coloring

Combine vodka, sugar syrup, vanilla, and anise extract in a 4-c. screw-top jar. Stir in just enough yellow food coloring to tint liquid a pale yellow. Close jar. Store in a cool, dark place for at least 1 week to age.

Apple Cinnamon Cream Liqueur

Makes about 1 qt.
1 (14 oz.) can sweetened condensed milk - NOT evaporated milk)
1 c. apple schnapps
1 c. whipping or coffee cream
4 eggs
1/2 tsp. ground cinnamon

In blender container, combine all ingredients; blend until smooth. Serve over ice. Garnish as desired. Store tightly covered in refrigerator up to 1 month. Stir before serving.

Cherry Bounce

1/2 lb. sugar cubes (about 1 c.)
1 qt. fresh tart cherries, stems removed
1 bottle (4/5 qt.)vodka

Place sugar and cherries in sterilized 2-qt container with tight-fitting lid. Pour vodka over cherries and sugar; shake. Store covered in cool dark place, shaking once a day for 1 week and then once a week for two months. Strain vodka; let stand 2 hours. Pour liqueur into sterilized jars, being careful not to disturb sediment. Makes about 3 cups. Traditionally served at Christmas.

Cherries from cherry bounce can be used again for an Easter drink, if desired. Pour 1 bottle (4/5 qt.) sauterne over cherries in 2-qt. glass container. Store covered in cool dark place, shaking once a day for 1 week and then once a week for 2 months. Strain; discard cherries. Place in clean jar or bottle.

Chocolate Liqueur

Makes about 1-1/4 pts.
1-1/3 c. vodka
1-1/4 c. basic sugar syrup #2
3 tsp. chocolate extract
2 tsp. vanilla extract

Stir in vodka, sugar syrup, chocolate extract and vanilla in a 4-c. screw-top jar until well blended. Close jar. Store in a cool, dark place for at least 1 week to age. Note: For Chocolate- Mint Liqueur, add 1/4 tsp. peppermint extract to above mixture.

Coffee Liqueur

Makes about 1-1/2 pts.
1-1/2 c. basic sugar syrup #2
1/4 c. instant coffee powder
1-1/3 c. vodka
2 tsp. vanilla

Stir sugar syrup and instant coffee until very smooth in a 2-c. measure. Pour into a 4-c. screw-top jar. Stir in vodka and vanilla. Close jar. Store in a cool, dark place for a minimum of 1 week to allow it to age.

Creme De Menthe

Makes about 1-1/4 pts.
1-1/3 c. vodka
1-1/4 c. basic sugar syrup #1
1/2 tsp. peppermint extract
2 tsp. vanilla
few drops green food coloring

Combine vodka, sugar syrup, peppermint extract and vanilla in a 4-c. screw-top jar; stir in just enough green food coloring to tint liquid a bright green. Close jar. Store in a cool, dark place for at least 1 week to age.

Daiquri Liqueur

Makes about 2 pts.
4 limes
3 c. light rum
1-1/2 superfine granulated sugar

Pare very thinly the bright-colored rind from the limes (no white). Blot peel on paper toweling to remove any excess oil. Put peel in a 4-c. screw-top jar. Add 2 c. of the rum. Close jar. Store in a cool, dark place for 2 days, or until the rum has absorbed the flavor and color of the peel. Remove peel; add sugar; shake vigorously until sugar dissolves. Add remaining 1 c. rum and stir until liquid becomes clear. Close jar and store in cool, dark place at least 1 week to age.

Orange Liqueur

Makes about 2 pts.
3 naval oranges
3 c. vodka
1-1/2 c. superfine granulated sugar

Pare very thinly the bright-colored rind from the oranges (no white). Blot peel on paper toweling to remove any excess oil. Put peel in a 4-c. screw-top jar. Add 2 cups of the vodka. Close jar. Store in a cool, dark place for 2 days, or until vodka has absorbed the flavor and color of the peel. Remove peel; add sugar; shake vigorously until sugar dissolves. Add remaining 1 c. vodka and stir until liquid becomes clear. Close jar; store in cool, dark place at least 1 week to age.

Raspberry Liqueur

Makes about 1-1/4 pts.
1-1/3 c. vodka
3/4 c. basic sugar syrup #1
1/2 c. bottled red raspberry syrup
2 tsp. vanilla

Combine vodka, sugar syrup, raspberry syrup and vanilla in a 4-c. screw-top jar. Close jar. Store in a cool, dark place at least 1 week to age.

Strawberry Liqueur

Makes about 1-1/4 pts.
1-1/3 c. vodka
1-1/4 c. basic sugar syrup #1
2 tsp. strawberry extract
2 tsp. vanilla
Few drops red food coloring

Combine vodka, sugar syrup, strawberry extract and vanilla in a 4-c. screw-top jar. Stir in just enough red food coloring to tint liquid a bright red. Close jar. Store in a cool, dark place for at least 1 week to age.

Coffee Flavored Liqueur

Nephew-Sam Darby - Normantown, WV

Into 2-1/2 c. boiling water dissolve 4 c. sugar and 2 oz. instant coffee. Add a fifth of vodka, 1/2 pt. brandy and 1 whole vanilla bean. Mix all together and pour into a large bottle or gallon jug and store three to four weeks. Remove vanilla bean. To serve; pour over chipped ice or serve as an after dinner drink in a glass. May also be served topped with sweet cream.

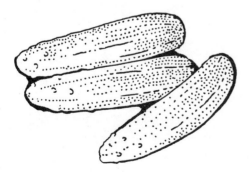

Pickling Spices

Niece-Theresa Darby - Normantown, WV

Mixed Pickling Spices

Use this mixture in sweet pickles or flavored vinegar for use in sweet and sour dishes.
1 T each of dill seed, fenugreek, mustard seed, celery seed, and coriander.
1 tsp. each of chopped ginger root and whole allspice.
1/2 tsp. each of black peppercorns, cloves and cut chilis.
2 whole bay leaves.
1 stick cinnamon, broken into pieces.

Dill Pickling Spices

This mix is excellent in salad dressing and tartar sauce.
4 T dill weed or seed (or a combination of the two)
1 T peppercorns
1 tsp. each of corainder seed, allspice, mustard seed and minced garlic
1/2 tsp. cut chili

Curried Pickling Spices

Use whole to pickle cucumbers, cauliflower of zucchini or grind to a powder for use in curry dishes.
4 T coriander seed
1 T each of celery seed and mustard seed
4 tsp. each of cumin and tumeric
2 tsp. each of cardamon seeds, mace pieces, peppercorns and chopped ginger root
1 stick cinnamon, broken into pieces
1 tsp. each of cut chilis, whole cloves and allspice

171

Pickling Spice II
Niece-Freda Keeney - Greenup, KY

1 T each of dill seed, mustard seed, whole coriander and
celery seed
1 tsp. dried ginger root, diced
1 tsp. whole allspice
1 cinnamon stick, 1 inch long, broken into pieces
2 whole bay leaves, crumbled
1/2 tsp. black pepper corns
1/2 tsp. hot red pepper flakes
1/2 tsp. whole cloves

Combine all ingredients. Use in making pickles.

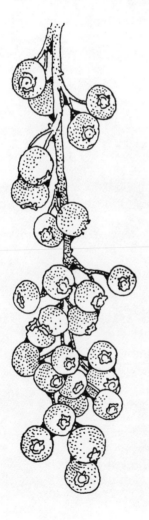

Just For Fun

Jared's Best Mud Pie
Cousin-Jared Arnold - Portsmouth, OH

Ingredients:
1. Best outfit (preferably light colored)
2. Sunday school shoes
3. Grandma's new pie plate
4. Papa's trowel
5. Large quantity of dirt (black)
6. Enough water to moisten

Splash water liberally over dry ingredients. Stir well with hands, occasionally wiping hands on pants. Knead to gooey consistancy. Pat lightly into pie plate and even out with trowel. Set in sun to dry 1-2 hours.

garnishes: Roses from Granny's garden, Papa's watch, Mommy's earrings.

Preparation Time: 15 minutes prior to leaving for Sunday school.

Play Dough
Cousin-Michael Steele - Dayton, OH

1 c. flour
1 c. sugar
1/2 c. water
food colorings

Mix above ingredients adding desired colors. This is fun

Meats

Beef

Barbecue Sauce
Seven Layer Casserole
Liver and Bacon
Basic Pot Roast
Corned Beef Casserole
Beef Roll Ups
Steak and Mango
Baked Steak and Gravy
Steak and Kidney Pie
Round Steak with Mushroom Gravy
Skillet Steak N' Potatoes
Crock Pot Steak
Stir-fry Steak and Vegetables (Wok)
Red Flannel Hash
Sweet and Sour Beef Ribs

Ground Beef

Barbecued Sauerkraut
Cabbage Rolls
Colorado Pie
Hamburger Pie
Hamburger Stroganoff
Lasagna
Meat Balls and Sauce
Sweet and Sour Meat Balls
Meat Loaf I
Meat Loaf II
Ribbon Meat Loaf
Sunday Meat Loaf
Meat Loaf (with boiled eggs)
Meatballs
Meaty Macaroni and Cheese
Pizza
Pizza Casserole
Up-side Pizza
Seven Layer Casserole
Sloppy Joes
Baked Spaghetti
Fancy Spaghetti
Spaghetti Sauce
Stuffed Green Peppers
Zippy Beef Casserole

Lamb

Barbecued Lamb Chops
Cheesy Topped Lamb Chops
To Bake or Roast a Leg of Lamb
Leg of Lamb, Buckingham Glaze
Lemon Lamb Marinade
Lamb Stew
Lamb-Yam Stew

Pork

Bacon, Sauerkraut and Potato
Barbecue Sauce (for pork)
Barbecue Sauce (for spareribs)
Barbecue Ribs
Chinese Pork
Ham 'N' Broccoli
Baked Ham in Beer
Country Ham with Buttermilk Biscuits
Fried Country Ham and Red Eye Gravy
How to Sugar Cure a Ham
Grandma's Ham and Apple Dumplings
Grilled Ham Steak with Sweet Potatoes and
Pineapple Wedges
Ham Loaf
Ham with Raisin Sauce
Liver and Onions
Pork Chop Bake
Pork Chops and Rice I
Pork Chops and Rice II
Baked Pork Chops With Carrots and Potatoes
Pork Chop Vegetable Skillet
Pork Roast (or ribs) and Sauerkraut
Marinated Pork Roast
Slow Cooked Pork Roast
Glazed Smoked Sausages
Sausage and Cabbage
Sausage Breakfast
Sausage-Rice Casserole
Souse

Meats

Poultry and Stuffings

Chicken-Bacon Nuggets
Chicken and Beef
Chicken and Broccoli Casserole I
Chicken and Broccoli Casserole II
Chicken 'N' Broccoli Crepes
Chicken and Feather Dumplings
Feather Dumplings
Chicken and Noodles
Chicken and Rice
Chicken and Mushroom Sauce
Chicken Casserole
Fried Chicken
Fried Chicken Breasts
Grandma's Fried Chicken and Cream Gravy
Jayant's Boned, Fried Chicken
Chicken Supreme
Continental Chicken

Chicken Divan
Chicken and Wild Rice Casserole
Hot Chicken Salad
Wrapped Chicken
Pineapple-Glazed Cornish Hen with
  Wild Rice Stuffing
Old Fashion Roast Duckling
Goose with Fruit Stuffing
Cider Baked Turkey Breast
Turkey-Noodle Casserole
Skillet Turkey in Cream
Roast Turkey
Turkey Souffle
Country Corn Bread Sausage Dressing
Spinach Almondine Stuffing
Zucchini Dressing

Young Grandfather Nathan Hylton

Jesse's grandfather - Nathan Hylton. 90 years old - Lived to be 92.

Under that yellow sun of yesterday
That shone in Aprils of forgotten past,
Those heavy muscled legs stepped on the clay
That has converted them to it at last.
Those heavy legs and arms and shoulders stout
Followed the cattle through the root-bound field.
The crust broke open and the loam turned out,
The dead-leaf loam that gave the heaviest yield.
Under the yellow sun and furrows done
Men learned that mighty strength lay in the land,
That light was sweet from the almighty sun,
And from the first, nature was in command.
Under the yellow sun they leave their past;
It was a shame their bodies could not last.

*Stuart, Jesse, *Album of Destiny*, (New York: E. P. Dutton & Co., Inc., 1944), p.33.

175

L to R. Jesse's Aunt Mary Hilton Johnson, his Uncle Jesse Hilton, his mother Martha Hilton Stuart and his Uncle, Jiles Hilton

Jesse's Uncle Martin Hilton

Autumn has come upon us; summer and spring
Have passed into the golden wind-strewn leaves;
And death knells for the spring and summer ring
Above us in the wind among the leaves.
We feel the stir of dead leaves in our blood,
The wailing wind is music to create in us the mood
Arriving only with the passing years.
Autumn has come upon us and we stand
Together here, not as we were in spring,
When we like flowers were blooming on the land
And carefree as a white moth on the wing.
Autumn has come upon us; can't you see
Autumn has changed the looks of you and me?

*Stuart, Jesse, *Album of Destiny*, (New York: E. P. Dutton & Co., Inc., 1944), p. 117.

Barbecue Sauce

Brother-James Stuart - Greenup, KY

1/2 c. Wesson oil
1/2 c. chopped onion
1/3 c. lemon juice
3/4 c. tomato catsup
3/4 c. water
3 T Worcestershire sauce
2 T prepared mustard
2 tsp. salt
1/2 tsp. pepper
3 T sugar

Cook onion till soft in Wesson oil. Add other ingredients and simmer 15 minutes. Makes enough sauce to baste and serve 4 cut up chickens. Also good with hot-dogs, hamburgers, steaks, and other favorites. Note: Recipe may be doubled and placed in a container for freezing.

Seven Layer Casserole

Cousin-Susan Ellington - Louisville, KY

1 c. uncooked rice
1 can whole kernel corn, drained
salt & pepper
1 (8 oz.) can tomato sauce
1/2 c. water
1/2 c. finely chopped onion (optional)
3/4 lb. ground beef, uncooked
salt & pepper
1/2 c. green pepper, finely chopped (optional)
1 (8 oz.) can tomato sauce
1/4 c. water
4 strips bacon, cut in half

Preheat oven to 350 degrees. Combine ingredients in layers in the order listed above in a 2 quart baking dish. Bake covered at 350 degrees for 1 hour. Uncover and bake about 30 minutes longer.

Liver and Bacon

Niece-Freda Keeney - Greenup, KY

Calves liver is the best. Slice liver 1/4 inch thick. Pour hot water over liver and let it stand a few minutes to clear it of blood, then dry on paper towel. Take 1/2 lb. of bacon and fry until crisp; lay on platter and keep hot. Dredge liver in flour and season with salt and pepper. Fry the liver to a nice brown in the same pan. Serve with a slice of bacon on the top of each slice of liver.

Basic Pot Roast

Sister-in-law-Lucille Norris - Greenup, KY

Rub roast with seasoned flour, allowing 1 tsp. salt for each pound of meat. Or, omit flour, just season meat. Brown meat on both sides in small amount of hot shortening in heavy skillet, allowing 12 to 20 minutes for browning. Add 1 c. water, tomato or vegetable juice or bouillon and 1/2 c. sliced onions. Cover tightly, simmer over low heat or cook in moderate oven (350°) until meat is fork-tender, about 1 hour per pound. Turn meat occasionally; add more water if needed. Carrots and potatoes (peeled and cut in large pieces) may be placed around roast last 1/2 hour of cooking, if desired.

Corn Beef Casserole

Sister-in-law-Lucille Norris - Greenup, KY

1 can corn beef
1 (8 oz.) pkg. noodles, prepared
1/4 lb. sharp cheese
1 can cream of chicken soup
1/2 c. chopped onion (optional)
1-1/2 c. milk

Combine above ingredients in a casserole and top with buttered bread crumbs. Bake at 350° for 45 minutes.

Beef Roll-ups

Niece-Betty S. Baird - Wadestown, WV

Round steak, 8 pcs. (approx. 6 x 4 inches each, pounded
  to 1/4")
3 T butter
3 T salad oil
2 (10 1/2 oz.) cans beef broth
2 c. red wine
2 bay leaves
1 lb. small white onions, peeled
1 (8oz.) pkg. fresh mushrooms

For filling:
4 T butter
1 1/2 c. onion, chopped
1/2 c. celery, chopped
2 tsp. garlic, minced
1/3 c. green pepper, chopped
2 c. parsley, chopped
2 tsp. salt
2 tsp. white pepper
1 tsp. black pepper
1 tsp. dry mustard
1 tsp. ground cayenne pepper

To make filling: Combine first five filling ingredients and
cook until onion is tender. Remove from heat and add
remaining filling ingredients. Mix well.

On each slice of pounded steak, place 1/4 c. filling, fold
over the ends and tie with string. Mix oil and butter in
Dutch oven (or electric skillet) and brown beef bundles.
Add wine, beef broth and bay leaves. Bring to boil, reduce
heat and simmer for 1 hour. Add onions and mushrooms,
simmer until tender. Lift out beef bundles, place on
platter and remove strings. Allow broth and onion mixture to cook uncovered to reduce liquid, if necessary.
When liquid thickens, pour over bundles. You may use a
little flour (sprinkle in some Wondra) if too much liquid
remains.

Steak and Mango

Niece-Ellen Keeney Douglas - Lexington, KY

2 lb. top round steak
1 green med. mango
1 large onion
1 small can mushrooms
1/3 c. Worcestershire sauce

Cut steak bite size; brown in oil and drain. Add vegetables
cut to your liking. Add Worcestershire sauce. Cover and
simmer until vegetables are tender. Serves 4.

Baked Steak and Gravy

Cousin-June Stewart Haney - Huntington, WV

6 to 8 pieces of cubed steak
flour
salt and pepper
shortening or oil

Dip steak in flour covering both sides well. Brown steak
in skillet in heated shortening or oil. Salt and pepper each
piece. Remove steak from skillet and place in 9 x 13"
baking pan. Combine flour, drippings, and hot water in
skillet. Cook and stir until mixture starts to thicken. Pour
over steak in pan. Cook at 375° for 1-1/2 to 2 hours. If
browner gravy is desired, add Worcestershire sauce or
Kitchen Bouquet gravy mix, towards end of cooking time.

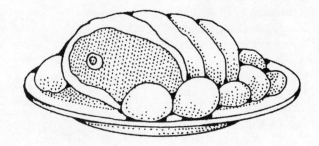

Steak and Kidney Pie (single crust goes on top)

Brother-James Mitchell Stuart - Greenup, KY

1-1/2 lb. round steak
3 lamb kidneys
flour
salt and pepper
2 T butter or margarine
1 large onion, minced
1 c. boiling water
1 T Worcestershire
pastry for one 10" crust
milk

Trim fat from round steak. Cut meat into 3/4 inch cubes. Remove skin, fat, and tubes from kidneys. Cut kidneys in 1/2 inch cubes. Dredge steak and kidney cubes in 3 T flour mixed with 1 tsp. salt and 1/4 tsp. pepper. Melt butter in heavy pan. Add onion and brown lightly. Remove onion and brown meat cubes, a few at a time, in remaining drippings. Add onion, boiling water, and Worcestershire. Cover tightly. Simmer gently 30 minutes, or until meats are tender. Mix 2 T flour in a little cold water and add to gravy to thicken. Pour mixture into 10" pie pan. Invert a small funnel or custard cup in center to support crust. Roll out pastry and cover pie. Cut small slits in pastry to allow steam to escape. Trim edge of pastry to rim of pie pan. Brush pastry with milk. Bake in hot oven (425°) about 30 minutes. 6 servings.

Round Steak with Mushroom Gravy

Niece-Shirley Stuart - Greenup, KY

2 lb. round steak
1 can mushroom soup

Trim steak and cut into small pieces. Roll steak pieces in flour and brown in skillet. Put browned steak into pressure cooker. Add soup and one can of water. Cook for 15-20 minutes.

Skillet Steak 'N' Potatoes

Nephew-Phillip K. Douglas - Lexington, KY

1-1/2 lbs. boneless round steak, 1/2" thick
1/4 c. all-purpose flour
2 tsp. salt
1/4 tsp. pepper
2 T vegetable oil
1 (10 1/2 oz.) can beef broth, undiluted
1 c. water
4 med. potatoes, thinly sliced
2 med. onions, thinly sliced
chopped fresh parsley (optional)

Trim excess fat from steak and cut into serving-size pieces. Combine flour, salt and pepper. Dredge steak in flour mixture. Brown steak in hot oil. Add broth and water, cover and simmer 30 minutes. Turn meat and top with potatoes and onions. Cover and simmer 20 minutes or until potatoes are done. Sprinkle with parsley, if desired. 6 servings.

Crock Pot Pepper Steak

Cousin-Mahala Hilton - Frankfort, KY

2 lbs. round steak
2 green peppers cut into strips
2 onions, sliced
1 c. beef broth
1/4 c. soy sauce
1/2 tsp. ground ginger
1/2 tsp. garlic powder

Cut meat into cubes or strips. Place 1/2 of the steak, pepper, and onions into pot; pour into 1/2 of broth mixture. Add the rest of the steak, pepper, onions and broth mixture. Cover and cook on low setting 8-10 hours; high setting 3-4 hours. Make 6 servings.

Stir-fry Steak and Vegetables (WOK)

Niece-Shirley Stuart - Greenup, KY

2 lbs. top sirloin steak
1 pkg. Japanese style frozen veg.
1 pkg. Chinese style frozen veg.
peanut oil
soy sauce
garlic salt
cooked rice

Trim and slice steak into small strips. (About 2 in. long and 1/8 thick). Heat 2 T of peanut oil in wok. Fry quickly, a small amount at a time, stirring often. Season meat with soy sauce and garlic salt during frying. Keep steak on a warm platter. Cook and stir vegetables, one pkg. at a time. Add more oil and seasoning. Serve over hot rice.

Red Flannel Hash

Niece-Eileen McCarten Nelson - Greenup, KY

The beets in this New England dish are reminiscent of the Long John red flannel underwear worn eight months a year up East. Red Flannel Hash was a favorite quick dinner for the family while I was growing up. It also works well as a camp meal when the fish aren't biting.

1 can corned beef, cut into cubes
1 T butter or oil
3 medium potatoes
2 small onions, halved and sliced lengthwise
1 can sliced beets, drained
1/4 c. milk
2-3 squirts of Worcestershire sauce
salt and pepper to taste

Scrub and slice potatoes. Steam or fry potatoes until just tender. Drain the water from the potatoes if you steamed them. Saute the onions with butter in a large skillet until the onions are translucent. Add corned beef, potatoes, beets, milk and Worcestershire sauce to the onions. Gently stir the hash until the ingredients are well combined. Cook over low heat until the hash is hot. Adjust the seasonings. Serve Red Flannel Hash with biscuits and a dark green leafy vegetable or salad.

Sweet and Sour Beef Ribs

Cousin-Jimmie L. Stewart, Jr., - Kenova, WV

3 lbs. beef short ribs
1 c. sliced onion
1 clove garlic
1 sm. bay leaf
3 T brown sugar
1/4 c. raisins
1/8 tsp. pepper
1-1/2 c. hot water
1/4 c. vinegar
1/3 c. catsup
1 tsp. salt
small can crushed pineapple

Wipe short ribs with damp cloth. Cut into serving pieces. Remove excess fat. Dredge in seasoned flour and brown well on all sides in hot fat in skillet. Remove ribs - saute onions and garlic. Combine remaining ingredients. Pour over ribs. Cover; simmer 2 to 2-1/2 hours or until tender. Serve over rice.

Ground Beef

Barbecued Sauerkraut

Cousin-Beverly Jane Benner Murphy - Lucasville, OH

1 lb. ground beef
1 med. onion, chopped
1 med. can kraut, drained
1 c. brown sugar
2 c. tomato juice

Brown beef and onion. Drain. Add kraut, brown sugar, and tomato juice. Bake uncovered at 350° for 1 hour. Surprisingly delicious.

Cabbage Rolls

Cousin-Betty Adkins Hotopp - Dayton, OH

1 lg. head cabbage
1 lg. jar sauerkraut
1 lb. sausage
1 lb. lean ground round
1 lg. onion, chopped
2 eggs, beaten
2 cans tomato sauce
2 c. Minute Rice
salt

Cut leaves from cabbage and wash. Cut out the hard part of vein from each leaf. Heat water to boiling in a large pan. Put cabbage leaves into boiling water a few at a time until wilted. Remove leaves from water and place in colander. Run cold water over the leaves to cool.

Mix sausage, ground round, onion, eggs, rice and salt thoroughly. Roll into meat balls. Roll each meat ball up in a cabbage leaf and secure with toothpicks. Place in a large pan and pour one can of tomato sauce over the meatballs. Spread the sauerkraut over the sauce and pour the remaining tomato sauce over all layers. Bake at 350 ° until cabbage is tender.

Colorado Pie

Niece-Martha Stuart Wheeler - Knoxville, TN

Prepare pastry for 2 crust pie, using 1 tsp. onion salt in pastry if desired. Line 9" pie pan with half the pastry. Roll out top crust.

Brown in skillet:
1 lb. ground beef
1/2 c. chopped onion

Stir in:
1 T sugar
1/4 tsp. pepper
1/2 tsp. salt
2 c. cooked mixed vegetables, drained
1 (10 oz.) can tomato soup

Pour into pastry-lined pan, add top crust and cut slits in the crust to allow steam to escape. Bake at 400° for 25 minutes. Serves 4-6.

Hamburger Pie

Cousin-Katherine Stewart Martin - Racine, WS

1 lb. ground beef
1 egg
1 tsp. salt
1/8 tsp. pepper
1 T instant minced onion
1/4 c. catsup
1 c. milk
potato buds instant puffs (enough for 8 servings)
1/2 c. shredded sharp cheddar cheese

Preheat oven to 350°. Mix the first seven ingredients with 1-1/2 c. of instant puffs (dry). Spread into ungreased pie pan, 9 x 1-1/2". Bake uncovered 35 to 40 min.

Prepare remaining puffs as directed on pkg. for 4 servings. Top baked meat loaf with potatoes; sprinkle with cheese. Bake 3 to 4 minutes longer until cheese melts. 4 to 5 servings.

Hamburger Stroganoff

Cousin-Katherine Stewart Martin - Racine, WS

1 lb. ground beef
1/2 c. onion
1/4 c. butter or margarine
2 T flour
1 tsp. salt
1 clove garlic, minced
1/4 tsp. pepper
1 can (4 oz.) mushroom stems and pieces, drained
1 can (10 1/2 oz.) condensed cream of chicken soup
1 c. dairy sour cream
Poppy seed noodles

In large skillet, cook meat and onion in butter until brown. Stir in flour, salt, garlic, pepper, and mushrooms; cook 5 minutes, stirring constantly. Stir in soup; heat to boiling, stirring constantly. Reduce heat; simmer uncovered 10 minutes. Stir in sour cream; heat throughly. Serve over poppy noodles.

Poppy Seed Noodles:

Cook 8 oz. medium noodles as directed on pkg. Drain. Stir in 2 tsp. poppy seed and 1 T butter.

Lasagna

Sister-in-law-Betty Stuart - Greenup, KY

1-1/2 to 2 lb. ground beef
1 c. minced onion
2 tsp. salad oil
1 tsp. garlic powder
1 tsp. salt
1 qt. Italian tomatoes
2 (6 oz.) cans tomato sauce
1 tsp. oregano
dash pepper
1/2 lb. lasagna noodles
3/4 lb. Ricotta or cottage cheese
1/2 lb. Mozarella cheese
1/2 c. Parmesan cheese

Saute onions and garlic in oil; add beef and salt. Brown in skillet. Combine tomatoes, tomato sauce, oregano and pepper in pot; add meat and cook slowly for 2 hours or until thick. Cook and drain noodles. Put in baking dish in layers; 1st layer-sauce; 2nd layer-noodles; 3rd layer-cheese. Repeat and finish with a layer of sauce. Bake 50 minutes at 350°.

Meat Balls and Sauce

Cousin-Marie Hilton Ellington - Ashland, KY

1 lb. ground beef
1 tsp. salt
1 tsp. onion salt
1/2 c. all bran (1 minute oats)
1/2 c. milk (can substitute V-8 juice or tomato juice)
1 egg
2 T Worcestershire Sauce
1/2 tsp. sage or poultry seasonings

Mix ingredients and shape into 2" balls. Place in greased casserole dish; cover with sauce and bake for about 1 hour at 350°. I usually double this recipe and freeze one casserole. Just put into oven frozen and bake a little longer.

Sauce:
1/2 c. catsup
1/2 c. water
1 T sugar
1 T vinegar
2 T Worcestershire sauce

Sweet and Sour Meat Balls

Cousin-James Stewart - E. Liverpool, OH

1 pkg. Lipton's dry onion soup mix
2 lb. ground beef (chuck)
2 eggs
1/2 c. water

Stir soup mix, water, and eggs together. Add ground beef, mix well and form into balls.

Sauce:
1 (16 oz.) can sauerkraut, rinse and drain
1 (8 oz.) can plain cranberry sauce
3/4 c. water
1/3 c. brown sugar
3/4 c. chili sauce

Mix ingredients together. Pour 1/2 of the sauce into a large baking dish or casserole. Place meat balls on top and cover with remaining sauce. Cover and bake at 350° for 20 minutes, then remove cover and bake for an additional 20 minutes. Serve over hot rice.

Meat Loaf I

Cousin-Lola Hilton - Moraine, OH

1 lb. ground round
1/2 lb. ground pork
1 lb. ground chuck
2 eggs
2/3 c. crackers, crushed
2 T barbeque sauce
2 T. veg. flakes
1 c. tomatoes
1 small onion
1 tsp. salt
1/4 tsp. pepper
1 small green pepper

Mix well and bake in greased pan for 1 1/2 hours at 325°.

Meat Loaf II

Niece-Kathy Abdon - Greenup, KY

1 lb. hamburger
1/2 green pepper, chopped
1 med. onion, chopped
1 egg
1 sm. can tomato sauce
2 slices of bread, cubed
salt and pepper to taste

Mix all ingredients well. Form into a loaf. Top with catsup and bake at 450° for 45 minutes, covered. Bake for an additional 15 minutes uncovered. (Tastes good made in iron skillet).

Ribbon Meat Loaf

Cousin-Katherine Stewart Martin - Racine, WS

3 slices soft bread, torn into small pieces
1 c. milk
1 lb. ground beef
1/2 lb. ground lean pork
1 egg yolk
1/2 c. minced onion
1 1/4 tsp. salt
1/4 tsp. pepper
1/4 tsp. dry mustard
1/4 tsp. sage
1/4 tsp. celery salt
1/4 tsp garlic salt
1 T Worcestershire sauce

Heat oven to 350°. Stir together bread and milk; mix in remaining ingredients except filling. Pat one half of meat mixture into greased loaf pan, 9 x 5 x 3". Cover with cheese filling. Top with remaining meat mixture. Bake 1 hour 30 minutes. 6 to 8 servings.

Cheese Filling:
1 egg white, slightly beaten
1 T water
2 slices soft bread, torn into pieces
4 oz. crumbled or shredded blue cheese

Combine egg white and water; toss lightly with bread crumbs and cheese.

Sunday Meat Loaf

Cousin-Linda Stewart Spence-Huntington, WV

1 lb. whole hog sausage (hot)
2 lbs. ground beef
2 eggs
1-1/2 cups crushed cornflakes
1 small can tomato sauce
1 med. onion (chopped)

In a large mixing bowl blend sausage and ground beef together with hands as if kneading dough. Add eggs and gradually add corn flakes, onion and all but 1/4 c. of tomato sauce. After ingredients are well blended shape in loaf pan and bake at 375° for 1 1/2 hours. During last 15 minutes of baking time spread remaining tomato sauce over top of meat loaf and continue baking.

Meat Loaf (with boiled eggs)

Cousin-Ethel Hilton-Raceland, KY

1-1/2 lbs. ground beef
1 egg, slightly beaten
1 c. bread crumbs
1/2 c. milk
1-1/2 tsp. pepper
1 T Worcestershire sauce
3 hard boiled eggs (shelled)

Mix above ingredients except hard boiled eggs. Put a layer of the mixture in a loaf pan. Place the eggs on the mixture so they will slice as the meat loaf is sliced. Cover eggs with rest of meat mixture. Spread with catsup and bake for about 1 1/2 hours at 350°. This was always a favorite of the family.

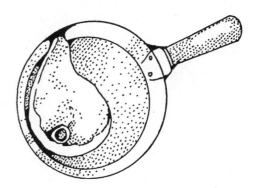

Meatballs

Niece-Kathy Abdon-Greenup, KY

1 egg, beaten
1/2 c. tomato juice
1 T sugar
3 slices light bread, cubed
1 lb. ground beef
1/6 tsp. black pepper
1 tsp. salt
1/2 tsp. chili powder

Mix above ingredients well and form into medium size balls. Brown lightly in oil. Then simmer until meat is well done in the following sauce.

Sauce:
1/2 c. tomato juice
1/4 c. sugar
1/4 c. plain barbecue sauce
1/4 tsp. red chili powder

Meaty Macaroni and Cheese

Niece-Freda Kenney - Greenup, KY

2 c. elbow macaroni (uncooked)
1 lb. ground beef
1/2 c. chopped onion
1/2 c. sliced celery
1 T butter
1-3/4 c. tomato sauce with tomato bits, (15 oz. can)
1 tsp. salt
1 tsp. pepper
1 c. shredded cheddar cheese (4 oz.)

Cook macaroni according to package directions; drain. Brown beef, onion, and celery in butter in large skillet; drain off excess fat. Stir in tomato sauce, salt, and pepper. Combine with macaroni and pour into 2 qt. casserole. Top with shredded cheese. Bake at 350° for 25 minutes or until hot and bubbly. 4 to 6 servings.

Pizza

Niece-Ruth Nelson - Greenup, KY

Crust:
1 c. lukewarm water
1 pkg. yeast
1 egg, beaten
1 tsp. sugar
1 tsp. salt
1 T shortening or oil
3 c. all-purpose flour or bread flour

Dissolve yeast in water and let stand 5 minutes. Then stir in sugar, salt, egg, and shortening; blend well. Add 1-1/2 c. all-purpose flour or bread flour. Beat until smooth. Add another 1-1/2 c. flour. If necessary use more flour to make the dough just barely firm enough to handle. Knead until smooth. Divide the dough into thirds. Knead each piece into a ball. Flatten, then pull and stretch gently to fit a 9 inch cake tin, lightly greased. Press up around the edges to make a slight rim. Let rise 15 minutes. Brush lightly with olive oil (any oil will do).

Sauce:
1 (16 oz.) can whole peeled tomatoes
1 (8 oz.) can tomato paste
1/4 tsp. garlic powder

Combine ingredients in blender and spread evenly over pizza dough. Sprinkle with oregano and basil, then top with grated Parmesan cheese.

Cover with any or all of the following:
browned ground beef
ham
pepperoni
mushrooms
grated Mozzarella cheese
anchovies - the list is endless.

Bake 25 minutes at 425°. Makes three 9-inch pizzas.

Pizza Casserole

Cousin-Mary Catherine Stewart Martin - Racine, WS

1-1/2 to 2 lb. hamburger (browned)
1 lg. can tomato sauce
1 sm. can tomato paste with 1/2 can water added
2 pkgs. cooked Creamets
1 tsp. garlic salt
1 tsp. oregano
salt and pepper to taste

Mix above ingredients in cake pan, cover with package of shredded pizza cheese and sprinkle Parmesian over this. Cover with foil. Bake 45 minutes at 350° - uncover and bake another 15 minutes.

Up-side Pizza

Cousin-Anne Hilton Short - Forestville, MD

2 lb. lean ground beef
2 lg. eggs, slightly beaten
1 jar (15 1/2 oz.) pizza or spaghetti sauce
2 c. shredded Cheddar cheese (8 oz.)
8 oz. Mozzarella cheese, sliced
1 can (8 oz.) refrigerated cresent dinner rolls

Heat oven to 350°. Have a 13 x 9 x 2 inch baking pan ready. Brown beef in a large skillet over medium heat, breaking up meat with a wooden spoon. Remove from heat; drain off excess fat and let stand 3 to 5 minutes to cool slightly. Add all but 1 T of the eggs to beef, then stir in sauce until well blended. Spread into ungreased baking pan. Sprinkle with Cheddar and arrange Mozzarella on top. For crust, unroll dough on a lightly floured surface. Firmly press edges and perforations to seal. Roll to form a 13 x 9 x 2 inch rectangle. Place over cheese and brush with reserved beaten egg. Bake 20 minutes or until beef mixture is hot and crust well browned. Let stand 5 minutes before cutting into squares. Makes 8 regular or 12 buffet servings.

Seven Layer Casserole

Cousin-Mary Beth Stewart Martin - Racine, WS

In Baking Dish, Place
1 c. uncooked rice
1/2 c. chopped onion
1 can whole kernel corn and liquid
1 lb. ground beef, browned and drained
salt and pepper to taste
1 can tomato sauce
bacon

Bake for 1 -1/2 hours at 350°.

Sloppy Joes

Cousin-Marie Hilton Ellington - Ashland, KY

1 lb. ground beef
onion (optional)
1 tsp. salt
1/8 tsp. pepper
2 T flour
1 T Worcestershire sauce
3/4 c. tomato sauce

Cook the above until meat looses color. Sprinkle flour over meat mixture. Add Worcestershire sauce and tomato sauce. Simmer until meat is cooked. Serve on hamburger buns. Can be doubled.

Baked Spaghetti

Cousin-Norma Jean Pennington Darnell - Greenup, KY

4 T butter
3 or 4 medium onions
1 lb. ground beef
1 green pepper, cut fine
1 qt. or more tomatoes
8 oz. spaghetti
1 tsp. salt
pepper to taste
1/2 lb. grated cheese

Cook spaghetti and drain. Cook onions in butter until well browned. Add beef, seasoning, green peppers, and tomatoes. Then add spaghetti and cook until mixture thickens. Add cheese and pour into a greased pan. Bake at 300° for 30 minutes. This freezes well.

Fancy Spaghetti
Sister-in-law-Lucille Norris - Greenup, KY

1 (7 oz.) pkg. thin spaghetti
1 T butter
1-1/2 lb. lean ground beef
salt and pepper
2 (8 oz.) cans tomato sauce
1/2 lb. small curd cottage cheese
1 (8 oz.) pkg. softened cream cheese
1/4 c. sour cream
1/3 c. chopped onion (or chives)
1 T green pepper
2 T melted butter

Prepare spaghetti according to package directions; add butter, set aside. Saute beef with salt and pepper; drain and add tomato sauce. In a separate bowl, combine remaining ingredients. Place 1/2 spaghetti in 2 qt. buttered casserole. Cover with cheese mixture. Spread remaining spaghetti over cheese. Pour 2 T butter over all. Spread beef and tomato mixture on top; cover and refrigerate 24 hours. Remove 20 minutes before baking. Bake covered 1 hour at 350°. Remove cover and bake 15 minutes. (I use more meat).

Spaghetti Sauce
Cousin-Anna Laura Adkins - Ceredo, WV

2 lb. ground chuck
1 onion, chopped
1/3 mango pepper, chopped
1 tsp . sweet basil
1 tsp. salt
1 tsp. pepper
1 lg. can tomato sauce
1/2 c. water

Brown together meat, onion, pepper, and spices. Add tomato sauce and water and simmer 1 hour. You may use 1 tsp. hot sauce, if desired.

Stuffed Green Peppers
Niece-Naomi Vivian Kenney - Greenup, KY

4 large green peppers
1/2 lb. chuck beef, ground
3 T minced onion
8 tsp. fat or salad oil
2 tsp. salt
Dash pepper
3/4 tsp. powdered sage
1 1/4 tsp. bottled thick meat sauce
2 c. boiled rice (optional)
1 1/4 c. tomatoes
1/3 c. bread crumbs

Wash peppers, cut a thin slice from stem end. Remove seeds. Cover with boiling salt water and simmer about 5 minutes. Drain. Meanwhile, cook beef and onions in 4 tsp. fat in a skillet or until meat loses its red color. Add salt, sage, pepper, meat sauce, rice and tomatoes. Combine thoroughly. Stuff peppers with meat mixture and top with bread crumbs, which have been combined with remaining 4 tsp. fat. Arrange peppers upright in a greased baking dish and bake at 375° for 35-40 minutes. Ground lamb, veal, or left over cooked meats may replace the beef.

Zippy Beef Casserole
Cousin-Katherine Stewart Martin - Racine, WS

1 lb. ground beef
4 oz. uncooked elbow macaroni
1 can (10 1/2 oz.) condensed cream of mushroom soup
3/4 c. milk
2/3 c. catsup
1/2 c. shredded cheddar cheese
1/4 c. chopped green pepper
1 to 2 T instant minced onion
1 tsp. salt
1 c. crushed potato chips

Cook and stir meat until brown. Drain off fat. Cook macaroni as directed on pkg., drain. In ungreased 2 qt. casserole, mix all ingredients except potato chips. Bake at 350° for 40 minutes. Uncover, sprinkle with chips and bake 5 minutes longer. 4 to 6 servings.

Lamb

Barbecued Lamb Chops

Nephew-Jim Lush - Bowling Green, KY

6 lamb loin or rib chops (1 inch thick)
marinade:
1 c. sugar
1 c. soy sauce
1 c. dry white wine or unsweetened apple juice
fresh ginger, grated
fresh garlic, grated

Marinate chops in marinade in covered container in the refrigerator for 2 days. Barbecue chops over coals for 5-6 minutes per side.

Cheesey Topped Lamb Chops

Nephew-David Abdon - Greenup, KY

8 lamb chops (cut 1" thick)
2 T cooking oil
3 T butter or margarine
1/3 c. flour
2/3 c. milk
1 egg, beaten
1/2 c. grated Parmesan cheese
2 tsp. grated onion
1/4 tsp. pepper
paprika

Brown chops in skillet in hot oil, about 10 minutes. Drain. Place chops in 8 x 8 x 2 inch baking dish. In a small saucepan melt butter, stir in flour. Add milk; cook and stir until thickened. Stir 1/2 of the thickened mixture into beaten egg. Return to sauce pan. Cook 1 minute more, stirring constantly. Stir in cheese, onion, and pepper. Spoon about 2 T of the mixture a top each chop. Sprinkle with paprika. Bake uncovered in 350° oven for 30 minutes or until meat is done and topping is lightly browned. Makes 4 servings.

To Bake or Roast a Leg of Lamb

Sister-Glennis Liles - Greenup, KY

Be sure the lamb you choose is bright red color with white fat, and it is best when 2 months old. The season for butchering is from April to September.

Place the leg of lamb on rack in broiler pan. Cut small gashes on the surface of the lamb. Tuck a few small cloves of garlic into the gashes. Mix thyme, sage, and marjoram together and run over the surface of the lamb. Bake at 325°, 35 minutes per pound. About one half hour before lamb is done, remove from oven and brush surface with 1/2 cup jelly mixed with 1/2 cup hot water. Return to oven and finish baking. Very good. Served with mint sauce.

Mint Sauce:

1/2 c. vinegar
1-1/2 c. water
1/2 c. chopped fresh mint leaves
1/4 c. lemon juice
2 T granulated sugar
1/4 tsp. salt

Simmer vinegar, 1 c. of the water and 1/4 c. of the mint until liquid has been reduced one-half. Strain and add remaining ingredients except the 1/4 c. of mint. Chill, then add the remaining mint. Serve cold with lamb or fish. Makes about 1 c. of sauce.

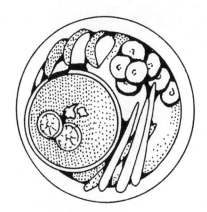

187

Leg of Lamb, Buckingham Glaze

Niece-Jean Keeney Lush - Bowling Green, KY

1 leg of lamb
salt and pepper to taste
1/2 c. dry sherry
1/2 c. apple jelly
parsley
1/2 c. catsup
1/2 tsp. marjoram leaves
lemon wedges

Sprinkle lamb with salt and pepper, put in 325° oven. Roast 30-35 minutes per pound until meat thermometer registers 175°. Combine other ingredients making a sauce and brush lamb as it roasts during last hour and half. Heat remaining sauce and serve with lamb. I double the sauce as we use it for left overs. It really does wonders for lamb.

Lemon Lamb Marinade

Niece-Anne Liles O'Hare - Ashland, KY

Grated peel and juice of 1 lemon
2 T vegetable oil
1 T grated onion
1 medium clove garlic, minced
1 tsp. dry rosemary leaves
1 tsp. dry tarragon leaves
1/4 tsp. black pepper
1 boneless sirloin lamb roast (1 1/4 - 2 lbs.)
1/2 c. chicken broth
2 tsp. cornstarch

In large bowl, combine lemon peel, juice, oil, onion, garlic, herbs, and pepper. Add lamb and coat with marinade. Cover and refrigerate two hours or longer, turning occasionally. Reserve marinade. Roast lamb on rack in shallow baking pan at 350° for 30-35 minutes per pound. In small sauce pan, combine marinade, broth, and cornstarch. Cook over low heat, stirring until thickened. Pour over sliced lamb. 6-8 servings.

Lamb Stew

Nephew-Jim Lush - Bowling Green, KY

2 lbs. boneless lamb shoulder
1/4 c. flour
3 T vegetable oil
1 lg. onion, chopped
1 clove garlic, minced
3 c. water
1 can (1 lb.) tomatoes
3 tsp. salt
1/4 tsp. pepper
3 lg. carrots, pared
3 stalks celery
3 medium potatoes, pared

Cut lamb into 1" cubes; dust lightly with flour. Heat oil in a 4 qt. sauce pan. Gradually add lamb and brown on all sides; remove. Saute onion and garlic in drippings until soft. Add browned lamb, water, tomatoes, salt and pepper. Cover, heat to boiling. Reduce heat and simmer for 35 minutes. Cut carrots and celery into 1/2 inch slices, potatoes into one-inch cubes. Add to pan, simmer until meat and vegetables are tender, about 25 minutes. Serves 6-8.

Lamb-Yam Stew

Cousin-Helen Johnson Shultz - Portsmouth, OH

1 lb. boneless lamb stew meat
2 T cooking oil
1 med. onion, chopped
1 clove garlic, crushed
1 tsp. ground coriander
1/4 tsp. each: ground cumin, ginger, and cloves
2 T soy sauce
3 med. carrots, thinly sliced
2 med. yams or sweet potatoes, peeled and halved
1 (16 oz.) can tomatoes, cut up
1/4 c. flour
1 large can mushrooms, drained

Brown meat in hot oil. Place in 2 1/2 qt. casserole, add onion, garlic, seasonings, and 1/2 tsp. salt. Pour 3/4 c. water and soy sauce on top. Bake covered, in a 350° oven for 1 hour. Add carrots and yams. Drain tomatoes, reserving juice; add tomatoes to stew. Blend tomato juice into flour and stir into stew. Bake covered 45 minutes; add mushrooms; bake 5 minutes. Makes 6 servings.

Pork

Hog butchering was a big day at our house. We had to wait for cold weather so the meat would keep. By that time of year the smokehouse was empty, and we were ready for fresh meat. Dad (Mitchell Stuart) always had two or three fat hogs fastened in the hoghouse when fall came. He fattened them on corn to make the meat firm and so there would be lots of fat for lard. Usually only one hog was killed at a time. Then the process was repeated until all the hogs were butchered.

The day before the butchering, Dad placed a block and tackle in the big hickory tree in the backyard. He filled the big iron kettle with water, sharpened the knives razor sharp, and filled the woodlot with wood.

At daybreak the neighbors came to help. Their pay was a "mess" of fresh meat to take home. First, they put a fire under the kettle and heated the water to a boil. Then they went to the hoghouse and let the hog, they were going to kill, come out into the lot. The best marksman in the group shot the hog. The hog was shot in the head so it would die instantly and not break a bone as it fell. Dad then slit its throat from side to side so it would bleed. The men loaded it onto a sled, and the horse pulled it to the kettle. They poured boiling water over the hog so it would be easy to scrape. Each man scraped a section until only skin remained. Then they placed a single tree between the hog's hind legs to hold them apart and pulled it up by the block and tackle so that it hung, head down, from the tree. Next they gutted it, by splitting it down the middle and putting the insides in a tub. They took the liver to the kitchen for Mom to make liver and onions for dinner that day. The heart was saved and the fat was removed from the intestines for lard. All the rest was thrown away. The hog was then washed inside and out with cold water and let hang to cool until the next day.

After the meat cooled, Dad took it to the smoke-house and placed it on a long bench. He cut off the feet for pickled pigs feet. He then cut the remaining into sections: hams, shoulders, middlings (bacon) and the backbone and ribs. Either pork chops or tenderloin, which ever was preferred, he cut from the backbone. Most of the fat he cut from all sections for lard. The ham and middlings he salted with coarse salt so it would keep until spring when he

would smoke it with smoke from hickory or sassafras wood. He covered the meat with black pepper and stored it in bran in a big oak box. Sometimes he smoked the shoulders; sometimes he put them in sausage.

The women's job was to cut the fat meat into small pieces and cook it in a large iron kettle, stirring constantly with a big wooden paddle, until all the grease was cooked out of the meat, leaving cracklings for cracklin bread or lye soap. They separated the lard from the cracklings by running it through a lard press. Next day, strained it into tin lard cans, covered it and stored it in a cool place.

The lean scraps they ground on a sausage grinder, seasoned them with salt, pepper, and sage, and made them into patties. These patties were fried until done (brown on both sides) and placed in stone jars. The hot sausage grease was poured over them, and the stone jar was covered with a cloth or lid.

In later years, glass jars were used. They could be sealed.

In those days we had no refrigerator. Pork could be preserved.

Butchering hogs was a big event at our house because that was our main source of meat until the next butchering season.

Sister-Sophie Stuart

189

Bacon, Sauerkraut and Potato

Niece-Jean Keeney Lush - Bowling Green, KY

This is a recipe designed after eating potatoes and kraut at the same meal, growing up in W-Hollow. It gets raves when taken to a picnic. You may do any combination of the kraut and potatoes. I always cooked on a wood stove and it's hard to specify temperature, but baking about 350° is good.

Combine mashed potatoes and kraut well. Crumble bacon and sprinkle onto mixture. Place on top one cup of grated cheese and bake until cheese is melted and bubbly. Excellent served with weiners, bratwurst, or pork. Serve hot.

Barbecue Sauce (for pork)

Cousin-Beverly Stewart - Winter Haven, FL

2 qts. vinegar
2 small cans cayenne pepper (1 1/4 oz. each)
salt to taste
2 c. sugar
1/4 c. butter
2 qts. water
1 c. flour

Combine all above ingredients and cook 15 minutes. This is an excellent sauce for pork. Be very careful as this is a hot sauce.

Barbecue Sauce for Spareribs

Cousin-Faye Stewart Lester - Kenova, WV

1 c. catsup
1 c. water
1 T chili powder
2 T Worcestershire sauce
1 tsp. mustard

Mix well, pour enough in bottom of baking dish to lightly cover. Lay country style spareribs in dish, salt and pepper. Pour remaining sauce over spareribs. Slice onion over top. Cover and bake at 350° for 2 or 2 1/2 hours. Uncover last hour. Sauce may be used for chicken also.

Barbecued Ribs

Cousin-Betty Stewart Walker - Huntington, WV

3-4 lbs. ribs
1/2 c. brown sugar
1 tsp. salt
1/2 tsp. pepper
1/2 c. tomato sauce
1/2 tsp. garlic powder

Simmer ribs in water for 30 minutes. Drain and put in baking dish. Mix other ingredients in bowl. Bake ribs for 15 minutes and then pour ingredients over the ribs. Bake for about 20 minutes more. (Oven should be set at 350°).

Chinese Pork

Nephew-Walter Stuart Keeney - Greenup, KY

1-1/2 lb. lean pork, cut in 1-inch strips
3 T Worcestershire sauce
1 green pepper, chopped
1 onion, chopped
4 oz. can mushroom stems and pieces

Coat meat in seasoned flour and brown in fat. Drain excess fat after meat is browned. Add sauce to meat and simmer for 20 minutes. Add 2 cups water and cook slowly until meat is tender. Add pepper and onion, cook 20 minutes. Add mushrooms and thicken, if desired. Serve over rice or noodles.

Ham 'N' Broccoli

Cousin-Katherine Stewart Martin - Racine, WS

1 pkg. of Au Gratin Potatoes
1 pkg. (10 oz.) frozen chopped broccoli; partially thawed and broken apart.
1-1/2 to 2 c. cut-up cooked ham or 1 can pork lunche on meat, cut-up

Prepare potatoes as directed on pkg., except use 2 qt. casserole and omit butter. Stir in broccoli and ham. Bake uncovered 45 to 50 minutes. Makes 4 to 5 servings.

Baked Ham in Beer

Nephew-Sam Darby - Normantown, WV

Spread a boiled ham with prepared mustard. Cover with a thick paste of corn syrup and brown sugar. Stud with cloves. Place in a baking pan and pour in a bottle of beer. Bake in very hot oven (450°), basting occasionally with the beer, for about 1/2 hour, or until crust is nicely set.

Boiled Country Ham

Niece-Nancy Sue Darby Lake - Berea, KY

Cut off hock; soak ham overnight. Wash ham and trim off hard surface of cut side of ham. Fill a large roaster 1/2 full of water. Put ham in skin side up. Start ham at 450° and reduce heat to 300° when water boils. Cook 20 minutes to the pound or until internal temperature of ham reaches 170°. When done, allow to cool in liquid for 4 to 5 hours. Trim the ham of excess fat, leaving 1/4" to 1/2" of fat.

Glaze:
A mixture of corn meal, brown sugar, cloves and cinnamon. Brown about 1/2 hour in a hot oven.

Ham should not be overcooked. If the ham is tender near the bone in the thickest part or if meat begins to pull away from bone at ends, the ham is done.

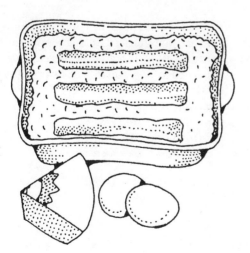

Country Ham with Buttermilk Biscuits

Niece-Sandy Nelson Perrine - Greenup, KY

1/4 c. Dijon or grainy mustard
1/4 c. butter, room temperature
24 thin slices (1 lb.) country ham

1. Make buttermilk biscuits.
2. Split warm biscuits in half. Spread bottom half with mustard, top half with butter. Place 2 slices of ham on bottom half, cover with top and serve warm.

Buttermilk Biscuits:
1 c. all-purpose flour
1 c. whole-wheat flour
1 tsp. baking powder
1 tsp. baking soda
1/2 tsp. salt
1/8 tsp. fresh ground pepper
10 T cold, unsalted butter (1 1/4 sticks)
1 c. buttermilk

Heat oven to 450°. Mix flours and other dry ingredients in mixing bowl. Cut 6 T butter into small pieces and add to flour mixture. Cut in with a pastry blender until mixture resembles fine meal. Melt 4 T butter and set aside. Pour buttermilk into flour mixture and gradually work flour into buttermilk with a fork. Turn dough onto lightly floured surface, roll or pat evenly 1/2" thick. Cut with 2-1/2" biscuit cutter. Brush both sides with melted butter and place on an ungreased baking sheet. Bake until golden, 10-12 minutes. Cool 5 minutes before splitting.

Fried Country Ham with Red Eye Gravy

Niece-Nancy Sue Darby Lake - Berea, KY

Slice ham 3/8" thick or less. Place in heavy frying pan with a little water (about 1/4 c. per skilletful of ham) and cook slowly until done. As the water evaporates the ham will brown.

Red Eye Gravy:
After removing fried ham from pan, add a little water to the drippings. Simmer about three minutes and pour over grits or biscuits.

How to Sugar Cure a Country Ham

Nephew-John Drew Lake - Berea, KY

When the daytime temperature reaches 32° - 40° in the fall its time to cure hams. Trim all the loose fat and skin from a freshly killed ham and rub the following mixture into the ham.

For one ham:
1-1/2 c. brown sugar
3 c. white salt
3 T black pepper
1-1/2 T red pepper

Mix this combination of ingredients thoroughly. Then rub the ham with the mixture being very careful to pack the hock and all holes or indentations. Lay the ham on a shelf with extra mixture under and over it until it "takes" the mixture, about three weeks. Add time to the curing if the ham gets cold enough to freeze. Try to keep the temperature between 32° and 40°.

After the curing is done, brush off the extra mixture and sack the ham first in a brown paper bag and then into a tightly woven cloth sack. Tie the top securely and hang in the smokehouse. The ham will drip the first summer and has to go through the "June Sweat" to develop a true country ham flavor.

Grandma's Ham and Apple Dumplings

Cousin-Helen Shultz - Portsmouth, OH

1 meaty ham bone
2 c. dried apples
dumpling dough

In large pan combine the ham bone with the dried apples. Cover with liquid (use plenty of water to ensure enough broth for dumplings) and cook for approximately 3 to 3-1/2 hours. When apples are done, make dumpling dough and add to the apple ham bone mixture.

Dumpling Dough

Cousin-Helen Shultz - Portsmouth, OH

2 c. all-purpose flour
1-1/2 tsp. baking powder
1 tsp. salt
1/3 c. lard
3/4 c. milk

Mix dry ingredients together, then cut in lard. Add milk and stir well. Drop by T into pan of ham bone and apples. Grandma (Mary Hilton Johnson) always made this when her father Nathan Hilton came to visit her. She and Grandpa Hilton were the only ones in the family who partook of this dish.

Grilled Ham Steak with Sweet Potatoes and Pineapple Wedges

Cousin-Alma Martin - Racine, WS

1 fully cooked ham steak (1-1/2 lbs.) about 1 inch thick
1 T soy sauce
2 tsp. dry mustard
1 med. pineapple, peeled, cored and quartered length wise. (drained canned pineapple can be substituted for fresh)
1 can (17 oz.) sweet potatoes
4 T honey, divided

Slit edges of ham in several places to prevent curling; set aside. Mix soy sauce and mustard until smooth. Brush on both sides of ham; set aside. Place a pineapple quarter and a sweet potato on each of 4 squares of heavy-duty foil. Drizzle each with 1 T honey. Seal tightly. Over medium-hot coals arrange foil packets around edges of grill. Cook 15 minutes or until hot and bubbly. Place ham in middle of grill; cook, turning once, 15 minutes or until browned and heated thoroughly. Makes 4 servings.

Ham Loaf

Cousin-Essie Hilton Rowland - Chillicothe, OH

1-1/2 lb. fresh ham, ground
1 lb. cured ham, ground
1 c. milk
3 eggs
1 c. cracker crumbs

Mix all together in a bowl and shape into loaf. Bake at 350° until done, approximately 1 hour. Put a mixture of the following on top of loaf.

1/2 c. brown sugar
1/4 c. water
1/8 c. vinegar
1/2 tsp. mustard
1 tsp. flour

Ham with Raisin Sauce

Niece-Connie Keeney - Greenup, KY

1 c. brown sugar
1 c. water
2 T cornstarch
1/4 c. vinegar
1/4 to 1/2 c. raisins

Warm cooked ham slices. Combine sugar, water, cornstarch, vinegar, and raisins in a saucepan. Stir constantly until raisins are plump and mixture thickens. Pour over warm ham and serve.

Liver and Onions

Niece-Betty Stuart Baird - Wadestown, WV

Slice pork liver about 1/4" thick. Salt and pepper liver slices and dredge in flour. Fry in hot fat over medium heat until brown on one side. Turn liver and place slices of onion on top of liver slices and cover skillet. When liver is brown on the under sides turn slices again so that onions will be on the bottom of skillet. Fry a few more minutes (covered) until liver is tender and onions are done. Beef liver may be substituted for pork liver if preferred.

Note: If necessary, add small amount of water last few minutes of frying to keep onions from burning and insure tenderness of liver.

Pork Chop Bake

Cousin-Mary Beth Stewart Martin - Racine, WS

1 c. rice (cooked)
1 onion, sliced thin
1 (16 oz.) can stewed tomatoes
4 pork chops

Fry pork chops until browned well. Place pork chops in a baking dish. Lay onion on top, then place 1/4 cup cooked rice on onion. Then top with stewed tomatoes. Bake 1 hour at 350°.

Pork Chops and Rice I

Cousin-Nancy Ellen Stewart Fannin - Kenova, WV

4 thick pork chops
salt
oil
1 c. rice
flour
pepper
1 can cream of chicken soup

Roll pork chops in flour. Place in frying pan with about 1 T oil. Salt and pepper to taste. Brown meat on both sides. Remove meat from pan. Put remaining flour in grease. Stir, then add the soup and 1 can of water. Add rice. Stir. Put the meat back in the pan. Cover and cook on medium low heat for about 1 hour.

Pork Chops and Rice II

Niece-Melissa (Lissie) Liles - Greenup, KY

2 c. instant rice, prepared according to package
  directions
Pork chops - 4 or 5 lean, cut in small pieces
green onions - about 2, cut fine
soy sauce
fresh mushrooms - about 1 cup
1 egg

Prepare rice, set aside. Saute' mushrooms and onions in butter. Add pork chops and cook until brown. Combine with rice and simmer, covered, 5 minutes. Separate mixture in middle and add an egg. Mix and add soy sauce to taste.

Baked Pork Chops with Carrots and Potatoes

Nephew-Walter Stuart (Ted) Kenney - Greenup, KY

6 pork chops
6 potatoes, peeled and quartered
6 carrots, halved
1 medium onion

Gravy:
Combine chop drippings with 1 can (10 3/4 oz.) cream of chicken soup, diluted with 1/2 can of water.

Brown chops. Make layer of potatoes and carrots on bottom of casserole. Lay chops on top. Make gravy and pour over all. Place sliced onion rings on top. Bake 50 minutes at 350°.

Pork Chop Vegetable Skillet

Cousin-Lola Hilton - Moraine, OH

4 pork chops
4 potatoes, sliced
2/3 c. green peppers, coarsley diced
1 c.celery, diced
1 c. onions, sliced
2 tsp. salt
1/8 tsp. pepper
1 can tomato soup
1/4 tsp. tabasco sauce
1/2 c. water

Use 2 qt. skillet and brown pork chops. Remove from skillet. Start with potatoes and put vegetables in layers; sprinkle with salt and pepper (each layer). Place pork chops on top. Top with remaining green peppers, onions and celery.

Mix together tomato soup, water, and tabasco sauce. Pour over meat; cover and simmer for 1 to 1-1/2 hours.

Porkroast (or ribs) and Sauerkraut

Niece-Melissa Liles - Greenup, KY

Wash and drain sauerkraut and place on bottom of baking dish. Add one chopped medium onion and a few dashes of Worcestershire sauce. Place pork roast or pork ribs on top of kraut mixture (salt and pepper meat if desired). Bake at 350° uncovered until meat is tender.

Marinated Pork Roast

Cousin-Melinda Shultz Arrick - Lucasville, OH

3 T vegetable oil
1 clove garlic, crushed
1 tsp. dry mustard
1 tsp. dried whole thyme
1 tsp. dried rosemary
1 tsp. minced fresh parsley
1/2 tsp. salt
1/2 tsp. pepper
1 (4-5 lb.) rolled boneless pork loin roast
1 c. white wine

Combine first 8 ingredients. Score roast; rub on seasonings. Wrap roast in foil, and refrigerate overnight. Remove roast from foil. Place roast, fat side up, on rack in a shallow baking pan. Insert meat thermometer (not touching fat). Bake, uncovered, at 325° for 2-1/2 to 3 hours or until thermometer reaches 170°, basting frequently with wine. Let stand 10-15 minutes. Yield: 12-15 servings.

Slow Cooked Pork Roast

Cousin-Mary Beth Stewart Martin - Racine, WS

In slow cooker put pork roast. Add 1 lg. can sauerkraut and liquid. Salt and pepper to taste. Add 1/2 cup brown sugar, 1 quartered onion, and 2 apples cored and quartered. Cover and cook on low, all day or faster, if wished.

Glazed Smoked Sausages

Cousins-David and Thomas Adkins - Lucasville, OH

1/4 c. firmly packed brown sugar
1 T cornstarch
1/4 tsp. cinnamon
1/8 tsp. nutmeg
1/8 tsp. cloves
1 c. apple juice
2 lbs. smoked sausage links cut into serving size or small
  sausages may be used

In large frying pan, combine brown sugar, cornstarch, and seasonings. Stir in apple juice and cook over medium heat until thickened and bubbly. Add sausage - turning to coat with glaze. Cook until sausages are heated through. These may be served from chafing dish.

Sausage and Cabbage

Cousin-Steven D. Arnold - Portsmouth, OH

1/2 medium cabbage, coarsley shredded
1/2 c. green pepper, chopped
4 T water
1 German or Polish sausage, cut into 1 inch slices
salt and pepper to taste

Combine cabbage and green pepper in a medium skillet; season with salt and pepper. Add water, and heat until water begins to boil. Reduce heat, and place sausage on top of cabbage mixture. Cover and simmer about 15 minutes; yields about 4 servings.

Sausage Breakfast

Cousin-Phyllis Hilton Parker - Portsmouth, OH

6 slices bread
butter or margarine
1 lb. (bulk) pork sausage
1-1/2 c. (6 oz.) shredded longhorn cheese
6 eggs, beaten
2 c. half and half
1 tsp. salt

Remove crusts from bread; spread with butter. Place in a greased 13 x 9 x 2" baking dish and set aside. Cook sausage until browned, stirring to crumble; drain well. Spoon over bread slices, sprinkle with cheese. Beat eggs and combine with half and half and salt; mix well and pour over cheese. Cover casserole and chill over-night. Remove from refrigerator 15 minutes before baking. Bake casserole uncovered at 350° for 45 minutes or until set. Serves eight.

Sausage-Rice Casserole

Nephew-Walter Stuart Kenney - Greenup, KY

1c. uncooked regular rice
2 c. carrots, chopped
1 lg. onion, chopped
1 c. celery, chopped
1/2 c. green peppers, chopped
1 (14-1/2 oz.) can chicken broth
1/4 c. water
1 lb. (bulk) pork sausage

Spread rice evenly in a lightly greased 3 qt. casserole. Spoon vegetables over rice. Pour chicken broth and water over the vegetables.

Cook sausage until browned; drain well. Spoon sausage over vegetables. Cover and bake at 350° for 30 minutes. Remove from oven, and stir well; cover and bake an additional 30 minutes.

Souse

Sister-Glennis Liles - Greenup, KY

Clean the ears, feet and gristly part (not the fat) of the hog's head; let them soak 12 hours in brine, then take out, scrape clean, and soak again in fresh brine. Then wash and put in cold water, and boil gently until the bones loosen from the meat. Pick meat from bones and tear up in small pieces with hands. Season with salt, pepper and sage to taste. Press down in a crock and keep in a cool place. Very good for a sandwich with a slice of onion.

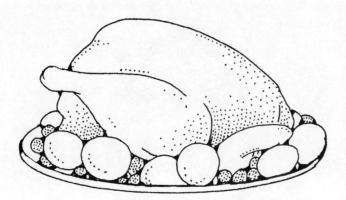

Poultry and Stuffings

Chicken-Bacon Nuggets

Cousin-Lynn Hunt Newton - Hamilton, OH

2 whole chicken breasts
1/4 c. orange marmalade
2 T soy sauce
1/2 tsp. salt
1/2 tsp. ground ginger
1 (8 oz.) pkg. sliced bacon
1/4 tsp. garlic powder

Halve breasts; skin and bone; then cut each half into 6 chunks. In medium bowl, mix chicken, marmalade, soy sauce, salt, ginger and garlic powder; set aside. Preheat broiler. Arrange bacon on rack in broiling pan. Broil bacon 4 minutes, until partially cooked, turning once. Cut each bacon slice crosswise in half. Wrap each piece of chicken with a piece of bacon. Secure with toothpick. Place on broiling pan. Broil 5 minutes or until chicken is fork tender, turning once and brushing with remaining marmalade mixture. Remove toothpicks. Serves 4.

Chicken and Beef

Wife-Naomi Deane Norris Stuart - W-Hollow, KY

4 whole chicken breasts (boned and halved)
8 slices bacon (1/2 slice on each)
1/4 lb. chipped beef
1 can (10-1/2 oz.) mushroom soup
1/2 c. sour cream
paprika

Wrap bacon around chicken. Line 8 x 8 in. shallow baking dish with beef. Place chicken on top. Spread soup and sour cream on top. Do not salt. Sprinkle with paprika. Pepper. Bake 2 hours at 275°. Yields 6 servings.

Chicken and Broccoli Casserole I

Sister-in-law-Betty Stuart - Greenup, KY

4 chicken breasts (split)
2 pkg. frozen broccoli, chopped
2 c. regular rice
2 c. water
3/4 c. onion, chopped
1 c. celery, chopped
1 stick butter, melted
1 jar of cheese whiz (little dabs all over)
2 cans of mushroom soup
1 tsp. salt

Put in casserole in layers:
1 c. rice
1 c. water
1 box of broccoli
1/2 c. of chopped onion
1/2 c. of chopped celery
1/2 of cheese whiz
1 can mushroom soup

Repeat layers ending with cheese on top. Bake at 350° about 30 minutes.

Chicken and Broccoli Casserole II

Cousin-Faye Stewart Lester - Kenova, WV

4 chicken breasts
1 can cream of mushroom soup
1 can cream of celery soup
1/2 to 3/4 c. mayonnaise
2 pkg. (or 1 bag) chopped broccoli
salt
sliced water chestnuts
cheddar cheese, shredded

Cook and debone chicken. Combine cream of mushroom soup and cream of celery soup and mayonnaise together. Cook and drain broccoli. Layer in long Pyrex in this order: Cooked chicken, soups and mayonnaise mixture, seasoning salt, sliced water chestnuts, broccoli and shredded cheddar cheese (enough to cover broccoli) and bake at 350° for 30 minutes.

Chicken 'N' Broccoli Crepes

Niece-Regina Nelson Stout - Greenup, KY

6 T butter
6 T flour
3 c. milk
dash salt
1/2 c. medium sharp cheddar cheese, grated
1/2 c. dry white wine
1 (2-1/2 oz.) jar sliced mushrooms, drained
1 (10 oz.) pkg. frozen broccoli
2 c. cooked chopped chickens
12 basic crepes (recipe follows)

Sauce: In medium saucepan, melt butter; blend in flour and salt. Add milk all at once. Cook, stirring constantly until thickened and bubbly. Stir in cheese and wine until cheese melts. Remove 1/2 c. of sauce and set aside. Stir mushrooms into remaining sauce.

Filling: Cook broccoli according to package directions; drain. Combine broccoli, chicken and the 1/2 cup of sauce.

Crepes:
1 c. flour
1-1/2 c. milk
2 eggs
1 T cooking oil
1/4 tsp. salt

In a bowl combine all ingredients; beat with rotary mixer until blended. Heat lightly greased 6" skillet. Remove from heat; spoon in about 2 T batter, tilting the skillet to spread batter evenly. Return to heat; brown on one side only. To remove, invert pan over paper toweling; remove crepe. Repeat with remaining batter, greasing pan occasionally. Set aside. Place wax paper between crepes if they are to be stored.

To assemble: Spread 1/2 c. filling over unbrowned side of crepe, leaving 1/4 inch around edges. Roll up crepe. Place seam side down in chaffing dish. Repeat with remaining crepes. Drizzle with remaining mushroom sauce. Cook covered, over low heat until bubbly. Makes 6 servings.

Chicken and Feather Dumplings

Niece-Naomi Vivian Kenney - Greenup, KY

Cut up and stew a large stewing hen (4-5 lb.). Simmer gently until tender (2-3 hours). Add more water if necessary. Remove meat in pieces from bones to add to dumplings.

Feather Dumplings:
2 c. sifted flour
1 tsp. salt
3 tsp. baking powder
1/4 tsp. pepper
1 egg, well beaten
2 T melted butter
1/3 c. milk

Sift dry ingredients together. Add egg, melted butter, and enough milk to make a moist, stiff batter. Drop, by small teaspoons, into boiling liquid. Cover very loosely and cook for 18 minutes. Makes 2 dozen dumplings. (These are so good you'll want to double the recipe for more dumplings). Add the chicken gently to cooked dumplings.

Feather Dumplings

Cousin-Rosalie Stewart - Ravenswood, WV

2 c. flour
1 tsp. salt
4 tsp. baking powder
1/4 tsp. pepper
1 egg, well beaten
3 T melted butter
2/3 c. milk

Mix ingredients together and drop by teaspoon in boiling liquid. Cover and cook 18 minutes.

Chicken and Noodles

Cousin-June Stewart Haney - Huntington, WV

6 to 8 pieces of chicken (chicken breasts are better)
1 pkg. noodles
1 can cream of chicken soup
2 T margarine
salt and pepper

Cook chicken in slow cooker (crock pot) until tender. Season with salt and pepper at beginning of cooking. Cook noodles in pan on stove according to directions. Drain, add margarine, and cream of chicken soup. Remove chicken from crock pot, drain liquid from pot. Place noodles in crock pot. Place chicken back in pot on top of noodles. Heat a little while longer. Remove from pot and serve.

Chicken and Rice

Niece-Melissa (Lissie) Liles - Greenup, KY

2-1/2 to3 lb. frying chicken pieces
1/4 c. oil
salt and pepper
2 med. onions, sliced thin
1 lg. green pepper, chopped
1 clove garlic, minced
2 c. uncooked rice
1 (8 oz.) can tomato sauce
3 (10-3/4 oz.) cans chicken broth
1/2 tsp. cumin
1/4 tsp. powdered saffron (optional)

Brown chicken pieces in oil. Sprinkle with salt and pepper. Remove from skillet. Cook and stir onions, green pepper, garlic, and rice in skillet until all oil is absorbed. Place rice mixture in large baking dish or pan. Stir in tomato sauce, chicken broth, cumin, and saffron. Arrange chicken pieces on top. Bake at 350° until chicken and rice are done. Garnish with pimiento strips and sliced ripe olives, if desired.

Chicken in Mushroom Sauce

Niece-Carrol Abdon - Greenup, KY

2 lb. chicken legs and breasts
1/4 c. all-purpose flour
1 tsp. salt
1/4 tsp. pepper
2 T butter or margarine
1 (13 oz.) can ready to serve mushroom soup, undiluted
1 (10 1/2 oz.) can condensed cream of chicken soup, undiluted

Coat chicken pieces in mixture of flour, salt and pepper. Brown in butter in skillet. Combine soups; pour over chicken. Cover; reduce heat and simmer 45 minutes or until tender. Makes 6 servings.

Chicken Casserole

Cousin-Faye Hilton - Frankfort, KY

1 sm. to med. frying chicken
1 can mushroom soup
1 (8 oz.) carton sour cream
1 can sliced water chestnuts
1 sleeve butter crackers
1 stick margarine

Stew chicken in salted water until tender. Remove skin from chicken when cool. Cut into small pieces. Mix with soup, sour cream, and water chestnuts. Put into lightly buttered casserole. Crush crackers (not too finely) and mix with melted margarine. Put on top of chicken. Bake at 350° for 30 minutes or until soup bubbles up around. Serves 6-8. You may use leftover chicken or turkey and double amount of course.

Fried Chicken (One of Jesse's favorites)

Sister-Mary Nelson - Greenup, KY

Use 1 or 2 fresh chickens (depending on need) skinned or unskinned, if desired. Cut into pieces desired. Put about 3 handfuls flour (more if needed) in a large paper bag, add the chicken and shake to flour it. Using an iron skillet, fill 1/3 full with vegetable oil or shortening. Heat oil and add chicken and salt. Cook over medium high to high heat. Cover with lid. Constantly turn the chicken until it fries to a golden brown.

Fried Chicken Breasts

Cousin-Linda Stewart Spence - Huntington, WV

5 or 6 boneless chicken breasts (split)
1-1/2 c. flour
1 T black pepper
1 tsp. oregano
1 T garlic powder

Mix flour, pepper, oregano, and garlic powder together in bowl. Dip each chicken breast in dry mixture, making sure both sides are evenly coated. Fry in Crisco on medium heat until both sides are a golden brown.

Grandma's Fried Chicken and Cream Gravy

Cousin-Helen Shultz - Portsmouth, OH

Fryer, cut up
flour
salt
pepper

Combine flour, salt and pepper. Dredge chicken pieces in mixture. Heat iron skillet and melt shortening (Grandma used plenty of lard) until just ready to start smoking. Fry chicken pieces on all sides until crispy brown. Remove to platter if more room is needed in skillet; do not crowd. When all chicken pieces are brown, put back into skillet with thicker meated pieces on the bottom. Add 1/2 cup water and cover with tight fitting lid. Turn heat to low and cook until fork tender. Remove to warm platter while making gravy.

Cream Gravy:
4 T chicken drippings
(remove excess fat from skillet, but use crusty brown pieces in bottom of skillet).
4 T all-purpose flour
2-1/2 to 3 c. warm milk
salt and pepper

Add flour to drippings and stir until just starting to turn brown. Gradually add warm milk; cook, stirring constantly until thickened. Add salt and pepper to taste.

Jayant's Boned, Fried Chicken

Niece-Rebecca Sue Callihan - Lexington, KY

2 fryers, cut-up (boned pieces will be about 3" x 3"; some
  smaller)

Marinade:
6 T soy sauce
2 T sherry
1-1/2 tsp. garlic powder
1 tsp. pepper
10 shakes accent

Combine ingredients, and marinate chicken overnight. Flour, and fry in Crisco.

Chicken Supreme

Cousin-Lynn Hunt Newton - Hamilton, OH

3 oz. softened cream cheese
3 T melted butter
2 c. cooked chicken, cubed
1/4 tsp. salt
1/8 tsp. pepper
2 T milk
1 T chopped onion
1 (8 oz.) can cresent rolls
3/4 c. crushed croutons

In medium bowl blend 2 T melted butter and cream cheese until smooth. Add next 5 ingredients; mix well. Seperate rolls into 4 rectangles. Press perforations together. Spoon 1/2 c. chicken mixture on rectangle. Fold corners together and twist. Brush with butter and sprinkle with croutons. Cook on ungreased cookie sheet for 25 minutes at 350°.

Continental Chicken

Niece-Regina Nelson Stout - Greenup, KY

1 frying chicken, cut into pieces
1/3 c. all-purpose flour
1/4 c. melted butter
1 (10 3/4 oz.) can condensed cream of chicken soup
2-1/2 T dried onion
1 tsp. salt
dash pepper
1 T celery flakes
1 T parsley flakes
1/2 tsp. ground dried thyme
1-1/3 c. water
2 c. precooked rice

Dredge chicken in flour; brown in butter. Remove chicken. Combine soup, onion, seasonings, and water with drippings; cook and stir until mixture boils. Spread rice in 1-1/2 qt. shallow casserole. Pour all but 1/3 cup soup mixture over rice. Stir to moisten. Top with chicken and remaining soup mixture. Cover; bake at 375° for 30 minutes. Yield: 4 servings.

Chicken Divan

Wife-Naomi Deane Norris Stuart - W-Hollow, KY

2 chicken breasts, halved
1 pkg. frozen broccoli
1/4 tsp. curey powder (or more)
Parmesan cheese
1/4 c. mayonnaise
1 can cream chicken soup
1/2 tsp. lemon juice
bread crumbs

Cook chicken. Cook broccoli. Place chicken in greased casserole. Cover with broccoli. Mix soup, lemon juice, mayonnaise, and curey powder. Pour over chicken and broccoli. Sprinkle bread crumbs and cheese on top. Bake at 350° for 20 minutes. Serves 4.

Chicken and Wild Rice Casserole

Daughter-Jane Stuart Juergensmeyer - Gainsville, FL

1 c. uncooked wild rice
1/2 c. onion, chopped
1 stick butter
1/2 c. flour
1 (6 oz.) can sliced mushrooms
1 c. chicken broth
1-1/2 c. half and half
3 c. diced cooked chicken
2 T diced parsley
1/2 c. sliced almonds

Cook rice. Saute onion in butter, stir in flour. Drain mushrooms (save liquid). Combine chicken broth and mushroom liquid to make 1-1/2 c. Gradually add broth mixture into onion mixture. Slowly add half and half, cook and stir until thick. Add rice, mushrooms, chicken, parsley, and salt and pepper to taste. Pour into ungreased 2 quart casserole. Sprinkle with almonds. Bake 25-30 minutes at 350°. Serves 6-8.

Hot Chicken Salad

Cousin-Susan Shultz Arnold - Portsmouth, OH

4 c. cooked chicken, cubed
2 c. celery, coarsely chopped
3/4 c. mayonnaise
3/4 c. cream of chicken soup
2 T lemon juice
1 tsp. salt
1 T grated onion
4 hard cooked eggs, sliced

Topping:
1 c. (4 oz.) grated cheddar cheese
1-1/2 c. crushed potato chips
2/3 c. toasted slivered almonds

Combine all the salad ingredients and toss well. Line a 9 x 13 inch baking dish with salad. Top with layers of cheese, potatoes chips, and almonds, refrigerate overnight. Let come to room temperature and bake at 400° for 25-30 minutes.

Wrapped Chicken

Cousin-Phillis Hilton Parker - Portsmouth, OH

1 large pkg. chipped corn beef or ham
8 boned chicken breasts
8 slices of bacon
1 can cream of mushroom soup
1 c. of sour cream

Line a 9 x 13 inch pan with chipped corn beef or ham. Cover with 8 boned chicken breasts, wrapped with bacon. Mix the mushroom soup with the sour cream and pour this over the chicken. Bake uncovered at 275° for 3 hours.

Pineapple-Glazed Rock Cornish Hens

Niece-Anne Liles O'Hare - Ashland, KY

4 Rock Cornish hens
1/4 c. dry white wine
salt and cracked pepper to taste
Wild Rice Stuffing, recipe follows
1/4 c. melted butter
2 (8-1/2 oz.) cans pineapple slices
1/2 c. chicken broth
2 T. sugar
1/4 tsp. ginger
1 tsp. cornstarch

Rub cavity of hens with wine, salt and pepper and fill loosely with Wild Rice Stuffing. Skewer openings. Place remaining stuffing in a casserole and cover. Brush hens with some of the butter and place, breast side up, in a shallow baking pan. Drain the pineapple and reserve 1/2 cup syrup. Mix 1/4 cup reserved syrup with the chicken broth and pour over hens. Bake hens and stuffing at 350° for about 1 hour, basting hens every 15 minutes with remaining butter and pan drippings. Top each hen with a pineapple slice. Mix the sugar, ginger and cornstarch with remaining reserved syrup and spoon over hens. Place remaining pineapple slices in baking pan. Remove casserole from oven. Increase temperature to 400° and bake about 15 minutes longer, or until hens are glazed, basting occasionally. Serve pan liquid as sauce.

WILD RICE STUFFING

1 c. washed wild rice
1/4 c. butter
1-1/2 c. chicken broth
1 tsp. salt
6 green onions, chopped
1 c. celery, chopped
1/2 c. toasted almonds, chopped
1 (8 oz.) can sliced mushrooms
1/2 tsp. marjoram
1/8 tsp. nutmeg

Soak the rice in hot water to cover for 1 hour. Drain and dry on paper towels. Saute in the butter in a sauce pan until golden. Add the chicken broth and salt and cover tightly. Simmer for about 25 minutes or until tender. Add the green onions, celery, almonds, mushrooms, marjoram, and nutmeg.

Old Fashion Roast Duckling

Niece-Freda Keeney - Greenup, KY

1 frozen duckling (4 1/2 to 5 lb.), defrosted
1 tsp. salt
1-1/2 c. coarsley chopped onion
1-1/2 c. diced celery
1/3 c. butter
4 c. toasted bread cubes
1 egg, well beaten
1/3 c. hot water
1/2 tsp. poultry seasoning
pepper to taste

Wash, drain and dry duckling. Sprinkle 1/2 tsp. salt over neck and body cavities. Cook onion and celery slowly in butter until tender, but not brown. Pour vegetable mixture over bread cubes. Add egg and mix gently. Add remaining 1/2 tsp. salt, poultry seasoning and pepper; mix well. Fill neck and body cavity loosely with stuffing. Skewer neck skin to back. Cover opening of body cavity with aluminum foil and tie legs together loosely. Place on rack in shallow roasting pan. Bake in 325° oven until drumstick is very tender, about 2 1/2 to 3 hours. Makes 4 servings.

Goose with Fruit Stuffing

Niece-Carrol Keeney Abdon - Greenup, KY

1 (9-10 lb.) dressed goose
3-1/2 c. soft bread crumbs
1-1/2 c. peeled, chopped apples
1/2 c. raisins
1/2 c. chopped onion
1/2 c. butter, melted
2. tsp. salt
1 tsp. rubbed sage
1 tsp. dried whole rosemary
1 tsp. pepper
Fresh parsley springs, grapes, apples and oranges
  (optional)

Remove giblets and neck from goose; reserve for gravy, if desired. Rinse goose thoroughly and pat dry. Combine next 9 ingredients and mix well. Spoon dressing into cavity of goose; close with skewers. Place breast side up on roasting rack. Bake at 350° for about 4 hours, or until drumsticks move easily. Baste occasionally with pan drippings. Place goose on serving platter; garnish with parsley, grapes, apples, and oranges, if desired. Serves 5-7.

Cider Baked Turkey Breast

Cousin-Melinda Shultz Arrick - Lucasville, OH

1 (5 to 5 1/2 lb.) turkey breast
1-1/2 c. apple cider
1/4 c. soy sauce
1/2 c. apple cider
2 T cornstarch

Place turkey breast, skin side up, in a large roasting pan; bake at 450° for 30 minutes or until skin is crisp.

Combine 1-1/2 c. cider with soy sauce; pour over turkey. Insert meat thermometer in meaty portion of breast, making sure it does not touch bone. Cover and bake at 325° about 1-1/2 hours to 2 hours until meat thermometer registers 185°; baste turkey frequently with cider mixture.

Sauce:
Combine 1/2 c. cider and cornstarch, mixing well; stir into pan drippings. Return to oven and bake, uncovered, until sauce is thickened. Transfer turkey to serving platter; serve with sauce. Yields: 12-16 servings.

Turkey-Noodle Casserole

Niece-Hilde Darby - Greenup, KY

12 oz. egg noodles, cooked
2 (8 oz.) pkg. broccoli spears, cooked and diced
6 c. diced turkey
3 (8 oz.) pkg. mild cheddar cheese, shredded
2 cans cream of celery soup
2 c. water
2 chicken bouillon cubes

Combine water and bouillon and boil until cubes are dissolved. Mix turkey, noodles, and broccoli in a large bowl. Place mixture in 3 - 8" x 8" baking dishes. Mix bouillon with celery soup until creamy and pour over turkey mixture. Sprinkle with cheddar cheese. Bake at 350° for 30-40 minutes, uncovered.

Skillet Turkey in Cream

Niece-Pam Abdon - Greenup, KY

4 slices bacon, cut in half
2 med. onions, sliced
3 T flour
1/2 tsp. salt
1/2 tsp. oregano
1/8 tsp. pepper
2 c. diced cooked turkey
1 c. water
1/2 c. sour cream

Cook bacon until crisp. Drain on paper towels and crumble for garnish. Pour off all but 2 T drippings. Add onions to drippings. Cover and cook over low heat 10 minutes, or just until tender. Remove from heat. Stir in a mixture of flour, salt, oregano, and pepper. Add turkey. Stir in water. Stir over medium heat until mixture boils. Boil one minute. Remove from heat, fold in sour cream. Serve over toast and sprinkle with bacon. Makes 4 servings.

Roast Turkey

Niece-Freda Keeney - Greenup, KY

1 (12-14 lb.) turkey
salt
melted butter

Remove giblets, and rinse turkey thoroughly with cold water; pat dry. Sprinkle cavity with salt. Tie ends of legs to tail with cord or string, or tuck them up under flap of skin around tail. Lift wingtips up and over back so they are tucked under bird.

Brush entire bird with melted butter; place on roasting rack, breast side up. Bake at 325° about 4 1/2 to 5 hours. If using a meat thermometer it should reach 185°. If turkey starts to brown too much, cover loosely with aluminum foil.

When turkey is 2/3 done, cut the cord or band holding the drumstick ends to the tail; this will ensure that the inside of the thighs are cooked. Turkey is done when drumsticks are easy to move up and down. Let stand 15 minutes before carving. Yield 20-24 servings.

Turkey Souffle

Niece-Kathy Abdon - Greenup, KY

2 small onions, minced
3 lg. fresh mushrooms, minced
1 pimiento, minced
1/4 c. butter
3 T flour
1/2 tsp. salt
3/4 c. turkey broth
1/4 c. heavy cream
4 egg yolks, beaten
1 c. diced cooked turkey
1 tsp. minced dill
4 egg whites, stiffly beaten

Cook onion, mushroom, and pimento in butter until onion is yellow. Blend in flour and salt until smooth. Gradually stir in broth and cream. Stir over low heat 2 minutes. Stir a little of this hot cream sauce into egg yolks. Pour yolk mixture into sauce and stir in turkey and dill. Fold egg whites into turkey mixture. Pour into greased 1-1/2 qt. casserole. Bake at 350° for 40-45 minutes. Make 4-6 servings.

Country Corn Bread Sausage Dressing

Cousin-Nellie Adkins - Defiance, OH

1 sm. box of corn bread mix
1 pkg. (1 lb.) pork sausage
2 c. celery, diced
1 c. onion, diced
6 c. soft bread cubes
1/4 c. margarine or butter, melted
1-1/2 T sage
1 can (10 3/4 oz.) chicken broth
3/4 c. water
2 eggs, beaten

Bake corn bread according to directions; cool. Crumble into large bowl, set aside. Brown sausage with onion and celery, drain. In large bowl, combine sausage mixture, corn bread, bread cubes, butter, and sage. Mix well. Add broth, water, and beaten eggs; toss lightly until bread is well moistened. (If a more moist dressing is desired, add 1/2 c. more water).

This is enough dressing for a 12 to 16 lb. turkey.

Spinach Almondine Stuffing

Sister-in-law-Betty Stuart - Greenup, KY

1/2 c. butter or margarine
1 c. fresh mushrooms, sliced
1/2 c. onion, chopped
1/2 c. celery, chopped
1 can Swanson clear ready-to-serve chicken broth
1 pkg. (16 oz.) Pepperidge Farm Herb Seasoned Stuffing
1 pkg. (10 oz.) frozen spinach thawed, well drained
3/4 c. (3 oz.) sliced toasted almonds

In 4 qt. sauce pan, over medium heat, cook mushrooms, onions, and celery in hot butter until tender. Toss lightly with stuffing, spinach, and almonds. May be used to stuff 14 to 16 lb. turkey or spooned into greased 12 x 8 inch baking dish and bake at 350° for 30 minutes, until lightly browned. Makes 7 cups or 8 servings.

Zucchini Dressing

Cousin-Mary Arnold - Hillsboro, OH

3 eggs
1 tsp. oregano
1/2 c. oil
1/2 tsp. pepper
1 lg. onion
1-1/2 c. grated cheese
4 c. zucchini, chopped

Combine ingredients and top with 1/2 c. grated cheese. Pour in greased 8 x 10 pan and bake at 350° for 40-45 minutes.

Microwave

Meats

Smoky Barbecued Chicken
Microwave "Oven Fried" Chicken
Chicken Parmesan
One Step Chili
Enchiladas
Delicious Lasagna
Microwave Manicotti
Cheesy Meat Loaf
Pork Chops
Pork Chops and Dressing
Pork Roast
Salmon Loaf

Vegetables

Green Beans with Tomatoes
Cabbage with Sweet-and-Sour Sauce
Corn Chowder
Herbed Corn
Calico Stuffed Peppers
Hot German Potato Salad
Zesty New Potato Salad
Acorn Squash
Squash Parmesan
Summer Squash Toss

Other Microwave Dishes

Almond Carnival Brittle
Cheese Sticks
Caramel Corn
Microwave Peach Crisp
Apple Wheat Germ Muffins
Graham Cracker Dessert
Southern Jam Cake
Lemon Cake
Southern Nut Baskets
Frosted Oatmeal Squares
Orange-Coconut Apple Crisp
Wintertime Breakfast Pudding

L to R. Gene Darby and Walter Stuart (Ted) Keeney

L. to R. Vivian (Bibbie) Keeney, Jean Keeney, Carrol Keeney and Betty Darby

Grandma and Grandpa Stuart usually had a yard full of grandchildren, especially in the summer. We loved to play on the rocks in the pasture, in the backyard and down in the hollow in W-Hollow Creek. The older group consisted of Aunt Sophia' s four children and my mother's (Mary) three. Sometimes we all went home at night, but often we stayed and caught jars of lightning bugs and fussed over who got to sleep with Grandma. Looking back, I marvel at their patience with us. We frequently climbed the young apple trees, or tried to catch Grandpa's corn-crib blacksnake, or made so much racket that Uncle Jesse scolded us and chased us away from the bunkhouse where he was writing .We followed Grandma to the barn to watch her milk the cows and we searched for hens' nests. We also brought her wild strawberries, picked from the 1ittle flat above Uncle Jesse and Aunt Deane's house, and she made strawberry preserves . We caught frogs in W-Hollow Creek and she fried them and made biscuits and gravy for us. She would cook anything we brought to her. There was always time for us.

Grandma Stuart could bake bread on the hearth, using a dutch oven and hot coals. She cooked on a woodburning cookstove, then an electric range and was one of the first women in the family to use a pressure cooker. There is no doubt that she would have tried and enjoyed the microwave cooking available to us. Martha Hilton Stuart was not afraid to try new methods. She was creative and progressive.

Betty Stuart Baird

Nancy Sue Darby

Meats

Smoky Barbecued Chicken

Niece-Shirley Stuart - Greenup, KY

3/4 c. commercial barbecue sauce
2 T Worcestershire sauce
2 tsp. liquid smoke
1/4 tsp. onion powder
1/4 tsp. celery seed
1/8 tsp. garlic powder
1 (2 1/2- to 3-pound) broiler-fryer, cut up and skinned
Fresh parsley sprigs

Combine first 6 ingredients in a small bowl, mixing well. Arrange chicken in a 12 x 8 x 2-inch baking dish, placing thicker portions of chicken to outside of dish. Brush half of sauce over chicken. Cover with waxed paper and microwave on HIGH for 7 to 9 minutes. Drain off excess fat.

Turn chicken and rearrange so that uncooked portions are to outside of dish; brush with remaining sauce. Cover with waxed paper and microwave on HIGH for 10 to 12 minutes or until done. Transfer to serving platter; garnish with parsley. Yield: 4 servings.

Microwave "Oven-Fried" Chicken

Niece-Martha Stuart Wheeler - Knoxville, TN

2/3 c. Bisquick baking mix
1-1/2 tsp. paprika
1-1/4 tsp. salt
1/4 tsp. pepper
2-1/2- to 3 1/2-pound broiler-fryer chicken, cut up

Mix baking mix, paprika, salt and pepper; coat chicken. Arrange pieces, skin sides up, in rectangular microwavable dish, 12 x 7 1/2 x 2 inches, with thickest parts to outside edges. Cover with waxed paper and microwave on high (100%) 10 minutes; rotate dish 1/2 turn. Microwave until done, 8 to 12 minutes longer, 6 servings.

Chicken Parmesan

Niece-Lori Ann Stuart - Greenup, KY

1/4 c. butter
1/2 c. Parmesan cheese
1/2 c. bread crumbs
1 T paprika
1/4 to 1/2 tsp. garlic powder
1-1/2 tsp. Italian seasoning or 1/2 tsp. each of rosemary, oregano, and basil.
6 chicken breast halves, boned, skinned (1-1/2 lbs.)
(Chicken parts may be substituted for chicken breasts)

Allow 7 minutes per pound of chicken for cooking.

Melt butter in 8 x 12 inch glass pan. Dip both sides of chicken in butter. Combine remaining ingredients on paper plate; roll chicken in mixture. Place chicken in dish, with thicker edges toward outside. Cover loosely with waxed paper. Microwave on HIGH for 12 minutes, rotating dish once. Yield: 6 servings.

Conventional Method: Omit waxed paper and bake at 350° for 35-45 minutes.

One Step Chili

Nephew-Ron Wheeler - Knoxville, TN

1 lb. lean ground beef
1 can (15 oz.) pinto or kidney beans plus liquid
1 can (14-1/2 oz.) whole tomatoes and juice, cut up
1 can (6-oz.) tomato paste
1/2 c. chopped onion
1/4 c. chopped green pepper
1 garlic clove, crushed
2 T chili powder
1 tsp. salt
1/2 tsp. ground cumin
1/4 tsp. red pepper flakes (optional)

Microwave crumbled ground beef in 2-qt. casserole on HIGH for 5 minutes, stirring once to break meat into pieces. Drain. Add remaining ingredients. Cover; microwave on HIGH for 20 minutes, stirring every 5 minutes. Yield: 6 servings.

Enchiladas

Niece-Melissa Liles - Greenup, KY

1-1/2 lbs. ground beef or pork
1 can (12 oz.) tomato paste
1 c. water
1/2 c. chopped onion
1 pkg. taco seasoning mix, optional
salt, if desired
12 flour tortillas
1 jar (8 oz.) Cheese Whiz
1 can (4 oz.) chopped green chili peppers, drained

Crumble meat in large microwavable dish; microwave on HIGH 6-8 minutes or until meat loses pink color. Drain. Add paste, water, onion, taco seasoning (if desired) and salt to meat; microwave on HIGH 3 minutes. Set aside. Wrap tortillas in dampened paper towels and microwave on HIGH 1-2 minutes until soft. Spoon 2 T meat mixture on each tortilla; roll up tightly. Place in lightly greased 9 x 13 inch baking dish. Combine Cheese Whiz and green chilies; microwave on HIGH for 1-2 minutes until heated thoroughly. Pour over tortillas. Top with remaining meat mixture. Microwave on HIGH 5 minutes; rotate dish. Cover with plastic wrap; microwave on HIGH 5 minutes more. Let stand, covered, 5 minutes. Yield: 10-12 servings.

Delicious Lasagna

Niece-Theresa Darby - Normantown, WV

1/2 lb. ground beef
1/2 c. water
1 jar (32 oz.) spaghetti sauce
1-1/2 c. cottage cheese
1 egg
1/2 tsp. pepper
1/2 lb. shredded Mozzarella cheese
8 lasagna noodles, uncooked
1/2 c. grated Parmesan cheese

Crumble ground beef in large glass bowl. Microwave on HIGH 2-3 minutes or until meat is no longer pink. Drain. Stir in spaghetti sauce and water. Set aside. Combine cottage cheese, egg and pepper. Layer 1/2 c. of sauce, half of noodles, egg mixture, mozzarella cheese and sauce. Repeat layers; cover with plastic wrap. Microwave on HIGH 8 minutes; reduce setting to MEDIUM-LOW. Microwave 20-25 minutes or until noodles are tender. Top with Parmesan cheese; let stand, covered, 15 minutes before serving. Yield: 8 servings.

Microwave Manicotti

Cousin-Janet Mayo - Kenova, WV

1/2 lb. lean ground beef
1 c. refried beans
1 tsp. dried oregano, crushed
1/2 tsp. ground cumin
8 manicotti shells
1-1/4 c. water
1 (8 oz.) can picante sauce or taco sauce
1 (8 oz.) carton dairy sour cream
1/4 c. finely chopped green onion
1/4 c. sliced pitted ripe olives
1/2 c. shredded Monterey Jack cheese

Combine beef, beans, oregano and cumin. Fill uncooked manicotti shells with meat mixture. Arrange in a 10 by 6 by 2-inch baking dish. Combine water and picante sauce; pour over shells. Cover with vented plastic wrap. Microcook on 100 percent power (high) 10 minutes, giving dish a half-turn once. Using tongs, turn shells over. Microcook, covered, on 50 percent power (medium) 17 to 19 minutes or until pasta is tender, giving dish a half-turn once. Combine sour cream, green onion and olives. Spoon down center of casserole; top with cheese. Microcook, uncovered, on high 2 to 3 minutes or until cheese melts. Makes 4 servings.

Cheesy Meat Loaf

Cousin-Brenda Marcum - Kenova, WV

1-1/2 lbs. lean ground beef
1 egg
3/4 c. cracker crumbs
2 T minced onion
1 tsp. salt
1/8 to 1/4 tsp. oregano
1/2 tsp. pepper
1 can (8 oz.) tomato sauce, divided
2 c. shredded Mozzarella or cheddar cheese or combination of both
1/4 tsp. Italian seasoning

Combine beef, egg, crumbs, onion, salt, oregano, pepper and 1/3 can tomato sauce. Mix well. Shape into flat rectangle about 8 x 12 in. on waxed paper. Pat or roll to even thickness, about 1/4 in. Sprinkle cheese evenly over meat; roll up like jelly roll, pressing ends to seal. Place roll in a 9 x 12 in. glass baking dish. Pour remaining tomato sauce mixed with Italian seasoning over top. Cover with waxed paper; microwave 12-15 minutes on HIGH. Let stand at least 10 minutes before serving. Yield: 6-8 servings. Conventional Method: Bake at 350° for 1 hour.

Pork Chops

Cousin-Scott Stewart - Ceredo, WV

4 thin slices onion
1 can (11 oz.) cheddar cheese soup
1-1/2 c. packaged cube stuffing mix
1-1/2 c. diced tart apples
2 T chopped parsley
4 thick pork chops (about 1-1/2 lbs.)
paprika
salt
pepper

In 1-1/2 quart shallow glass dish (10 x 6 x 2-inch), cook onion in microwave oven 1 minute. Stir in soup, stuffing, apples and 1 T parsley. Cover with waxed paper; cook 5 minutes, giving dish a half turn after 2 minutes. Sprinkle chops with paprika, salt and pepper. Arrange on top of casserole and sprinkle with remaining parsley. Cover; cook 10 - 12 minutes or until done, giving dish a half turn every 4 minutes. Makes 4 servings.

Pork Chops and Dressing

Cousin-Kay (Cookie) Stevens - Kenova, WV

4 loin pork chops, 1/2 inch thick
Kitchen Bouquet
3 c. herb-seasoned croutons
1/4 c. diced onion
1/4 c. melted butter
1 egg, slightly beaten
1/4 c. water
1 can (10 3/4 oz.) cream of mushroom soup
1/3 c. milk

Brush both sides of chops with Kitchen Bouquet; set aside. Combine croutons, onions, butter and egg mixed with 1/4 cup water. Spread in bottom of 8 x 12 inch glass baking dish. Place chops on dressing. Cover with plastic wrap; microwave on HIGH for 5 minutes. Remove wrap carefully; turn chops. Pour soup mixed with milk over all. Re-cover and microwave on 70 percent POWER for 10 minutes. Let stand for at least 5 minutes, covered, before serving. Yield: 4 servings. Conventional Method: Bake at 350° for 1 hour. Omit plastic wrap; cover with foil.

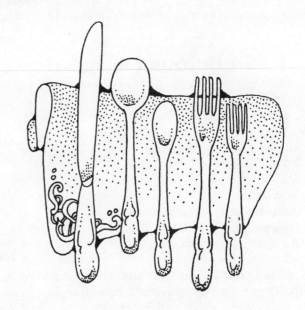

Pork Roast

Cousin-Al Lester - Ceredo, WV (Rota, Spain)

1 (12 oz.) pkg. fresh or frozen cranberries, unthawed
1/3 c. Grand Marnier (or 3 T undiluted orange juice
 concentrate and 2 T water)
1 tsp. grated orange peel
1/3 c. finely chopped onion
1 c. sugar
1/2 tsp. Tabasco hot pepper sauce
6 T butter or margarine
1/2 tsp. browning and seasoning sauce
1 (3-4 lb.) pork loin roast, with bones
3 unpared apples, cored and cut into rings
salt, to taste
parsley sprigs, for garnish
12 oz. hot cooked noodles

To prepare cranberry sauce: Combine cranberries, Grand Marnier, orange peel, onion, sugar and pepper sauce in microwave bowl. Cover and microwave on High for 12 minutes, stirring once.

Microwave butter in medium bowl on High, uncovered, for 40 to 50 seconds, until melted. In small bowl, blend half of butter with browning and seasoning sauce. Brush over pork loin.

Place pork fat-side up in shallow microwave pan; cover with waxed paper. Microwave on High for 10 minutes. Baste with pan juices. Microwave on Medium for 15 minutes more. Pour off and discard excess pan juices. Spoon 1 cup of cranberry sauce over pork roast. Cover loosely with tent foil; allow to rest 10 minutes.

Meanwhile, brush remaining 3 T butter over apple slices. Sprinkle with a pinch of salt, if desired. Place in large, shallow microwave dish; cover and cook on High for 3 minutes. Allow to stand, covered, for 5 minutes.

To serve, place pork loin on platter. Garnish with apple slices and parsley; surround with cooked noodles. Serve remaining sauce in bowl with roast. This recipe makes 8 servings.

Salmon Loaf

Cousin-Ruth Smith - Ceredo, WV

LOAF:
1 can (15-1/2 oz.) salmon, drained, boned and skinned
2 eggs, lightly beaten
1 c. soft bread crumbs
1/4 c. evaporated milk
1/2 c. diced celery
1/4 tsp. salt
2 T chopped onion
2 tsp. lemon juice
1 jar (2 oz.) diced pimiento

SAUCE:
1 can (10 3/4 oz.) cream of celery soup
2 T fresh lemon juice, optional
2 T cultured sour cream, optional
1/2 tsp. dill weed

In medium mixing bowl, combine salmon, eggs, crumbs, milk, celery, salt, onion, lemon juice and pimiento. Place in plastic ring mold or arrange around inverted glass placed in center of 6-cup round glass dish. Microwave on HIGH for 9 minutes, rotating 1/4 turn each 3 minutes. Let stand 5 minutes. Meanwhile, mix sauce ingredients together in 2-cup measure. Microwave on HIGH 3 minutes, stirring every minute. Serve warm over loaf. Yield: 4 servings. Conventional Method: Put loaf in greased 4 -1/2 x 8-inch pan. Bake at 400° for 30-35 minutes.

Vegetables

Green Beans with Tomatoes

Niece-Freda Keeney - Greenup, KY

1/2 lb. fresh green beans
1/2 c. water
1/3 c. chopped green pepper
1/4 c. chopped green onions
1 T vegetable oil
1 medium tomato, peeled and chopped
1/2 tsp. salt
1/2 tsp. sugar
1/2 tsp. dried whole basil

Wash beans, trim ends, and remove strings. Cut beans into 1-1/2 inch pieces. Place beans in a 1-1/2 quart casserole and add water. Cover with heavy-duty plastic wrap and microwave at HIGH for 7-9 minutes, stirring twice. Let stand, covered, for 3 minutes.

Place green pepper, onions, and oil in a 1-quart casserole. Cover and microwave at HIGH for 3 minutes or until tender.

Drain beans, Add green pepper mixture and remaining ingredients; stir well. Cover and microwave on HIGH for 2 to 2 1/2 minutes or until thoroughly heated. Yield: 2 servings.

Cabbage with Sweet-and-Sour Sauce

Cousin-Ethel Stewart Terry - Ceredo, WV

1 small cabbage, shredded
2 T water
1/8 tsp. salt
2 T butter or margarine
2 T all-purpose flour
1 T sugar
1/8 tsp. salt
1/4 tsp. white pepper
1/2 c. whipping cream
1/4 c. milk
3 T vinegar
paprika

Place cabbage in a 1-quart casserole. Add water and 1/8 tsp. salt; cover with heavy-duty plastic wrap and microwave on HIGH for 10 to 11 minutes. Let stand, covered, 3 minutes.

Put butter in a 1-quart casserole and microwave on HIGH for 40 seconds or until melted. Add flour, sugar, salt, and pepper; stir until smooth. Gradually stir in whipping cream and milk. Microwave on HIGH for 2 to 3 minutes or until thickened, stirring twice. Stir in vinegar. Pour sauce over cabbage; mix well, and sprinkle with paprika. Yield: 4 servings.

Corn Chowder

Cousin-Geraldine Holbrook - Greenup, KY

1 c. chopped onion
1/2 c. chopped celery
2 T butter, melted
3 c. corn, fresh or frozen
1-1/2 c. peeled cubed potatoes
1-1/2 c. water
3 chicken-flavored bouillon cubes
1 tsp. salt
1/4 tsp. pepper
1/4 tsp. dried thyme
2 c. milk, divided
2 T flour
1 c. half and half or cream

Combine onion, celery and butter in 3-qt. casserole; microwave on HIGH for 2 minutes. Add corn, potatoes, water, bouillon, salt, pepper and thyme. Microwave on HIGH until potatoes are tender, about 10 minutes. Heat 1 cup milk and 2 T flour to boiling; stir into soup. Add remaining milk and half and half or cream. Microwave until thoroughly heated. Yield: 6 servings.

Herbed Corn

Nephew-Ron Wheeler - Knoxville, TN

2 T butter or margarine
2 c. fresh corn, cut from cob
1/2 c. water
1/2 tsp. dried whole basil
1/2 tsp. sugar
1/4 tsp. salt
1/8 tsp. pepper
2 tsp. chopped fresh or frozen chives

Place butter in a 1-quart casserole and microwave at HIGH for 40 seconds or until melted; stir in corn and water. Cover with heavy-duty plastic wrap and microwave at HIGH for 2 minutes; stir well, and give dish a half-turn. Cover and microwave at HIGH for 7 to 8 minutes or until corn is tender. Stir in remaining ingredients. Cover and microwave on HIGH for 1 to 2 minutes or until thoroughly heated. Yield: 4 servings.

Calico-stuffed Peppers

Cousin-Margaret Terry Waller - Ceredo, WV

3 large green peppers, halved lengthwise, seeded, membrane removed
1 lb. extra lean ground beef
3/4 c. chopped onion
1 can (8 oz.) whole kernel corn
3 T catsup
1/4 tsp. garlic powder
1/2 tsp. chili powder
1 can (8 oz.) tomato sauce
1 tsp. chili powder
1/2 c. grated cheddar cheese

Arrange peppers in 4-qt. casserole or on 14-in. round glass tray. Cover with plastic wrap, turning back one corner to vent steam. Microwave on HIGH 4 minutes. Set aside. In 2-qt. casserole, crumble beef and add onion. Microwave on HIGH 5 minutes, stirring once. Drain. Add corn, catsup, garlic, and 1/2 tsp. chili powder to beef. Mix; spoon into pepper shells. Combine tomato sauce and 1 tsp. chili powder; spoon over pepper halves. Cover; microwave on HIGH 5 minutes. Sprinkle with cheese; microwave on HIGH, uncovered, 1 minute. Let stand 2 minutes before serving. Yield: 6 servings.

Hot German Potato Salad

Cousin-Melinda Shultz Arrick - Lucasville, OH

4 slices bacon
1 pkg. (5-1/2 oz.) scalloped potatoes
2 c. water
1/4 T sugar
2 T vinegar
1/2 tsp. celery seeds

Place bacon in glass pie pan; cover with sheet of waxed paper. Cook in microwave oven until crisp, about 4 minutes. Reserve 2 T bacon fat; drain bacon.

Place potatoes and water in 2-quart glass casserole; cover. Cook in microwave until potatoes are tender, 10 to 15 minutes. Stir in remaining ingredients (including reserved bacon fat); cover. Cook 1-1/4 minutes.

Zesty New Potato Salad

Niece-Connie Keeney - Greenup, KY

1 lb. small new potatoes, unpeeled
2 T water
1/8 tsp. salt
1/4 c. Zesty Italian salad dressing
2 T minced green onions
2 T chopped fresh parsley
2 tsp. chopped pimiento

Scrub new potatoes, and cut into 1/4-inch thick slices. Place in a 1-1/2 quart casserole; add water and salt. Cover and microwave on HIGH for 8 to 10 minutes or until potatoes are almost done. Let stand 3 minutes. Drain carefully.

Combine salad dressing and remaining ingredients, stirring well. Pour mixture over potatoes, tossing gently to coat thoroughly. Cover and chill at least 3 hours. Yield: 4 servings.

Acorn Squash

Niece-Kathy Abdon - Greenup, KY

2 (1-lb.) acorn squash, washed
1/4 c. hot water
4 tsp. butter or margarine
8 tsp. honey
1/4 fresh lemon
salt

Cut acorn squash in half crosswise and remove seeds with a spoon. Place squash cut side up in a 9-inch square nonmetallic baking dish. If necessary, cut a thin slice from the bottom to prevent squash from toppling.

Pour hot water over the squash halves.

Heat, uncovered, in microwave oven 9 to 10 (11-1/2 to 13) minutes. Turn dish 1/2 turn and heat, uncovered, in the microwave oven 8-10 minutes or until squash is fork tender.

Place 1 tsp. butter, 2 tsp. honey, a few drops of lemon juice and a sprinkling of salt on each half.

Heat, uncovered, in microwave oven an additional 3-4 minutes. Serves 2 to 4.

Squash Parmesan

Niece-Sandy Nelson Perrine- Greenup, KY

2 yellow squash, cut in julienne strips
2 zucchini, cut in julienne strips
1 T minced onion
1-1/2 tsp. vegetable oil
3/4 tsp. minced fresh basil or 1/4 tsp. dried whole basil
1/4 tsp. salt
1/8 tsp. pepper
1 small tomato, peeled and chopped
2 T grated Parmesan cheese
fresh basil

Combine first 7 ingredients in a 2-quart casserole. Cover with heavy-duty plastic wrap and microwave on HIGH for 3 to 4 minutes or until squash is crisp-tender, stirring after 2 minutes.

Stir in tomato. Cover and microwave on HIGH 1 minute or until tomato is tender. Sprinkle with cheese. Garnish with fresh basil, if desired. Yield: 4 servings.

Summer Squash Toss

Nephew-John O'Hare - Ashland, KY

1 lb. medium-sliced yellow squash (about 4)
1 lb. medium-sized zucchini (about 4)
1 (2 oz.) jar chopped pimiento, drained
1/2 tsp. salt
1/4 tsp. pepper
1/4 tsp. dried whole basil
1/4 tsp. garlic powder
2 T water
2 T butter or margarine
1 to 2 T grated Parmesan cheese

Wash yellow squash and zucchini, and cut into 1/2 inch thick slices; place in a 2-quart casserole. Add next 6 ingredients; toss well. Dot with butter. Cover with heavy-duty plastic wrap and microwave on HIGH for 9 to 10 minutes, stirring twice. Let stand, covered, 3 minutes before serving. Sprinkle with Parmesan cheese before serving. Yield: 4 to 6 servings.

Other Microwave Dishes

Almond Carnival Brittle
Niece-Lori Ann Stuart - Greenup, KY

2 c. whole blanched almonds, lightly toasted
1/2 c. packed brown sugar
1/2 c. granulated sugar
1/2 c. honey
1/2 tsp. almond extract
1 T butter
1 tsp. baking soda

Using butter or margarine lightly grease a cookie sheet.

With a wooden spoon, stir the two sugars and honey into the 2-qt. casserole. Microwave on high (100 percent) for 4 minutes. Mixture will be bubbly.

Stir in almonds and microwave on High (100 percent) 3-4 minutes, until light brown and bubbly.

Stir in butter and extract. Microwave on High (100 percent) for 2-3 minutes. Nuts will be a light brown and the syrup a rich golden brown.

Remove casserole from oven and beat in baking soda until syrup is light and foamy. Quickly transfer mixture to greased cookie sheet.

Allow to cool and break into pieces. Yields 1-1/2 lbs.

Cheese Sticks
Niece-Jennifer Stuart - Greenup, KY

1/2 c. butter, room temperature
1/2 c. shredded cheddar cheese
1/2 c. shredded Swiss cheese
3 drops pepper sauce
1 c. flour
1/4 tsp. onion salt
grated Parmesan cheese or garlic salt

In a medium mixing bowl cream butter, cheeses and pepper sauce. Mix flour and onion salt; add to creamed mixture, blending thoroughly.

On floured board, roll dough to 1/8 inch thickness, flouring lightly as needed. Cut into strips, 1/2 inch x 2 inches. If dough is sticky, refrigerate for 1/2 hour, then roll as directed.

Line flat side of the Imperial Bake and Roast Grill with waxed paper. Place cheese sticks on paper 1/2 inch apart. Microwave on high for 4 to 6 minutes or until firm.

For extra flavor, sprinkle with either garlic salt or grated Parmesan cheese before microcooking. 3-1/2 dozen sticks.

Caramel Corn
Niece-Amber Wheeler - Knoxville, TN

1/3 c. butter or margarine
2/3 c. firmly packed brown sugar
1/3 c. light or dark corn syrup
1/4 tsp. baking soda
1/2 tsp. vanilla
1 pop-and-serve bag (3.5 oz.) microwave popcorn, butter or natural flavor, popped.

In a large shallow baking dish, microwave butter on High until melted, about 1-1/2 minutes. Stir in brown sugar and corn syrup. Microwave on High until mixture boils, about 3 minutes, stirring once. Microwave on High 3 to 4 minutes without stirring. Stir in soda and vanilla. Stir in popped corn, mixing well. Microwave on 75 percent power for approximately 6 minutes, stirring every 2 minutes to coat popcorn evenly. Cool completely. Break apart and store in tightly covered container. This recipe makes about 2 quarts.

Microwave Peach Crisp

Nephew-Aaron Wheeler - Knoxville, TN

4 medium peaches, sliced (about 3 cups), or 2 cans
(16 oz. each) sliced peaches, drained
3/4 c. Bisquick baking mix
1/2 c. quick-cooking oats
1/2 c. packed brown sugar
3 T margarine or butter, softened
1/2 tsp. ground cinnamon
1/4 tsp. ground nutmeg

Arrange peaches in square microwavable dish, 8 x 8 x 2 inches. Mix remaining ingredients until crumble; sprinkle over peaches. Microwave uncovered on high (100 percent) 6 minutes; rotate dish 1/2 turn. Microwave uncovered until peaches are tender, 4 to 6 minutes longer. Serve with ice cream or whipped cream if desired. 6 servings.

Conventional Oven Directions: Heat oven to 375°. Prepare as directed except use square baking dish, 8 x 8 x 2 inches. Bake until peaches are tender, 30 to 35 minutes.

High Altitudes Directions: For microwave (for fresh peaches), increase second microwave time to 6 to 8 minutes. For canned peaches, no adjustments are necessary. For conventional oven, bake 40 to 45 minutes.

Apple Wheat Germ Muffins

Niece-Ellen Keeney Douglas - Lexington, KY

1/2 c. sugar
1/4 c. butter or margarine, softened
2 eggs
1-1/2 c. all-purpose flour
1/2 c. Kretschmer regular wheat germ
1 T baking powder
3/4 tsp. ground cinnamon
1/2 tsp. salt
1/4 tsp. ground nutmeg
1/2 c. milk
1 c. cored, pared and diced Golden Delicious apple
1/2 c. currants or raisins
wheat germ topping*

Cream sugar, butter and eggs thoroughly. Combine flour, wheat germ, baking powder, salt and spices. Add dry ingredients to creamed mixture alternately with milk. Blend well. Stir in apple and currants. Spoon batter into paper-lined microwave- safe muffin cups or custard cups about 1/2 full. Sprinkle about 1/2 tsp. wheat germ topping on each. Microwave 6 muffins at MEDIUM (50 percent power) 3 to 3-1/2 minutes; turn once halfway through cooking time. Remove from microwave oven. Let stand 2 to 3 minutes before serving. Makes 12 to 16 muffins.

*Wheat Germ Topping: Combine 2 T regular wheat germ, 1 T sugar and 1/8 tsp. ground nutmeg; mix well. Makes 3 T.

**Recipe developed for 600 to 700 watt microwave oven.

Conventional Method: Mix batter as above. Spoon batter into greased or paper-lined muffin pans about 2/3 full. Sprinkle 3/4 tsp. wheat germ topping on each. Bake at 400°, 20 to 25 minutes. Makes 12 muffins.

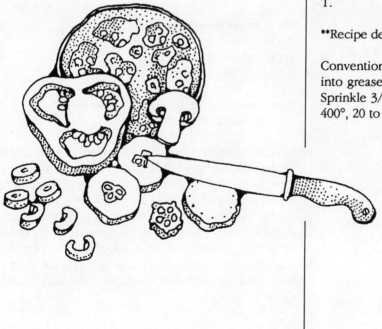

Graham Cracker Dessert

Nephew-David Abdon - Greenup, KY

Pudding:
2 c. milk
2 eggs, separated
2 T cornstarch
1/2 tsp. salt
1 c. sugar
1 tsp. vanilla

In medium sized glass bowl mix milk and sugar; add egg yolks (beaten), cornstarch and salt. Put in micorwave until it bubbles and thickens (around 5 minutes). Stir occasionally. Add vanilla.

Crust:
While pudding is cooking, prepare crust as follows: Roll fine, 18 graham crackers and mix with 1/2 c. sugar. Chunk 1/2 c. margarine on mixture. When pudding is done put graham cracker mixture in oven to melt butter, then stir and press into 9 x 9 inch pan. Reserve some cracker mixture to put on top of dessert.

Beat egg whites until stiff, then add 2 T powdered sugar. Pour pudding into crust, top with egg whites and cracker crumbs.

Bake at 350° for 20 minutes in conventional oven.

Southern Jam Cake

Niece-Marty Abdon - Greenup, KY

1-1/2 c. all-purpose flour
2/3 c. sugar
1/2 tsp. soda
1/2 tsp. salt
1 tsp. cinnamon
1/4 tsp. cloves
1/4 tsp. nutmeg
2/3 c. shortening
1/2 c. fruit preserves, jam or marmalade (cherry, plum, apricot or orange)
4 eggs
1/3 c. milk
1 T lemon juice
1/2 c. finely chopped nuts

Place all ingredients in mixing bowl. Blend at low speed, then beat at medium speed 2 minutes.

Grease fluted cake pan well. Coat with graham cracker crumbs. Spread batter in pan. Place on turntable. Microwave at medium heat (50 percent) for 12 minutes. If not using turntable rotate 1/4 turn every 3 minutes. Increase power to high (100 percent), and microwave 1 to 6 minutes, or until done. Cool directly on countertop 10 minutes. Turn out on wire rack. Makes 1 cake.

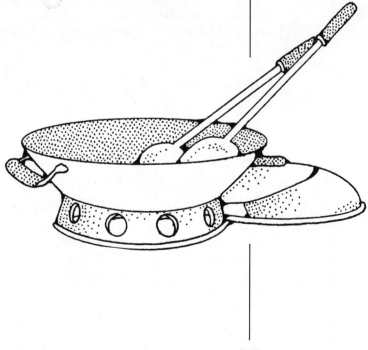

Lemon Cake

Daughter-Jane Stuart Juergensmeyer - Greenup, KY

1 c. flour
2 tsp. shredded lemon peel
1/2 tsp. baking powder (just guessed)
1/4 c. margarine
3/4 c. sugar
2 egg yolks
1 T lemon juice
1/2 c. milk
2 egg whites
cinnamon sugar
strawberries (optional - I used canned raspberries)

Stir together flour, lemon peel, baking powder. Beat margarine, add sugar, add egg yolks, and lemon juice. Combine well. Add flour mixture and milk one at a time. (I used a wooden spoon).

Beat egg whites, fold into batter, put into microwave safe baking dish. Cook uncovered on 100 percent power 4-6 minutes or until done, turning dish every 2 minutes. Mine took about 5 minutes to cook. Sprinkle with cinnamon sugar, cut into portions and serve warm with berries.

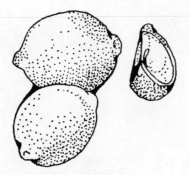

Southern Nut Baskets

Niece-Lori Ann Stuart - Greenup, KY

24 cupcake liners
1/4 c. butter or margarine
1 c. graham cracker crumbs
2 T sugar

Filling:
1/2 c. light or dark corn syrup
1/3 c. packed brown sugar
2 T butter or margarine, melted
1 T flour
1 tsp. vanilla
2/3 c. chopped pecans or walnuts
3 eggs

Place 2 liners in each cup of two muffin pans. In side dish, microwave butter at High (100 percent) 45 to 60 seconds, or until melted. Stir in crumbs and sugar. Place rounded tablespoonful of crumb mixture in each liner. Press down firmly with bottom of small glass.

Place a scant tablespoon of pecans in each cup. Blend remaining filling ingredients; place 2 tablespoosn in each cup. Place one muffin pan on turntable. Microwave at High (100 percent) 2 to 4 minutes, or until mixture bubbles in spots and tops are quite firm. If not using turntable, rotate pan every minute. Repeat for remaining muffin pan. Cool. Serve topped with whipped cream. Makes 12 servings. NOTE: If necessary to re-use muffin pan for remaining desserts, cool 2 to 3 minutes, then transfer desserts to paper towel.

Frosted Oatmeal Squares

Cousin-Dorothy Holbrook - Greenup, KY

4 c. quick cooking rolled oats
1 c. brown sugar
1 c. soft margarine
1/2 c. white syrup

Mix oats, brown sugar, margarine and syrup thoroughly. Divide mixture between two 2-quart glass dishes. Press evenly into dishes and bake each 3-1/2 to 4 minutes, until bubbly. Cool. Store in refrigerator. The squares will seem hard to cut, but will soften at room temperature. Makes 48 squares.

Frosting for Oatmeal Squares:
1 (6 oz.) pkg. chocolate bits
3/4 c. chunky peanut butter

Melt chocolate bits and peanut butter for 1-1/2 minutes; stir halfway through. Mix until smooth and spread on top of oatmeal mixture.

Orange-Coconut Apple Crisp

Niece-Jean Keeney Lush - Bowling Green, KY

6 c. sliced pared apples
2 T orange juice
2/3 c. brown sugar, packed
1/3 c. flour
1/2 tsp. grated orange rind
1/3 c. butter or regular margarine
1 c. flaked coconut
sweetened whipped cream

Arrange apples in 8-inch square glass baking dish. Sprinkle with orange juice. Combine brown sugar, flour, and orange rind in small bowl. Cut in butter with pastry blender or two forks until crumbly. Add coconut and toss. Sprinkle mixture over apples.

Microwave (high setting) 12 minutes or until apples are tender, rotating dish one-half turn after 6 minutes. Cool slightly. Spoon into dessert dishes. Top with whipped cream. Makes 6 servings.

Wintertime Breakfast Pudding

Nephew-Scott Lake - Berea, KY

2 T butter
3 eggs, lightly beaten
1-1/4 c. half and half
1 tsp. vanilla
3/4 c. packed brown sugar
1/2 tsp. cinnamon
1/2 tsp. coriander
1/4 tsp. salt (optional)
1/2 c. raisins
1/2 c. walnuts, chopped
1 can (30 oz.) fruit cocktail, drained
7 c. popped popcorn

In a 2-qt. casserole microwave butter on High (100 percent) for 30-45 seconds or until melted. Beat into the butter, half-and-half, eggs and vanilla, until ingredients are well blended.

Stir into the egg mixture, the brown sugar, cinnamon, coriander, salt, raisins, walnuts, and drained fruit cocktail. Stir until well blended.

Add the popcorn. Stir until the popcorn absorbs some of the liquid and it becomes half its size.

Transfer the mixture into the 1-qt casserole. Microwave, uncovered, on High (100 percent) for 12-15 minutes or until center is just about firm. Allow pudding to stand 10-15 minutes before serving. Serve plain or with half-and-half. Serves 6-8.

To keep pudding "serving warm", cover, and set the 1-qt. casserole in a pan of hot water.

Jesse and Naomi Deane Stuart's Grandchildren

Conrad Juergensmeyer

Erik Juergensmeyer

Pies, Pastries and Meringues

Pies

Apple Pie
Jenny's Apple-Cranberry Pie
Dutch Apple Pie
Apple Sauce Pie
Banana Cream Pie
Blackberry Pie
Blueberry Pie
Buttermilk Pie
Old Fashioned Butterscotch Pie
Cherry Pie
Chess Pie
Chocolate Pie
Coconut Cream Pie I
Coconut Cream Pie II
Coconut Macaroon Pie
Miniature Coconut Tarts
Custard Pie I
Custard Pie II
Grape Nuts Southern Pie
Grasshopper Pie
Hickory Nut Pie
Hawaiian Pie
Lemon-Pineapple Pie
Mincemeat (for pies)
Parisienne Pie
Grandma's Fried Peach Pies
Super Peach Custard Pie

Fresh Peach-Blueberry Pie
Pecan Pie I
Pecan Pie II
Toasted Pecan-Coconut Pie
Pecan Fudge Pie
Pecan Tarts
Damson Plum Pie
Pumpkin Pie
Raisin Pie
Rhubarb Pie
Strawberry Pie
Vinegar Pie

Pastries

Cream Cheese Pastry (for 2-9" pie shells)
Graham Cracker Pie Crust
Busy Wife Pie Crust
Never Fail Pie Crust I
Never Fail Pie Crust II
Standard Pastry
Vanilla Nut Crust

Meringues

Beautiful Meringue for Pie
Never-Fail Meringue
Chocolate Chip Pie
Meringue Shells

Jesse's grandmother - Violet Anne Pennington Hylton

Grandmother Violet Anne Pennington Hilton (B. 1855, D. 1895). Her mother was Sally Rosie Gullett and her maternal grandmother was a full blooded member of the Cherokee Nation, Wild Potato Clan, who died at Fontana Village near Cherokee, N.C. soon after Sally Rosie was born. Grandmother Violet Anne never saw her mother or grandmother. Her paternal grandmother Elizabeth Smith Pennington Thompson took violet Anne when she was a baby. She lived with her until she married Nathan Hilton. This lady was known as "Granny Thompson" because she was a midwife. Nathan Hilton (B. 1851, D. 1943)

Granny Thompson - Great, great grandmother Elizabeth Smith Pennington Thompson.

The two black horses pulled the children back
To their deserted pine-log mountain shack.
They left her there to sleep among the dead;
Tall Sextons, Penningtons and Leadinghams;
Shoveled her under after the prayer was said,
Among grave-stones with Bibles and White-lambs.
One crumpled dirt and put into her box:
"Ashes to ashes and dust to dust," he said.
And at her head and feet one put field rocks.
Violet Hylton was sister to the dead.
And forty years have passed—her grave is flat.
And no one now would know a grave is there.
No one would know here-by five children sat
And look last on their mother's straight black hair.

Jesse Stuart, *Man With a Bull-tongue Plow,* (New York: E. P. Dutton & Co., Inc., 1934), p. 181, sonnet 354.

Pies

Apple Pie
Sister-Sophie Keeney - Greenup, KY

6 apples
1/2 to 2/3 c. sugar
1/4 tsp. salt
1 tsp. cinnamon
2 T flour
1 recipe for standard pie pastry
1 T butter
1/4 tsp. nutmeg

Pare and slice apples. Sift dry ingredients together and mix with apples. Line pie pan with pastry, fill with apple mixture, dot with butter. Bake in very hot oven (450°) 15 minutes; reduce temperature to moderate (350°) and bake 45 minutes longer.

Jenny's Apple-Cranberry Pies (makes 2-9" pies)
Sister-Glennis Stuart Liles - Greenup, KY

3 c. sliced apples
2 c. cranberries (raw)
1/4 c. flour
1 tsp. cinnamon
1-3/4 c. sugar
Crusts for 2-2 crust pies

Mix sugar, flour, and cinnamon in a bowl. In pie shells, place 1 layer of apples and cranberries, sprinkle with sugar mixture and 3 or 4 slices of butter. Then place top crust on and bake 1 hour and 10 minutes at 400°.

Dutch Apple Pie
Cousin-Helen Johnson Shultz - Portsmouth, OH

1 c. light brown sugar, packed
2 T flour
1/2 tsp. salt
1 tsp. cinnamon
3/4 c. water
1 T lemon juice

Mix dry ingredients, stir in liquids and cook, stirring until fairly thick. Remove from heat and add:

2 T butter or oleo
1 tsp. vanilla extract

6 apples; peeled & sliced

Cool to lukewarm. Line pie pan with half of pastry. Put apples in lined pan and cover with cooled mixture. Crumble remaining pastry
with:
1/2 c. light brown sugar, packed

Sprinkle over top of pie. Bake in 450° oven 10 minutes. Reduce heat to 400° and bake about 30 minutes longer. Serve warm or cold.

Apple Sauce Pie
Cousin-Joyce (Jimmie) Carter McKinney - Scarbro, WV

1 c. apple sauce
1 c. milk
1 egg
1 tsp. lemon flavoring
1 tsp. butter
1/2 c. sugar
1/4 tsp. salt

Mix ingredients and pour in unbaked pie shell. Bake in 350° oven for 30-40 minutes.

Mother (Grace Hilton Carter) - "Girl in the Slipover Sweater" has made this pie ever since I can remember. I still make it often. It's simple, very refreshing to the taste.

Banana Cream Pie

Cousin-Betsy Shultz - Portsmouth, OH

3/4 c. sugar
1/4 c. flour
1/4 tsp. salt
2 c. milk
2 eggs, separated
2 T margarine
1 tsp. vanilla
2 bananas, sliced
1 baked 9" pie shell

Mix 1/2 c. sugar, flour, and salt in top of double boiler and stir in a little of the milk. Stir in remainder of the milk and cook, stirring constantly, over boiling water until thick. Cover and cook fifteen minutes longer, stirring occasionally. Beat egg yolks and add a small amount of the hot mixture to them. Stir it and the egg yolks back into the hot mixture and cook for several minutes. Add margarine and vanilla and stir until margarine is melted. Place bananas in pie shell and pour filling over them. Cool slightly. Beat egg whites in bowl until stiff, add remaining sugar gradually. Spread over filling. Bake at 400° until brown.

Blackberry Pie

Niece-Pam Abdon - Greenup, KY

3 c. fresh blackberries
1 c. sugar
2 T flour
2 T lemon juice
1/8 tsp. salt
1 recipe (or double crust pie) pastry
1 T butter

Combine berries, sugar, flour, lemon juice, and salt. Line pie pan with pastry, add filling, dot with butter and cover with top crust. Bake in hot oven (450°) for 10 minutes. Reduce temperature to moderate (350°) and bake 20-30 minutes longer. Makes 1 (9 in.) pie.

Blueberry Pie

Niece-Pam Abdon - Greenup, KY

4 c. blueberries
1 c. sugar
4 T flour
1/8 tsp. salt
1-1/2 T lemon juice
1 recipe standard pastry

Mix berries with sugar, flour, salt, and lemon juice. Line pie pan with pastry, pour in filling, and cover with top crust. Bake in hot oven (450°) 10 minutes; reduce temperature to 350° F and bake 20-30 minutes longer. Makes 1 (9 in.) pie.

Buttermilk Pie

Niece-Carrol Keeney Abdon - Greenup, KY

1-1/3 c. sugar
3 T all-purpose flour
2 eggs, beaten
1/2 c. butter or margarine,, melted
1 c. buttermilk
2 tsp. vanilla extract
1 tsp. lemon extract
1 unbaked 9" pastry shell

Combine sugar and flour, mixing well; add eggs, butter, and buttermilk. Beat well. Stir in flavoring. Pour into pastry shell. Bake at 400° for 10 minutes. Reduce heat and bake at 325° for 30 to 35 minutes. Yield: 1 (9 in.) pie.

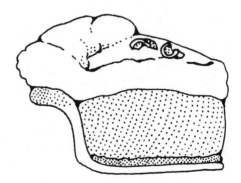

Old Fashioned Butterscotch Pie

Niece-Carrol Abdon - Greenup, KY

1 c. light brown sugar (firmly packed)
2 c. boiling water
5 T flour
3 egg yolks, beaten
4 T butter
1/4 tsp. salt
1 tsp. vanilla
1 baked 9" pie shell

Mix sugar, flour, and salt together thoroughly. Add boiling water and cook over medium heat until thickened. Add butter and cook until melted. Have 3 egg yolks beaten in small bowl. Add small amount of cooked mixture to egg yolks and mix. Put back into mixture and cook 2 minutes, stirring constantly. Take from heat and add vanilla. Let cool. Pour into pie shell. Cover with meringue and bake in 350° oven until browned.

Cherry Pie

Cousin-Mary Bell Johnson - Portsmouth, OH

2 (16 oz.) cans pitted tart cherries
1 c. sugar
1/4 c. all-purpose flour
pastry for lattice-top 9" pie.
1/4 c. milk

Drain cherries, reserving 3/4 c. juice. Set cherries aside. Combine juice, sugar, and flour in medium saucepan. Cook over medium heat, stirring constantly, until thickened and bubbly. Remove from heat and stir in cherries. Spoon filling evenly into pastry lined 9" pie pan. Arrange strips of pastry in lattice design over filling; seal edges. Pastry strips may be brushed with milk to insure even browning. Bake at 375° for 45 minutes.

Chess Pie

Niece-Connie Keeney - Greenup, KY

1/2 stick butter
1-1/2 c. sugar
3 large eggs or 4 small
1/2 c. evaporated milk
1 T corn meal
1 tsp. vanilla
1 tsp. vinegar
1/2 tsp. butter flavoring
1/4 tsp. rum flavoring

Cream all together except vinegar. Add it last and mix well. Pour into unbaked pie crust and bake 45 minutes at 350°.

Chocolate Pie

Niece-Jennifer Stuart - Greenup, KY

1-1/2 c. sugar
1/2 c. cornstarch
1/2 c. cocoa
1/4 tsp. salt
2-1/2 c. milk
3 egg yolks, beaten
1/2 tsp. vanilla
1 9-inch baked pie shell
1/2 pint whipping cream, whipped

Mix the sugar, cornstarch, cocoa, and salt in the top of a double boiler. Add 1/2 c. milk and egg yolks and blend well. Add remaining milk. Place over boiling water and cook, stirring constantly, until thick. Add vanilla. Pour into pie shell and top with whipped cream. Chill.

Coconut Cream Pie I

Niece-Hilde Darby - Greenup, KY

Crust:
1 c. flour
1/2 tsp. salt
1/3 c. Crisco
2 T water

Mix flour and salt. With pastry blender, cut in the shortening. Sprinkle with water and mix with fork until dough is moist. Press into ball and roll out. Place into pie pan and bake in preheated oven on 475° for 8-10 minutes. Cool

Filling: Mix in saucepan:
2/3 c. sugar
3 T cornstarch
1/2 tsp. salt

Gradually stir in *3 c. milk.*

Cook over medium heat, stirring constantly until it thickens and boils. Boil for 1 minute. Remove from heat. Separate 3 eggs and beat egg yolks slightly, with fork. Stir about half of the hot mixture into egg yolks. Now stir this into the hot mixture in saucepan.

Stir in:
4 T butter
1-1/2 tsp. vanilla
1 can "Angel Flake" Coconut

Meringue:
3 egg whites
1/2 tsp. vanilla
6 T sugar

Beat egg whites until frothy. Gradually add sugar and keep beating until mixture is no longer grainy. Add vanilla. Pile meringue on coconut cream pie, then sprinkle with coconut. Bake in preheated 400° oven for 8-10 minutes or golden brown. Cool at room temperature. Note: To cut meringue pie neatly, dip a sharp knife into water between each cut.

Coconut Cream Pie II

Niece-Carrol Abdon - Greenup, KY

Mix in saucepan:
2/3 c. sugar
1/2 tsp. salt
2-1/2 tsp. cornstarch
1 T flour

Stir in gradually 3 c. milk. Cook over moderate heat, stirring constantly, until mixture thickens and boils. Boil 1 minute. Remove from heat. Slowly stir half the mixture into 3 egg yolks, slightly beaten. Then blend into hot mixture in saucepan. Boil 1 minute more, stirring constantly. Remove from heat.

Blend in:
1 T butter
1-1/2 tsp. vanilla
3/4 c. shredded coconut

Spread whipped cream or meringue on top. Sprinkle with 1/4 c. shredded coconut (toast, if desired).

Coconut Macaroon Pie

Cousin-Connie Frazier Stewart - Kenova, WV

1 9" unbaked pie shell
1-1/2 c. sugar
1/2 c. milk
1/2 c. margarine
1-1/2 c. coconut
2 eggs
1/4 c. flour
1/2 tsp. salt

Beat sugar, eggs, and salt until mixture is lemon yellow. Add margarine and flour and blend well. Add milk and fold in coconut (1 cup). Pour into pie shell and top with remaining coconut (1/2 cup). Bake in 325° oven (about 60 minutes).

Miniature Coconut Tarts
Cousin-Beverly Jane Benner Murphy - Lucasville, OH

Pastry:
1-1/3 c. plain flour
1/3 c. sugar
1/4 tsp. salt
3/4 c. butter
1 egg, slightly beaten

Filling:
1 egg, beaten
1 pkg. (3-1/3 oz.) flaked coconut
2/3 c. sugar

To make pastry, cream butter and sugar; add egg, flour, and salt.

Refrigerate several hours wrapped in wax paper. Preheat oven to 375°. To make the filling, add coconut and sugar to the beaten egg. Make tart dough 1/8 inch thick. Use 1 tsp. filling for each tart. Bake 12 minutes until filling is golden. Makes 40.

Custard Pie I
Cousin-Cynthia Smith Lewis - West Portsmouth, OH

2-1/2 c. scalded milk
4 eggs, beaten
1/2 c. sugar
1 tsp. vanilla
pinch salt

Combine eggs, sugar, and salt. Add milk and vanilla. Pour into an unbaked pie shell. If desired, sprinkle nutmeg over mixture. Bake at 475° for 15 minutes, then at 400° for 5 minutes.

Custard Pie II
Sister-Glennis Stuart Liles - Greenup, KY

4 eggs, slightly beaten
1/2 c. sugar
1/2 tsp. salt
3 c. milk
1 tsp. vanilla
1/4 tsp. nutmeg
1 unbaked pie shell

Combine eggs, sugar, and salt. Add milk, vanilla, and nutmeg and pour into pie shell. Bake in hot oven at 450° for 10 minutes; and then in a moderate oven of 350° for 30 minutes or until a silver knife inserted in center comes out clean.

Grape Nuts Southern Pie
Cousin-Ginny Belle Smith - Lucasville, OH

1/2 c. grape nuts
1/2 c. lukewarm water
1 c. brown sugar
1 c. dark corn syrup
1/4 c. butter
3 eggs
1/8 tsp. salt
1 tsp. vanilla

Soak grape nuts in water until water is absorbed. Combine sugar, syrup, butter, and salt in saucepan. Bring to a boil, stirring until the sugar is dissolved. Remove from heat. Beat eggs until foamy. Add small amount of hot syrup mixture to the eggs, beating well. Stir in softened grape nuts and the vanilla. Pour into a pastry lined pan. Bake at 375° for 45-50 minutes. Serve with whipped cream, if desired.

Grasshopper Pie

Niece-Sally Ann Staph - Greenup, KY

4 T butter
20 cookies (use Oreo cookies)
24 marshmallows
2/3 c. milk
2 jiggers creme de menthe
2 jiggers white cream de cocoa
1 c. whipped cream

Crush cookies and mix with melted butter. Put in pans, then in 350° oven for 5 minutes to get hot. Melt marshmallows in milk in double boiler-cool. Add cream de menthe, white cream de cocoa and whipped cream. Freeze overnight. Recipe makes 2 fillings.

Hickory Nut Pie

Sister-Sophie Stuart Kenney - Greenup, KY

1 c. kernels
1 c. brown sugar
1/2 c. white sugar
2 eggs
1/4 c. butter
1/2 tsp. salt
1/2 tsp. vanilla
2 T milk
2 T cornmeal

Mix all ingredients thoroughly. Add nuts and pour into an unbaked pie shell. Bake at 325° for 55-60 minutes or until done.

Hawaiian Pie

Cousin-Goldie Adkins - East Liverpool, OH

1 can (12 oz.) unsweetened pineapple juice
3/4 c. sugar
7 medium cooking apples, pared, cored and cut in wedges
3 T cornstarch
1 T butter or margarine
1/2 tsp. vanilla
1/4 tsp. salt
A baked, cooled pastry shell

In large saucepan, combine 1-1/4 c. of pineapple juice and sugar. Bring to a boil, add apple wedges. Simmer covered until tender, but not soft. 3-4 minutes. Lift apples from syrup-set aside to drain. Combine cornstarch and the remaining pineapple juice, then add to syrup in saucepan. Cook and stir until thickened and bubbly. Cook 1 minute more. Remove from heat, add butter, vanilla, and salt. Cool 10 minutes, without stirring. Pour half the pineapple mixture into pastry shell. Spread to cover bottom. Arrange cooked apples on top. Spoon remaining sauce over apples. Chill. Garnish with whipped cream. Sprinkle with chopped macadamia nuts.

Lemon-Pineapple Pie

Cousin-Katherine Stewart Martin - Racine, WS

1 (20 oz.) can crushed pineapple
1 pkg. (3-3/4 oz.) instant lemon (pie filling pudding)
1 pkg. (2 oz.) dry whipped cream (Dream Whip)

Make instant pudding mix as directed on pkg. Drain crushed pineapple. Prepare dry Dream Whip. Fold all ingredients together and pour into a 9 inch graham cracker crust. Top with whip cream.

Mincemeat

(Originally, venison neck meat was used).
Cousin-Ron Arrick - Lucasville, OH

2 lbs. beef, coarsely ground
1 lb. suet
5 lb. apples
3 lb. raisins
2 lb. currants
3/4 lb. citron
2-1/2 lb. brown sugar
2 T cinnamon
2 T mace
1 T cloves
1 T salt
1 tsp. nutmeg
1 qt. sherry
1 pint brandy

Peel and chop apples. Combine all ingredients together. Cook very slowly, uncovered for about an hour and a half, or until the mincemeat reaches the right consistency. Can hot, or store in an earthenware crock or plastic tub in the refrigerator. The mincemeat will be protected by a coating of suet. This makes enough for 10 medium size pies and keeps forever improving with age.

Parisienne Pie

Cousin-Ramona Adkins - Defiance, OH

1 c. flour
3/4 c. crushed walnuts
1 stick oleo
2 tubs Cool Whip
1 c. powdered sugar
1 (8 oz.) pkg. cream cheese
1 lg. pkg. instant chocolate pudding
3 c. milk

Mix flour, 1/2 c. nuts and oleo; press into 9 x 13 inch pan and bake for 15 minutes - cool crust.

Layer 1: Mix 1 c. Cool Whip, sugar and cream cheese.
Layer 2: Mix pudding and milk according to directions on pkg.
Layer 3: Top with remaining Cool Whip. Sprinkle with 1/4 cup crushed nuts. Chill and serve.

Grandma's Fried Peach Pies

Cousin-Helen Shultz - Portsmouth, OH

2 (8 oz.) pkg. dried peaches (may use apples)
1/2-3/4 c. sugar
1/2 tsp. cinnamon
1/2 tsp. ground nutmeg
egg pastry
shortening

Cover peaches with boiling water and cook over medium heat until very tender. Drain, reserving 1/4 cup liquid; cool. Mash peaches and combine with reserved liquid, sugar, and spices; set aside. Roll out pastry and cut out circles, using a 5 inch saucer as a measure. Place about 3 T peach mixture on half of each pastry circle. Fold in half and crimp edges together. Heat 1 inch shortening in skillet to 375°. Cook pies until brown on each side, turning only once. Drain well on paper towels.

Egg Pastry:
3 c. all-purpose flour
1 tsp. salt
1 c. shortening
1 egg, beaten
4 T water
1 tsp. vinegar

Combine flour and salt; cut in shortening until mixture resembles coarse cornmeal. Combine egg and water; sprinkle over flour mixture. Add vinegar and lightly stir until mixture forms a ball. Wrap in waxed paper and chill at least 1 hour or until ready to use. Yield: about 1-1/2 dozen pies.

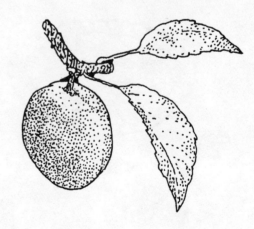

Super Peach Custard Pie

Cousin-Ila Shanks - Zelienople, PA

This is a prize winning recipe. It is unique because it is made without milk. A great dessert and so easy to make.

1 c. sugar
2 T flour
2 large eggs, well beaten
sliced fresh peaches
1 T butter
1/2 tsp cinnamon
1 9-in. unbaked pie shell

Mix flour and sugar together. Add to well-beaten eggs. Slice enough pared fresh peaches (thick slices) to fill unbaked pie shell and cover with egg, sugar, flour mixture. Sprinkle with cinnamon and dot with butter.

Bake 10 minutes at 450° - reduce temperature to 350° and bake for 30 minutes or until custard is done. Be careful not to overbake.

Fresh Peach-Blueberry Pie

Niece-Betty Stuart Darby Baird - Wadestown, WV

5 to 5-1/2 c. fresh peaches, sliced
1 c. fresh blueberries
1 T lemon juice
1 c. sugar
3 T quick cooking tapioca
1/4 tsp. salt
2 T butter or margarine

Combine peaches, blueberries, and lemon juice. Add sugar, tapioca, and salt; toss gently. Spoon fruit mixture into crust-lined pan. Dot with butter. Top with second crust and flute; cut several slits for steam to escape. Bake at 425° for 40 - 50 minutes or until golden brown. Serve warm or cold. Garnished with whipped cream.

Tips: Frozen fruit can be substituted for fresh. Thaw it and drain it well. Cover edge of crust with strip of foil during last ten to fifteen minutes of baking to prevent excessive browning.

Pecan Pie I

Niece-Naomi Vivian Keeney - Greenup, KY

Make pastry for one-crust 9" pie or double recipe, if desired. Line pie pans.

3 eggs
2/3 c. sugar
1/3 tsp. salt
1/3 c. butter, melted
1 c. dark corn syrup

Beat ingredients together with rotary beater.

Mix in ...
1 c. pecan halves

Pour into pastry-lined pan. Bake at 375° for 40-50 minutes until set and pastry is nicely browned. Cool. Serve cold or slightly warm.

This is a traditional recipe from Virginia. It is the choice among all desserts served at renowned Williamsburg Inn in restored colonial Williamsburg.

Pecan Pie II

Niece-Shirley Stuart - Greenup, KY

1-1/2 c. light corn syrup
1/2 c. sugar
1/4 c. butter or margarine
1 c. coarsley chopped pecans (or use halves)
1 unbaked 9-inch pastry shell
3 eggs
1 tsp. vanilla
dash salt

In saucepan, combine corn syrup, sugar, and butter or margarine; bring to boiling. Boil gently, uncovered 5 minutes, stirring occasioinally. Cool syrup mixture slightly. Place the pecans in bottom of pastry shell. Combine eggs, vanilla, and salt. Pour cooled mixture into egg mixture; beat well. Pour over nuts (pecans will rise to top). Bake at 375° until knife inserted in center comes out clean, 30 to 35 minutes.

Toasted Pecan-Coconut Pie

Cousin-Ethel Hilton Porter - Ashland, KY

3 eggs, beaten
1-1/2 c. sugar
1/2 c. margarine, melted
2 tsp. lemon juice
1 tsp. vanilla
1 c. coconut
1/2 c. pecan halves

Mix all ingredients together and pour in pie shell. Bake at 350° for 45 minutes.

Pecan Fudge Pie

Cousin-Al Lester - Kenova, WV

1 9-inch, unbaked pastry shell
1 (4 oz.) pkg. sweet cooking chocolate or 2 (1 oz.)
  squares unsweetened chocolate
1/4 c. margarine or butter
1 (14 oz.) can Eagle Brand sweetened condensed milk
  (not evaporated milk)
1/2 c. hot water
2 eggs, well beaten
1 tsp. vanilla extract
1/8 tsp. salt
1-1/4 c. pecan halves or pieces

Preheat oven to 350°. In medium saucepan, over low heat, melt chocolate and margarine. Stir in Eagle Brand, hot water, and eggs; mix well. Remove from heat; stir in remaining ingredients. Pour into prepared pastry shell. Bake 40 to 45 minutes or until center is set. Cool. Chill 3 hours.

Pecan Tarts

Cousin-Betty Adkins Hotopp - Dayton, OH

Mix:
1 c. brown sugar
1/2 c. sugar
1 T flour

Beat in thoroughly:
2 eggs
2 T milk
1 tsp. vanilla
1/2 c. butter, melted

Fold in:
1 c. pecans

Pour into muffin pan lined with pastry shells. Bake at 375°, just until set.

The Friday after Thanksgiving we always have a family reunion. Every year a menu is made out and each person is assigned a dish (or dishes) to bring. I am always asked to bring my pecan tarts.

Damson Plum Pie

Niece-Nancy Sue Darby Lake - Berea, KY

4 c. stoned, sliced plums
2 T flour
2/3 c. granulated sugar (or more)
1/4 tsp. nutmeg
1/8 tsp. salt
1/4 tsp. cinnamon
1 tsp. lemon juice
1 T butter

Line 9" pan with pastry and fill with sliced plums. Mix sugar, flour, nutmeg, salt, cinnamon, and lemon juice. Sprinkle over plums and dot with butter. Bake at 425° for 40 minutes.

Pumpkin Pie

Niece-Pam Abdon - Greenup, KY

2 eggs, slightly beaten
1 lb. can pumpkin
3/4 c. sugar
1/2 tsp. salt
1 tsp. cinnamon
1/2 tsp. ginger
1/4 tsp. cloves
1-2/3 c. evaporated milk or light cream
9" unbaked pie shell

This can be doubled easily for 2 (8 inch) pies.

Mix ingredients in order given. Pour into pie shell. Bake in hot oven (425°) for 15 minutes. Reduce temperature to moderate (350°) oven and continue baking for 45 minutes or until knife inserted in center of pie filling comes out clean.

Delicious with whipped cream.

Raisin Pie

Niece-Pam Abdon - Greenup, KY

Filling for 9" pie

2 c. seeded raisins
2 c. boiling water
1/2 c. sugar
2 T flour
1/2 c. chopped nuts (optional)
2 tsp. grated lemon rind
3 T lemon juice

Cook raisins covered in water until tender (about 5 minutes). Stir in mixture of sugar and flour. Cook over low heat, stirring constantly until boiling. Boil 1 minute. Remove from heat. Stir in nuts, lemon rind, and lemon juice. Pour into pie shell and cover with top crust. Bake until nicely browned. Serve slightly warm.

Temp.: 425° (hot oven)
Time: Bake 30-40 minutes

Rhubarb Pie

Niece-Carrol Keeney Abdon - Greenup, KY

3 T flour
1 c. sugar
1 egg, beaten
2 c. rhubarb, cut into small pieces
1 pastry shell (unbaked)

Mix all the above ingredients together. Pour into pie shell and bake at 425° F. for 10 minutes. Reduce heat to 350° for 35 minutes.

Strawberry Pie

Niece-Melissa (Lissie) Liles - Greenup, KY

2 c. water
3/4 c. sugar
3 T cornstarch
1 T lemon juice
dash of salt

Mix above ingredients together and cook until thick. Remove from heat and add 1 (3 oz.) pkg. strawberry jello. Put a layer of strawberries in baked pie shell. Pour mixture over berries and refrigerate.

Uncle Jesse loved fresh strawberries. He always got the first quart from our patch. From the time I was old enough to go by myself, Dad let me take them to him. He called me his "Strawberry Girl."

Vinegar Pie

Sister-Mary Nelson - Greenup, KY

3 egg yolks
1/2 c. cold water
1 c. sugar
1 T lemon juice
4 T flour
1-1/2 c. boiling water
1/2 c. vinegar
1/2 tsp. salt

Mix flour and cold water. Add egg yolks and sugar, then boiling water and vinegar. Cook over low heat. Add salt and lemon juice after cooking. Let cool and pour into baked pie shell. This is an old recipe used many years ago by us country people for Sunday dinner.

233

Pastries

Cream Cheese Pastry (for 2-9" pie shells)

Cousin-Faye Lester - Kenova, WV

2 c. sifted flour
3/4 tsp. salt
2/3 c. vegetable shortening
12 oz. cream cheese

Mix flour and salt. Work in shortening and cream cheese. This crust is good for open fruit pies or citrus chiffon pies.

Graham Cracker Pie Crust

Cousin-Grace Carter - Sophie, WV

1-1/4 c. fine graham cracker crumbs
1/4 c. soft butter
1/4 c. sugar
1 egg

Mix together and press into a 9 inch pie pan. Flute edge. Bake at 350° for 10 minutes. This crust cuts without so much crumbling.

Busy Wife Pie Crust

Cousin-Loretta Adkins Benner - Lucasville, OH

3 c. of flour
salt to taste
1 c. shortening

Place 1/3 c. of water in a pan and heat; then add shortening, stirring until mixture is hot. Stir into flour and salt and mix well. Cool in refrigerator until ready to use for pies.

Never Fail Pie Crust I

Sister-in-law-Betty Stuart - Greenup, KY

5 c. flour
2-1/2 c. Crisco
1 tsp. salt
1 egg
2 tsp. white vinegar

Sieve flour and salt together. Beat egg in a measuring cup with vinegar, then add enough water to fill the cup.

Combine liquid with dry ingredients. Mix with pastry blender. Roll into oblong shape, or divide into 6 rolls (makes 6 crusts for 9" pies). Wrap and place them all in a plastic bread wrapper, fastened up. Use as needed. It will keep a month or longer.

Never Fail Pie Crust II

Cousin-Mae Pennington Fellows - Albuquerque, NM

2 c. flour
1 tsp. salt
1/2 c. cold milk
1/2 c. cooking oil

Measure flour and salt in bowl. Measure milk and oil in cup (together). Dump it into the flour-stir lightly. Makes a soft dough. Roll between 2 pieces of wax paper-lift bottom paper to place in pie tin.

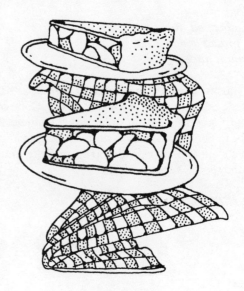

Standard Pastry (2 crust 8" or 9" pie or 2 shells)
Niece-Martha Stuart Wheeler - Johnson City, TN

2 c. flour, sifted
1 tsp. salt
2/3 c. vegetable shortening (solid)
1/2 c. lard
4 to 5 T cold water

Mix flour and salt; cut in shortening and lard. Add water, a few drops at a time, mixing with a fork, until all flour can be held together in a ball. Enough for 2 8" or 9" or 2 shells.

Variety Pastries-Using Standard Recipe:

Cheese: Cut 1/3 c. grated cheddar into flour with shortening to standard recipe.

Nut: Substitute 1/2 c. finely ground walnuts or pecans for 1/2 c. flour in standard recipe.

Coffee: Add 1 T instant coffee powder with salt in the standard recipe.

Spice: Add 1 tsp. cinnamon, 1/2 tsp. nutmeg, dash of cloves to standard recipe.

Sesame: Add 1/4 c. toasted sesame seed to standard recipe.

Vanilla Nut Crust (for one 9" pie)
Niece-Lori Ann Stuart - Greenup, KY

1 c. all-purpose flour
1/4 c. finely crushed vanilla wafers
1/2 tsp. salt
1/3 c. lard (or shortening)
3 T pecans finely chopped
3 to 4 T water

Combine dry ingredients and cut in shortening until pieces are the size of small peas. Stir in chopped pecans. Sprinkle 1 T water over part of mixture and gently toss with a fork. Push to side of bowl. Repeat, using 2 to 3 T more water until all is moistened. Form dough into a ball.

On lightly floured surface, flatten dough with hands. Roll into 12 inch circle; transfer to 9 inch pie plate. Trim pastry, leaving 1/2 inch beyond edge of plate. Flute edge. Prick bottom and sides with fork. Bake at 450° for 11 to 12 minutes or until pastry is golden. Cool on wire rack. Makes one 9 inch crust.

Meringues

Beautiful Meringue for Pie
Niece-Connie Keeney - Greenup, KY

1/2 c. water
1 T cornstarch
1/2 c. sugar
3 egg whites
3/4 tsp. cream of tartar

Combine the water, cornstarch, and 2 T sugar in a saucepan and mix well. Cook until thick, stirring constantly, then cool. Beat egg whites with cream of tartar in a bowl until stiff. Add remaining sugar and beat until glossy. Fold in cornstarch mixture and spread on pie, so meringue touches edge of crust. Bake at 350° until brown.

Never-Fail Meringue
Niece-Connie Keeney - Greenup, KY

3 egg whites
1/4 tsp. cream of tartar
6 T sugar
1/2 tsp. vanilla

Beat egg whites and cream of tartar in a bowl until fluffy. Add the sugar gradually and beat until stiff peaks form. Add vanilla and beat well. Spread on pie so meringue touches edge of crust. Bake at 400° for 8 to 10 minutes or until brown.

Chocolate Chip Pie
Cousin-Susan Ellington - Louisville, KY

1 can Angel Flake coconut
1 pkg. chocolate chips
1 stick margarine
5 eggs
1 1/2 c. sugar
1 T flour
1 tsp. vanilla
1 tsp. vinegar

Prepare 2 pie shells. Divide coconut evenly and spread in bottom of pie shells. Divide chocolate chips evenly and spread over coconut. Combine the next 6 ingredients in a mixing bowl and beat until creamy. Pour mixture over coconut and chocolate chips. Bake at 325 degrees for 35 minutes.

Tastes excellent with marshmallows and butterscotch chips added.

Meringue Shells
Niece-Lori Ann Stuart - Greenup, KY

For a special occasion dessert, scoop any homemade frozen dessert into these beautiful meringue shells and top with fresh fruit and syrup.

Makes 8 Meringues.

6 egg whites, at room temperature
1/2 tsp. cream of tartar
dash salt
1/4 tsp. almond flavoring
1-3/4 c. granulated sugar

In large bowl of electric mixer, combine egg whites, cream of tartar, salt, and almond extract. (Be certain bowl beaters are free from oil or fat before you begin).

Beat egg whites until frothy. Gradually add sugar, several tablespoons at a time, until mixture is very stiff.

Preheat oven to 225°. Cover 2 cookie sheets with foil. Grease foil with vegetable cooking spray or oil.

Spread some meringue to make four 4-inch rounds (about 1/8 inch-thick) 2-inches apart, on each tray.

Spoon remaining meringue into a large pastry bag with large star tip and pipe a row of stars, 1-inch high, around the edge of each meringue round. Or, spoon remaining meringue into swirls around the edge of each meringue round.

Bake meringue shells 1 hour. Turn off oven, but do not open it. Allow meringues to sit in oven 2 hours or overnight, until crisp. Store, tightly covered in a tin, until ready to use.

Salads and Salad Dressings

Salads
Antipasta Salad
Four-Bean Salad
Green Bean and Bacon Salad
Best Yet Salad
Marinated Broccoli
Broccoli Salad I
Broccoli Salad II
Broccoli-Mushroom Salad
Buttermilk Salad
Chicken Salad
Hot Chicken Salad
Cucumber and Red Onion Salad
Florida Salad
Killed Lettuce
Linguine Salad
Macaroni Salad I
Macaroni Salad II
Pea Salad
Potato Salad I
Potato Salad II
Potato Salad III
Grandma's German Potato Salad
Sourcream Potato Salad
Sauerkraut Salad
Cole Slaw

Cole Slaw Parfait Salad
Slaw
Freezer Slaw I
Freezer Slaw II
Spinach Salad I
Spinach Salad II
Taco Salad I
Taco Salad II
24 Hour Bean Salad
24 Hour Cole Slaw
Vegetable Salad
Raw Vegetable Salad

Salad Dressings
Buttermilk Salad Dressing
French Dressing
Hollandaise
Homemade Mayonnaise
Deluxe Honey Dressing
Lemony Vegetable Dressing
Red Salad Dressing
Roquefort or Bleu Cheese Dressing
Russian Dressing
Slaw Dressing
Thousand Island Dressing
Vinaigrette Dressing

Jesse and daughter, Jane

Jesse Stuart and daughter, Jane

Let her know actual beauty inwardly,
Not artificial beauty second-hand;
Let her be free as mountain wind is free
To know, observe, and love her native land.
Let her touch rugged bark of sister trees,
Pull percoon petals, tearing them apart
To feel and see the beauty that's in these,
The strength to feed her growing brain and heart.
Let her know mandrake and the sawbriar tendril
And wild sweet williams blooming in the hollow;
And let her have strong legs to climb the hill
And find the magic road she is to follow.
Let her blow milkweed furze across the meadow
And course each runlet to the valley stream;
Let her run with a spring cloud's shifting shadow . . .
Give her the world and time wherein to dream.

Jesse Stuart, *Album of Destiny*, (New York: E. P. Dutton & Co., Inc., 1944), p. 250.

Salads

Antipasta Salad

Cousin-Connie Frazier Stewart - Kenova, WV

Cook: 1 lb. shell macaroni
Drain, cool and combine with following:

2 green peppers, diced
3 stalks celery, diced
1 onion, diced
black and green olives
1/4 lb. salami, diced
1/4 lb. Provolone cheese, diced
1/4 lb. pepperoni, diced
3 tomatoes, cut small

Mix all together.

Dressing:
Combine and shake in jar:

1 T salt
1 tsp. pepper
1 tsp. oregano
1/2 c. vinegar
1/4 c. oil

Pour over salad and let stand overnight.

Four-Bean Salad

Sister-Sophie Stuart Kenney - Greenup, KY

1 can green beans
1 can yellow beans
1 can dark red kidney beans, washed
1 can garbanzas (chick peas), washed
1 stalk celery, sliced thin
1 green pepper, chopped
1 medium onion, sliced thin
1 c. sugar
1/2 c. salad oil
3/4 c. vinegar
salt

Combine sugar, salad oil, vinegar, and salt. Beat well or run a few minutes in a blender. Pour over ingredients and stir gently. Stir several times during the first day. Make this salad at least 24 hours before serving. (Keeps for several days). Serves 6 or more.

Green Bean and Bacon Salad

Niece-Sandy Nelson Perrine - Greenup, KY

Serve as a side dish at room temperature.

5 slices bacon, coarsley chopped
3 T olive oil
Pepper to taste
1-1/2 lb. fresh green beans, trimmed, cooked crisp, tender and drained, or 2 pkgs. (9 oz.) frozen whole green beans, thawed.
1 medium yellow or red bell pepper, chopped coarse (1/2 c.).

Cook bacon in skillet over medium heat until crisp, stirring once or twice. Remove with a slotted spoon to paper towel and drain. Pour all but 1 T drippings from skillet. Add remaining ingredients except for bacon. Cook about 3 minutes, heating through, stirring constantly. Transfer to a medium size bowl. Stir in bacon; cool completely. Cover and refrigerate at least 6 hours or up to 2 days, tossing occasionally. Makes 5 cups, 6 servings.

Best Yet Salad

Cousin-Linda Adkins Meyers - Defiance, OH

Using 9 x 13 in. casserole, place enough shredded crisp lettuce in bottom of casserole to cover well. Shred 2 medium carrots and dice 1/4 cup onion, 1/4 cup cauliflower buds, 8 oz. frozen early peas. Spread these vegetables over lettuce. Make dressing of: 1-1/2 c. mayonnaise, 1 T lemon juice, 1 T sugar or 1 pkg. equal. Mix well together and spread over vegetables. Top with 1 cup shredded cheddar cheese. Sprinkle with real bacon bits. Cover with saran wrap and refrigerate over night.

Marinated Broccoli

Cousin-Al Lester - Ceredo, WV

2 lbs. fresh broccoli
1-1/2 c. vegetable oil
1 c. distilled vinegar
1 T sugar
1 T dill seed
1 tsp. garlic salt
1 tsp. pepper
1/2 tsp. salt

Trim off large leaves of broccoli and remove tough end of lower stalks. Wash broccoli thoroughly. Cut off flowerettes (reserve stems for another use) and place in a large bowl; set aside.

Combine remaining ingredients in a jar. Cover tightly, and shake vigorously. Pour marinade over broccoli; toss gently. Cover and chill 8 hours. Serve with a slotted spoon. Yield: 8 to 10 servings.

Broccoli Salad I

Cousin-Goldie Adkins - East Liverpool, OH

1 bunch broccoli, cut up (use flowers and stems)
diced onion to taste
1 c. shredded cheddar cheese
1/2 lb. fried bacon, crumbled
1/2 c. Miracle Whip
1/2 c. or less sugar
2 T vinegar

Mix together the last three ingredients and pour over broccoli and mix well. Top with cheese and bacon.

Broccoli Salad II

Cousin-Katherine Stewart Martin - Racine, WS

1 (10 oz.) pkg. broccoli
1 diced cucumber
2 medium tomatoes, diced
2 chopped green onions
cucumber dressing

Add enough cucumber dressing to cover. Toss all ingredients and chill 2 hours.

Broccoli-Mushroom Salad

Niece-Martha Deane Callihan North - Champaign, IL

1 lb. fresh mushrooms
1 head broccoli
2 chopped green onions

Wash broccoli, break off flowerettes, wipe mushrooms and slice. Mix the following for dressing:

1/2 c. sugar
1 tsp. salt
1 tsp. paprika
1 tsp. celery seed
1 T onion powder
1 c. oil
1/4 c. vinegar

Allow dressing ingredients to meld for 1 hour. Mix together mushrooms, broccoli and onion powder. Pour dressing over broccoli mixture and refrigerate for another hour, stirring now and then.

Buttermilk Salad

Cousin-Grace Carter - Sophie, WV

Bring 1 (20 oz.) unsweetened can crushed pineapple to a boil and add 1 (16 oz.) pkg. apricot flavored jello and stir to dissolve. Chill until almost sets. Add 2 cups buttermilk, chill again. Fold in 8 oz. Cool Whip and 1/2 c. nuts. Pour in 9 x 13 x 2 in. pan.

Chicken Salad

Niece-Martha "Marty" Abdon - Greenup, KY

Toss together:
2 c. cut-up cold cooked chicken
1 c. cut-up celery (1/2" pieces)
1 T lemon juice
salt and pepper to taste

Mix in:
1/2 c. mayonnaise

Carefully fold in:
2 or 3 cut-up hard-cooked eggs.

Chill thoroughly. Arrange a mound in each lettuce cup and garnish with olives or little sweet pickles.

Tomato flower cups: cut tomatoes almost through into 6 sections so they will open like flowers. Fill with chicken salad. Garnish with sieved hard-cooked eggs.

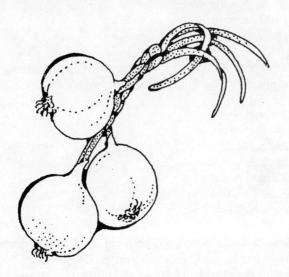

Hot Chicken Salad

Cousin- Almma Stewart Webb - St. Clair Shores, MI

4 c. cooked chicken
2 c. chopped celery
2 T lemon juice
1 T minced onion
1 tsp. salt and pepper
1 tsp. Accent
1 c. toasted slivered almonds and croutons
1/2 c. mayonnaise
1/2 c. sour cream
3 hard boiled eggs

Mix well and turn into casserole.

Sprinkle on top of casserole:
1 c. grated American cheese
2 c. potato chips, crumbled

Add:
1 can cream of chicken soup
1 c. seasoned croutons

Add:
1 can water chestnuts or 1 c. mushrooms

Bake for 20 minutes at 350°.

Cucumber and Red Onion Salad

Cousin-Bob Hall - Huntington, WV

3 medium-size cucumbers
2 T salt
2 c. water
1 large sweet red onion
3/4 c. white vinegar
1/4 c. pure vegetable oil
2 T sugar
Few strips fresh dill, chopped or 1/2 tsp. dill seed
Pepper to taste

Remove ends from cucumbers. Slice unpared cucumbers lengthwise thinly. Mix salt and water; pour over cucumbers; let stand 1 hour. Drain well. Slice peeled onion thinly; separate into rings. Toss with cucumbers. Combine remaining ingredients; pour over vegetables; toss until well coated. Chill. Carry to picnic in container with tight-fitting lid. Makes 8 servings. Recipe may be doubled.

Florida Salad
Cousin-Beverly Stewart - Winter Haven, FL

1/4 lb. endive or small head Boston lettuce
1/2 lb. spinach
6 T frozen grapefruit juice concentrate, thawed and
 undiluted.
1 T vinegar
1 T flour
1 tsp. sugar
1/2 tsp. salt
1/4 tsp. pepper
1/4 c. salad oil
6 slices of bacon, cooked and crumbled
2 c. grapefruit sections, drained
1 Florida orange, sliced
1 purple onion, sliced

Wash endive or lettuce and drain. Put in refrigerator to stay crisp. Clean spinach and tear into bite size.

Dressing:
Combine, grapefruit juice, vinegar, flour, sugar, salt, pepper and salad oil in medium saucepan. Heat, stirring gently, until mixture begins to boil. Remove from heat, add crumbled bacon. Pour over spinach in a large bowl and toss; let stand for 15 to 20 minutes. A few minutes before serving add drained grapefruit sections, orange slices, onion and endive or lettuce. Toss lightly. Makes 8 servings.

Killed Lettuce
Niece-Betty Stuart Darby Baird - Wadestown, WV

Grandma Stuart made this salad often. It was a real "Springtime Treat".

4 slices bacon or (3 T bacon greese)
2 bunches garden lettuce (loose leaf)
2 T sugar
3 small green onions, chopped (including tops)
1/3 c. vinegar

In you have bacon, cut it into small pieces and fry it until crisp. Put lettuce and onions in crock, sprinkle with sugar and vinegar. When bacon is ready, pour it on all at once. If using bacon grease, just heat it very hot and pour it on.

Linguine Salad
Cousin-Goldie Adkins - East Liverpool, OH

1 lb. box linguine
16 oz. bottle Italian Wishbone Dressing
Jar salad supreme-McCormacks
1 or 2 small onions, chopped
2 small tomatoes, chopped
1 small cucumber, chopped
1 green pepper, chopped

Cook linguine in 4 qts. water 20-22 minutes. Drain in colander and cool. Mix together. Refrigerate over night.

Macaroni Salad I
Cousin-Linda Stewart Spence - Huntington, WV

1 lb. macaroni
2 cucumbers
1 large onion
1/2 small jar sweet pickles
pinch salt/pepper
1 lb. cheddar cheese
3 stalks celery
1 green pepper
1 large bottle Wishbone Deluxe French salad dressing.

Cook and drain macaroni. Cut up all vegetables into small cubes. Put all vegetables together in a large bowl. Pour in whole bottle of dressing, 1/2 jar of pickle juice. Add salt and pepper to taste. Refrigerate over night. Makes 1 gallon.

Macaroni Salad II
Niece-Ellen Keeney Douglas - Lexington, KY

1 lb. macaroni
2 small tomatoes
1 green pepper
1 cucumber
1/2 bottle Italian dressing
1/2 bottle of salad dressing

Boil macaroni, rinse. Chop vegetables fine and pour salad dressing and all ingredients together. Mix and chill.

Pea Salad

Cousin-Katherine Stewart Martin - Racine, WS

1 head lettuce
1/2 c. chopped onion
1/2 c. chopped celery
1 pkg. peas, cooked and cooled
1/2 c. chopped green pepper

Arrange in layers as listed in covered dish. Spread top with: 1 pt. mayonnaise, 2 T sugar, 1 c. cheddar cheese. Fry about 10 slices of bacon and crumble. Cover and store for 24 hours. Toss just before serving.

Potato Salad I

Niece-Martha Deane Callihan North - Champaigne, IL

8 boiled medium potatoes
1-1/2 c. mayonnaise
1 c. sour cream
1-1/2 tsp. horseradish
1 tsp. celery seed
1/2 tsp. salt
1 c. fresh chopped parsley
2 medium onions, minced

Cut potatoes in 1/8 in. slices. Combine mayonnaise, cream, horseradish, celery seed, and salt; set aside. In another bowl mix parsley and onion. In large bowl, layer potatoes (salted), mayonnaise mixture, onion-parsley. Continue, and end with parsley-onion. Do not stir, cover and refrigerate at least 8 hours.

Potato Salad II

Cousin-Susan Stewart Gump - Spencer, WV

8-10 potatoes
sweet pickles, chopped
1 medium onion, chopped
3 stalks celery, chopped
1 jar mayonnaise
3 T mustard

Boil potatoes and dice into small pieces. Drain and add next three ingredients. Then the next two. Salt to taste.

Potato Salad III

Cousin-June Stewart Haney - Huntington, WV

9-10 potatoes, cooked with peeling on, drained, peeled and cut up.
6-8 hard boiled eggs, sliced or chopped
1 to 1-1/2 c. sweet pickle or sweet pickle relish
2 medium onions, chopped
1 c. celery, chopped
1 c. salad dressing or amount needed for right consistency
1/4 c. mustard
1 T sugar
salt and pepper to taste

Combine all ingredients, mix well, chill several hours. Top with sliced boiled eggs, and paprika.

Grandma's German Potato Salad

Cousin-Alma Martin - Racine, WS

1 (5-lb.) bag red salad potatoes cooked w/skins on and then peeled and sliced thinly
6 slices of bacon, chopped and fried
3 T oleo melted with bacon and grease
4 T vinegar (I always add 3 and then taste it).
salt and pepper to taste

Take a coffee cup and slowly beat an egg. As you are beating, add cooking oil until cup is full and mixture is slightly thickened. One small chopped onion may be added, if desired. Mix all ingredients thoroughly. Garnish with tomatoes and cut up hard-boiled egg. Serves 10 to 12 people.

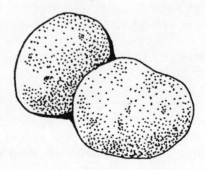

Sour Cream Potato Salad

Cousin-Faye Stewart Lester - Kenova, WV

Cook 7 medium potatoes with skin on. Peel and cube while warm. Pour 1/3 cup zesty Italian dressing over and mix well. Chill for 2 hours. Then add:

3/4 c.celery, diced
1/3 c. green onions, diced
4 hard boiled eggs, diced
1 c. mayonnaise
1/2 c. sour cream
1-1/2 tsp. horseradish mustard
1/3 c. sweet pickle relish

Salt to taste and chill for another 2 hours.

Sauerkraut Salad

Nephew-Roy Abdon - Greenup, KY

15 oz. can sauerkraut
1 c. diced celery
1 c. chopped onion
1 can pimiento
3/4 c. sugar

Drain kraut. Mix with other ingredients. Let stand in refrigerator over night. Ready to serve.

Cole Slaw

Niece-Ellen Keeney Douglas - Lexington, KY

1/2 c. sour cream
2 T mayonnaise or salad dressing
1/4 tsp. seasoned salt
1/4 tsp. mustard
dash of pepper
1/4 medium head green cabbage, finely chopped or shredded (about 2 cups)
1/2 small onion, chopped (about)
2 T paprika

Mix sour cream, mayonnaise, seasoned salt, mustard and pepper; toss with cabbage and onion. Sprinkle with paprika. About 4 servings.

Cole Slaw Parfait Salad

Cousin-Goldie Adkins - East Liverpool, OH

1 pkg. lemon flavored gelatin
1 c. hot water
1/2 c. mayonnaise
1/2 c. cold water
2 T vinegar
1/4 tsp. salt
1-1/2 c. finely shredded cabbage
1/2 c. radishes, sliced
1/2 c. diced celery
2 to 4 T green pepper
1 T onion

Dissolve gelatin in hot water. Blend in mayonnaise, cold water, vinegar, and salt. Chill until partially set. Then beat until fluffy; add vegetables. Pour into dish and set. Garnish with a few more radish slices.

Slaw

Sister-in-law-Laura Avanelle Norris Callihan
Greenup, KY

2 lg. heads cabbage
3 lg. white onions
1-1/2 green peppers
1 medium can pimientos
1 pt. vinegar
3/4 c. sugar
1 T salt
1/2 c. Wesson oil

Shred cabbage; cut onions and peppers into rings. Mix all ingredients together and store in covered container in refrigerator. Marinate 24 hours. Drain before serving.

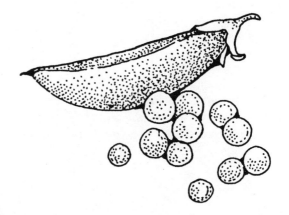

Freezer Slaw I

Cousin-James E. Hilton - Frankfort, KY

1 head cabbage, shredded
1 carrot, shredded
1 green pepper, chopped
1 tsp. salt

Sprinkle salt over cabbage; let stand 1 hour. Squeeze excess liquid from cabbage and add carrots and peppers.

Sauce:
1 c. vinegar
2 c. sugar
1-1/4 c. warm water
1 tsp. celery salt
1 tsp. mustard seed

Mix and boil 1 minute. Cool to lukewarm and pour over cabbage. Freeze.

Freezer Slaw II

Cousin-Betty Stewart Walker - Huntington, WV

1 large cabbage, shredded
1 carrot, grated
1 bell pepper, chopped
1 tsp. salt
1-1/2 tsp. sugar
2 onions, chopped

Mix salt and sugar with cabbage and let stand for 1 hour. Squeeze out excess moisture and add carrot, pepper and onions. While cabbage is standing, make dressing.

Dressing:
1 c. vinegar
1 tsp. dried mustard
2 c. sugar
1 tsp. celery seed
1/4 c. water

Mix and boil 1 minute. Cool to lukewarm. Pour over cabbage mixture and let stand 4 hours. Put into plastic containers, cover, and freeze.

Spinach Salad I

Niece-Martha Deane (Marty) Callihan North Champaign, IL

1 pkg. fresh spinach
1 medium onion, chopped
1/2 lb. crisp bacon
croutons
hard-boiled egg

Combine first four ingredients. Top with slices of egg.

Sauce:
3/4 c. sugar
1/2 c. water
1/2 c. vinegar
1 tsp. salt
1 egg, beaten

Sauce:
Bring to a boil over medium heat; cook about 10 minutes in all. Stir constantly. Cool and pour over spinach mixture. Sauce can be made in advance and stored in refrigerator 1 to 2 weeks.

Spinach Salad II

Cousin-Beverly Stewart - Winter Haven, FL

10-12 oz. fresh spinach, washed, stems removed, drained & torn.
4 strips bacon, saute', drain, cool and crumble
1 medium size sweet onion, sliced thin
1 can water chestnuts, drained and sliced
6 fresh mushrooms, sliced thin

Combine all above ingredients in a large bowl and pour dressing over; toss.

Dressing:
5 T good white wine vinegar
3 T water
1/2 c. salad oil

Combine above ingredients and shake well. Pour over salad.

Taco Salad I

Cousin-Ila Shanks - Zelienople, PA

This is a big hit with everyone. Teenagers consume this in quanity. It's great to take to outdoor functions.

1 lb. ground beef, browned
1 large onion, diced
1 head lettuce, cut in small pieces
2 c. tomatoes, cut up
1 c. grated cheddar cheese
1 lb. (1 can) kidney beans, optional
green olives, sliced
1 bag Nacho cheese flavored chips (Doritos), broken in small pieces.
1 pkg. Good Season Italian dressing, prepared

Toss lettuce, onion, beef, and cheese together. Add tomatoes, kidney beans (if desired), green olives, and nacho chips. Pour prepared dressing over salad and mix well before serving.

Taco Salad II

Cousin-Alma Martin - Racine, WS

1 small head lettuce, cut in small pieces
1 medium tomato, chopped
1 medium onion, chopped
1 c. cheddar cheese, grated
1 can chili beans
1 bag taco chips
1 (8 oz.) bottle Thousand Island Dressing
1 lb. ground beef

Toss lettuce, tomato, onion, and cheese. Brown ground beef and add chili beans. Mix with vegetables, crushed taco chips (reserve 1 c. for topping), and dressing. Top with reserved chips. Serves 6.

24 Hour Bean Salad

Cousin-Geraldine Holbrook - Greenup, KY

1 med. can lima beans
1 med. can green beans
1 med. can kidney beans
1 med. can wax beans
3/4 c. chopped celery
1 c. sliced onions
1/2 c. salad oil (Crisco)
1/2 c. cider vinegar
3/4 c. white sugar
1/2 tsp. black pepper
1/2 tsp. salt

Drain beans. Put oil, vinegar, sugar, black pepper, and salt in a jar and shake to mix well. Pour this over the vegetables and mix well. Set in refrigerator for at least 24 hours before serving. Stir occasionally.

24 Hour Cole Slaw

Cousin-Ila Shanks - Zelienople, PA

This recipe is great for company. Women love it. The men devour it. It's my husband's favorite coleslaw. Must be made 24 hours ahead.

1 medium head cabbage, shredded
1/2 c. green pepper, diced
1/4 carrots, grated
1-1/2 c. chopped celery
1 small onion, finely chopped
1 c. sugar
1/2 c. apple cider vinegar
1 tsp. salt
1 tsp. mustard seed

Mix sugar and vinegar together. Add to other ingredients and stir well. Refrigerate in covered container for 24 hours. Stir again before serving. This will keep in refrigerator for 2-3 weeks.

Vegetable Salad

Cousin-Joyce (Jimmie) Carter McKinney - Scarbro, WV

1 can of LeSueur peas
1 can white shoe peg corn
1 can french style green beans
1 can pimientos
1 c. chopped celery
1 c. green onions, chopped
1/2 c. green peppers, chopped

Mix and drain the first four ingredients. Add celery, onions, and peppers.

Mix:
1/2 c. red wine vinegar
1/2 c. sugar
1/2 c. oil (Wesson)
1 tsp. salt

Add to vegetables and set overnight. Serve anytime, but especially during Christmas holiday season.

Raw Vegetable Salad

Cousin-Phyllis Hilton Parker - Portsmouth, OH

1/2 head raw cauliflower
3-4 stalks broccoli
1 bunch green onions, chopped
1/2 pkg. frozen peas
1 small jar pimientos
black olives (12 to 14), chopped

Slice cauliflower and broccoli lengthwise and cut into small bits. Add rest of ingredients and seal tightly. Refrigerate overnight. Add dressing before serving.

Dressing:
1 (8 oz.) carton sour cream
1/2 c. mayonnaise
1 pkg. ranch style Hidden Valley dressing mix

Blend well and chill several hours before serving over vegetables. Serves 12.

Salad Dressings

Buttermilk Salad Dressing

Niece-Sally Ann Staph - Greenup, KY

8 T salt
4 T monosodium glutamite
3 T garlic powder
2 T onion powder
2 T ground pepper
4 T dried parsley flakes

Mix and store in jar in cupboard.

Dressing:
2 rounded tsp. salad dressing mix.
1 c. mayonnaise
1 c. buttermilk.

Stir together and store in refrigerator. Add sugar for cole slaw dressing, mustard for potato salad. Good on baked potatoes and green vegetables.

French Dressing

Cousin-Beverly Stewart - Winter Haven, FL

1 can tomato soup
1 tsp. dry mustard
1/2 tsp. (or more) Worcestershire sauce
2/3 c. Wesson oil
1/2 c. sugar
1/2 tsp. pepper
1/2 c. vinegar
1/2 tsp. salt
1/2 tsp. paprika
onion or garlic to taste

Combine all the above ingredients in blender. Blend until thoroughly mixed.

Hollandaise

Cousin-Wanda Lee Maynard - Huntington, WV

2 egg yolks
pinch of cayenne
1 to 1-1/2 T lemon juice
1/3 c. hot melted butter or margarine

In top part of double boiler, heat first 3 ingredients until well blended. (A small wire whisk is helpful for this). Gradually drip in melted butter. Continue beating over 1" hot, not boiling water until thickened. Makes about 1/2 cup. Note: Hollandaise in jars or packaged hollandaise mix is quick and convenient.

Homemade Mayonnaise

Cousin-Rena Stewart - Magee, MS

3 egg yolks
1/2 tsp. salt
1/2 tsp. sugar
1/4 tsp. dry mustard
1-1/2 c. salad oil
3 T cider vinegar

In small bowl with mixer at medium speed, beat egg yolks, salt, sugar, and dry mustard 2 minutes. Continue beating and gradually add 1/2 c. salad oil, 1/2 tsp. at a time, until mixture is smooth and thick. Gradually beat in vinegar, then beat in remaining salad oil, 1 T at a time, until all the oil is absorbed and mixture is smooth. Cover and refrigerate mayonnaise up to 1 week. Use in recipes as any mayonnaise. Makes 2 cups.

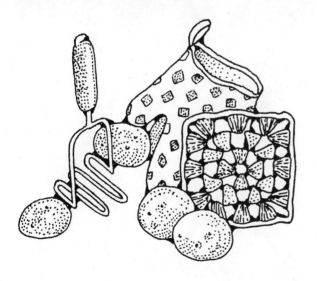

Deluxe Honey Dressing

Cousin-Connie Frazier Stewart - Kenova, WV

2/3 c. sugar
1 tsp. dry mustard
1 tsp. paprika
1/4 tsp. salt
5 T vinegar
1 T lemon juice
1 tsp. grated onion
1/3 c. honey
1 tsp. celery seed

Mix all ingredients and beat well. Add slowly 3/4 to 1 cup oil; beat for 15 minutes. Use blender or mixer.

Lemony Vegetable Dressing

Cousin-Thelma Edwards - Ceredo, WV

1 medium lemon
1/2 c. olive oil
1 tsp. salt
1 tsp. sugar
1/2 tsp. seasoned pepper
1/4 tsp. day mustard

Into small bowl, grate 1 tsp. peel from lemon and then squeeze juice. Add remaining ingredients; stir until well blended. Cover and refrigerate up to 1 week. Serve with cooked or fresh vegetable salads or tossed green salads. Makes about 3/4 cup.

Red Salad Dressing

Cousin - Connie Frazier Stewart - Kenova, WV

1 bottle chili sauce
3/4 to 1 c. sugar
1 c. Mazola oil
1 sm. chopped onion
1 tsp. salt

Mix in blender.

Roquefort or Bleu Cheese Dressing

Cousin-Faye Hilton - Frankfort, KY

2 or 3 oz. Roquefort or Bleu Cheese
3 T oil
3T vinegar
3/4 c. mayonnaise
6 or 8 T sweet or sour cream

Crumble cheese into oil. Add vinegar, mayonnaise and cream. Mix well. Keeps well. (Very small recipe - I double or more and keep tightly covered in refrigerator).

Russian Dressing

Cousin-Brian Lester - Jacksonville, FL

Mix:
1 c. mayonnaise
1 T horseradish
1/4 c. chili sauce or catsup
1 tsp. grated onion

Store in refrigerator. Makes about 1-1/4 cups.

Slaw Dressing

Cousin-Mary Belle Johnson - Portsmouth, OH

Combine:
3 T butter
2 T flour
2/3 tsp. salt
1/2 tsp. pepper
1/2 c. sugar
2 eggs, well beaten
1 c. milk

Cook slowly until mixture thickens. Gradually add 1/3 c. vinegar (more or less, depending on sourness desired). May be seasoned with dry mustard or celery seed.

Thousand Island Dressing

Cousin-Cristi Arnold - Hillsboro, OH

1/2 c. salad dressing or mayonnaise
3 T chili sauce or catsup
1/4 c. sweet pickle relish, well drained
1 hard cooked egg, chopped

Put the salad dressing or mayonnaise in the mixing bowl. Add the chili sauce, relish, and egg; mix well. Store dressing, covered in the refrigerator. When the meal is ready to serve, spoon a little dressing over lettuce wedges.

Vinaigrette Dressing

Niece-Lori Ann Stuart - Greenup, KY

3/4 c. oil
1/2 c. white wine vinegar
1 T chopped parsley
2 tsp. chives
1 tsp. basil
1/2 tsp. dry mustard
1/4 tsp. pepper
1/8 tsp. garlic powder

Combine all ingredients, mix well. 1-1/4 cups.

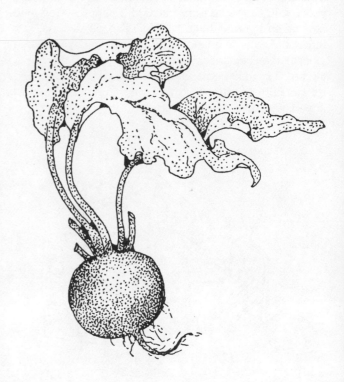

Soups and Stews

Soups

Bean and Bacon Soup
Broccoli Soup
Chicken Corn Soup
Chili
Chili Con Carne
Ron's Chili
Chili Mac
Creamy Chicken Soup
Jesse Stuart's Cheese Soup
Fish Chowder
Oyster Bisque
Pea Soup (Split)
Potato Cheese Soup

Potato Soup
Potato Soup-Cheese Chowder
Creamed Pumpkin Soup
Sheep Shanty Soup
Danish Vegetable Soup

Stews

Beef Stew
Burgoo
Five-hour Stew
Four-hour Stew
Oven Beef Stew
Western Stew
Nine Bean Soup Mix
Nine Bean Soup

Fireside-snack

Wife Naomi Deane Norris Stuart, W-Hollow, KY

When Jesse and I came here housekeeping in 1940, the W-Hollow road was impossible to drive on in wet weather.

If we went anywhere evenings we had to park the car at Glenn Hilton's home on the hard road and walk to our home. We kept warm coats, boots, lantern or flashlight in the car for such walks.

By the time we reached home we were cold, often wet, always muddy and hungry. Jesse always brought in more logs for the fire and I went to the kitchen to make ready our favorite snack. We had no electricity in the early days and anything warm had to be heated in the fireplace. Jesse's favorite was cream of tomato soup and a cheese sandwich. We found a special pan to use in the fireplace; however the handle was short and he had a problem reaching the hot coals. Later he took the pan to Dave Meyers Blacksmith shop and had a long handle welded to the pan.

I liked hot tea, so we heated water first to pour over tea leaves in a tea pot warming on the hearth. Then we poured soup in the pan for Jesse to heat while I made sandwiches from a tray on the hearth. Jesse liked mustard on one side of the bread and mayonnaise on the other. I left off mustard for mine; it didn't seem good with tea.

Of course we removed our shoes and sat on pillows on the floor by the hearth, warming and enjoying our snack. This seldom ever varied

unless there was cold fried chicken in the refrigerator. That was Jesse's choice with an olive-mayonnaise sandwich, especially if the soup happened to spill. It sometimes did, nearly putting out the fire.

253

Soups

Bean and Bacon Soup

Niece-Freda Keeney - Greenup, KY

1 lb. dried navy beans
6 c. water
2 tsp. salt
1/4 tsp. pepper
2 cloves garlic, minced
1 bay leaf
4 slices bacon
2 medium onions, finely chopped
1 sm. green pepper, finely chopped
1/2 c. finely chopped carrots
1 (8 oz.) can tomato sauce
1 tsp. minced parsley

Sort and wash beans; place in large pot. Cover with water 2 inches above beans; let soak overnight.

Drain beans, cover with 6 cups water. Add salt, pepper, garlic and bay leaf.

Cook bacon until crisp; remove bacon, reserve drippings. Crumble bacon and set aside. Add onion, and green pepper to drippings, saute' until tender. Add onions, green peppers and carrots to beans. Bring to a boil; cover and simmer 1 hour.

Add tomato sauce and parsley to soup; cover and simmer an additional 30 minutes. Ladle into serving bowls, sprinkle with reserved bacon. Yield: about 3 quarts.

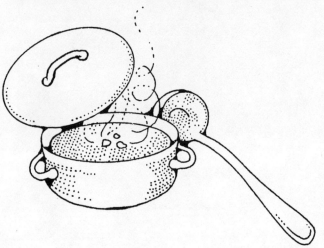

Broccoli Soup

Niece-Sandy Nelson Perrine - Greenup, KY

1/4 c. celery, chopped
1/4 c. green onion, chopped
2 T butter or margarine
2 (10 oz.) pkgs. frozen chopped broccoli, thawed
2 c. chicken broth
1 c. milk
1/2 tsp. salt
1/2 tsp. pepper

Saute celery and onion in butter in Dutch oven until vegetables are tender. Add broccoli and broth, bring to boil. Cover and simmer 5 minutes or until broccoli is tender. Let cool slightly.

Spoon half of broccoli mixture into blender and process until smooth. Repeat with remaining mixture.

Return broccoli mixture to Dutch oven; stir in milk and seasonings. Cook over low heat; stirring occasionally until heated thoroughly. Yield: 5-1/2 cups.

Chicken Corn Soup

Cousin-Ila Shanks - Zelienople, PA

A good old Pennsylvania Dutch recipe. A great favorite in the "Dutch" country. At family reunions, church and fire company picnics, while the corn seasons last, gallons and gallons are simmered in big iron kettles.

1 stewing chicken
2 hard-boiled eggs
8 ears of corn
1 onion
rivels
pepper
salt
chopped parsley

Cut up chicken and put in pot with 3 qts. of water. Add 1 onion, 1 T salt, and 1/4 tsp. pepper and stew until tender. Remove the chicken. Cut meat into 1 inch pieces, return to broth with corn cut from ears. Make rivels by combining 1-1/2 cups flour, a little salt, and 1 beaten egg. Mix together with fingers to form crumbs. Add these to broth and boil for 15 minutes more. Drop in the chopped hard-boiled eggs and parsley.

Chili

Cousin-Ethel Stewart Terry - Ceredo, WV

2 T shortening
1 lb. ground beef
1 can kidney beans
1 can tomato soup
1 can water
1 medium onion
2 T chili powder
1 tsp. garlic

Brown meat and onion. Mix in other ingredients and cook slow for about 45 minutes.

Chili Con Carne

Cousin-Geraldine Holbrook - Greenup, KY

1-1/2 lbs. ground beef
2 medium onions sliced
1 (28 oz.) can tomatoes
1 (6 oz.) can tomato paste
1 c. water
1 beef bouillon cube
1 (16 oz.) can kidney beans
2 T diced green peppers
2 cloves garlic, minced
2 tsp. salt
2 tsp. oregano
2 tsp. chili powder
1/2 tsp. crushed red pepper
1 bay leaf

Combine first two ingredients in a large saucepan. Brown meat, drain off fat. Add remaining ingredients, stir to blend. Cover and simmer 1-1/2 hours, stirring occasionally, then remove bay leaf.

Ron's Chili

Nephew-Ron Wheeler - Knoxville, TN

1/2 lb. cooked pinto beans
15 oz. Hunts Special Tomato Sauce
1 medium onion, diced
2 (15 oz.) cans of whole tomatoes
1-1/2 lb. hamburger, browned
1 pkg. French's chili seasoning
2 T chili powder
Dash garlic powder
1/2 c. water
1/2 tsp. pepper
1 T salt

Combine ingredients and add more garlic powder to taste. Let simmer, covered, all day until ready to eat and enjoy!

Chili Mac

Cousin-Margaret Terry Waller - Ceredo, WV

1 lb. ground beef
1 c. macaroni
1/2 green pepper (large)
1 onion
1 (15 oz.) can of tomato sauce
1 c. water
1 c. pork and beans
3 T chili powder

Brown ground beef and green peppers and onion together. Add water, tomato sauce, macaroni, pork and beans and chili powder. Cook slow for about 30 minutes.

255

Creamy Chicken Soup

Cousin-Lynn Hunt Newton - Hamilton, OH

1-1/2 stick butter
3/4 c. flour
1 c. milk
1 c. heavy cream
6 c. chicken stock
2 c. chopped chicken (cooked)
1/2 tsp. salt
1 tsp. pepper
1 tsp. Dijon mustard

In a saucepan, blend butter and flour and cook over medium heat for 2 minutes. Heat milk, cream and stock. Add a little at a time to butter/flour mixture, stirring constantly until mixture is smooth and thickened. When it begins to boil, add chicken and seasonings. Serves approximately 10.

Jesse Stuart's Cheese Soup

Sister-Mary Stuart Nelson - Greenup, KY

1/2 stick butter
3 grated onions
3 stalks celery, chopped, including leaves
3 grated carrots
3 (10 3/4 oz.) cans potato soup, undiluted
2 (10 3/4 oz.) cans chicken broth
1 oz. (3 slices) American cheese
8 oz. sour cream

Mix all ingredients except cheese. Stir in chopped parsley, coarse pepper and bottled hot sauce to taste. Simmer 30 minutes. Drop in cheese and stir until cheese melts. Serves 10-12.

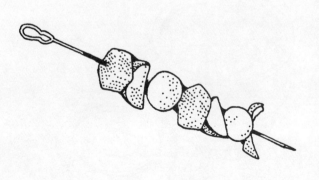

Fish Chowder

Niece-Anne Liles O'Hare - Ashland, KY

1 T butter
2 c. diced potatoes
2 c. sliced carrots
2 c. sliced onions
2 whole cloves
1 T fresh or dried dill
1 bay leaf
salt
2 c. hot water

Melt butter in saucepan. Add remaining ingredients. Cook until vegetables are tender. Add 1 lb. thick fish fillets (halibut, cod or haddock) cut in 1/2" pieces and 1/2 c. dry white wine. Cover and cook 10 more minutes. Mix: 2 T flour and 1 c. milk. Stir into soup. Cook until thickened. Sprinkle finely chopped parsley on each serving.

Oyster Bisque

Cousin-Melinda Shultz Arrick - Lucasville, OH

2 qts. standard oysters, undrained
1 c. butter
1 sm. clove garlic, minced
8 c. whipping cream
2 T instant minced onion
1 tsp. salt
1/4 tsp. white pepper
1/4 c. dry sherry

Drain oysters, reserving liquid. Place oysters in container of food processor or electric blender. Process just until coarsely chopped. Set aside. Melt butter in a large Dutch oven; add garlic and saute until tender. Add whipping cream, reserved oyster liquid, onion, salt, and pepper; heat thoroughly (do not boil). Add oysters to cream mixture; simmer 5-8 minutes or until edges of oysters curl. Stir in sherry. Yield: about 4 qts.

Pea Soup (Split)

Sister-Glennis Stuart Liles - Greenup, KY

2 c. dried green split peas
1 ham bone
2 medium onions, diced
4 carrots, diced
4 celery stalks, sliced
2 bay leaves

Wash peas and soak overnight in cold water. Add about 2 more quarts of water and all other ingredients. Bring to a boil. Reduce heat and simmer two hours. Remove bay leaves and ham bone. Press entire mixture through sieve. Reheat. 10-12 servings. Very good eating at low cost.

Potato Cheese Soup

Niece-Connie Keeney - Greenup, KY

5 c. potatoes, chopped
1 c. carrots, chopped
1 c. celery, chopped
1 c. onion, chopped
5 c. of water
4 chicken bouillon cubes
2 cans cream of chicken soup
1 lb. of Velveeta cheese

Dissolve bouillon cubes in boiling water. Add carrots, celery and onion. Cook 20 minutes. Add potatoes and cook 20 more minutes. Add soup and mix well. Add cheese (in pieces). Cook until cheese is melted. Serve with crumbled bacon on top. Serves 8.

Potato Soup

Niece-Kathy Abdon - Greenup, KY

6 to 7 potatoes
2 T butter
1 can celery soup
1 can condensed milk (small size)

Dice potatoes like you are stewing them. Add salt, pepper, and butter. Cook until potatoes are tender. In another pan, combine celery soup and milk. Warm. Drain potatoes, stir in celery soup mixture. If too thick, stir in a little water.

Potato Soup-Cheese Chowder

Cousin-Mae Pennington Fellows - Albuquerque, NM

2 c. potatoes (diced)
1 c. celery
1 c. onion
Left over chicken, turkey, ham, chopped
2 c. water, salted
2 cubes chicken bouillon
2 c. milk
2 T butter
2 T flour
1 c. cheddar cheese (grated)

Boil potatoes until almost soft, drain and save water. Melt butter and saute' celery and onion; add flour and stir together. Add potato, water, and milk gradually; stir occasionally on medium heat until it boils. Should be thickened. Add potatoes and broccoli and stir. Add cheese and let melt. Put some cheese in bowl and serve.

"This is delicious and makes a complete light meal. I sometimes serve it to company for a light supper - they love it".

Creamed Pumpkin Soup

Niece-Sandy Nelson Perrine - Greenup, KY

4 T (1/2 stick) butter
1/2 c. minced onion
2 shallots, minced
1 rib celery, minced
1 carrot, pared, minced
4 oz. mushrooms, minced
2 c. canned pumpkin puree (or fresh cooked)
2 c. chicken stock
1/2 c. heavy cream
1 c. half and half
1/4 c. fresh orange juice
1 c. sour cream
1 T snipped fresh chives
1 tsp. grated orange zest
3/4 tsp. salt
3 dashes hot pepper sauce

Heat butter in medium saucepan; add onions, shallots, celery, and carrots; cook, stirring constantly, until softened, about 7 minutes. Add mushrooms, stir and cook 5 minutes longer. Stir in pumpkin and broth; simmer uncovered 10 minutes. Transfer to a blender, puree until smooth. Return to saucepan, stir in half and half, cream, and orange juice. Heat to boiling. Reduce heat-simmer uncovered 10 minutes. Combine sour cream, zest, and chives in a bowl. Season soup with salt and pepper sauce. Ladle into soup bowls and top with dollop of sour cream mixture. Serve at once.

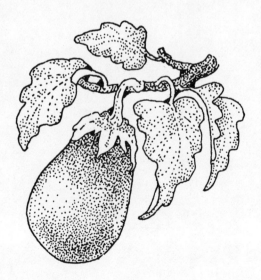

Sheep Shanty Soup

Niece-Jean Keeney Lush - Bowling Green, KY

Cook a bony piece of beef until tender such as shank, chuck, etc. Salt to taste, pepper. Add potatoes and cut cabbage in strips, with canned tomatoes, corn, peas, green beans, onions, celery, carrots in porportions you like or may have. We like lots of tomatoes. At the end, if there is a sour taste a few T of sugar may be added. Serve with oyster crackers or corn bread. This was a meal for us many a night when we lived at the sheep shanty and took care of Uncle Jesse's sheep. Sometimes in the corner by the stove, there would be a new born lamb or two the mother did not own. We ate soup and petted them. The cabbage was a must and how good it was to get something fresh and green. Daddy would walk to town and get it on soup day. Any other vegetable you may like may be added.

Danish Vegetable Soup

Niece-Regina Nelson Stout - Greenup, KY

1 sm. onion, chopped fine
3 T butter
2 T flour
2 c. milk
1 (16 oz.) pkg. frozen Danish mix vegetables (carrots, broccoli, cauliflower)
1/2 c. white wine
1 c. half 'n' half
1 c. grated swiss cheese

In a saucepan, melt butter, add onion and saute'; add flour and stir. Slowly blend milk while stirring with wire whisk. Stir over medium heat until mixture begins to thicken. Transfer to double boiler over medium heat. Add frozen vegetables and simmer 30 minutes. Add half 'n' half, swiss cheese and wine, simmer another 30 minutes. Salt to taste. Serves 8.

Stews

Beef Stew

Niece-Martha Deane Callihan North - Champaign, IL

1-1/2 lb. chuck beef, cubed
1 small can tomatoes (1 lb.)
1 c. celery, cut in large pieces
6 carrots, cut in large pieces
3 onions, cut in large pieces
1 T salt
1 tsp. sugar
3 T tapioca
1 clove garlic
pepper to taste

Bake in covered pan 5 hours at 250°. Add diced potatoes the last 2 hours.

Burgoo

Wife-Naomi Deane Norris Stuart - W-Hollow, KY

1 lb. beef
1/2 lb. veal
1 sm. hen
(2 or 3 lbs. venison may be substituted for beef and veal)
4 carrots
1 turnip
1 slice red pepper
celery tops
1 T Worcestershire sauce
2 green peppers
4 stalks celery
2 med. potatoes
1 qt. tomatoes
4 onions
1 lb. okra
1 pt. butterbeans
1/4 head cabbage
4 ears corn
6 qts. water

Cook meats separately 4-5 hours. Cool and combine. Add water to stock to make 6 qts. liquid. Add all vegetables, except corn and potatoes. Cook 2 hours, add corn and potatoes and cook 1/2 hour. Season to taste. Stores well in refrigerator, freezes well too.

Five-Hour Stew

Cousin-Alma Martin- Racine, WS

2-3 lbs. stew meat
3 onions
1 pkg. carrots
3 stalks celery
1-1/2 tsp. salt
4 T tapioca pudding
1-1/2 green pepper (cut)
1/8 tsp. pepper
1 c. tomato juice
1 can tomatoes
4 big potatoes
1 pkg. brown gravy mix

Meat may be browned. Cook 5 hours at 250°, covered.

Four-Hour Stew

Cousin-Lola Hilton - Moraine, OH

2 lbs. chuck cut in pieces
1 onion, cut up
3 carrots, cut up
2 potatoes, cut up
1 stalk celery, cut up
1 small green pepper
1 tsp. salt
1 T sugar
1/2 c. V-8 juice

Cook 4 hours at 250°.

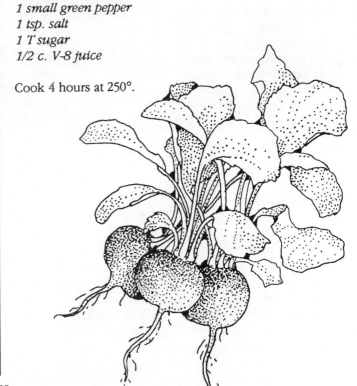

Oven Beef Stew

Cousin-Ramona Adkins - Defiance, OH

2 T flour
1-1/2 tsp. salt
1-1/2 lb. beef chuck, cut into cubes
2 T shortening
2 cans tomato soup
1-1/2 c. diced onion
1/2 tsp. crushed, dried basil
4 medium potatoes, pared and cubed
4 medium carrots, cut in one inch pieces
1/2 c. water

Combine flour, salt, and dash of pepper. Coat meat cubes in seasoned flour. Brown in hot shortening with diced onion in dutch oven. Add soup and 2-1/2 c. water. Cover and bake in 375° oven about 1 hour. Add potatoes and carrots and 1/2 c. water; cover and bake until tender. Serve with hot bread or rolls.

Western Stew

Cousin-Fred Hilton - Ashland, KY

2 T flour
1/2 tsp. salt
1-1/2 lbs. lean beef (or venison) cut in 1-1/2 inch cubes
2 T shortening
1-1/2 c. strong coffee
2 T molasses
1 T Worcestershire sauce
1 clove garlic, crushed
1/2 tsp. dried oregano
1/2 tsp. salt
1/4 tsp. red pepper
3 medium potatoes, cut into 1-1/2 inch pieces
4 medium carrots, cut into 1/2 inch slices
4 small onions, quartered
3 T flour
1/4 c. cold water

Combine first two ingredients; dredge meat in flour mixture and brown in 2 T hot shortening in Dutch oven. Stir in next seven ingredients and bring to a boil. Cover and simmer 1-1/2 hours or until meat is tender. Add 1 -1/2 c. water and all vegetables. Cover and simmer 25 minutes or until vegetables are tender. Combine flour and 1/4 c. water in small bowl. Gently stir mixture into stew and simmer 5 minutes or until stew has thickened. Yield: 2-1/2 quarts.

Nine Bean Soup Mix

Cousin-Simon Benner-Lucasville, OH

1 Lb. Barley Pearls
1 Lb. dried Black Beans
1 Lb. dried Red Beans
1 Lb. dried Pinto Beans
1 Lb. dried Navy Beans
1 Lb. dried Great Northern Beans
1 Lb. dried Lentils
1 Lb. dried Split Peas
1 Lb. dried Black-Eyed Peas

Combine all beans. Divide into ten 2-cup packages for gift giving along with the recipe and ingredients for Nine Bean Soup as listed below.

Nine Bean Soup

2 c. Nine Bean Soup Mix
2 quarts water
1 Lb. ham, diced
1 large onion, chopped
1 clove of garlic, minced
1/2 to 3/4 tsp. salt
1 (16-oz.) can tomatoes, undrained and chopped
1 (10-oz.) can tomatoes and green chilies, undrained

Sort and wash bean mix and place in a dutch oven. Cover with water 2 inches above the beans. Let soak overnight. Drain beans and add the 2 quarts water, ham, onion, garlic, and salt. Cover and bring to a boil. Reduce heat and simmer 1-1/2 hours or until beans are tender. Add tomatoes and simmer for 30 minutes, stirring occasionally. Yield 8 cups soup.

Vegetables

Asparagus Simmered in Onions, Garlic,
  Lemons and Herbs
Blanched Asparagus
Big Sandy Baked Beans
Baked Beans
French Cut Green Beans
Green Beans with Water Chestnuts
Lima Bean-Broccoli Casserole Supreme
Brussel Sprouts (Sweet-Sour)
Harvard Beets
Broccoli Casserole I
Broccoli Casserole II
Broccoli Casserole III
Broccoli Casserole IV
Broccoli Casserole V
Cabbage Casserole I
Cabbage Casserole II
Candied Carrots
Copper Carrot Pennies
Baked Shredded Carrots
Baked Cauliflower
Fried Corn
To Cut Corn From the Cob
Southern Corn Pudding
Corn Oysters
Corn Oysters or Fritters
Corn Pudding
Skillet Corn
Fried Eggplant in Fritter Batter
Eggplant Parmesan
Green Casserole
Candied Parsnips
Lux Peas and Celery
Hopping John
Creamed Peas and New Potatoes
Purple Hull Peas
Fried Banana Peppers

Potato Bake (Scalloped)
Potato Cakes
Creamed New Potatoes and Peas
Fried Potatoes and Onions
Hopplepoppel
Roast Potatoes
Scalloped Potatoes
Stovetop Cheese Potatoes
Tasty Potatoes
Candied Sweet Potatoes
Sweet Potato Casserole I
Sweet Potato Casserole II
Sweet Potato Casserole III
Sweet Potato Casserole IV
Sweet Potato Dish
Henry Keeney Sweet Potatoes
Sweet Potato Souffle
Sauerkraut and Potato Bake
Yellow Squash Casserole
Baked Acorn Squash
Butternut Squash with Thyme
Glazed Squash
Thanksgiving Stuffed Squash
Baked Tomatoes
Flavorful Tomatoes
Tomatoes in Creamed Sauce
Fried Green Tomatoes
Scalloped Tomatoes
Stewed Tomatoes
Buttered Turnips
Turnip Supreme
Vegetable Stew
Veggi Pizza
Zucchini Skillet Dinner
Zucchini Patties
Zucchini Squares
Leather Breeches Beans

L to R. Mitchell Stuart, Martha Hylton Stuart and their children Jesse, Sophie, Mary, James and Glennis (World War II)

Everything for churning and making butter. Churn at left is a walking churn to be held under the arm-churn while you stand or walk.

262

Jesse's cousin - Glen Hilton. Jesse and Glen were very close.

He stays close to the land and tills the land,
His flesh is brown, his hands are calloused by
The handles of the plow, the ax and spade.
Gleen Hylton is as rugged as his land,
He sees years come and ripen and roll by,
He does not laugh at them nor does he sigh,
But solemnly he stands as years roll by.
No finer hill farmer has ever made
Furrows in earth then Gleen Hylton has made—
A man of earth, he lives close to the earth,
And such has been Gleen Hylton's heritage.
And he has lived among these hills since birth,
Though young in years hard work has made him age.
Gleen Hylton is as honest as the day,
His metal is as true as native clay.

Stuart, Jesse. *Man With a Bull-Tongue Plow,* E.P. Dutton & Co. Inc., New York, 1934, Pg. 24.

Asparagus Simmered in Onions, Garlic, Lemon, and Herbs

Cousin-Janet Mayo - Kenova, WV

1 c. onion, thinly sliced
1/3 c. olive oil
2-4 large cloves garlic, peeled and sliced
1 lemon peel, cut in strips
1/2 tsp. thyme
1 bay leaf
1/2 tsp. peppercorns
1/2 c. dry white wine
1/4 c. fresh lemon juice
2 c. water (about)
1/2 tsp. salt
fresh minced parsley
2-3 lbs. fresh asparagus

In heavy saucepan, cook onions, garlic, lemon peel, herbs and bay leaf slowly for 10 minutes. Add peppercorns, wine, lemon juice, water and salt. Cover and simmer very slowly for 20 minutes.

Wash and peel asparagus. Lay in a pan, adding water if necessary so asparagus is just covered. Bring to a boil, cover and simmer slowly for 20 minutes. Remove asparagus to serving dish. Rapidly boil down liquid until syrupy. Pour over asparagus.

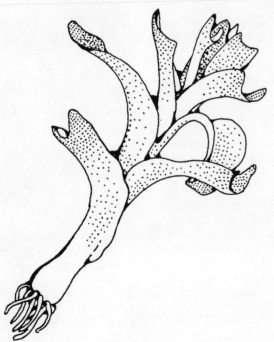

Blanched Asparagus

Cousin-Connie Stewart - Ceredo, WV

1/2-3/4 lb. asparagus per person
1 tsp. salt per qt. of water
1/2 T melted butter per serving

Preparing Asparagus: Wash asparagus carefully. Peel the tough outer skin of the stalk about halfway up with a sharp knife. Do not press too hard or you will break the stalk.

Blanching: Fill a rectangular pan 3/4 full water, add salt and bring to a boil. Drop in asparagus. Partially cover pan and bring to a rapid boil. Uncover pan and cook until spears are tender, about 4 minutes. Test spears with point of a sharp knife. The asparagus should still be crisp and bright green. Remove immediately from water and place on dry, clean towel to soak up excess water. Arrange on warm platter and drizzle melted butter over asparagus.

Big Sandy Baked Beans

Sister-Mary Stuart Nelson - Greenup, KY

2 c. dried pea beans
1/4 lb. lean salt pork
1 medium onion, sliced
1 tsp. salt
1/4 c. molasses
1/2 tsp. dry mustard
1-1/2 T brown sugar
2 c. cooked tomatoes (with juice)

Cover washed beans with 6 cups water, bring to a boil and boil 2 minutes. Cover and let stand 1 hour; then cook until tender (3/4 - 2 hours depending on variety of bean). Drain (use liquid for some other purpose). Put beans in pot. Cut through salt pork rind every 1/2", making cuts 1" deep. Bury in pot and add remaining ingredients. Cover and bake in slow oven (300°) 6-8 hours. Uncover pot last hour. Serves 6.

Baked Beans

Niece-Shirley Stuart - Greenup, KY

1 (31 oz.) can pork and beans
1/2 c. brown sugar
1/3 to 1/2 c. ketchup
1 T mustard

Combine all ingredients in baking dish. Cover top with strips of bacon. Bake uncovered 45 minutes in 400° oven.

French Cut Green Beans

Sister-in-Law-Laura Avenelle Norris Callihan Greenup, KY

1 can cream mushroom soup
1/2 T onion powder
1/2 tsp. mushroom powder
salt and pepper
celery, cut up
ground up potato chips
1 lg. can green beans (drained)

Combine all ingredients in greased casserole and top with slices of green pepper. Bake 30 minutes in 350° oven.

Green Beans with Water Chestnuts

Niece-Martha Stuart Wheeler - Knoxville, TN

2 pkgs. frozen style green beans
1 (3 oz.) can broiled mushroom crowns
1 (8 oz.) can water chestnuts, drained and sliced
1 can cream of celery soup

Allow beans to defrost until they can be separated. Mix in the remaining ingredients. Bake in greased 2 qt. casserole, covered, in moderate oven (350°) about 50 minutes or until green beans are tender. Makes 6-8 servings.

Lima Bean-Broccoli Casserole Supreme

Cousin-Ila Shanks - Zelienople, PA

A special favorite. You'll love it.

1 (10 oz.) pkg. frozen chopped broccoli
1 (10 oz.) pkg. frozen lima beans
1 pkg. Liptons dry onion soup mix
1 (10 oz.) can sour cream
1 small (8 oz.) can water chestnuts, chopped
3 c. Rice Krispies for topping

Cook broccoli and lima beans according to directions on packages. Don't overcook. Drain well and put in large mixing bowl. Mix together sour cream, mushrooms soup, and onion soup mix. Fold in water chestnuts. Add to vegetables and stir well. Place in casserole dish. Melt 1/4 cup margarine and pour over Rice Krispies. Mix well and spread over top of vegetables. Bake at 350° for 35 minutes.

Brussel Sprouts (Sweet-Sour)

Cousin-Faye Lester - Kenova, WV

1-1/2 lbs. brussel sprouts
3 T butter
1 onion, finely chopped
1/4 c. flour
2 c. beef broth
salt, pepper, and cloves to taste
2 T brown sugar
2 T lemon juice or vinegar

Cook brussel sprouts in boiling salted water until barely tender. Heat butter in saucepan, add onion, and cook until tender. Sprinkle in flour and stir until flour browns. Gradually add beef broth, stir until smooth and bubbly. Season with salt, pepper and ground cloves. Stir in brown sugar and lemon juice or vinegar. Add sprouts to sauce and simmer 5 more minutes. Good with sausage.

Harvard Beets

Niece-Naomi Vivian Keeney - Greenup, KY

1/3 c. granulated sugar
1/2 tsp. salt
1 T cornstarch
1/2 c. vinegar
2 T butter, margarine, fat or oil
1 tsp.onion, minced
2 c. hot cooked beets, diced

Blend sugar, salt, and cornstarch in top of double boiler. Add vinegar, stir until mixed and cook over boiling water until smooth and thickened; stirring constantly. Add butter, onion, and beets. Let heat over boiling water for about 20 minutes. Serves 6.

Broccoli Casserole I

Cousin-Margaret Terry Waller - Ceredo, WV

2 pkgs. chopped broccoli (frozen)
8 oz. Velveeta chesse-slices
1/4 lb. Ritz crackers (finely crushed)
1/2 stick margarine

Cook broccoli accoring to directions on pkg. Melt margarine and mix well with crushed crackers. Grease casserole dish. Place a layer of broccoli and top with cheese; then top with crackers. Repeat - ending with crackers. Bake about 20 min. at 350°.

Broccoli Casserole II

Cousin-Linda Stewart Spence - Huntington, WV

2 bunches broccoli or 2 boxes of frozen broccoli
2 ozs. sharp cheddar cheese
8 ozs. Veleveeta cheese
1 sm. can Carnation milk
1 stick butter
1 c. graham cracker crumbs

Cook broccoli until tender and then drain. Place broccoli in 9 x 13 in. glass baking dish. In a double boiler melt the cheddar and velveeta cheese on low heat while slowly adding the milk. Pour this mixture over the broccoli. In another pan melt the butter and crumble the graham cracker crumbs in to soak up the butter. Place over broccoli and cheese. Bake at 350° for 20 minutes.

Broccoli Casserole III

Niece-Martha Stuart Wheeler - Knoxville, TN

2 pkgs. frozen broccoli pieces
1 c. uncooked minute rice
1/2 c. Cheese Whiz
1 can cream of chicken soup
1/2 can milk
1 small chopped onion
1 T butter

Cook broccoli as directed. Mix other ingredients. Drain broccoli and mix together. Pour into buttered casserole. Bake uncovered at 350° for 30 minutes.

Broccoli Casserole IV

Cousin-Mae Pennington Fellows - Albuquerque, NM

1/4 c. minced onion
1/4 c. butter
2 T flour
1/2 tsp. salt
1/2 c. water
1 (8 oz.) jar Cheese Whiz
2 pkgs. thawed chopped broccoli
3 eggs, well beated
1/2 c. Ritz buttered cracker crumbs

Cook onion in butter for 5 minutes. Blend in flour, salts, and water until thick and smoother. Stir in cheese. Blend with broccoli and eggs. Turn mixture into buttered 1-1/2 qt. casserole. Top with cracker crumbs. Bake at 325° on 40 minutes.

Broccoli Casserole V

Sister-in-law-Laura Avenelle Norris Callihan
Greenup, KY

2 pkgs. chopped broccoli, cooked and drained
1 can mushroom soup
1/4 lb. butterm melted
Pepperidge Farm stuffing

Add 1 c. hot water and butter to soup, then add Pepperidge Farm stuffing til thick as oatmeal (you will have some left over). Mix with drained broccoli. Put in casserole and top with dressing crumbs. Bake til hot.

266

Cabbage Casserole I

Cousin-Cynthia Smith Lewis - West Portsmouth, OH

1 sm. head cabbage
1 lb. ground beef
1/2 c. rice
1/4 tsp. pepper
1/2 c. onions, chopped
1 tsp. salt
1 can tomato soup
1-1/2 c. water
1/4 c. grated Italian cheese

Chop cabbage into medium pieces. Spread in bottom of greased 13 x 9 x 2 in. baking dish. Brown meat and onion in lg. skillet, breaking meat as it cooks. Stir in rice, salt, and pepper. Spoon over cabbage. Heat soup and water to boiling. Pour over ingredients. Sprinkle with cheese. Cover with foil and bake 1-1/2 hours at 350°. Fluff lightly with fork beofre serving.

Cabbage Casserole II

Cousin-Phyllis Hilton Parker - Portsmouth, OH

1 head chopped cabbage (about 2 lb. head)
1 can cream of celery soup
1/2 c. mayonaise
1/2 c. milk
8 ozs. shredded mozzarella cheese
1/2 c. butter
1-1/4 tube of townhouse crackers

Cook cabbage 8 to 10 minutes; drain and melt butter in baking dish, crumble 3/4 tube of Townhouse crackers in bottom of dish. Place cooked cabbage over crumbs. Pour mixture of soup, mayonnaise, and milk over cabbage. Sprinkle cheese over soup mixture. Crumble 1/2 tube of crackers on top. Cover and bake 1 hour at 350°.

Candied Carrots

Niece-Naomi Vivian Keeney - Greenup, KY

About 3 lbs. carrots, pared and diagonally sliced
1/4 c. + 2 T butter
3/4 c. jellied cranberry sauce
1/4 c. + 2 T firmly packed brown sugar
3/4 tsp. salt

Cook carrots in small amount of water until crisp tender. Drain. Melt butter in small saucepan; add remaining ingredients. Cook, stirring constantly, until cranberry sauce melts. Pour sauce over carrots. About 10 servings.

Copper Carrot Pennies

Niece-Lori Ann Stuart - Greenup, KY

2 lb. carrots, sliced
1 small green pepper, cut in rings
1 medium onion, thinly sliced
1 can tomato soup
1/2 c. salad oil
1 c. sugar
3/4 c. vinegar
1 tsp. prepared mustard
1 tsp. Worcestershire sauce
salt and pepper to taste

Boil carrots in salted water until tender. Set aside. Cut green pepper in rings. Alternate layers of carrots, pepper rings, and onion slices in a dish. Combine remaining ingredients, blend well. Pour over vegetables and refrigerate until serving time. Keeps well. Serve cold. Serves 12-15.

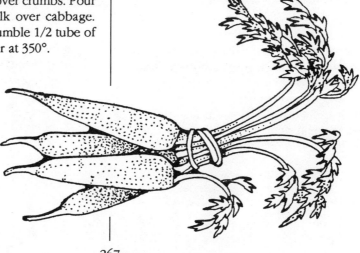

267

Baked Shredded Carrots

Cousin-Anne Hilton Short - Forestville, MD

3 c. carrots, coarsley shredded (about 1 lb.)
1/4 c. pecans, coarsley chopped
2 T melted or liquid margarine
2 T orange juice
1 T lemon juice
1 T chives, chopped
1/4 tsp. salt

Heat oven to 350°. Coat a shallow 1 qt. baking dish with vegetable cooking spray. Mix all ingredients in a bowl, then transfer to prepared baking dish. Cover and bake for 30 minutes or until carrots are tender. Makes 6 servings.

Baked Cauliflower

Cousin-Ila Shanks - Zelienople, PA

A delightful casserole. Adapted from Chef Imre Szego St. Gellert Hotel, Budapert, Hungary

1 large head of cauliflower, trimmed of blemishes and
   broken into flowerettes
1/2 c. buttered fine bread crumbs
1/2 c. grated Parmesan cheese
2 eggs and yolks, separated from whites
2 T flour
2 c. thick sour cream
1 c. cooked ham, cubed

Allow prepared cauliflower to stand in salted cold water first. Cook until tender, but firm, about 20 minutes. Mix and set aside buttered bread crumbs and cheese.

Mix:
Two egg yolks, slightly beaten with flour. Blend the sour cream into egg mixture. Beat egg whites until rounded peaks form. Fold into sour cream and egg mixture. Drain cauliflower and arrange on bottom of casserole. Spoon cubed ham over cauliflower. Pour half of sauce over ham. Arrange remaining cauliflower over sauce and add remainder of sauce. Sprinkle crumb mixture over top. Bake at 350° for 20 - 30 minutes, or until top is lightly browned.

Fried Corn

Sister-Glennis Stuart Liles - Greenup, KY

8 to 10 ears fresh corn, cut from cob
3 T butter
salt to taste
1 to 1-1/2 T sugar (may be added if corn is not sweet
   enough)
1/4 c. water

Melt butter in skillet and add corn. Add salt, sugar and water. Cook until thickened, stirring often. Add more water if needed.

To Cut Corn from the Cob

The best way to cut corn from the cob is to stand the ear on the small end, and with a sharp knife, cut off about half the kernel. Pressing on the back of the knife scrape with the sharp edge. This will carry many of the hulls with it, and they are not wanted. This is the best method for cutting off corn for canning or cooking.

Southern Corn Pudding

Niece-Carrol Keeney Abdon - Greenup, KY

2 c. fresh corn or 1 pkg. frozen corn
3 eggs
1/4 c. flour
1 tsp. salt
1/2 tsp white pepper
2 T butter, melted
2 c. light cream or milk

Cut corn from cob or thaw frozen corn. Beat eggs vigorously. Stir in corn and a mixture of flour, salt, and pepper. Add butter and cream. Pour into a buttered 1-1/2 qt. baking dish or casserole. Place in pan of hot water and bake in a preheated 325° oven for 1 hour or until a knife tested in center comes out dry. Serves 6 to 8.

Corn Oysters

Cousin-Marie Pennington Hardymon - Greenup, KY

2 c. grated fresh corn
2 eggs, beaten
3/4 c. flour
3/4 tsp. salt
1/4 tsp. black pepper
1 tsp. baking powder

Cut corn off cob and scrape cob; add eggs, flour, salt, pepper and baking powder. Stir well. Drop from T into 1 inch oil, hot enough to brown bread cubes in 40 seconds. Makes 12.

Corn Oysters or Fritters

Sister-Glennis Stuart Liles - Greenup, KY

1 c. grated fresh corn (3-4 ears)
1 egg yolk, beaten
2 T flour
1/4 tsp. salt
few grains black pepper
1 egg white
1/4 to 1/2 c. shortening

Combine corn, egg yolk, flour, salt, and pepper. Beat egg white until forms medium stiff peaks and fold into the corn mixture. Heat 2 T shortening over high heat until a light haze forms over it. Drop batter by teaspoonfuls into fat and fry for a minute or two on each side (watch carefully and regulate heat as needed). Drain on paper toweling, batch by batch, adding shortening to the skillet as needed. Makes about 20 oysters the size of silver dollars. If desired, sprinkle with more salt before serving. Terrific with chicken dishes or cold soup and salad.

Corn Pudding

Niece-Martha Stuart Wheeler - Knoxville, TN

2 cans creamed corn
1 c. milk
1 T flour
1 T butter
1/2 tsp. salt
2 eggs, well beaten
1 tsp. sugar

Mix together and bake in preheated oven at 375° for 25-30 minutes, or until pudding rises to an oval in the middle.

Skillet Corn

Cousin-Helen Shultz - Portsmouth, OH

3 c. fresh corn, cut off cob
1/2 tsp. salt
1/8 tsp. pepper
1 T sugar
1/4 c. butter
1/2 c. water
1 T all-purpose flour
1/4 c. milk

Combine corn, salt, pepper, sugar, butter, and water in 10 inch iron skillet. Cover and simmer 15 minutes over medium heat, stirring occasionally. Combine flour and milk, blending until smooth, stir into corn. Cook another 15 minutes over low heat, stirring constantly. Serves 4-6.

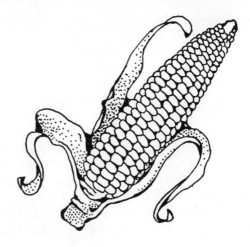

Fried Eggplant in Fritter Batter

Niece-Anne Liles O'Hare - Ashland, KY

Peel a medium-sized eggplant, cut in 1/4 inch slices. Soak in cold water 1 hour. Drain and dry between towels. Sprinkle with salt and pepper, dip in batter and fry in deep hot fat.

Fritter Batter:
1 c. flour, sifted
1/2 tsp. salt
few grains white pepper
2/3 c. milk
2 tsp. cooking oil
2 eggs, well-beaten

Mix flour, salt and white pepper. Add milk slowly, stirring until batter is smooth; add cooking oil and eggs.

Eggplant Parmesan

Niece-Sally Ann Stapf - Greenup, KY

1-1/2 lbs. eggplant, peeled and cut into about 1/4 inch slices
2 eggs, beaten and seasoned with salt and pepper
flour, seasoned with salt and pepper
about 8 ozs. Mozzarella cheese, thinly sliced
about 1/2 c. or more grated Parmesan cheese
4 or 5 hard-boiled eggs
tomato sauce recipe

Dip slices first in beaten eggs, then in seasoned flour. Heat 1/4 cup of Wesson (or similar oil) in heavy 10 or 12 inch skillet. Brown slices a few at a time (on both sides) working quickly to prevent them from soaking too much oil. Add more oil as it cooks away. As eggplant browns, transfer the slices to fresh paper towels to drain.

Pour 1/4 inch of tomato sauce into oiled 1-1/2 to 2 quart baking dish. Spread drained eggplant slices over the sauce. Top with Mozzarella and sliced hard-boiled egg scattered here and there. Pour tomato sauce over layer. Sprinkle with some Parmesan cheese. Repeat layers until dish is full, ending with sauce and cheese on top. Cover snugly with foil. Bake in middle of oven at 350° for 45 - 55 minutes, must be hot and bubbly. Serves 4.

Note: Sauce should not be too thick, but of rather medium consistency.

Tomato Sauce:
Cook 1/4 c. onions in 2 T olive oil until soft, but not brown, about 7 to 8 minutes. Add 1 can tomato paste (8 oz.) (I like Contadina brand) and 1 can water; 2 or 3 cans of tomato sauce (Contadina, 8 oz.) and half amount of water. Stir well; add 1 or 2 T finely cut fresh parsley, 1 tsp. dried basil, pinch of oregona, 1 tsp. sugar, 1/2 tsp. or more salt, black pepper and garlic powder to taste. Simmer with the pan partially covered at least 2 hours or more.

Note: A browned pork chop, sausage, chicken legs, and piece of beef simmered in the sauce (all or only one meat) gives it added flavor. For variation, add 1/4 cup sherry; also mushrooms.

Ready made sauce is used if in a hurry; for example, Progresso, Annarino or Ragu. However, I dilute it a little with water and add my favorite seasonings along with a can of tomato sauce.

Green Casserole

Sister-in-law Laura Avenelle Norris Callihan
Greenup, KY

Precook:
about 1 pt. green beans with 1/4 c. green sweet pepper

Combine with:
1 (10 oz.) pkg. frozen chopped broccoli
1 (10 oz.) pkg. frozen cut asparagus
1 (8 oz.) can water chestnuts, slivered

Drain until all excess liquid is gone. Then add 1 zucchini about the size of large banana that has been diced in bite size pieces. Toss the vegetables gently to mix. Then add 1 can cream of chicken soup (undiluted). Mix well. Salt to taste. Use 2 qt. buttered casserole. Cover with toasted bread crumbs. Bake at 350° for 1/2 hour. Note: Do not precook the zucchini, add last.

Candied Parsnips

Cousin-Nancy Fannin - Kenova, WV

6-8 medium sized parsnips
1/3 c. butter
1/3 tsp. salt
1 c. brown sugar

Wash and peel parsnips and cook until tender. Drain and slice length wise. Arrange in shallow baking pan. Melt butter in saucepan, stir in salt and sugar, add 1/3 c. water, and cook 5 minutes. Pour syrup over parsnips. Bake in 350° oven until transparent.

Lux Peas and Celery

Niece-Martha Stuart Wheeler - Knoxville, TN

1 T butter
1/2 c. bias cut celery
3 oz. can broiled sliced mushrooms
2 T pimiento, chopped
2 T onion, finely chopped
1/2 tsp. salt
1/4 tsp. savory dash pepper
1 lb. can of peas drained or 10 oz. frozen peas
   cooked and drained

Melt butter in skillet. Add all ingredients, except peas. Cook uncovered, stirring frequently until celery is crisp-done, about 5-7 minutes. Add peas. Heat until just hot.

Hopping John

Nephew-John D. Baird - Wadestown, WV

1 c. black-eyed peas (or beans)
6 c. water
1/2 lb. sliced bacon
1 dried hot red pepper
1 c. uncooked rice

Wash peas and add water, bring to a boil and boil 2 minutes. Cover and let stand 1 hour, then add bacon and pepper. Bring to boil and simmer, covered, 1 hour or until beans are tender. Add rice and cook 15 minutes, or until tender, adding boiling water if more liquid is needed. Season to taste. 6 servings.

Creamed Peas and New Potatoes

Cousin-Ruth Smith - Ceredo, WV

1-1/2 lbs. tiny new potatoes
1 to 1-1/2 lb. fresh green peas
3 T green onion, sliced
1/4 c. butter
1/4 c. all-purpose flour
1 c. milk
1/4 tsp. salt
1/8 tsp. pepper

Wash potatoes; peel a thin strip around center. Cook in boiling salted water until tender, drain. Shell and wash peas. Add peas and onions to small amount of boiling salted water. Reduce heat and cook until tender (8-12 minutes). Drain.

Melt butter in saucepan, blend in flour. Cook one minute, stirring constantly. Gradually add milk; cook over medium heat, stirring constantly, until thickened. Add salt and pepper. Combine vegetables and top with sauce. 4-6 servings.

Purple Hull Peas

Brother-in-law-H. C. (Whitey) Liles - Greenup, KY

Pick and shell crowder peas when the hulls turn purple and peas are mature (before they dry). Put shelled peas in saucepan with just enough water to cover; add salt and seasoning and cook until peas are tender.

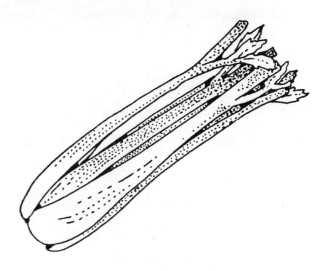

271

Fried Banana Peppers

Brother-in-law-H. C. (Whitey) Liles - Greenup, KY

*Fresh sweet or hot banana peppers (if hot better wear
  rubber gloves)*
1-1/2 c. milk
1-1/2 c. flour
1/2 c. cracker meal

Split peppers in half length wise and remove seeds. Dip
peppers in milk, then in one cup of the flour. Let peppers
stand 10 minutes. Then re-dip peppers in milk and coat
with 1/2 c. flour and 1/2 c. cracker meal mixed. Fry in hot
fat until brown on both sides. Onion ring mix may also be
used to coat peppers, instead of the above. Follow package directions for coating onion rings.

Potato Bake (Scalloped)

Sister-in-Law-Betty Stuart - Greenup, KY

3 T butter or margarine
3 T all-purpose flour
2 c. milk
*4 or 5 large potatoes, peeled and sliced (depending on the
  size of pan, you may need more)*
1 large onion, chopped
1 c. cubed, cooked ham, or use bacon bits (I use bacon)
1 tsp. salt
1/4 tsp. pepper
1 T dry parsley
1 (8 oz.) pkg. shredded cheese

Melt butter in heavy saucepan over low heat; add flour,
stirring until smooth. Cook 1 minute, stirring constantly.
Gradually stir in milk, cook over medium heat, stirring
until thick and bubbly.

Put together in a 2-1/2 quart casserole in this manner: Use
1/2 potatoes in bottom of pan, 1/2 of onions, ham or
bacon bits, salt, pepper, cheese, white sauce. Repeat in the
above order. Sprinkle parsley on top of cheese and last of
white sauce. Bake at 350° for 1 hour and 15 minutes.

Potato Cakes

Cousin-June Stewart Haney - Huntington, WV

A good way to use left over mashed potatoes.

Left over mashed potatoes
1 or 2 eggs, depending on amount of potatoes
3 or 4 T flour, depending on amount of potatoes
Small amount of minced onion

Mix ingredients well, then drop by T into hot bacon grease
or oil in skillet. Fry until brown on both sides. Remove,
place on paper towels in plate to absorb excess fat. Serve
hot.

Creamed New Potatoes and Peas

Niece-Freda Keeney - Greenup, KY

1 lb. new potatoes
1 c. water
*1-1/2 lbs. fresh peas, shelled, (one 10 oz. package of
  frozen peas may be substituted for fresh peas.)*
1/2 tsp. salt
2 T butter
1/4 c. flour
1 tall can evaporated milk (1-2/3 cups)

Scrape or peel potatoes. Cut them in half, if too large.
Place in medium sized sauce pan with 1 cup water. Cover,
bring to a boil, and boil over medium heat 10-15 minutes,
or until fairly tender. Add peas and salt and cook 4
minutes longer. Add butter and stir until melted. Remove
from heat and gradually stir in flour, then evaporated
milk. Return to low heat and cook, stirring occasionally,
until sauce is thickened and peas are tender, about 15
minutes. Makes 6 servings.

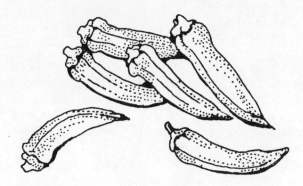

Fried Potatoes and Onions

Nephew-Sam Darby - Normantown, WV

6-8 medium size potatoes, peeled and sliced
1 large onion, peeled and sliced
Bacon grease or cooking oil for frying
Salt and pepper for seasoning

Uncle Jesse Hilton always sliced his potatoes crosswise. He claimed that they cooked more evenly this way. I do it too–because he did.

Put the grease or oil in the skillet (cast iron preferred) and get it hot. Dump in the potatoes and brown them on one side. Then add the onions and seasoning. When the potatoes brown on the second side, stir them a little to be sure they are all cooked.

At this point, you can add 2-3 eggs to the skillet and stir carefully until cooked. This is called a "Buckskinner's Breakfast".

Hopplepoppel

Cousin-David Shultz - Portsmouth, OH

1/4 c. butter
3 c. potatoes, cooked and sliced
1 medium onion, sliced
1 T parsley, minced
1/2 tsp. paprika
8 eggs
1/2 c. milk
salt and pepper to taste

Melt butter in large skillet. Add potatoes, onion, parsley, and paprika and cook, stirring occasionally until potatoes begin to brown and onion is tender. Reduce heat to medium. Meanwhile, beat eggs, milk, salt, and pepper with a fork. Pour egg mixture over potatoes. As eggs begin to cook, draw a pancake turner across the bottom and sides of the skillet, breaking mixture into large soft curds, but do not stir constantly. Cook until eggs are done, but still moist. 4 servings.

Roast Potatoes

Niece-Freda Keeney - Greenup, KY

4 medium potatoes, pared
1/2 c. butter or margarine, melted
1 small clove garlic, minced
1/4 tsp. pepper
dash of salt

Cut each potato lengthwise into 8 wedges. Place in large bowl of ice water. Cover and chill 45 minutes. Preheat oven to 475°. Drain potatoes, then pat dry with paper towels. Place wedges in 9" square baking dish.

In small bowl, combine butter, garlic, pepper and salt; pour over potatoes, stirring to coat each wedge evenly (butter will set on cold potatoes). Bake 40-45 minutes, spooning butter over potatoes and turning occasionally, until potatoes are browned and fork tender. Serves 4.

Scalloped Potatoes

Cousin-Brenda Stewart Marcum - Kenova, WV

8 medium potatoes, sliced
1 medium onion
1/2 c. milk
6 to 8 slices cheese (Velveeta)
salt
pepper
parsley flakes
3 T flour

Cover the bottom of a 9 x 12 in. baking dish with the sliced potatoes. Sift flour over potatoes until lightly covered. Pour part of the milk over the layered potatoes and flour. Cover layer with cheese and add parsley flakes. Add another layer of potatoes and continue the same as first layer. Bake at 350° for 2 hours on center rack. (Add 2 T, butter on top, if desired).

Stovetop Cheese Potatoes

Niece-Freda Keeney - Greenup, KY

4 large potatoes, peeled and cut into 1/4 in. slices
1 medium onion, minced
4 T butter or margarine, cut into small pieces
1 tsp. salt
1/4 tsp. pepper
1 (4 oz.) pkg. shredded sharp cheddar cheese

Spray 12 inch skillet with vegetable cooking spray; place skillet over medium heat. In skillet, melt butter or margarine; add potatoes, onion, salt, and pepper. Cover and cook potato mixture until potatoes are browned, about 15 minutes, turning potatoes occasionally with pancake turner. Remove skillet from heat, sprinkle potato mixture with cheddar cheese. Cover skillet until cheese melts.

Tasty Potatoes

Nephew-Phillip K. Douglas - Lexington, KY

5 medium size potatoes, peeled and sliced
2 onions, sliced
1 green pepper, seeded and chopped
salt and pepper to taste
2 T margarine
4 slices bacon, cut into 1 inch pieces
milk, if desired

Combine first 3 ingredients in a baking dish, season with salt and pepper. Dot with margarine and top with bacon pieces. Add milk, if needed. Cover, bake at 325° for 40 minutes. 5 servings.

Candied Sweet Potatoes

Niece-Naomi Vivian Keeney - Greenup, KY

6 large sweet potatoes
1 c. brown sugar
1/4 c. water
1/4 c. butter or margarine
1/2 tsp. salt

Wash, pare, and boil sweet potatoes until tender. Drain and slice cooked potatoes. Place in greased casserole. Add a syrup made of brown sugar, water, and butter, plus salt. Bake at 350° (mod. oven) for 45 minutes. Baste occasionally.

Sweet Potato Casserole I

Niece-Connie Keeney - Greenup, KY

3 c. of mashed sweet potatoes
1 c. of sugar
1/2 tsp. salt
1/2 stick butter, melted
2 eggs, beaten
1/2 c. milk
1/2 tsp. vanilla

Topping:
1 c. brown sugar
1/3 c. flour
1/2 c. chopped pecans
1/3 stick of butter, melted

Combine first 7 ingredients. Pour into casserole dish. Combine topping ingredients and pour over mixture. Bake at 350° for 35 minutes.

Sweet Potato Casserole II

Cousin-Margeret Terry Waller - Ceredo, WV

1 large can sweet potatoes, rinsed
3/4 stick butter
2 eggs, well beaten
1-1/2 c. sugar
2 T corn starch
1 c. milk
dash cinnamon

Dissolve corn starch in a little of the milk. Mix all ingredients together and put in a casserole dish. Bake 15-20 minutes at 400°.

Topping:
1 c. crushed corn flakes
1/2 c. brown sugar
3/4 c. butter
1 c. coconut

Mix together over low heat. Spread topping over sweet potato casserole. Return to oven and bake 15-20 minutes more.

Sweet Potato Casserole III

Cousin-Faye Stewart Lester - Kenova, WV

2 c. mashed sweet potatoes
1-1/4 c. sugar
1/2 c. margarine, melted
1/2 tsp. nutmeg
2 eggs, beaten
1 c. milk
1/2 tsp. cinnamon

Mix above ingredients together and place in a greased 10 x 10 in. casserole. Bake uncovered at 400° for 20 minutes. Spread topping over baked mixture and continue baking another 5 or 10 minutes.

Topping:
3/4 c. crushed cornflakes
1/2 c. chopped pecans
1/2 c. brown sugar
3/4 stick margarine (melted)

Mix well.

Sweet Potato Casserole IV

Cousin-Helen Shultz - Portsmouth, OH

3 c. cooked mashed sweet potatoes
1 c. sugar
1/2 c. butter, melted
2 eggs, well beaten
1 tsp. vanilla
1/3 c. milk

Combine all ingredients and mix well. Place in 2 qt. casserole. Cover with topping. Bake at 350° for 25-30 minutes.

Topping:
1/2 c. firmly packed brown sugar
1/4 c. all-purpose flour
2-1/2 T butter, melted
1/2 c. chopped pecans

Combine all ingredients and mix well. Sprinkle over the sweet potato mixture before baking. Serves 6-8.

Sweet Potato Dish

Sistser-in-law-Betty Stuart - Greenup, KY
Niece-Martha Stuart Wheeler - Knoxville, TN

3 c. cooked mashed sweet potatoes
1 c. sugar
3 eggs, beaten
1 tsp. vanilla
1/2 tsp. salt
1/2 c. milk
1 tsp. nutmeg

Mix well and put in greased baking dish, cover with topping.

Topping:
1 c. brown sugar
1/3 c. flour
3 T butter

Mix until crumbly, then cover top of sweet potatoes. Use chopped nuts, also, if desired. Bake at 350° for 35 minutes.

Henry Keeney Sweet Potatoes

Niece-Jean Keeney Lush - Bowling Green, KY

Cook large sweet potatoes just until skin starts to peel. Cool and peel off skin. Slice in half and line a flat baking pan with potatoes flat side up. Butter each flat side well and sprinkle with white sugar. Bake at about 350° until sugar crystalizes. Be generous with butter and sugar. Daddy would have a big pan of these when we came home from school and how delicious they were with sweet milk!

Jean was the first grandchild of Martha and Mitchell Stuart. She was loved and spoiled by grandparents, aunts and uncles, as well as her parents, Henry and Sophie Stuart Keeney.

Sweet Potato Souffle

Cousin-Judith Ellington DeChirico - Charleston, SC

3 c. (or 4) of mashed sweet potatoes (boil 4-5 lg. sweet
  potatoes)
1/3 c. butter or margarine, softened
1 tsp. vanilla
1/4 c. sugar
1/3 c. milk
2 eggs

Boil sweet potatoes, peel and mash with above ingredients. Put in greased 9 x 13 in. baking dish.

Topping:
1 c. brown sugar
1/3 c. flour
1/3 c. butter
1/2 to 1 c. chopped nuts (pecans or walnuts)

Mix well. Sprinkle topping over potato mixture. Bake at 350° for 30 minutes.

Sauerkraut and Potato Bake

Niece-Jean Keeney Lush - Bowling Green, KY

about six strips of bacon
about 2 c. mashed potatoes (without butter)
1 c. kraut
1 c. grated cheese

Fry bacon until crisp and place on paper towel to drain. Reserve drippings. Boil and mash potatoes with milk and salt. Fry kraut in three or four T of bacon fat (more if desired).

Combine mashed potatoes and kraut, mixing well. Crumble bacon and add to potato mixture. Place mixture in casserole and top with cheese. Bake at 350° until cheese is melted and bubbly. Serve hot with wieners, bratwurst, or pork.

When I grew up in W-Hollow, this recipe was designed to use left over mashed potatoes. It was cooked on the old wood stoves. It is difficult to tell what temperature to bake at, but 350° works well for me.

Yellow Squash Casserole

Cousin-Joyce (Jimmie) Carter McKinney - Scarbro, WV

1 qt. cooked yellow squash, cut up in pieces
1/2 c. cut up green pepper
1 medium onion, chopped
1 stick margarine
1 c. Pepperidge Farm Herb dressing

Saute the pepper and onion in margarine. Add to squash. Blend in dressing. Pour into Pam-sprayed casserole dish. Sprinkle shredded cheese on top. Bake in 350° oven for 30-45 minutes until slightly browned.

Baked Acorn Squash

Sister-Glennis Stuart Liles - Greenup, KY

squash
brown sugar
cinnamon
butter

Wash and cut squash in half. Clean out the center of each half. Fill center with brown sugar, sprinkle on cinnamon and dot with butter. Bake at 350° until squash is tender. Cushaw may also be baked this way.

Butternut Squash with Thyme

Cousin-Brenda Marcum - Kenova, WV

1 lg. butternut squash
1 T butter
1 T skim milk
1 tsp. honey
dash of cinnamon or nutmeg
1 T fresh thyme leaves (or 1 tsp. dried)

Cut squash in half lengthwise. Scoop out seeds. Place squash in pan with about one inch of water. Cover and cook until it is easily pierced with a fork, about 35 minutes. Be careful that the water does not boil away. With a spoon, remove pulp from squash, mash it well. Add remaining ingredients to pulp. Whip until fluffy.

Glazed Squash

Cousin-Helen Shultz - Portsmouth, OH

2 lg. butternut squash
1/2 c. sugar
1/2 c. brown sugar
1/2 c. water
2 T butter
1/8 tsp. ground allspice

Parboil whole squash about 15 minutes or until tender; drain. Peel and halve crosswise; remove seeds and membrane and cut into thick slices. Place in 11 x 7 3/4 inch baking dish. Combine sugar, water and allspice; pour over squash. Dot with butter. Bake at 350° for 25-30 minutes, basting frequently. Servings 6-8.

Thanksgiving Stuffed Squash

Niece-Betty Stuart Darby Baird - Wadestown, WV

1 whole blue hubbard
1/4 c. water
2 T veg. oil
1-1/2 c. onion, diced
1-1/2 c. celery, minced
1/2 tsp. dried marjoram
1 orange
2 c. cranberries, roughly chopped
4 c. turkey or chicken, cubed
1/4 c. pure maple syrup
3 T butter
1 c. bread crumbs
salt and pepper

Preheat oven to 375°. Cut squash in half and take out seeds. Place squash, cut side down, in pan covered with 1/4 c. water. (Water should cover bottom of pan); bake 30 minutes.

Filling:
Heat oil; saute onion and celery until limp (3-5 minutes); add marjoram. Peel orange and sliver 1 T of the rind. Squeeze juice of orange. Add orange rind, juice and cranberries to onion and saute briefly. Add turkey and maple syrup and remove from heat.

In separate pan, melt butter and stir in bread crumbs. Add 3 T of bread crumbs to turkey and toss. Season to taste with salt and pepper. Remove squash from oven and divide stuffing between halves. Sprinkle with remaining bread crumbs and bake one hour.

Baked Tomatoes

Cousin-Brian Lester - Jacksonville, FL

4 medium tomatoes, cut in half crosswise
1/4 tsp. salt
1/8 tsp. pepper
1/2 c. soft breadcrumbs, toasted
3 T fresh parsley, chopped
2 cloves garlic, minced
1/4 tsp. dried thyme
1/4 tsp. dried oregano
2 T vegetable oil

Place tomatoes, cut side up, in a lightly greased baking dish. Sprinkle salt and pepper over cut side of each tomato half. Combine next 6 ingredients; mix well, and spoon over surface of each tomato. Bake at 350° for 12-15 minutes or until tomatoes are thoroughly heated. Yield: 8 servings.

Flavorful Tomatoes

Cousin-Helen Shultz - Portsmouth, OH

4 ripe tomatoes
1 Spanish onion, sliced and separated
1/4 tsp. sugar
1/2 tsp. salt
1 T fresh chives, chopped
1 T fresh basil, chopped
1 T dill weed
1 tsp. celery seed
1/4 c. French dressing
ground black pepper
lettuce leaves

Slice tomatoes into 1/2 inch thick slices. Arrange tomatoes and onion rings in a shallow dish; sprinkle with sugar and seasonings. Pour French dressing over tomatoes. Cover and refrigerate overnight. Serve on lettuce leaves. Serves 4-6.

Tomatoes in Creamed Sauce

Cousin-Dottie Hatten - Morganfield, KY

4 T butter or margarine
6 firm tomatoes, red or green
4 T flour
1 tsp. salt
1/8 tsp. pepper
3 T brown sugar
1 c. heavy cream

Cut tomatoes into thick slices; dip in flour mixed with salt and pepper. Sprinkle with brown sugar.

Heat butter in a large skillet. Add tomatoes and cook slowly. Turn once and sprinkle again with brown sugar. When the tomatoes are tender, add cream and cook until it bubbles. Arrange the tomatoes on a serving platter and pour the sauce over them. Very good for breakfast with crisp bacon.

Fried Green Tomatoes

Nephew-Roy Abdon - Greenup, KY

4-6 sliced green tomatoes (leave skins on)
1 egg, beaten
1/2 c. flour and 1/2 c. cornmeal, mixed with salt and pepper

Dip tomato slices in egg and then in flour and cornmeal mix. Fry until brown.

Scalloped Tomatoes (For a large number)

Sister-in-law-Nancy Norris Curry - Greenup, KY

4 large cans tomatoes, mashed
11 slices bread, toasted and cut in squares
2 sticks butter, melted
1-3/4 c. sugar
1-1/2 tsp. salt
1/2 tsp. pepper

Mix tomatoes with sugar, salt, pepper and butter. Put a layer of tomatoes in bottom of small roaster; then a layer of toast; another layer of tomatoes. Top with a layer of the rest of toast on top. Bake at 300° until bubbly.

Stewed Tomatoes

Cousin-Virgie Litchfield - Ceredo, WV

2 lbs. tomatoes
1 tsp. salt
1/8 tsp. pepper
2 tsp. sugar (more, if desired)
1 T butter
2 slices bread, torn in small pieces
1 T minced onion (if desired)

Wash tomatoes, peel and cut into pieces. Place in tightly covered saucepan and cook about 15 minutes. Add other ingredients and cook until tomatoes are thickened, stirring often. Serves 6-8. Note: Canned tomatoes may also be used.

Buttered Turnips

Niece-Ruth Nelson - Greenup, KY

3 bunches young turnips
water for cooking
salt to taste
1/2 tsp. sugar
1/3 c. melted butter
1 T minced parsley

Peel turnips; sprinkle with salt and cook until tender. Caramelize sugar, then melt butter in same pan. Add parsley and pour this over turnips. Let stand ten minutes before serving.

Turnip Supreme

Cousin-Dorothy Holbrook - Greenup, KY

6 to 8 medium turnips
1 lg. onion
4 slices bacon
1/2 tsp. sugar
1/2 tsp. cayenne pepper
1 tsp. paprika

Peel and quarter turnips and onion. Cook in boiling salted water until tender. Drain and set aside. Fry bacon until crisp; drain and reserve drippings. Crumble bacon. Add bacon, bacon drippings, sugar and seasonings to vegetables; toss well. Spoon into a greased 2 qt. casserole. Bake at 350° for 15 minutes or until heated thoroughly. Yield: 6 servings.

Vegetable Stew
Cousin-Orville Shultz - Portsmouth, OH

4 T butter
1 medium eggplant, peeled and diced
1 large green pepper, chopped
2 large onions, diced
2-3 small zucchini, diced
4 large tomatoes, peeled and diced
garlic or garlic powder
minced parsley
oregano
salt and pepper

Place garlic (or garlic powder) and butter in large skillet and heat. Saute eggplant, zucchini, onion, and green pepper in butter until lightly browned, then add tomatoes and other seasonings to taste. Cover and simmer until vegetables are tender. The addition of browned ground beef before simmering makes a good one dish meal. Serve with grated Parmesan cheese, if desired.

Veggie Pizza
Cousin-Lynn Hunt Newton - Hamilton, OH

2 pkg. cresent rolls
8 ozs. cream cheese
1 c. mayonnaise
1 pkg. Hidden Valley Ranch dressing mix
1 c. carrots, grated
1 c. broccoli flowerettes
1 c. tomatoes, diced
1/2 c. green peppers
1 c. cheddar cheese, grated

Lay out cresent rolls in a jelly roll pan together (no gaps). Bake 10 minutes. Mix cream cheese, mayonnaise, and dressing mix. Spread on top of cresent rolls. top with carrots, broccoli, tomatoes, green peppers, and cheese. Refrigerate. when ready to serve, cut into bars.

Zucchini Skillet Dinner
Nephew-Walter Stuart Keeney - Greenup, KY

1-1/2 lbs. ground beef
1 lg. zucchini, peeled and cut up
1 med. onion, chopped
2 or 3 good sized tomatoes, chopped
2 banana peppers or 1 lg. green pepper, cut in strips

In skillet, brown ground beef; drain. Add remaining ingredients and cook at low heat 20 minutes.

Zucchini Patties
Niece-Ruth Nelson - Greenup, KY

3 c. grated zucchini
1 medium onion, grated
1/2 tsp. garlic salt
1 tsp. salt
1/4 tsp. pepper
1 egg, beaten
3 T flour, heaping

Mix ingredients. Fry by spoonfuls until brown.

Zucchini Squares
Cousin-Geraldine Holbrook - Greenup, KY

3 c. thinly sliced zucchini
1 c. Bisquick
1/2 c. onion, chopped
1/2 c. Parmesan cheese
2 T parsley flakes
1/2 tsp. salt
1/2 tsp. seasoned salt
1/2 tsp. oregano
Dash of black pepper
1 clove garlic, or garlic powder
1/2 c. vegetable oil
4 eggs, beaten

Mix ingredients and bake in a 9 x 13 inch pan (best in glass ones) in a 350° oven for 25 minutes or until the top is light brown. Cut into squares. Best to serve warm.

Leather Breeches Beans

Cousin-Loretta Adkins Benner - Lucasville, OH

Wash and string tender green beans that are not filled out too much. I use Missouri Wonder pole beans. Thread a darning needle with a long piece of twine or thread such as crochet cotton. Push the needle through the center of the first bean pushing it to the end of the thread. Tie the string around this first bean. It will hold all the other beans on the string. Keep adding beans until the string is nearly full. Save enough room to make a loop to hang the beans for drying. Do not dry in the open sun or attempt to dry them too fast. I dry mine in a hallway. A spare room upstairs is a good place also.

To cook later in the winter drop a string of the beans in a pot of boiling water. Turn off the burner and let them soak about an hour. Empty the water from the pot and remove the beans from the string. Place the beans back into the pot, add some smoked ham hocks or bacon, cover with water and continue to cook until nice and tender and almost dry.

Make a pan of corn bread to eat with them.

Wild Game and Other Wild Foods

Wild Game
Preparing Wild Game for the Kitchen
Baked Coon
Dove Risotto
Doves with Sausage Rice
Orange-Glazed Wild Duck
Wild Duck in Chili Sauce
Stuffed Wild Duck
Frog Legs
Crispy Goose
Roast Wild Goose with Bourbon Sauce
To Skin a Groundhog
Groundhog
Groundhog and Kraut
Grouse in Casserole
Grouse with Orange Slices
Roasted Orange Grouse
Roast Grouse
Freshwater Mussel Fritters
Stuffed Roast Pheasant
Sunchoke Pheasant
Pheasant Tarragon
Possum and Sweet Potatoes
Braised Quail
Country-Style Quail
Saute'd Quail with Rosemary
Hasen Pfeffer
Rabbit Stew

Saddle or Rack of Rabbit
Country Style Squirrel
Hunting Camp Squirrel
Fried Turtle
Easy Barbecued Venison
Venison Chops
Venison Cutlet
Jesse James' Jerky
Cider Basted Roast Venison
Deer Roast
Venison Stew
Venison and Wild Rice
Stuffed Sassafras Leaves

Other Wild Foods
Wild Greens
Pennsylvania Dutch Sweet and Sour
  Dandelion Greens
Jerusalem Artichokes Saute'd in Butter
Fried Morels
French Fried Morels
Wild Mountain Tea
Poke Sallet
Stir Fried Pokeshoots and Fiddleheads
Wild Raspberry Jelly
Wild Raspberry Jelly Roll
Sumac Candy
Maple Syrup

L to R. Jesse Stuart and brother James Stuart

282

Wild Game

There was no refrigerator in W-Hollow as we grew up in the 1920's and 1930's. We cooled our milk by lowering it in a bucket into the well where we got our drinking water.

The only real meat we ever had come from hogs we raised or game from the woods. We never had beef. Beef had to be aged in cold storage for a week or ten days, depending upon the size of the animal.

About June or July, young rabbits were large enough to fry; we called it "getting ripe". They were good fried, with gravy, hot biscuits, wild honey and cold milk or hot coffee. The young chickens were good for frying all summer. They made a good Sunday morning breakfast or dinner with new potatoes, gravy, and other fixins.

In the autumn, we had squirrel, opossum coon, grouse and quail to furnish meat for our table. Ground hog was in abundance all summer long. Jesse and I spent many hours, including Sunday, in the woods with old Black Boy, our dog and the Columbia single barrel shotgun. If we came home with squirrels and/or ground hogs, our Dad's eyes would really light up. He liked all wild game. He would pull out his razor sharp pocket knife and make short work of skinning whatever we had caught.

When I was four years old, my Dad took me back to Seaton Ridge where we, in the coolness of early morning, sat under shell bark hickory trees. Here he killed two gray squirrels with two shots from the old Columbia single barrel shotgun. He showed Jesse and me how to stalk squirrels and other game. He told us never to kill what we couldn't eat unless it was an owl, hawk or copperhead snake.

After Jesse went away to college, he lost interest in hunting, but he always loved any wild game that I would give him to eat.

After electric lines came into W-Hollow in the 1940's to provide power for refrigerators and freezers, our way of cooking and eating was altered. We had more income with all the family working and soon were like much of the outside world. We learned what steaks, roasts, and chops were. That was over forty years ago, but it will never replace the sound of my Dad singing on Sunday morning as he came from the barn with a frying (Dominicker) rooster in each hand for Mom to fry for breakfast with gravy, hot biscuits and wild honey.

James Stuart (Jesse's brother)

283

Maude Wright Hilton - wife of Uncle Jesse Hilton

Uncle Jiles Hilton and his wife Agnes.

*L to R. Jesse's mother - Mary Hilton Johnson and
Jesse's mother Martha Hilton Stuart*

Women Pioneers

*We know we owe you mothers of our past,
Who were so strong a part of destiny.
You were eternal as our skies and vast,
A portion of rock-ribbed eternity.
We owe our hearts to you as these greenbriars
Owe their first tender leaves to warm spring earth;
We owe our blood to you and living fires
Stirring our mortal brains from birth.
Yours was the will too strong for turning back
To your Atlantic coast, Virginia skies.
But here you helped clear the land to build the shack,
Where mountain barriers shoulder to the skies.
You sleep, Blue Dreamers here of yesteryears,
Unmarked in weedy cells, women pioneers!*

*Stuart, Jesse, *Songs of a Mountain Plowman*, (Ashland, Kentucky: The Jesse Stuart Foundation, Inc., 1986), p. 18.

Preparing Wild Game for the Kitchen

Nephew-Stacy Nelson - Greenup, KY

Perhaps the single most important step in any wild game recipe is the proper care and butchering of the game before cooking ever takes place. Even though most of us, including the rugged out-door types, find that process anything but pleasant, it is essential to go slowly, carefully, and cleanly. Cooking wild meats not properly dressed and butchered causes the unpleasant gamey, musky, or wild taste meats so often complained about. The tips and suggestions given here are general and very basic. For a more detailed understanding, I would suggest your reference sporting magazines, your local library, or book store. Of course, there is no reference like experience.

In the hardwood forest mountains of Eastern Kentucky, tradition and traditional methods have been passed from generation to generation ever since the first settlers built their log homes upon the mountain slopes. Among them was an old folk law by which we all have hunted, "Don't kill what you won't eat and eat what you kill." This simple rule had its greatest impact on those hunters who, through their skills, provided meat for the family table. The methods of preparing wild game they used are proven methods, and are the standard of today's practices developed over many generations of practical application. It is a very basic sketch of those skills that I have put down here, but with a little inovation and experience you should be able to turn your successful hunting into enjoyable feasting.

Game Birds:

The dressing of game birds is like that of domestic foul of similar species. Small game birds, such as quail, woodcock, dove, or grouse, differ only from the larger birds, such as geese, turkey, or ducks, in that they are smaller and their feathers are more easily removed. To remove the feathers on these small birds, simply hold them by the feet and pull the feathers down sharply. The feathers should come off easily. To remove the feathers from larger birds, you may find it necessary to dip them in boiling water. When the feathers have been removed, rotate the larger bird over an open flame to singe away the

fine hairs and pin feathers. With a sharp knife, cut the loose skin away between the neck and breast and remove the neck. From this opening the chest organs can be removed. Next, make an incision from the breast peak to the anal opening. During this procedure, be careful with your knife; cutting too deeply can pierce the intestine and stomach which will contaminate the meat. Now, cut around the anal opening and pull it away from the body. Remove the intestines and other body organs, saving the liver, gizzard, and neck for giblets, if you so desire.

If you keep the liver (and this is true of any small or large game you must first remove the gall bladder. The gall bladder is a small fleshy sack attached in the folds of the liver, that contains bitter gall. If you rupture the gall bladder the liver is contaminated and probably should be discarded. Something else you may want to keep in mind is that if you puncture the intestines or they are shot damaged, you have not necessarily lost the meat. Wash the entire body with hot water and mild soap. Rinse it thoroughly and it should be alright, if the contamination is not wide spread or very old. Intestional contamination of meat is a prime cause of salmonella, which can cause flu-like symptoms or death in extreme cases.

Furbearing Animals:

Dressing a furbearing animal is a similar process to that of fowl. A rabbit is probably the easiest of all furbearing game to skin. Simply hang the rabbit by its back feet and pull down sharply on the fur and the skin will peel away. Always hang the furry creatures and work down in the skinning process; this helps eliminate hair contamination. To skin other animals, an incision must be made along the stomach from the tail to the neck. Remove the tail and begin peeling the whole skin down working it free from the flesh with a sharp knife. On large animals, you may find it necessary to make other incisions along the inside of each leg that joins with the stomach incision and around the ankle of each leg so that the entire skin can be peeled down. When the skin is peeled to the neck, remove the head with the skin. Next, slice through the sternum, which is the bone or cartilage between the ribs. Continue this cut along the stomach until it comes near the anal opening. Cut around this opening and remove it. On larger animals, such as deer, tie off this opening and remove the intestines. Once the body organs have been carefully removed, wash the body thoroughly.

The butchering of small game usually follows this procedure. First remove the feet. Next, cut the legs away. Watch for the place where the leg muscles attach to the body. Cut here and the leg can be easily removed. What you have left is ribs and back. At the point where the rib cage ends, cut through the backbone by cutting between two vertebras and so avoiding the bone. A deer can be parted out in the same manner for further cutting in more manageable portions.

A word of caution is in order. When butchering larger game animals, be aware of their scent glands. These glands are usually located in the arm pit and ankle areas. I would suggest you consult a diagram of their locations on different animals and remove them carefully. Scent gland contamination results in a musky, gamey odor and taste. When venison has been properly dressed, it should be sweeter and more flavorful than any beef you have ever eaten. If it is not, you have made a mistake somewhere in the dressing process.

Fish:

Without a doubt, the most popular and common method of cleaning fish is to filet them. To filet fish, you will need a knife designed specifically for this purpose. It should have a thin, flexible blade of spring steel and a sharp point. Now, find yourself a board twice as long as the fish you wish to clean. Drive a number eight finish nail at one end of the board somewhere close to the center of its width. This nail will hold the fish in place while you work on it. Next, using your fileting knife, make an incision along the back, next to the dorsal fin, from the head to the back of the rib cage. Cut down along the backbone until you encounter the ribs, then cut the filet away from the ribs providing the fish is large enough to have a filet over its ribs. Then, insert your knife through the fish and behind the rib cage and work flat along the backbone toward the tail. Stop before you reach the place where the skin attaches to the tail. Cut the filet away from the gill area and fold it back away from the fish. You should be looking at a nice filet.

Lay your knife flat on the skin that is still attached to the tail. Cutting between the skin and the filet, work the knife forward until the skin and flesh have been separated. Repeat this process on the other side and you should have two nice, boneless filets. It is a good idea to have plenty of water on hand during this process. As a general rule, I do my fileting just before I leave the place where I caught the fish. I take nothing but the filets home and leave the mess for the turtles and opossums.

Turtles:

Turtles take a little more preparation time, but are well worth the trouble. You will need to boil a container of water, large enough to dip the turtles in. A medium or large wash tub works fine for this. Some of the old timers dip their turtles while still alive. I find this method a little too nervy, so I remove the head and allow the blood to drain from them first. When the turtles have been sufficiently dipped in the boiling water, they will turn pale. When this happens, lay the turtle on its back and using a hatchet or very strong knife, cut the breast plate loose from the shell near the hinge around each leg. Remove the breast plate. Using a sturdy pair of pliers, pull the skin from the legs and remove the feet. Open the intestinal cavity and empty it. Next, using a sharp knife, cut between the turtle and the shell. The turtle is secured to its shell by a thin membrane and ligaments. Once these are cut away, the turtle will come from its shell. Butchering the turtle is like any other four legged creature; you cut away the legs and separate the back into two pieces. Wash the turtle thoroughly and leave it in the refrigerator to soak in strong salt water overnight.

The details of butchering the game we have discussed here vary from hunter to hunter and location to location. Most all butchering methods work well. The method you use is simply a matter of personal preference. With these basic instructions and some experience, you should be able to prepare your game properly for the kitchen. Remember, the test is in the taste. If the food tastes bad, you've done something wrong in the cleaning and butchering process. Most wild game and fish have a very pleasant taste. As Grandpa might have put it, "You need to weed your rows again".

Baked Coon

Cousin-William Everett Holbrook - Greenup, KY

1 racoon, dressed and cut in serving pieces
4 strips bacon (about)
1/4 tsp. salt
1/4 stick butter or margarine
2-3 bay leaves
1/8 tsp. pepper

Place pieces of raccoon in saucepan with bay leaves and enough water to cover. Boil over medium heat for about one hour. Drain. Save about 1 c. of the broth. Sprinkle raccoon pieces with salt and pepper and drizzle with butter. Roll in flour and place pieces of raccoon on rack in baking pan. Cut strips of bacon in half. Place a piece of bacon on each piece of raccoon. Bake 1-1/2 hours or until tender at 350°, basting occasionally with the reserved broth.

Dove Risotto

Brother-James Mitchell Stuart - Greenup, KY

6 slices bacon
12 dove breasts
1 medium onion, chopped
5 c. chicken broth
1-1/2 c. uncooked regular rice
1 T dried parsley flakes
1 bay leaf
1/8 tsp. hot sauce
Pinch of dried whole thyme
1 (4 oz.) can sliced mushrooms, drained

Fry bacon in a large skillet until crisp; remove bacon, reserving drippings in skillet. Crumble bacon and set aside. Brown dove breasts in skillet. Add onion; saute' 2 minutes. Add remaining ingredients except mushrooms; cover and cook over low heat 25 minutes or until rice is tender, stirring once. Remove bay leaf; add mushrooms and cook 2 minutes or until thoroughly heated. Yield: 4 servings.

Doves With Sausage Rice

Nephew-Walter Stuart (Ted) Keeney - Greenup, KY

1 medium onion, chopped
1 bell pepper, chopped
10 dove breasts
2 T bacon drippings
1-1/2 c. rice, uncooked
1 lb. link pork sausage, cut into 2-inch pieces
3-3/4 c. water

Saute' onion and bell pepper in bacon drippings. Remove, drain, and set aside. Salt and pepper dove breasts to taste. In large pot, add water and bring to a boil. Add doves, cover, and cook 5 minutes. Add rice, sausage, onion, and pepper; cover and simmer 40 minutes. It may be necesssary to add additional water as it cooks. Yield: Serves 5.

Orange-Glazed Wild Ducks

Nephew-Tony Abdon - Greenup, KY

2 (2 to 1-1/2 lb.) wild ducks, dressed
6 slices bacon
1 (6 oz.) can frozen orange juice concentrate, thawed and undiluted
1 clove garlic, crushed
3/4 tsp. dry mustard
1/2 tsp. salt
1/2 tsp. ground ginger
1 T cornstarch
1 c. water

Place ducks, breast side up, on a rack in a shallow baking pan; arrange bacon on top. Bake at 350° for 2 hours and 45 minutes. Combine remaining ingredients in a saucepan; stir well. Bring to a boil; cook over medium heat, stirring constantly, until smooth and thickened. Remove bacon from ducks; brush with sauce. Bake an additional 15 minutes or until ducks are done. Serve with remaining sauce. Yield: 4 servings.

Wild Duck in Chili Sauce (Serve with Wild Rice)

Cousin-Al Lester - Kenova, WV

4 (lb.) wild ducks, dressed
1 T chili powder
1-1/2 tsp. crushed red pepper
1 tsp. salt
1 tsp. pepper
2 c. celery, chopped
1 large onion, chopped
1 large green pepper, chopped
1 clove garlic, minced
1 (14 oz.) bottle catsup
1 (12 oz.) can beer
1 (10 oz.) can tomatoes and chiles, undrained
1 (8 oz.) can tomato sauce
1 (16 oz.) can tomato paste
2 T hot sauce
Hot cooked rice

Rinse ducks thoroughly with cold water; pat dry. Place ducks in large Dutch oven, breast side up. Sprinkle with chili powder and next 3 ingredients. Combine celery and next 3 ingredients; spoon evenly over ducks.

Combine catsup and next 5 ingredients; pour over ducks. Cover and bake at 350° for 3 hours. Reduce heat to 200° and bake an additional hour or until ducks are fork tender. Serve over rice. Yield: 4 servings.

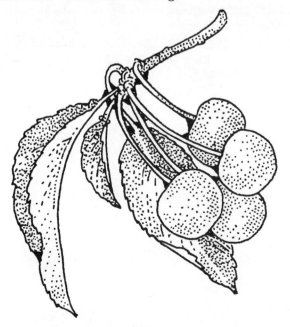

Stuffed Wild Duck

Niece-Betty Stuart Darby Baird - Wadestown - WV

Allow 1/2 duck per person
Clean, singe, wash and drain ducks
Sprinkle inside and out with salt

Stuffing:
1-3/4 c. water
1/4 c. butter or margarine
2-1/2 c. dry bread crumbs
1 egg, slightly beaten
1/2 c. cut up celery
1/2 c. onion, chopped
Salt and pepper

Saute the celery and onion in the butter and add all other ingredients. Stuff birds lightly and place in covered baking pan. Bake at 375° about 1-1/2 hours. Remove cover and bake uncovered at 400° for an hour or more, until brown and done.

Frog Legs

Nephew-Samuel Darby - Normantown, WV

These are real good. Only the hind legs are eaten. Cut the legs from the body and skin them. For about six frog legs, combine:

1/4 c. flour
Salt
Pepper

Dredge frog legs in mixture and brown in hot oil. Cover and cook on low heat until tender.

Crispy Goose

Niece-Regina Nelson Stout - Greenup, KY

2 geese, about 4 lbs. each, cleaned
2 T white vinegar
4 T salt
1 lemon
1 stick butter
4 stalks celery, sliced
1 large onion, diced
2-3 c. bread cubes, toasted (or 1 lb. pkg. quality stuffing mix)
Sage and Thyme to taste
2 eggs, beaten slightly
Salt and pepper to taste

Wash and soak the geese two hours in water, to which vinegar and salt have been added, just enough to cover. Drain geese and thoroughly pat dry, inside and out. Rub cavities with lemon. Melt butter in skillet; brush geese lightly. Add celery and onion to skillet with remaining butter and saute' until tender, about 3 minutes. In a bowl, combine bread cubes, seasonings, saute'd vegetables, eggs, and enough water to moisten slightly. Salt and pepper geese inside and outside. Stuff cavities loosely and roast in preheated 350° oven for 2 hours or until done. Yield: serves 6.

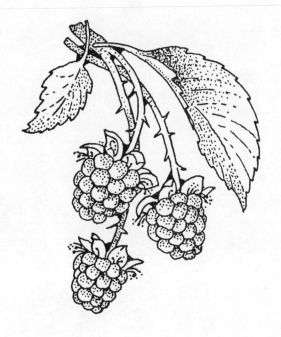

Roast Wild Goose with Bourbon Sauce

Nephew-Ken Stout - Greenup, KY

Goose:
1 goose, approximately 8 lbs., cleaned (anything larger, may be tough)
2 large onions
20 juniper berries or fresh cranberries

Sauce:
2 T cornstarch
1/2 c. chicken broth
1/2 c. Wild Turkey Bourbon
1/2 c. current jelly

Preheat oven to 325°. Wash and dry goose. Sprinkle with salt and pepper inside and out. Peel onions, remove center part and stuff each onion with 10 juniper berries or cranberries. Place onions in cavity of goose. Place goose, breast side down, on rack in standard roasting pan. Cover bottom of roasting pan with cold water. Place in preheated oven for 2-1/2 hours. Then turn and roast, breast side up, for another 2 hours (25 minutes/pound for total cooking time). Remove onions from cavity and transfer goose to another roasting pan and roast for 30 minutes more to crisp skin.

Wild Turkey Bourbon Sauce:
After goose has cooked, skim all fat from pan drippings. Blend cornstarch with a small amount of broth, then add remaining broth, bourbon, and currant jelly. Stirring constantly, loosen browned bits clinging to sides of pan. Simmer for about 15 minutes. Serve in sauce boat with goose. Yield: Serves 8.

To Skin A Groundhog

Nephew-John D. Baird - Wadestown, WV

Skinning a groundhog can be from relatively easy to practically impossible, depending on the age and size of the critter. The younger the animal, the easier to prepare and, in my opinion, the better tasting they are, but when times are hard and there are many mouths to feed, a fat old groundhog is not scorned just because he might prove difficult to shuck out of his hide. (Groundhog hide was often cut into long strips to use as shoe laces because of its toughness and resistance to breaking).

While rabbits and squirrels can be easily skinned by suspending them by their feet from two nails driven into a board or beam at a convenient height, only the younger groundhogs can readily be skinned in this manner. The big old rascals need a slightly different approach. The one I use is as follows:

I lay a 12 inch wide plank across two sawhorses or any similar support that will allow me to sit straddle of the plank comfortably. I then lay the groundhog on his back, head toward me, and drive an 8-penny nail through each of his rear feet. Using a sharp knife, I make an incision around the legs, just above the nails, and up each leg to a junction at the stomach. Then, being careful not to open the stomach cavity, I slit the belly skin up to a point between the front legs; then slit the skin on the under side of each front leg, from the feet down to the slit in the skin covering the chest.

I then proceed to work the skin off the animal, by pulling and cutting. When the legs are skinned up to the tail, I cut through the tail bone and leave the tail attached to the hide. As more hide is loosened from the carcass it becomes somewhat easier to grasp, but on more than one occasion I have resorted to pliers or a similar tool to get a good grasp on the slippery hide. At about this point you begin to lose your enthusiasm for a good meal of groundhog but hang in there; the results are worth the efforts.

Once you've got the rascal shucked out of his overcoat, cut the scent glands from under his forelegs, gut him out, and cut into serving pieces. You may find it necessary to wash him good in cold water before cutting him up, to get rid of the hair you have inadvertantly gotten on the carcass while getting the hide off. They say all things get easier with practice but I have found that I only get hungry for groundhog when I see a young one in the garden or in the meadow. I lose my appetite when I find myself with a big old brusier that I know is going to be tough to skin. But if you don't mind the trouble of skinning them out, an old groundhog tastes delicious, after he's been parboiled with two or three onions until he's fork tender, then tossed, onions and all, into a hot skillet of grease and fried until brown. A groundhog is a vegetarian, and will select only the finest plants in your garden to nibble on; if you can bring him to the skillet you'll be surprised at how good he tastes.

Groundhog

Niece-Betty Stuart Darby Baird - Wadestown, WV

When Grandpa brought in a groundhog, it was sometimes a quite mature animal (and a little tough). This recipe works for such a cooking challenge.

Clean and skin groundhog. Soak overnight in salt water.

Cut into serving pieces and parboil in water to which you have added 1/2 tsp. baking soda. It should be "fork tender". This will take about 30-35 minutes.

Combine:
1/2 c. flour
1/4 tsp. salt
1/4 tsp. pepper

Roll the pieces in this mixture and fry in hot oil (or bacon grease) until brown.

Groundhog and Kraut

Nephew-John Baird - Wadestown, WV

First, shoot one groundhog. Remove all fat and parboil with a little soda and onion. Remove bone and brown meat in skillet. Cook with kraut as you would pork. Most people would never know the difference. Rabbit would probably work well too.

Grouse in Casserole

Niece-Freda Keeney - Greenup, KY

2 grouse, cleaned and plucked
4 T butter
1 clove garlic
4 shallots
1/4 tsp. basil
1 c. mushrooms, sliced
2 c. dry white wine
1/2 c. flour
1 dash Tabasco sauce
1 T parsley, minced
1/4 lb. salt pork, diced
Salt and pepper

Cut the grouse into sections as when frying chickens. Rub the sections with salt and pepper and shake in a paper bag with flour. In a large skillet, fry the diced salt pork until nicely browned. Reserve and throw the liquid fat away. Brown the sections of grouse in hot butter, and then place them in the bottom of a large casserole. Saute' the livers and hearts in the skillet with the four shallots diced fine, and the minced clove of garlic for about three minutes.

Add the mushrooms, parsley, basil, Tabasco, diced pork, and one cup of wine. Bring to a boil and add to the grouse in the casserole. Add another cup of wine, stir and cover. Cook for about 1-1/2 hours in a 350° oven. Remove and stir in thoroughly one cup of sour cream. Bring just to a boil on the top of the range and serve immediately.

Grouse With Orange Slices

Nephew-Jim Lush - Bowling Green, KY

4 grouse
salt and pepper, to taste
4 (1/4-inch thick) orange slices, peeled and seeded
4 slices bacon, uncooked
1/4 c. butter, melted
rind of 1 orange, grated
2 T orange juice
1 tsp. lemon juice
2 T parsley, chopped

Sprinkle grouse inside and out with salt and pepper. Cover breast of each with an orange slice and a bacon slice: fasten with string. Place grouse breasts up in a baking pan. Roast in preheated 350° oven 15 to 20 minutes, or until tender, basting frequently with combined butter, orange rind, orange juice, and lemon juice. Remove string. Sprinkle with parsley. Serve with the roasted orange and bacon slices. Yield: Serves 4.

Roasted Orange Grouse

Nephew-Stacy Nelson - Greenup, KY

2 freshly dressed grouse
6 slices smoked bacon
1 large Valencia orange, thinly sliced
4 T butter
2 medium onions, peeled
1 T sage

Clean and rinse birds. Place in a roasting pan. Stuff each bird with a mixture of onions and sage. Drape grouse with bacon slices and cook for one hour, basting regularly with pan drippings, and butter. Just before the birds start to brown, lay orange slices over them and finish cooking. Serve on a cold winter day and enjoy.

Roast Grouse

Nephew-Jim Lush - Bowling Green, KY

4 grouse
2 slices wholewheat bread
4 T butter
1/4 c. chopped pecans
beef broth and sherry
salt and pepper

Clean and pluck the birds, then set them aside. Crumble bread into fine crumbs and cook in two tablespoons of butter for a couple of minutes. Combine with pecans and enough broth and sherry to just moisten. Season with salt and freshly ground pepper. Stuff birds until plump. If they are big birds, you may have to make more stuffing to fill them. Close the cavities with small skewers or toothpicks. Truss the legs and wings close to the bodies with twine and place on a rack in a shallow roasting pan. Brush the birds with the remaining melted butter, and roast the birds in a preheated 425° oven for 30 minutes. Baste frequently while roasting. Serve on fried bread which has been spread with a paste made with the cooked livers, hearts, gizzards and a little sherry.

Freshwater Mussel Fritters

Nephew-Stacy Nelson - Greenup, KY

Freshwater mussels are quite common in the local streams in Eastern Kentucky.

1 pint of small whole or large sliced fresh water mussels
1 c. flour
1 egg, beaten
1-1/4 c. cold water
1 c. flour for dipping

Lightly beat the flour, egg and water together to form a smooth, fairly thin, batter. Using chop sticks or small tongs, dip mussel pieces into flour then fritter batter. Deep fry the fritters in a skillet of 350° oil until golden brown. Serve with seafood sauce, hot mustard, sweet and sour sauce, or lemon.

Stuffed Roast Pheasant

Nephew-Walter Stuart (Ted) Keeney - Greenup, KY

2 pheasant (2 to 3 lbs.)
4 tart green apples, peeled, cored and chopped
4 stalks green celery, chopped
1/2 c. parsley, chopped
Salt and pepper
8 slices thick bacon
1 c. sherry wine
2 T red currant jelly
1-1/2 T fresh lemon juice

Wipe the pheasant inside and out with a damp cloth. Mix the apples, celery and parsley and saute' briefly in fresh butter. Rub the birds inside and out with salt and pepper. Stuff with the mixture when cool. Cover all exposed parts of the birds with strips of bacon, holding them in place with toothpicks. Roast for about one hour in a 325° oven. The last 15 minutes remove the bacon and baste with the remaining ingredients until done. Wild rice, braised celery and a fine California red wine goes well with this. Recipe serves six to seven.

Sunchoke Pheasant

Nephew-James Stephen Stuart - Greenup, KY

6 pheasant breasts
1 lb. Sunchokes (Jerusalem Artichokes), cut into half inch slices
2 c. fresh or frozen orange juice
12 oz. frozen or fresh pearl onions
Paprika, salt, pepper, garlic powder to taste

Preheat oven to 325°. Place pheasant and vegetables in oven dish. Sprinkle on seasonings, pour juice over, and bake one hour.

Pheasant Tarragon

Nephew-Scott Darby Lake - Berea, KY

1 pheasant, cut into frying pieces
1-1/2 tsp. salt
1/2 tsp. black pepper
1/8 tsp. paprika
1/2 c. margarine or butter
1 medium onion, thinly sliced
1/2 lb. fresh mushrooms, sliced
1 tsp. tarragon

Season pheasant pieces with salt, pepper, and paprika. Melt margarine in skillet on medium heat or in electric fry pan at 340°. Add pheasant and brown. Remove pheasant. Add onion and mushrooms and cook until tender, but not browned. Return pheasant to pan, sprinkle with tarragon, cover, reduce heat to simmer, and cook 30 minutes. Yield: Serves 4.

Possum and Sweet Potatoes

Niece-Betty Stuart Darby Baird - Wadestown, WV

1 possum, skinned, cleaned, and cut into serving pieces
3-1/2 c. water
Salt
Black pepper
4-6 red peppers, chopped
1 large onion, chopped
5-6 medium sweet potatoes, peeled and quartered

Combine possum and all ingredients except sweet potatoes and simmer 30 minutes. Remove possum to a baking pan. Cook the liquid until reduced by about half. Then add it and the sweet potatoes to the possum in the baking pan.

Bake in 350° oven about an hour, or until possum is tender. Baste with pan drippings as necessary.

Braised Quail

Brother-James Mitchell Stuart - Greenup, KY

1/4 c. + 2 T all-purpose flour
1/2 tsp. pepper
8 quail, dressed
1/2 c. bacon drippings
1 c. milk
1 c. chopped onion
2 (10-3/4 oz.) cans cream of celery soup, undiluted
1/2 tsp. dried whole caraway seed
Parsley sprigs (optional)

Combine flour and pepper; dredge quail in mixture and set aside. Melt bacon drippings in a Dutch oven; brown quail on both sides. Remove quail from Dutch oven and discard any remaining drippings. Combine milk and next 3 ingredients in a Dutch oven, stirring to mix. Add quail; cover and cook over low heat, basting frequently, 30 minutes or until done. Garnish with parsley, if desired. Yield: 4 servings.

Serve homemade biscuits with Braised Quail; you'll want to savor every bit of the creamy gravy seasoned with caraway seed.

Country-Style Quail

Nephew-John O'Hare - Ashland, KY

8 quail, dressed
1/4 c. all-purpose flour
1/2 c. vegetable oil
2 chicken bouillon cubes
1 small onion, sliced
1 tsp. salt
1/4 tsp. pepper
Milk or cream (optional)

Salt and pepper quail to taste; flour and place in oil in medium heated skillet. Turn frequently to ensure even browning. Remove birds and place on paper towels to drain. Pour excess oil from pan and add flour for gravy. After paste begins to brown, add water for desired thickness. Add chicken bouillon cubes to gravy. Place quail in gravy and top with onions. Sprinkle salt and pepper on top. Cover and cook on low heat one hour. It may be necessary to add additional water to keep gravy from becoming too thick. If you desire a richer gravy, milk, or cream may be added. Yield: Serves 4.

Saute'd Quail With Rosemary

Cousin-Orville Shultz - Portsmouth, OH

8 quail, dressed
Salt and pepper to taste
1/3 c. butter
2 T vegetable oil
1-1/2 tsp. fresh rosemary, chopped (or use 1 tsp. dried)
Juice of one lemon
2 T chives, chopped

Lightly sprinkle quail inside and out with salt and pepper. In large skillet on medium high, heat butter and oil (do not burn butter). Brown quail on all sides.

Add rosemary and lemon juice. Cover and simmer gently until birds are tender, about 30-35 minutes. Place quail on serving platter.

Add chives to pan juices and boil for one minute. Pour juices over quail and serve. Yield: Serves 6.

Hasen Pfeffer

Nephew-James Stephen Stuart - Greenup - KY

Hasen Pfeffer, which often appears as one word, means "hare pepper". It is in actuality a seasoned stew of rabbit, which has been marinated to make the meat more tender.

1 large rabbit or 2 small ones, cut into serving pieces
1 pint of water
1 pint vinegar
4 medium onions, sliced fine
6 whole cloves
1 tsp. salt and freshly ground pepper
1 bay leaf
1/2 tsp. tarragon
2 T flour
4 T butter
1 c. heavy sour cream
Salt and pepper

Mix the first eight ingredients in a large crock, and put in the rabbit. Place some small object, like a plate, on top of the pieces to make sure they are covered by the marinade. Place in a refrigerator or cool place for 48 hours. Remove pieces from marinade and pat dry. Strain and reserve the marinade. Fry the rabbit in a large skillet until brown, using two tablespoons of the butter. Add the rest of the butter and flour and cook until the flour is lightly brown. Add one cup of the marinade and bring slowly to a boil. Stir until thickened. Add more marinade to cover all the pieces. Season with salt and pepper to taste. Place a lid on the skillet and simmer over a low flame for about an hour or until tender. Remove the pieces of rabbit to a warm oven and add the sour cream to the remaining liquid. Stir thoroughly. Put the rabbit back in the skillet and heat to the boiling point, while stirring. Serve immediately with boiled noodles, sweet and sour red cabbage, and plenty of cold beer. (Serves six.)

Rabbit Stew

Nephew-Jim Lush - Bowling Green, KY

1 small rabbit, cut into serving pieces
2 c. dried lima beans, soaked overnight in 1-1/2 qts. water
5 medium carrots, sliced
2 green peppers, chopped
1 medium onion, diced
1 clove garlic
2 bay leaves
2 tsp. salt
1/4 tsp. pepper
2 T butter

Place rabbit in boiling water with the drained beans and 1-1/4 qts. of fresh water to cover. Add vegetables, garlic clove, bay leaves, and seasonings. Simmer one hour, adding more water, if needed. Add butter for the last 15 minutes of cooking time. Serves 4.

Saddle or Rack of Rabbit

Nephew-Mike Lake - Berea, KY

Season the whole rabbit with salt and pepper. Dust it with flour and brown it lightly in a combination of butter and Crisco. Place the rabbit on a rack in a hot oven (400°) and cook for about 25 minutes. Baste frequently with the butter-Crisco combination. When done, add 1/2 c. of brandy to the drippings along with some chopped parsley and serve as sauce with the rabbit. Serves three.

Country Style Squirrel

Niece-Betty Stuart Darby Baird - Wadestown, WV

2 squirrels, cleaned, rinsed, and cut into serving pieces
Flour to dredge, seasoned with salt and pepper
6-8 T oil or bacon grease (to fry)
2 c. water

Dredge squirrel pieces in seasoned flour and fry until golden brown. Remove from skillet and pour off grease, leaving about 2 T. Add water and bring to a boil. Return the squirrel to the skillet, turn heat to low, cover and cook until meat leaves the bone. This will probably be about 1 hour.

Hunting Camp Squirrel

Nephew-Stacy Nelson - Greenup, KY

4 young tender squirrels
6 large wild carrots
4 wild onions, diced
4 springs wild parsley
2 c. flour
1 large handful wild water cress
Salt and pepper

Cut squirrels into six pieces each. Place in a pot with carrots, onions, parsley, salt and pepper. Pour in enough water to cover the squirrels. Cook until the squirrels are tender. Remove the squirrels and save the broth. Bone out one squirrel and return the meat to the broth. Add water cress to the soup just before serving.

Add 1 tsp. salt and 1/2 tsp. pepper to 1 c. flour and dredge squirrel pieces in this mixture. Pan fry until brown. Then place fried squirrels near camp fire to keep them warm. Using the remainder of the flour, salt and pepper mixture, pour it into the pan of drippings where squirrels were fried to make gravy.

Serve, fried squirrels, gravy and soup with dutch oven biscuits or corn bread. It makes a hardy, stick to the ribs, meal that will satisfy even the heaviest eaters at camp.

Fried Turtle

Brother-in-law-Herbert (Whitey) Liles - Greenup, KY

1 turtle, cleaned and cut in pieces
1 tsp. salt
1/4 c. cooking oil
1/2 c. flour
1/2 tsp. pepper

Parboil turtle meat in enough water to cover for about 1 hour. Drain. Roll pieces of turtle in flour to which the salt and pepper has been added. Fry in the oil over medium heat until tender and brown on all sides.

Easy Barbecued Venison

Cousin-Orville Shultz - Portsmouth, OH

3 lb. venison roast
1 (16 oz.) can peaches with juice
1 (14 oz.) bottle ketchup

Blend peaches and ketchup in blender or food processor until smooth. Pour over meat. Bake covered in a Dutch oven at 200° for a minimum of one hour per pound. Can also be cooked in a slow cooker set on low for five to six hours, depending on size of roast.

Gauge cooking time according to the size of the meat. Allow about twice the time you would for beef, at half the cooking temperature. Slow simmering brings out barbecued flavor.

Note: Start with this recipe, and its success will motivate you to cook more game. This is an excellent barbeque sauce and almost too easy to believe. Use it on pork, chicken, or beef. It makes excellent barbequed spareribs and barbequed chicken. Serves four.

Venison Chops

Cousin-Steven D. Arnold - Portsmouth, OH

6 chops
6 c. warm salt water
3 c. milk
1 pkg. onion soup mix
2 c. water

Let chops soak in warm salt water for 2 hours. Drain and discard water. Soak in milk for 2 hours. Drain and discard milk. Place chops in 9 x 13 in baking dish. Top with dry onion soup mix and pour 2 cups of water in. Cover with foil and refrigerate over night. Bring to room temperature and bake at 350° for 60-90 minutes.

Vension Cutlet

Nephew-John Baird - Wadestown, WV

Pound steak thoroughly (similar to minute steaks). This is particularly well suited to the tougher cuts. Marinate for two hours in milk. Roll in seasoned crumbs and fry. Outstanding!

Jesse James' Jerky

Cousin-Randa Jane Murphy - Lucasville, OH

2 lbs. venison, sliced 1/8 inch thick, fat removed
2 T Worcestershire sauce
2 T soy sauce
1 T salt
1 tsp. ground red pepper
2 cloves of garlic, minced
1 c. of corn wiskey (may substitute 2 c. red wine)
1 c. water

Mix above ingredients, except venison, together in a covered casserole dish. Put meat into the above mixture. Let marinate for 2 days in the refrigerator. Take strips of venison out of marinade sauce. Drain as much as possible and pat dry. Bake at 150°. Leave oven door ajar so moisture will escape. Bake until dry and dark, usually 6 hours or more. For sweeter jerky, baste in honey or molasses before baking.

Cider Basted Roast Venison

Niece-Eileen McCarten Nelson - Greenup, KY

This recipe is based on a Native American recipe for venison. It will turn even the "gamiest" of deer meat into a gourmet delight.

1 (5 lb.) rump or sirloin venison roast
7-8 pieces of bacon
pepper corns

Marinade:
3 T honey
1/3 c. gin
2 c. cider

Place the venison in a large roasting pan. Stud the roast with peppercorns and lay the strips of bacon over the roast. Warm all the ingredients of the marinade in a saucepan. Roast the venison 1-1/2 hours in a 350° oven, basting often with the marinade. Cool the roast on a carving board for 15 to 20 minutes. Remove most of the grease from the drippings with a spoon. Make a cornstarch gravy with the drippings.

Deer Roast

Cousin-Brenda Stewart Marcum - Kenova, WV

1 lg. roast
1 onion
1 bay leaf
1 T garlic powder
1 tsp. garlic salt
water

Put roast in large pan and add onion, water, bay leaf, garlic salt and powder. Cook on medium heat until tender. (Approximately 3 hours). When roast is nearly done, add potatoes and carrots to complete meal.

Venison Stew

Nephew-Mike Lake - Berea, KY

Venison is particularly good for stews because of it's leanness. To make this dish more festive, flame it with 2 tablespoons of warmed cognac just before serving.

Makes 8 servings.

3 lbs. of venison, rump or round, cut into 1-1/2 inch cubes
1 T butter or margarine
1/4 lb. small mushrooms
4 medium carrots
3 stalks celery
2 cloves garlic, pressed
1/2 tsp. salt
1/8 tsp. ground black pepper
1/4 tsp. dried thyme leaves
8 whole cloves
7 small white onions, peeled
2 c. dry red wine, or 1 c. water and 1 c. prepared coffee
6 small potatoes, scrubbed and halved
1/4 c. water
3 T all-purpose flour
2 T cognac (optional)

Wipe venison cubes with damp all-natural (microwave) paper towels. Heat butter in a 5-quart Dutch oven. Saute venison cubes, one-third at a time, until they are lightly browned on all sides. Remove to a bowl and repeat until all cubes are browned.

While meat is browning, wash mushrooms, carrots, and celery. Finely chop enough to make 1/4 c. of each. When all meat is browned, add garlic and chopped vegetables to Dutch oven. Saute, stirring until lightly browned. Cut remaining carrots and celery into 1-inch chunks.

Add browned meat cubes, salt, pepper, and thyme to vegetables. Stir to combine well. Press cloves into one onion. add to stew. Halve remaining onions. Pour wine (or coffee mixture) over meat mixture. Cover tightly; bring to boiling. Reduce heat and cook until meat is almost tender, about 1-1/2 hours.

Scrub and halve potatoes. Stir the 1/4 c. water into the flour and fold into stew. Cook, stirring, until thickened. Add whole mushrooms, carrot and celery chunks, halved onions, and potatoes to stew. Stir to combine. Cook, covered, stirring occasionally, until meat and vegetables are tender - 30 to 45 minutes longer. Remove clove-studded onion.

If desired, heat cognac gently in a small saucepan. Ignite and carefully pour over stew. Present flaming; stir before serving.

Venison and Wild Rice

Cousin-Geraldine Holbrook - Greenup, KY

1 lb. ground venison
1-1/2 c. cooked wild rice
1 can cream of mushroom soup
1 can cream of chicken soup
1 c. of sliced celery
1 (8 oz.) can mushrooms, drained
1 c. water
1 onion, chopped
1 tsp. salt
3 T soy sauce

Brown venison in small amount of oil in large skillet. Drain off fat, if any. Add other ingredients and mix well. Pour into two-quart casserole, cover and bake in 350° oven for 30 minutes. Uncover and bake for 30 minutes more.

Stuffed Sassafras Leaves
Niece-Eileen McCarten Nelson - Greenup, KY

3-4 dozen large leaves from a red sassafras tree
1 lb. finely chopped or ground venison
8 red crab apples, peeled and diced
1/2 c. chopped beech nut or butter nut meats
1/4 c. minced wild onions with green
1/4 c. minced wild parsley roots and tops
1 large duck egg, beaten
1 tsp. sage
2 T sourwood blossom honey
2 c. apple cider
2 T butter or venison fat
Salt and pepper to taste
3/4 c. corn bread crumbs

Steam sassafras leaves in a 2 qt. pot and set aside to cool. Saute venison and onion until venison is brown and onion is translucent. Drain off most of the fat. Add nuts, apples, salt, pepper and sage. Cook until apples are tender. Remove from heat and cool. Stir in egg, crumbs, and honey.

Lay sassafras leaves on a cutting board. Place venison mixture on the upper middle end of a leaf. Tuck in the leaf fingers. Fold in sides and roll like a cabbage roll.

Melt butter on the bottom of a 2 qt. pot. Place rolls in the pot and carefully pour apple cider around them. Place a plate on top of the rolls and cover the pot with a lid. Cook on very low heat for 45 minutes, basting occasionally. Serve these sassafras rolls with fried potatoes, corn on the cob, brown or green beans, some cooked cabbage and scratch biscuits.

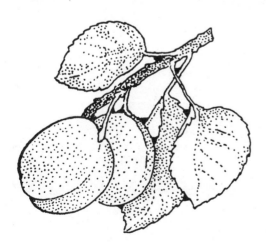

Other Wild Foods

Wild Greens
Niece-Nancy Sue Darby Lake - Berea, KY

Spring brought life back to W-Hollow. Early Sunday morning walks to Plum Grove Church were special times for me. Grandma Stuart (Martha Hilton Stuart) and I cut through the woods and across the creek by the Old Collins house to make our trip about one-third the distance it would be to follow the road. The crisp air made us hurry on and only occasionally notice the new plants and leaves beginning to show. On our return home, however, the warm sun pouring through the almost bare trees made a leisurely stroll more enjoyable. She would light up her pipe and talk or just walk along with a thoughtful expression. There was always one morning when she would spot the green patches along the roadside or by the creek or along the garden spot by the Old Collins barn.

"Well, Nancy, the greens are up," she'd say. "We'll come back after dinner and gather a mess."

After Sunday dinner, we'd take a big kettle and small knives and go back along the path and creek banks to gather creasies, lamb quarters, poke, dock, dandelion, mustard, plantal, sorrel, wild lettuce, or violets. There were others but over the years I've forgotton their common names. Many times she'd say, "There's not much _____ (one kind or another), so we'll leave some for seed."

Also, the kinds we found dictated how much of each we collected. Some combinations I remember are: mustard, dock and lamb quarters; or poke, dandelion, lamb quarters, violet leaves, and sour dock; or almost any kind to mix with mustard and creasies. However, we used very little sorrel and wild onions.

All the leaves should be gathered when they're very young and tender and full of "blood purifiers" (vitamins and iron). Poke stems can be used until they turn reddish purple when they contain a kind of poison. Some people say, "Look for poke when the frogs croak."

299

The mustard plant family can be recognized by their long deeply lobed leaves and pungent odor. If they're just a few inches tall, you can pick stems with the leaves.

Creasies are a dark green spinach type plants that grow along the creek-bank. The leaves are deeply-cut and grow in clumps before the tall stem appears.

There are different kinds of dock or sour dock. The leaves, I remember, were large dark shiny green with crinkled edges. We usually found it around the barn.

Dandilion and plantain were right in the edge of the yard, so I usually picked them while Grandma washed and prepared the others. When we put them all in the pot, she usually had a fully packed pot covered with water because greens shrink. After par-boiling and stirring until the greens were thoroughly wilted and a little lighter green color, she drained off the water. Then if they still had a strong odor, she par-boiled them again with fresh water for a few minutes. When the greens seemed to be wilted and no longer pungent, she would fry salted side meat (pork) and add the greens to the grease to fry until they were tender.

Another way to cook them is to pour the grease and a little water and salt to taste over the greens and simmer until tender.

These are methods I use today with domestic greens because you should never gather a plant unless you are familiar with it! Recognition of these wild greens from my memory is not reliable enough for me.

Pennsylvania Dutch Sweet and Sour Dandelion Greens

Niece-Eileen McCarten Nelson - Greenup, KY

1/2 lb. young fresh dandelion greens
3 slices bacon
1 hard boiled egg, still warm
2 T vinegar
2 tsp. sugar
Salt and pepper to taste

Dice bacon into small pieces and fry until very crisp. Remove the bacon from pan and drain the pieces on a folded paper towel. Reserve 3 T of bacon drippings in the pan. Rinse dandelion greens very well. The greens may be cut into large, bite size pieces or left whole. Steam the greens in a small amount of water until tender. While greens are cooking, add vinegar, sugar, salt and pepper to the bacon drippings. Heat the sauce until it bubbles. The sauce should be pleasantly sweet and sour, adjust salt or vinegar to suit your taste.

Drain the dandelion greens and place them in a serving dish. Pour the sauce over the greens. Sprinkle the bacon bits on the greens and decorate with sliced rounds of boiled egg.

This recipe was passed down in my family from my great grandmother who was Pennsylvania Dutch. It can be used as one of the traditional seven sweets and seven sours at a Pennsylvania Sermon Dinner.

lambs quarters

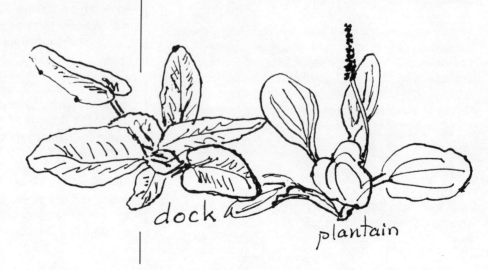

dock

plantain

Jerusalem Artichokes Sauted in Butter

Nephew-John Baird - Wadestown, WV

Jerusalem artichokes are the root of a plant in the sunflower family. They grow wild in North America and the Indians were cultivating them in their gardens long before the Colonists arrived.

Makes 4 servings.

1 lb. medium-size Jerusalem artichokes
1 T butter
1/4 tsp. salt (optional)

Scrub artichokes; place, unpeeled, in a medium saucepan. Cover with water; bring to boiling, Cook, covered, over medium heat until just tender, about 15 to 20 minutes.

Drain artichokes and cool under running water until they are comfortable to handle. Peel; cut into quarters.

In a heavy skillet, melt 1 T butter. Saute artichokes until golden on all sides, adding more butter as necessary. Salt, if desired, and serve hot.

Fried Morels

Cousin-Ken Smith, Jr. - Portsmouth, OH

In the Spring time, when the Hepatica has bloomed and the Trillium and Dog's Tooth Violet are emerging from the forest's loam, the time is right to find morels.

Morels are mushrooms which are found in the Spring from the first of April until mid-May. Sponge-like in appearance, they are often found near old apple orchards and under poplar trees. Usually, families will have a few select (and secret!) patches where morels are found each year. By using mesh bags when gathering morels, the spores are allowed to return to the soil and thus insure future pickings.

Clean morels by rinsing repeatedly and slice each in half. Soak them in salt water overnight in the refrigerator. Roll each half in cornmeal and fry them in butter. They can also be dipped in egg and rolled in cracker crumbs and fried.

French Fried Morels

Nephew-Gene Darby - Greenup, KY

Cut ends off the stems and split large morels lengthwise. Wash carefully in cold water. Soak in salt water for 1-2 hours. Wash again. Drain well.

beat together:
1 egg
1/4 c. milk

Mix together:
1 c. plain cornmeal
1/4 c. flour
1 tsp. salt
pepper

In a large skillet, heat about 1/2 inch oil. Dip morels in egg mixture, then roll in meal mixture. Fry until golden brown on both sides. Another way to prepare morels is to saute them in butter and diced onion, salt and pepper, until all the water has evaporated. Delicious served over steak.

Wild Mountain Tea

Nephew-Stacy Nelson - Greenup, KY

4 parts sassafras root
4 parts wild mint
4 parts mountain teaberry leaves
1 part ginseng
1 part sweet anise root

Combine ingredients in a large tea egg. Steep tea egg in 1 qt. of boiling water for 15 minutes. Serve in tea cups with a generous dollop of honey.

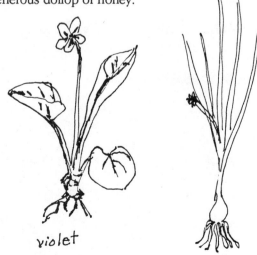

violet   onion

Poke Sallet

Sister-Glennis Liles - Greenup, KY

Select the desired amount of poke sallet, discard all except the most tender round sprouts. Clean thoroughly (rinse 3 times). Parboil and discard water. In large kettle cover greens with water and boil until tender, but not mushy. Fry 4 slices of bacon until crisp. Remove bacon from fat and set aside. Add the poke and 1 tsp. of salt to the fat. If desired, 1 dozen tender young chopped onions may be added at this time. Cook, stirring occasionally for about 20 minutes. When ready to serve, sprinkle with the crumbled bacon. Two chopped hard cooked eggs may also be sprinkled on sallet, if desired.

Stir Fried Pokeshoots and Fiddleheads

Nephew-Stacy Nelson - Greenup, KY

2 doz. pokeshoots
1 doz. fiddleheads
2 T butter
1/4 lemon
additional butter, if desired
salt and pepper to taste

Wash and trim pokeshoots and fiddleheads. Stir fry poke-shoots and fiddleheads in the butter in a wok or large skillet over high heat. Continue to cook, stirring constantly until pokeshoots and fiddleheads are bright green and are tender, yet crisp. Place the cooked greens in a serving dish. Squeeze the lemon over the greens, add more butter if you wish. Salt and pepper to taste.

Wild Raspberry Jelly

Niece-Regina Nelson Stout - Greenup, KY

3 qts. wild raspberries, red or black
7 c. sugar
2 T lemon juice
1 c. liquid pectin

Crush raspberries and drip through jelly bag. Measure 4 c. juice. Combine raspberry juice, sugar, and lemon juice. Cook over high heat until mixture boils. Add pectin, stirring constantly. Remove from heat and skim. Pour into hot sterilized glasses. Cover with paraffin. Makes 10 c. jelly.

Wild Raspberry Jelly Roll

Niece-Ruth Nelson - Greenup, KY

5 eggs, separated
1 c. sugar
3 T orange juice
1 c. sifted all-purpose flour
1 tsp. cornstarch
1/4 tsp. salt
confectioner's sugar
1 c. wild raspberry jelly

Beat egg whites until almost stiff. Add 1/2 c. sugar gradually, beating constantly until mixture is very stiff. Beat egg yolks until thick; add remaining 1/2 c. sugar gradually, beating constantly, until thick. Add orange juice. Fold egg yolk mixture into egg white mixture. Sift flour with salt and cornstarch. Add to egg mixture. Line a 11 x 16 inch jelly roll pan with waxed paper. Grease the paper. Turn batter into pan and spread evenly. Bake in 350° oven for 15 minutes. Turn out onto towel, sprinkled with confectioners' sugar. Remove paper and trim crusts. Roll up and allow to cool. Unroll to spread with jelly, then, reroll.

Sumac Candy

Niece-Theresa Darby - Normantown, WV

Make an infusion of:
8 c. boiling water
6 pyramidal heads of red Sumac berries, well rinsed (Smooth, Staghorn or Shining)
4 c. sugar
1 T butter
1 c. light corn syrup
1 tsp. cream of tartar

Steep berries in boiling water, covered, for 20 minutes. Strain liquid to obtain 2 qts., then add remaining ingredients.

Cook this mixture, stirring occasionally, until it reaches the hardcrack stage, 300° F. Skim off any scum. Pour into foil-lined, buttered 15 x 10 x 1 inch pan, and score into small pieces before it sets. Allow to cool and harden.

Mini-production of Maple Syrup

Cousin - Loretta Adkins Benner - Lucasville, OH

Suitable Maples
Sugar and black maples are the best source of sap. Red and silver maples can be tapped, but the sugar content is not as high, thereby requiring larger volumes of sap to produce a given volume of syrup.

Tapping the Trees
Late February and early March work best for us in southern Ohio. Good sap flows occur when night temperatures drop below freezing and are followed by mild temperatures the next day. Stop collecting sap just before bud expansion growth in late March or early April, depending on weather conditions.

Make tap holes by using a carpenter's brace and a 3/8 or 7/16 inch fast-cutting wood bit. Drill holes to a depth of 2 1/2 to 3 inches into sound wood, 2 to 5 feet above the ground. The south side of the tree is best but you can tap anywhere around the tree trunk. Slant the hole slightly upward to help the sap run out. On trees that have been tapped before, locate a new taphole 6 inches to one side and 4 inches higher than the old taphole.

The number of taps will depend on the size of the tree. Do not tap trees under 10 inches in diameter. Use one tap for 10 - 15 inch trees, two taps for 16 - 20 inch trees, three taps for 21 - 25 inch trees and no more than 4 taps on trees more than 25 inches in diameter.

When the sap begins to flow from the hole you will need a device called a spile to gently tap into the hole. Commercially made spiles have a hook attached for hanging a bucket. Make sure taphole is free of shavings and that some space is left between the end of the spile and the wood of the tree. Sap flow may start as soon as you bore the tap holes if the weather is right. Cover buckets to keep out rain and other foreign materials.

Sap collection
Collect sap at least once a day. When the sap is flowing it may fill a gallon bucket in less that 24 hours. Boil the sap down as quickly as possible to produce good tasting syrup. During the evaporation process, keep adding more sap because as the sap evaporates it yields very little syrup. Gradually add sap as not to slow the boiling process. Continue this boiling/evaporation process until

a suitable amount of concentrated sap is left in the pan, about a gallon of syrup from ten gallons of sap. Finish by boiling to a point 7 to 7 1/2 degrees above the temperature that water boils in your area. NOTE: Different altitudes cause a several degree variance in the point at which water boils. If a thermometer is not available, boil to a density similar to that of commercial maple syrup. Watch very carefully to prevent burning or scorching. Once the syrup had reached the proper density, it should be filtered and sealed in clean containers.

Spiles should be hammered into trees at an upward angle so that the sap flows directly into the juice cans.

Crumb Sugar

Boil maple syrup to 258 degrees F. Remove from heat and allow a minute or so for boiling to stop. Pour into a wooden bowl such as an antique butter bowl or a salad bowl and stir continuously with a heavy wooden spoon or paddle until the moisture is driven off and like magic before your eyes you will have a bowl of brown sugar! May be sifted through a flour sifter for a finer sugar and stored in a jar or plastic bag to prevent hardening.

For more information and recipes contact your county agricultural agent.

Teachers: Our school, Valley Elementary in Lucasville, Ohio, is in its 11th year of tapping the maples that border our playground. The sap is boiled down to syrup in the school cafeteria and when the sap season is over the whole school has a maple syrup and pancake breakfast. As a result, many people in the community have started tapping their own maple trees. Hopefully the art of making maple syrup is being kept alive in the community by this school project. If your school is bordered by maple trees, why not make this project an annual school event.

Uses of Maple syrup

Maple Taffy or Spotza

Boil maple syrup to 258 degrees F. Swirl a spoonful of syrup onto packed snow or finely shaved ice. Then pick the syrup up by twisting it onto a wooden fork or spoon.

This is a tasty taffy for use at "Spotza" parties. Spotza is a Pennsylvania Dutch name for taffy. The hot liquid may also be poured into a buttered pan or dish and stored in a freezer. When brittle it can be cracked into small pieces for eating.

Hollowed-out sumac branch for spout

one-gallon plastic milk jug

metal spout

Contributor Index

Additional Recipes

Additional Recipes

Additional Recipes

Additional Recipes